THE OUTLINE OF ART

Revised and Extended Edition, October 1940

PRINTED IN GREAT BRITAIN BY
MORRISON AND GIBB LTD., LONDON AND EDINBURGH

"CHEF DE L'HÔTEL CHATHAM," BY SIR WILLIAM ORPEN, R.A.

Diploma Gallery, Royal Academy.

In this portrait of the Chef of a Paris hotel, Sir William Orpen used all his amazing facility and dexterity in the handling of paint to put before us the rich humanity of a living being. Alike in its technical brilliance and in the human appeal of its democratic subject, this painting deserves to rank with Moroni's world-famous " Portrait of a Tailor."

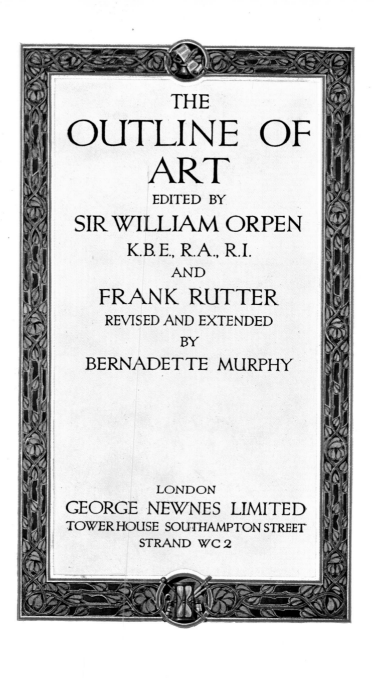

THE
OUTLINE OF ART

EDITED BY

SIR WILLIAM ORPEN

K.B.E., R.A., R.I.

AND

FRANK RUTTER

REVISED AND EXTENDED

BY

BERNADETTE MURPHY

LONDON
GEORGE NEWNES LIMITED
TOWER HOUSE SOUTHAMPTON STREET
STRAND WC 2

PREFACE

A NEW edition of this instructive and stimulating work being called for by reason of its continued popularity, the opportunity thus offered for revision has been made use of extensively. The last chapter of the first edition (now entitled " Art after the Great War ") has been brought up to date, and much new material added to the book in the form of a short survey of the art of the past twenty years. In the latter, particular attention has been paid to contemporary British artists, and to those French painters and sculptors whose work, already well known at the beginning of the period, had, by its close, become of world-wide fame. It is a very short period when art is considered as a whole, but it lies between events of tremendous importance for the world, and this gives its art a special interest and significance. In the main, and with some striking exceptions—among them Picasso's " Guernica " and the Mexican frescoes of Diego Rivera—there is but little reflection of the uneasy background of the times to be observed in the most notable pictorial and plastic art produced during the last two decades. But the period is rich in beautiful paintings the subjects of which—the countryside, the hills and the sea, the human face and form—can never cease to inspire artists or lose interest for art-lovers ; and it is also unique as the epoch in which there was first attempted by the group of artists known as the " surréalistes " the depiction of what they consider to be the less conscious regions of the mind.

The final chapter of the new edition has not been designed as a critical study, or as an exhaustive analysis of æsthetic trends and tendencies among contemporary artists, but

3

rather as a chronicle of events in the recent history of art, with the emphasis (as has been said) on the native achievement. In it will be found some account of the various movements or developments of modern art which belong to those years, and a record of what new reputations have been made, together with such biographical details as will enable the reader to fit artists into the general background of the art of our time. Brief descriptions are also given of acknowledged successes in painting and sculpture, and of much work of lesser fame but obvious merit.

There are twenty-two plates to illustrate the additional material, and although it was found impossible owing to the general dislocation of the art world consequent upon the war to obtain some of the reproductions originally chosen, a varied selection representative of many styles and schools has nevertheless been made.

The Bibliography has been considerably amplified, and in choosing the titles of works of reference special attention has been paid to their cost. The list therefore includes a number of moderately priced books suitable for private libraries, while in the case of the more costly publications, and of those standard works now out of print, only those which are to be found in the larger public libraries and in the principal art libraries have been included. There has also been added a general Index, which adds greatly to the book's practical value as a work of reference.

CONTENTS

5

CONTENTS

INTRODUCTION

FROM the earliest times, man has felt a need to express his joy in the world which surrounds him. In the caves of the Dordogne, the artists of the Stone Age made the first step towards picture painting when they scratched the outlines of reindeer and ibex on pieces of bone and drew a combat of animals with spirit and realism. These prehistoric drawings show both power of observation and skill with the hand. Less ancient than these Stone Age carvings are the three colour paintings of animals discovered in a cave near Santander, in Spain. They are at least fifty thousand years old. This prehistoric art is interesting because it shows that man, in a very early stage of his development, was eager to produce accurate representation of the nature with which he was familiar, and it is suggestive to notice the resemblance between this ancient work and the rude sketches and designs of such backward races in the modern world as the Australians, the South African bushmen, and the Esquimaux.

As we approach historic times, the instinct to record the beauty of form, colour, and movement becomes more strongly developed. The artists of ancient Egypt, for example, were most concerned with truth of contour. The human form was always conventionalised, but the characteristic poses of both men and beasts were graphically represented. Each phase of civilisation, indeed, has produced its own form of art, and it is largely from these monuments of bygone generations that we are able to reconstruct the history of man.

The monumental sculptures of Assyria and Egypt remain a living force and influence, and we cannot trace the beginning and development of Christian art without paying tribute to the miraculous genius of Greece. Four centuries before Christ, the Greeks had brought sculpture to a point of perfection and physical beauty which has never since been surpassed, and though nothing now remains of the paintings of the Greek artists Zeuxis and Apelles, we know not only from contemporary apprecia- tions but by the later wall-paintings of Pompeii and the memorial portraits of Alexandria that classical painting reached a high standard of realistic efficiency.   Under the Roman Empire the traditions of the Greeks were kept alive and maintained,[1] if not actually reinvigorated, but with the decline and fall of Rome the fine arts were tem- porarily submerged in the collapse of the ancient world.

During the dark ages, painting, as a secular art, almost entirely disappeared, and in the early days of the Church the Fathers gave little encouragement to art.   " Cursed be all who paint pictures " is a sentiment not infrequently found in their writings.   This antagonism to the joyous- ness of pagan art was natural in men who regarded this world as a vale of tears and only important as a preparation for the life to come.   The gloomy dogmatism of the new state religion of the Eastern Empire was satisfied with stiff formal mosaics for the basilicas of Constantinople.   The brush was too flexible an instrument for rendering the personages of their iron creed, and these emblems of ecclesiastical authority, rather than of heavenly love, were stony both in substance and sentiment.

When the new Gothic races had settled down in con- quered Italy, and Byzantine artists came over to decorate the interiors of the churches then building, they brought with them the frigid ceremonial ideals of the semi-oriental court from which they sprung.

The matter but not the manner of their art was changed when altar-pieces and mural decorations began to be painted instead of being built up by little cubes of coloured stones. The figures in these paintings are raised, like mosaics, from a gold background, red and blue are still the prevailing

[1] See wall-painting from Pompeii, " Ulysses and Penelope."

colours of the draperies, and the faces retain the fixed, staring solemnity of Byzantine types. The infant Jesus is a little wizened old man, the adult Christ is portrayed as an awful Judge, not as a loving Shepherd, and there is never a trace of emotion in the countenance of the almond-eyed Madonna.

The history of modern art begins with St. Francis of Assisi, the most lovable of all the Christian saints. He, the first forerunner of the Renaissance, substituted a religion of love for the sterile authority of orthodoxy, and in his infinite charity brought divinity nearer not only to mankind but to all creation. The birds and the fishes are his little brothers and sisters, and like the Psalmist of old he calls the hills and the valleys, the rivers and the woods, to join him in praising God. In a word, by his teaching, religion was reconciled to Nature, and with Nature again piously occupying the minds of men, art could progress.

It was only gradually that these new ideas popularised by St. Francis penetrated to the surface of painting. First of all, the change is limited to human psychology. Madonnas become more human in expression, and saints lose their severity to take on a mild and benevolent aspect. But still their figures are shown against a gold background which serves to isolate them from all terrestrial objects. Then this gilded screen is lowered, and in its place a landscape fills the background, at first a rather barren landscape with a few rudimentary trees, but soon enriched with shrubs and flowers, and ultimately completed by the presence of our little brethren the birds and animals.

The first great master to break away from the fixed type of Byzantine art was the Florentine painter, Giovanni Cenni, commonly known as Cimabue. He was born in 1240 and died in 1302. In his work a great change is perceptible. If in type his Madonna still adheres to the Byzantine tradition as regards features, a new softness has crept into her face, the Infant Jesus is no longer wizened but tender and more childlike, while there is a touch of human kindness in the angels who bear them company. It is extremely interesting that Cimabue was commissioned to decorate the church which was the burial-place of St. Francis, and there he was assisted in the work by his apprentice, the famous Giotto. It is with Giotto, whose work was directly inspired by " the little brother of the poor," that we begin our story.

In the OUTLINE there will be no attempt to print all the details of the history of art for six hundred years or to indulge in learned argument and criticism. We propose to reproduce as many as possible of the greatest pictures in the world and to say enough about their painters for the reader to understand what are their peculiar characteristics and what are the qualities of their work that make it beautiful and inspiring.

WILLIAM ORPEN

THE OUTLINE OF ART

I

THE BIRTH OF MODERN PAINTING

THE ART OF THE FLORENTINE MASTERS, FROM GIOTTO AND ANGELICO TO LIPPI AND BOTTICELLI

GIOTTO, a shepherd boy, was drawing pictures of his father's sheep on a slate, when Cimabue, the great artist of the time, happened to be passing by. Struck by the boy's talent, Cimabue obtained permission from his father and took the lad with him to Florence as his apprentice. When the artist was commissioned to decorate the church at Assisi, he entrusted his apprentice with painting the scenes from the life of St. Francis which were to adorn the walls of the upper church. In these frescoes the young Giotto proved himself, in the words of Ruskin, " a daring naturalist in defiance of tradition, idealism, and formalism." Besides his work at Assisi, Giotto also worked at Rome, and important frescoes by him, notably " The Bewailing of St. Francis " and " Herod's Birthday Feast," are in S. Croce at Florence, but the greatest and most famous of all his undertakings is the series of frescoes which he painted in the Chapel of the Arena at Padua. The date of this enterprise can be fixed with some certainty because it is known that in 1306 Dante was Giotto's guest at Padua, and the poet is said to have assisted the painter in his choice of subjects. Petrarch was also the friend of Giotto.

It is interesting to compare Cimabue's " Madonna and

Child " and his pupil's " The Bewailing of St. Francis,"
both reproduced here. To be fair to the elder artist, we
must remember what came before. We have only to look
at Margaritone's altar-piece in the National Gallery to
see the oppressive type of Byzantine art, destitute of any
feeling for beauty or truth to Nature. From whom
Cimabue received his training we know not—there was no
famous painter before him—but we do know he was held

Photo : Anderson.

" THE BEWAILING OF ST. FRANCIS," BY GIOTTO (*circa* 1266–1337)·

Santa Croce, Florence.

It is remarkable that St. Francis, the great apostle of Humanity, influenced the Italian
artists who brought back humanity to painting after the long period of Byzantine
artificiality that followed the fall of the Roman Empire.

in high esteem by his contemporaries. The " Madonna "
he painted for S. Maria Novella aroused such enthusiasm
that it was carried to the church preceded by trumpeters
and followed by a procession of Florentines. But whatever the advance made by Cimabue, Giotto advanced still
further.

§ 1

If we study Cimabue's " Madonna " at the National
Gallery we find that his figures, though not entirely lifeless

" ULYSSES AND PENELOPE."

Wall painting from Pompeii.

One of the few existing examples of Roman painting, showing the high standard of realism reached in classical art.

Photo : Rischgitz Collection.

" MADONNA AND CHILD ENTHRONED," BY CIMABUE (1240–1302).

National Gallery, London.

In Cimabue is seen the first sign of the softening of the Byzantine stiffness, shown in the expression on the face of the Virgin in this picture, and also in the more lifelike treatment of the Child. The gilt background, however, is still artificial, and we do not feel that the Virgin is really sitting on the formal throne. Note also the want of proportion between the Virgin and the angels who are supposed to surround her.

16

as the heavily gilded Byzantine figures, are wooden, formal, and conventional, while Giotto's figures have individuality and human feeling, and his groups have a new realism and dramatic vigour. Giotto had a more extended range of colour than Cimabue ; he showed a preference for gayer and lighter schemes, and he gave a more careful imitation of Nature than existed in the works of his predecessors. When we hail Giotto as a daring naturalist, we must think of him in relation to the artists who preceded him, and not to those later painters who gradually learnt to give accurate and complete expression to the truths of Nature. Yet his Paduan frescoes show, as it has been well said, " the highest powers of the Italian mind and hand at the beginning of the fourteenth century." Although a shepherd in his youth, it is strange that his drawings of sheep do not appear correct to modern eyes.

As will be seen from his " The Bewailing of St. Francis," his backgrounds, though in a sense true to Nature, are not realistic. His buildings and his trees are far too small, being drawn neither in true perspective nor in correct proportion to the human figures. His hills are bare and jagged cliffs, his trees have only a dozen leaves for foliage ; but it was an innovation for fields, trees, and animals to appear at all, and no imperfections in their rendering can rob the painter of the glory of having extended the subject-matter of his art. Giotto was the first Gothic painter to depict action, to substitute the dramatic human life for the eternal repose of the divine. To his contemporaries his realism must have seemed amazing, and we can understand Boccaccio, after looking at earlier Byzantine paintings, writing enthusiastically in the *Decamerone* :

Giotto was such a genius that there was nothing in Nature which he could not have represented in such a manner that it not only resembled, but seemed to be, the thing itself.

Giotto was not only a painter : he was also an architect. When he returned to Florence in 1334 the city honoured him and itself by appointing him Master of the Works of the Cathedral. Two great architectural works were

2

Photo : *Rischgitz Collection.*
GIOTTO'S TOWER,
FLORENCE.

Architect and sculptor, as well
as painter, Giotto is an example of the mediæval artists'
universality.

planned and begun by him at
Florence, the West Front of the
Cathedral and its detached Cam-
panile or bell-tower. The latter—
of which we give a reproduction
—exists to this day as a monument
of his genius, although its author
did not live to see its completion.
But its lower courses were completed from Giotto's design, and
he was able with his own hand
to carve the first course of its
sculptured ornaments, illustrating
arts and industries, before he died
on January 8, 1337.

Giotto was the first of the great
Florentine painters. Among his
immediate successors was Andrea
Orcagna, whose famous "The
Coronation of the Virgin" is in
the National Gallery. Orcagna
was painter, sculptor, architect, and
poet. More of a dreamer than
his shrewd practical predecessor,
Orcagna did not so much develop
the realistic side of Giotto as refine
and intensify his psychology. He
carried on the Giottesque tradition
of truth and simplicity, but drama
and action appealed to him less
powerfully than the expression of
emotion and deep religious feeling.
In his masterpieces we are arrested
not by any movement, but by the
variety and intensity of the feelings
expressed in the figures.

"In the work of Orcagna," Ruskin writes,
"an intense solemnity and energy in the
sublimest groups of his figures, fading away

Photo : Rischgitz Collection. "THE KISS OF JUDAS," BY DUCCIO (*circa* 1260–1339).
Museum, Sienna.

Note the introduction of a natural background in the pioneer work of this early Siennese master.

19

Photo: Anderson.

"THE CALUMNY OF APELLES" (DETAIL), BY BOTTICELLI (1444–1510).

This striking presentment of Calumny, typified by a black-cowled hag, retreating defeated from the pure presence of the naked Truth, is at once a brilliant re-creation of a
lost picture by the famous Greek artist Apelles, who flourished in the fifth century B.C.,
and is also an expression of Botticelli's indignation against those who calumniated the
great preacher Savonarola, even after his martyrdom. It represents the culmination
of the painter's devotion to Greek art and the beginning of his submission to the teaching
of this fanatical friar.

" JUDITH WITH THE HEAD OF HOLOPHERNES," BY BOTTICELLI.

Judith, the saviour of her country, is seen here after leaving the tent of Holophernes.
The sword is still in her hand, and behind her strides the maidservant bearing the head
of the tyrant whom Judith has slain. In the landscape background the discomfited
army of Holophernes is shown retreating in confusion across a spacious landscape. This
comparatively early work shows the graciousness of Botticelli's conception of womanhood and his power of rendering human beings and landscape with convincing truth.

as he touches inferior subjects, indicates that his home was among the
archangels, and his rank among the first of the sons of men."

This religious intensity led to a greater formality than
is found in Giotto and to a curious suggestion of a return
to Byzantine lack of humanity.

§ 2

While Giotto was laying the foundations of the art of
Florence, another school of painting arose in the quiet
hill city of Sienna. Its founder, Duccio di Buoninsegna,
is said to have been so much influenced by the Byzantine
style that he has been called " the last of the great artists of
antiquity," as opposed to Giotto, the "father of modern
painting." It is not easy to understand this comment if
one looks at Duccio's pictures, one of the most famous of
which—" The Kiss of Judas "—we reproduce. In spite
of their colour and their gilding the figures are human and
life-like, and the picture reflects human emotion entirely
in accord with the spirit of St. Francis. There is so much
sweetness and grace in the paintings of Duccio and his
fellows that they have been called the first lyric painters of
modern art.

Among his younger contemporaries the most gifted was
Simone Martini (c. 1283–1344), whose work has the pensive
devoutness that marks Siennese painting and a gay decorative
charm. There is a picture by him at Oxford, and another
in the Fitzwilliam Museum, Cambridge, but perhaps his
greatest achievement is the series of frescoes at Avignon.
These were once attributed to Giotto, but are now recognised to have been the work of Simone Martini and his
school. Among other Siennese artists the brothers Pietro
and Ambrogio Lorenzetti are noted for the dramatic
vigour in their work.

In the Florentine painting of the fifteenth century, the
impulse towards naturalism, first given by Giotto, branched
out in two opposite directions. One was psychic, the other
physical. The expression of intense and strong emotion,
together with action and movement was the aim of one

school; another strove after realistic probability and correctness of representation. This second school, pushed on by its love of truth, attacked and vanquished one by one various problems of technique. The approach to a closer representation of the appearance of realities involved three main inquiries : (1) the study of perspective, linear and aerial ; (2) the study of anatomy, of nude bodies in repose and action ; and (3) the detailed truth of facts in objects animate and inanimate.

§ 3

The most considerable figure in Florence after Orcagna was the Dominican monk Fra Giovanni da Fiesole, known as Fra Angelico (1387–1455), who belonged essentially to the psychic or spiritual school, and only approached the physical in his loving observation of nature. Here he was an innovator, for his eye dwells on gentle aspects, and in his landscape backgrounds he introduces pleasing forms of mountains and verdant meadows multicoloured with the budding flowers of spring. Indeed, all his painting is flower-like, but this delicate naturalism does not determine its character. It is the soulful quality of his work which gives it supreme distinction. The unworldliness of his art is explained partly by his cloistered existence and the fact that he lived until his fiftieth year in the little hill towns of Cortona and Fiesole. He led a holy and retired life, and, like St. Francis, was a little brother to the poor.

If Fra Angelico had his excellencies, he also had his limitations. His angels are so beautiful that, as Vasari wrote, " they appear to be truly beings of Paradise." But his devils inspire us with no terror ; they are too harmless and self-evidently ashamed of their profession to be anything but ludicrous.

" His pictures of martyrdom," says Muther, " create the impression of boys disguised as martyrs and executioners ; and his bearded men, weeping like women, are equally incredible. But when he does not leave his proper sphere, and the problem is to portray tender feelings, a great and silent joy of the heart, a holy ecstasy or tender sadness, his pictures have the effect of the silent prayer of a child."

"THE ANNUNCIATION," BY FRA ANGELICO (1387–1455).

St. Mark's, Florence.

The note of sweetness and simplicity introduced into art by Giotto is developed with appealing charm by Fra Angelico Note the perfect realism of the columns and the flowered background ; also the religious devotion expressed in the thoughtful countenances of the Virgin and the angel.

His frescoes in San Marco at Florence and in the Vatican at Rome remain the most enchanting visions of the heavenly world, a world he decked with bright joyful colours culled from the flower gardens of earth. Some idea of Fra Angelico's careful and tender art may be gathered from his " Annunciation," which we reproduce.

§ 4

In the expression of feeling, the most famous follower of Fra Angelico was Fra Filippo Lippi, but if unable to attain the ethereal spirituality of Angelico his art was full of humanity and delicacy. His Madonnas belong to Florence rather than to heaven and reveal the painter's fine feeling for feminine beauty more obviously than his piety. He was a genial painter, and in his comfortable satisfaction with the things of this life he shared with Angelico a love of flowers. " No one draws such lilies or such daisies as Lippi," wrote Ruskin. " Botticelli beat him afterwards in roses, but never in lilies."

Lippi's geniality is very evident in his " Annunciation," which we reproduce. The figures are human, the scene is homely, characteristics generally suggestive of the Dutch painters of a much later generation.

Fra Angelico and Fra Lippi stand for the imaginative development that followed the death of Giotto. In the other direction, the first great advance in the rendering of physical nature is found in the painting of Paolo Uccello, who first introduced perspective into pictures. Uccello was far more interested in the technical problems of fore-shortening and perspective than in anything else. Uccello represents the scientific spirit in the air of the Florence of Cosmo de' Medici, where not only artists, but mathematicians, anatomists, and great scholars were congregated. Among his achievements must be reckoned the recommencement of profane painting by his invention of the battle picture, a subject in which he had no predecessor and no successor till a century later. His early battle piece.

Photo : Rischgitz Collection.

" PORTRAIT OF JOHN HAWKWOOD," BY PAOLO UCCELLO (1397–1475).

Cathedral, Florence.

This equestrian portrait, in addition to its artistic merit, shown in the lifelike painting of the horse, is interesting as representing a famous English mercenary soldier, the son of an Essex tanner, who first went to the Continent with the English army that fought at Crécy.

the "Sant' Egidio,"[1] amuses us by the rocking-horse appearance of the horses.   In his absorption with technique, Uccello was indifferent then to realistic accuracy.   Truths of colour did not interest him—he painted horses red.   The third dimension in space, which Giotto could only suggest experimentally and symbolically, was conquered by Uccello, who clearly separated the planes in which his figures move and have their being.   Roses, oranges, and hedges were drawn with botanical precision, and no pains were spared to draw branches and even leaves in correct perspective. The splendid realism to which Uccello ultimately attained is best represented by the intensely alive animal and its rider in the picture we reproduce.   Uccello's equestrian portrait of the English mercenary John Hawkwood in the cathedral of Florence is a milestone in the history of art.

§ 5

Romantic mysticism, which budded with Fra Angelico, passed by Lippi to flower with all sweetness and beauty in the art of his pupil, Alessandro Filipepi, famed as Botticelli.   Sandro Botticelli was born in Florence about 1447, and was first apprenticed to a goldsmith.   To the end of his life he was a jeweller in colours, but owes little beside the name of Botticelli, by which we know him, to his goldsmith master, whom he soon left, to devote himself thenceforth entirely to painting.   The thing that differentiates the art of Botticelli from that of all his predecessors is the intensely personal, even egotistical note that he strikes in all his work.   The exquisite, delicate melancholy which pervades the expression, both of Christian saints and Pagan gods, in all his pictures, is his own, not theirs, as though he were sorry for them for being saints and gods, and so, by their very nature, deprived of all those ecstasies alike of faith and of doubt, of conviction and speculation, which are the compensating privileges of human imperfection.

[1] Though commonly known by this title, Uccello's masterpiece at the National Gallery is now held to represent the Rout of San Romano, 1432.

Photo : Hanfstaengl. "THE MOURNING FOR CHRIST," BY BOTTICELLI.

In this picture we have an extreme example of the tragic element introduced into Botticelli's last works due to his meditation on the gloomy preaching of Savonarola. There is a strained affectation in the poses of the Apostles which suggests that this picture was finished by pupils after Botticelli's death, but the tense feeling expressed in the central group is entirely in the master's last manner, though only the sweet face of the Magdalene, who is tenderly lifting the feet of Christ, remains to remind us of the earlier Botticelli, whose sole aim was the expression of beauty.

28

The Italy of Botticelli was not the Italy of Fra Angelico. Beauty was no longer the handmaid of religion. The Church was no longer the only patron of art, nor were church walls the only outlet for artists. Cosimo de' Medici and Lorenzo the Magnificent did not worry their painters with theological restrictions ; it was beauty that they wanted. It was not till his master Lippi left Florence in 1467 to undertake a commission at Spoleto, that Botticelli began to develop his own individuality. Pictures before that date, as " The Adoration of the Magi " in the National Gallery, reflect the art of Lippi. But as soon as the young painter was left alone in Florence, he mixed with other artists like the Pollaiuoli, who had greater knowledge of anatomy than Lippi, and his art made rapid progress. On another page is shown one of the most beautiful of these early works, " Judith with the Head of Holophernes." Muscular action is finely expressed in the swinging stride of the maid who follows bearing the head of the slain tyrant, while the heroine herself is depicted with all the fresh girlish charm of one of the young Florentine maids who frequented the artist's studio. In the distance the great army of invasion is seen retreating in confusion through a spacious landscape.

Botticelli's chief patron in Florence was not Lorenzo the Magnificent, but a distant kinsman of the Duke with the same name. For the villa at Castello, belonging to this younger Lorenzo de' Medici, Botticelli painted a number of pictures, among them, about 1477, the famous " Primavera." No more beautiful allegory of the coming of Spring has ever been painted than this picture, of which we give a reproduction. In the centre Venus, the Goddess of Love, awaits Spring's coming, with Cupid hovering over her. On her right are the Three Graces, with Mercury, the Messenger of the Gods ; on her left gaily-decked Spring advances, gently pushed forward by Flora, the goddess of flowers, and by Zephyr, who personifies the mild west wind. Where'er she treads the flowers spring to life. Beautiful as an interpretation of old Greek legends, which make a human story out of all the phenomena of Nature, this

Photo : *Anderson.*

"SPRING," BY BOTTICELLI.

In this exquisite allegory of the coming of Spring the vernal season is personified by a brightly garbed maiden, who is being gently pushed forward by Flora, the goddess of flowers, and Zephyr, the west wind ; preceding her as a herald (on the extreme left) is Mercury, the messenger of the gods. In the centre Venus, goddess of Love, welcomes Spring's coming, while hovering over her head, Cupid aims his arrow at the Three Graces.

picture is also an expression of the revived pagan delight in physical form which was typical of fifteenth-century Florence.

The fame of this and other pictures by Botticelli spread to Rome, whither in 1481 he was summoned by the Pope to assist in the decoration of the Sistine Chapel, where three great frescoes, the " History of Moses," " Destruction of Korah, Dathan, and Abiram," and " Temptation of Christ," remain to this day as a monument of his skill, his energy, and his sense of drama and beauty. After two years in Rome, Botticelli returned to Florence, where, in 1483, he painted the most exquisite of all his Madonnas, " The Magnificat." But the happy days of the painter were drawing to an end. After the death of Lorenzo in 1492 and the accession of his worthless son Piero, Florence was agitated by political troubles; and to that city, tired of pleasure and weary of knowledge, came Girolamo Savonarola, the great reformer priest.

When the Medici were expelled from Florence, the young Lorenzo went with them, and Botticelli lost his best patron. During these tumultuous years Botticelli devoted much of his time to executing a wonder-series of illustrations to Dante, the originals of which are still preserved in the Vatican Library and the Berlin Museum. These drawings reveal not only an intimate knowledge of the great poem, but also a profound sympathy with the feelings of the poet. Savonarola preached and Botticelli listened, though happily he did not follow the example of some of his contemporaries, and burn his earlier pictures of pagan subjects. Though his brother Simone, who lived with him in these later years, was a fanatical disciple of Savonarola, Sandro himself does not appear to have been wholly converted till the great preacher in turn became the victim of the fury of a fickle populace.

In the same year (1498) in which Savonarola was burned at the stake in the Piazza della Signoria, Botticelli painted his great picture, " The Calumny of Apelles." This work, which we reproduce, had a double purpose. Nominally it was an attempt to reproduce a famous lost picture,

Photo: Rischgitz Collection.

"THE ANNUNCIATION," BY FRA FILIPPO LIPPI (1406–69).

National Gallery, London.

An example of Lippi's decorative power, enlivened by accurate nature study. It will be noticed, however, on comparing this work with Angelico's rendering of the same subject, that Lippi, notwithstanding his increased technical dexterity, is less spiritual in his treatment and fails to express the devotional piety found in the work of his master.

Calumny," by the ancient Greek painter Apelles, from the description of it given by the Greek writer Lucian. But we can have little doubt that the inward and spiritual meaning of this picture, which shows black-robed Calumny (or according to another interpretation, Remorse) slinking from the radiant presence of the naked Truth, was directed against the calumniators of the martyred friar. Among all Botticelli's pictures this painting is distinguished by its exquisite finish and richness of detail, and we may regard it as the last great expression of his powers both as a classic and a humanist.   Distressed both by the disturbed state of his native city and by the tragic end of Savonarola, Botticelli fretted himself into melancholia during his last years.   The few religious pictures of this period which remain—many of them probably finished by pupils after the master's death—contain a strange exaggeration of gesture and facial expression, and an almost theatrical vehemence of action, which are entirely foreign to the poetical fantasies of his earlier manner.   As an example of the high-strung emotions of his last years, " The Mourning of Christ " may be compared in these pages with the serene tranquillity of Botticelli's early- and middle-period work. The happiest painting of his last period is the little " Nativity " in the National Gallery.

3

II

THE INVENTION OF OIL-PAINTING

THE ART OF THE VAN EYCKS, MEMLINC, AND THE EARLY
FLEMISH MASTERS

§ I

IN the whole history of painting there are no more remarkable figures than the two brothers Hubert and Jan van Eyck. Never before or since has Art made so mighty a stride in the space of one generation. We get some idea of what they achieved if we compare any King or Queen in a pack of playing cards with a modern photograph of a living monarch.

Just as Molière's " Bourgeois Gentilhomme " was astounded to find he had been talking prose all his life without knowing it, so some readers may be surprised to learn that they are perfectly familiar with mediæval Gothic art, for examples of it may be found in every pack of playing cards, in which the court cards are survivals of mediæval Gothic portraiture.

To obtain the best possible insight into the birth of Gothic art one ought to visit the Cathedral of Brunswick. Here we may see what are probably the best-preserved examples of mediæval wall-paintings. In the choir is a series of pictures, painted about the beginning of the thirteenth century, and one of the best of these represents " Herod's Birthday Feast." It is perfectly childish, of course, but it is childish in a totally different way from that in which the pictures of Giotto and Angelico are childish. Neither the Italian nor the Brunswick pictures show any sense of perspective or give any real effect of space and distance ; but the treatment of the figures greatly differs. In the Italian paintings there is still a faint trace of Greek

Photo : Annan & Sons.

"MARGARET TUDOR," BY MABUSE (*circa* 1472–1535).

Scottish National Gallery, Edinburgh.

" A rogue in porcelain "—George Meredith's famous phrase—might fittingly be applied to the subject of this portrait, an English Royal Beauty, the elder daughter of Henry VII. Though she looks so demure in her costume of 1500 or thereabouts, the painter has allowed the eyes to betray the real character of this self-willed princess, whose morals were said to be worse than those of her brother Henry VIII.

If we compare the polished softness of this portrait with Mabuse's earlier work, " The Adoration of the Kings," we learn the extent to which this Flemish painter altered his style after he had visited Italy and had become acquainted with the work of Leonardo da Vinci and his contemporaries.

35

draughtsmanship distorted by Byzantine dogma, but the Brunswick paintings show quite a new conception of the human body which has nothing to do with Greece or Rome ; it is *pure Gothic*.   In these Brunswick paintings the people pictured look like nothing so much as a row of court cards. Herod himself looks as much like a real human being as the King of Hearts looks like H.M. King George V.

Now we are in a position to appreciate the art of the brothers Van Eyck.   To realise the advance they made we must not compare their figures with the portraits of to-day or modern photographs, but with the Queen of Spades and the Jack of Diamonds.   And we must remember that little over a hundred years separates the style of court-card portraiture from the realistic forms of Hubert's mighty figures surmounting " The Adoration of the Lamb " and Jan van Eyck's " The Man with the Pinks."   Think of the court cards when you look at the illustrations of these paintings.

It is a great misfortune that we know so little about the lives of these amazing men.   Many interesting details about the early Italian artists have been preserved to us because Giorgio Vasari, himself an early sixteenth-century Florentine painter, wrote the lives of the preceding and contemporary Italian artists with a fullness and vivacity which make his accounts still fascinating and readable. But there was no biographer of the early Flemish artists, and the few meagre facts we know about them have slowly been unearthed by patient scholarship toiling amid the archives of the cities in which these artists lived.

Therefore it is by the pictures which remain, rather than by any written record, that we must endeavour to reconstruct the flowering of art in Flanders and Northern Europe.   But if we do study those works, then it is positively electrifying to behold the mysterious and rapid quickening of the artistic spirit in Flanders.

Of what came between the paintings of Brunswick Cathedral and the art of the Van Eycks, little is known and nothing certain.   The very names of the painters of some undoubtedly early pictures are unknown, and all we

"THE ADORATION OF THE LAMB," CENTRAL PANELS OF ALTAR-
PIECE BY HUBERT AND JAN VAN EYCK.

Though dating from the days when oil-painting was first invented, this gigantic altar-
piece—the painted surface of which extends to over 1000 square feet—has in many
respects never been surpassed. In its original form it consisted of the centre panel, from
which the whole takes its name, surmounted by three panels representing (from left to
right) the Virgin Mary, God the Father, and St. John. These three figures are certainly
the work of Hubert. This portion, all that now remains in the Cathedral at Ghent, is
shown above; but originally the polyptych was completed on either side by two tiers of
two panels each. Of these, two are now at Brussels and six are in the Berlin Museum.

37

Photo : Hanfstaengl.

"THE JUST JUDGES," BY HUBERT
AND JAN VAN EYCK.

Ghent Cathedral.

can say with certainty is
that from about the end
of the fourteenth century
to the middle of the
fifteenth century a group
of painters flourished on
the lower Rhine and be-
came known as the School
of Cologne. Several of
its members are merely
legendary, but the *Bimburg
Chronicle* of 1380 contains
an authoritative entry :
" In this time there was
a painter in Cologne of
the name of Wilhelm ; he
was considered the best
master in all German
Land ; he paints every
man, of whatever form, as
if he were alive." This
master has been identified
as William of Herle (or
Cologne), who died about
1378, and though he evid-
ently impressed his con-
temporaries by his pioneer
realism the work of his
school is esteemed in our
own time for its spiritual
calm and peaceful purity.
" St. Veronica " in the
National Gallery is prob-
ably painted by William
of Cologne or by one of
his pupils.

Now Hubert van Eyck
was born about 1365
near Maestricht, which

is no great distance from Cologne. Most probably he studied in the Rhineland capital before he migrated to Flanders and, with his brother Jan, settled in Ghent. The increasing commercial prosperity of Bruges and Ghent attracted artists from the banks of the Rhine, and the School of Cologne declined as the Early Flemish School arose.

Since the time of Vasari, the brothers Hubert and Jan van Eyck have generally received credit for having discovered oil as a medium for painting. Before their time artists had mixed their colours either with water (frescoes) or with yolk of egg (tempera paintings), and though modern scholarship is inclined to doubt whether the Van Eycks were actually the first to make use of oil, they were beyond question the pioneers of the new medium.

Tradition says that Jan, having one day " devoted the utmost pains " in finishing a picture with great care, varnished it and as usual put it in the

Photo : Hanfstaengl.

" CHRIST'S WARRIORS," BY HUBERT AND JAN VAN EYCK.

Ghent Cathedral.

sun to dry. But the heat was excessive and split the wooden panel which he had painted. Grieving at the destruction of his handiwork, Jan "determined to find a means whereby he should be spared such an annoyance in the future." After various experiments he discovered that linseed oil and oil of nuts dried more quickly than any which he had tried, and that colours mixed with these oils were more brilliant, proof against water, and blended far better than the tempera. Thus was oil-painting invented.

"The Adoration of the Lamb" at Ghent, executed by the two brothers, is not only the earliest monument of the art of oil-painting but it is the most splendid masterpiece produced by any Northern artist before the seventeenth century. Not till Rubens was born, some 200 years later, did Flanders produce the equal of the Van Eycks, and from this fact alone we may deduce the extraordinary mastery of their art.

"The Adoration of the Lamb," an elaborate polyptych, is not one picture but a whole collection of pictures. Originally it consisted of the long central panel showing "The Adoration of the Lamb" and above this three panels of "The Virgin," "God the Father," and "St. John" (all shown in our illustration) ; on the left of the "Lamb" panel—which measures $7\frac{1}{4}$ feet long by $4\frac{1}{2}$ feet high—were two panels of "The Just Judges" and "Christ's Warriors" (see pages 38 and 39), and these were balanced by panels showing "The Holy Hermits" and "The Holy Pilgrims" on the right. On the upper tier the three central figures were flanked by two double-panelled shutters, the painted subjects on one side being "Angels Singing," "Angels Making Music," and, at the extreme ends, "Adam" and "Eve" ; on the reverse of the shutters are "St. John the Baptist," "St. John the Evangelist," "Jodoc Vydt"— the donor of the altar-piece—and "Wife of Jodoc Vydt."

The complete altar-piece therefore consisted of twelve panels, four painted on both sides, making sixteen pictures in all. The whole painted surface of this composite picture, or polyptych, amounts to over a thousand feet. Six of these panels were formerly in the Berlin Museum, but, having been surrendered to Belgium under the Terms of the Treaty of

Versailles, they have now been added to the central panels together with the panels of " Adam " and " Eve," formerly at Brussels, so that the whole altar-piece is now seen in its original completeness in the Cathedral of Ghent.

The whole altar-piece was undoubtedly planned and begun by Hubert, who certainly painted the three tremendous central figures and the panel of " Angels Making Music." After Hubert's death in 1426 Jan van Eyck completed the altar-piece, and probably did not adhere altogether strictly to his brother's original designs. The difference between the work of the two brothers is one not so much of skill as of temperament. Hubert possessed a solemn spirituality and serious thoughtfulness which was not shared by his more worldly younger brother.

Jan van Eyck, born about 1385, is a more popular and no less eminent figure than his elder brother. He lived on in Ghent and Bruges till 1441 and his works are comparatively numerous, whereas few paintings by Hubert are extant. Shortly before completing the Ghent altar-piece, Jan entered the service of Philip of Burgundy, for whom he undertook several diplomatic missions. In this way he saw Portugal and other foreign countries, and his later paintings betray his affectionate remembrance of the country he had seen in southern climes. Jan was essentially a realist, with his keen gaze ever fixed on the beautiful earth and on human beings rather than on religious doctrines. His real bent is shown in many of his panels for " The Adoration of the Lamb." In the panel of " The Annunciation " his delight in the still-life, in the wash-basin and other furniture of the room, in the street view seen through the window, reveals him to be the true father of genre painting. His portraits of Jodoc Vydt and his wife, shown without flattery as a dull but prosperous Flemish burgher and his wife, prove him to be the father of modern portraiture. Both these qualities, his capacity for realistic portraiture and his infinite exactitude in rendering the detail of an interior, are magnificently displayed in our illustration, " Jan Arnolfini and his Wife " (page 56), one of the most precious things in the National Gallery.

While Hubert belongs to the austere company of monumental or architectural painters, Jan is a pioneer of domestic painting and one of the first producers of what we now know as a "picture." In this development Jan van Eyck was, doubtless unconsciously, meeting the demand of his time and place.

In Northern churches and cathedrals, which need more light than the Southern, the place occupied by wall-paintings was gradually given over to stained-glass windows, which are marked features in the Gothic architecture of Northern Europe. Wall-paintings, which still led the way in Italy, became secondary in Flanders to the decorative panels introduced into wooden screen-work. This much accomplished, it was a short step to meet the demands of a prosperous commercial community by (metaphorically) detaching a panel from its ecclesiastical frame and adapting its subject and style to a private dwelling-house.

Thus, while Italy remains the home of the religious picture, Flanders and the Netherlands become more and more the home of secular art. Though he painted other religious subjects beside "The Adoration of the Lamb" and the miniature "Altar-piece" which the Emperor Charles V. took with him on his travels, the most famous of the other paintings by Jan van Eyck are portraits. In his portraiture he is uncompromising in his endeavour to state the whole truth; such details as warts and wrinkles, furrows and stubbly beards, he renders with passionate delight and exactitude. A splendid example of Jan's rugged realism may be seen in our illustration from the portrait, in the Berlin Museum, known as "The Man with the Pinks" (on opposite page). Precisely drawn, true to every wart and wrinkle, the face is so full of life and character that we almost listen for speech to come from the slightly parted lips. Who this man was has never been discovered, but from his costume and the handsome ring on his finger we may deduce that he was a person of position.

§ 2

If little is known about the Van Eycks, still less is known concerning their successors. Patient research among

Photo : Bruckmann.

"THE MAN WITH THE PINKS," BY JAN VAN EYCK (*circa* 1385-1441).

Berlin Museum.

Painted about 500 years ago by one of the first artists to use oil-paint, this picture astounds us to-day by its lifelike realism, by its unswerving fidelity to every little detail that can help to give the character of a man and set his living presence before us. Note how the brocade collar of the tunic, showing above the fur collar of the coat, seems to be ornamented with the alternating letters Y and C. It is hoped these may one day afford a clue to the identity of the sitter, who is at present unknown. The bell which with a cross, hangs by a twisted chain from his neck, suggests that St. Anthony was the patron saint of the person represented.

43

municipal records in Flanders, however, has greatly increased our knowledge during recent years. Twenty years ago the very name of the painter of a fine altar-piece in the Abbey of Flemalle, near Liège, was uncertain ; he was alluded to vaguely as "The Master of Flemalle." To-day it has been established that he was a painter of Tournai, called Robert Campin, who was born about 1375 and lived till 1444. There are two good examples of his art in the National Gallery, and he is important, not only for his own work, but as being the master of Roger van der Weyden.

Among religious painters Roger van der Weyden (c. 1400–64), who was born at Tournai and settled in Brussels, had a considerable influence. Beside the calm solemnity of Hubert van Eyck, his pictures appear exaggerated in their dramatic intensity and fervour. He was essentially a tragic artist, dwelling on the sufferings of the Saviour and peopling his pictures with wailing figures, whose emaciated faces stream with tears, whose hands are convulsively clutched in agony or outstretched to heaven. In 1450 he visited Rome and is thought to have had some influence on Ferrarese and Paduan painting, and there he in turn may have imbibed something of a new spirit, for towards the end of his life his sentiment became more gentle and refined. Van der Weyden is seen at his best in "The Bewailing of the Body of Christ" in the Berlin Gallery, and in this picture his affinity with the school of Van Eyck is shown in the delicate and gently detailed landscape background.

Roger's fellow-pupil Jacques Daret, who died in 1466, is softer and more conciliatory in his religious themes, and his paintings are peculiarly sweet both in colour and temper.

The tragic painting of Van der Weyden was continued by Hugo van der Goes (c. 1435–82) of Ghent and Bruges, who is reputed to have begun life as a wild pleasure-lover. Suddenly he withdrew to a monastery near Brussels, and conscious-stricken at his own dissipation he henceforward devoted his talent to sacred subjects, usually accentuating the sorrows of Christ, but always avoiding the wailing and excessive gesticulation which marked the pictures of Van der Weyden. His art is deeper and more quiet, but is certainly not less expressive. The altar-piece with " The Adoration of Jesus " which, under the orders of Portinari, agent for the Medici in Bruges, he painted for Santa Maria Nuova in Florence, is generally accepted as the supreme masterpiece of Hugo van der Goes. We see the continuation of the Van Eyck tradition in the glimpse of landscape, in which light-green branches are boldly contrasted with the deep-blue sky, in the naturalism of the fire-red lily in the foreground, and in the realism of the rough, weather-beaten shepherds who on one side balance the sturdy figure of St. Joseph, who stands praying, on the other. When this picture, which we illustrate (page 57), arrived in Florence, it created a great sensation, and it has been thought that many famous Italian artists, among them Piero di Cosimo, Ghirlandaio, Piero Pollaiuolo, were influenced to the extent of changing their style after they had seen this masterpiece by Hugo van der Goes.

§ 3

The first great figure in Flemish painting who appears to owe little to either of the Van Eycks is Hans Memlinc (c. 1430–94), who probably studied at Cologne before he settled in Bruges about 1467. His paintings in the Hospital of St. John at Bruges are world-famous, and round them has been woven a pretty legend.

Young Memlinc, the story goes, while fighting as a soldier of Charles the Bold, was desperately wounded and dragged himself to the Hospital of St. John at Bruges, where he was kindly received and his wounds tended. When cured, out of gratitude and for no fee, he painted the pictures still to be seen in the Hospital.

Unfortunately, historical research has demolished the legend and reveals Memlinc as no soldier of fortune but as a prosperous citizen and house-owner in Bruges. Yet the legend well accords with the character of Memlinc's paintings, which have been likened to " the visions of a sick man in convalescence."

Just as the name of Michael Angelo is indissolubly

linked to the Sistine Chapel in Rome, so is that of Memlinc to the Hospital of St. John at Bruges. But while we are awed by the heroic figures and magnitude of the Italian's paintings at Rome, in Bruges we are fascinated and bewitched by the bijou qualities of the Fleming's art. Memlinc's large triptych in the Hospital, " The Virgin and Child Enthroned," with panels on either side of " St. John the Baptist " and of " St. John the Evangelist at Patmos," is not the work that takes our breath away : it is the " Shrine of St. Ursula," a wonderfully painted casket—made to hold relics of the saint. Though only 3 feet long and less than 3 feet high, this casket is covered with eight panel paintings, and six medallions on the roof slopes. Five of the scenes illustrating the story of St. Ursula are reproduced (pages 47 and 48), and the beauty of their workmanship is manifest.

Looking at these poetical pictures of a romantic story, it seems ungracious to recall that the legend of St. Ursula, according to modern science, rests on no surer foundation than the discovery in mediæval times of an old Roman burial-ground. From these unknown remains, it is now said, the tale of Ursula and her 11,000 virgins was constructed. Many versions of the legend are in existence ; but none nearer than five or six centuries to the date when the events were supposed to have happened. This is the version followed by Memlinc.

Ursula, daughter of a King of Brittany or Cornwall, either to delay marriage with a pagan prince, or alternately to escape the persecution of the British Emperor Maximian, was enjoined to go on a pilgrimage and make 11,000 virgins her companions. The company sailed up the Rhine via Cologne to Basle, and thence went by foot to Rome, where they were received by the Pope with every honour and attention. Returning, they sailed up the Rhine from Basle, with papal benedictions, but on arriving at Cologne they were slaughtered by the Huns. After the martyrdom, their relics were piously collected and buried.

That is the story, and it will be noted that Memlinc, to

(3)   (4)

(1) ST. URSULA ARRIVING AT COLOGNE.   (2) THE PILGRIMS ARRIVING AT BASLE.
(3) THE POPE AND PILGRIMS EMBARK AT BASLE.   (4) THE MARTYRDOM OF THE PILGRIMS.

"THE MARTYRDOM OF ST. URSULA," BY MEMLINC (*circa* 1430-94).

Hospital of St. John, Bruges.

Memlinc's " Shrine of St. Ursula," in the Hospital of St. John at Bruges, is one of the
art wonders of the world.   It is an oblong gabled casket, the sides of which are adorned
with six miniatures illustrating the legend of St. Ursula.   Four of these are shown above.
At the ends are " The Virgin and Child with two Nuns " and " St. Ursula with Ten
Companions " ; on the roof-slopes are medallions showing " The Coronation of the
Virgin," " St. Ursula and her Companions," and four angel-musicians.

The whole casket only measures 3 ft. in length, 2 ft. 10 in. in height, and 1 ft. 1 in.
in breadth.

"THE MARTYRDOM OF ST. URSULA," BY MEMLINC.

Hospital of St. John, Bruges.

This illustration, about half the size of the original painting, illustrates the final episode in the story of St. Ursula. Accompanied by a maiden and one of the Pope's suite, the Saint stands undismayed before the General of the Huns and, refusing to deny her faith, calmly awaits death by the arrow which an archer is ready to let fly. It is characteristic of Memlinc's gentleness and delicacy of feeling that he has preferred suggesting the Saint's martyrdom to painting the Saint's death with the grim realism which we find in the works of other Flemish masters.

Photo : W. A. Mansell & Co.

"THE DUKE OF CLEVES," BY MEMLINC.

National Gallery, London.

The grace and spirituality of this picture admirably illustrate the portraiture of Memlinc who, it has been said, " saw not only with his eyes but with his soul."

4

show how absolutely the Pope was in sympathy with St. Ursula, actually makes him embark with her at the start of the return journey. Incidentally these miniature paintings show that Memlinc knew Cologne well, for in all the scenes which take place in the city he has effectively introduced the Cathedral and other of its principal buildings.

The spirituality of Memlinc's portraiture, his power to paint the soul as well as the surface, is beautifully exemplified in " The Duke of Cleves," reproduced from the picture at the National Gallery. His romanticism, a new note which Memlinc definitely contributed to painting, is bewitchingly exhaled from his " Betrothal of St. Catherine " and the " Legend of St. Usrula," both of which are touching in their simplicity, their girlish freshness, and miniature daintiness.

Already the city, so wealthy in the days of the Van Eycks, had become in the time of Memlinc *Bruges-la-Morte*. Something of its sad poetic solitude pervades his pictures. The great house of the Medici had collapsed, the rich merchants had gone elsewhere, and the next great Flemish painter, Quinten Massys (1466–1530), was domiciled in Antwerp.

§ 4

Tradition relates that Quinten Massys, the " smith of Antwerp," became a painter only because his sweetheart would not marry a smith. The swinging brushwork and broad handling which he substituted for the small detailed touches of the earlier painters well accord with the vigour demanded by the work of a smithy. His handling of colour is also new, for instead of placing unbroken blues, reds, yellows, etc., in immediate juxtaposition, he marshals his hues into a uniform colour-scheme. Disliking smallness in all things, he painted figures almost life-size ; and when the size of his picture forbade the full-length, he contented himself with half figures rather than reduce his scale to miniature proportions. " The Banker and his Wife " at the Louvre is a fine example of this innovation (page 52).

Photo : W. A. Mansell & Co.

" THE ADORATION OF THE KINGS," BY MABUSE (*circa* 1472–1535).

National Gallery, London.

In this remarkable picture we see one of the last masterpieces of pure Flemish art before it became influenced and changed by Italian painting. The words " Roi Jaspar," inscribed on the lid of the chalice offered to the Virgin, reveals the identity of the kneeling king. Behind him stands Melchior with his gift, a monstrance, in his right hand, while on our left is the swarthy figure of Balthasar holding before him a gold reliquary. In the original at the National Gallery the signature of the artist " IENNINE GOS . . . " may be deciphered on the torque of the turbaned attendant and also on Balthasar's turban.

THE BANKER AND HIS WIFE " BY QUINTEN MASSYS (1466–1530).

The Louvre, Paris.

This delightfully intimate portrait of a fifteenth-century Banker and his Wife is deservedly the most popular of Massys' paintings.   It is full of charming human touches, and there is no hint of the miser in the expression of the man who is counting and weighing his money.   He is just getting on with a necessary piece of business, and both he and his wife, who has turned from her illuminated book—to see if he will be much longer—seem to tell us they will be glad when the day's work is over and nothing is to be done except enjoy their own domestic happiness.

Note how the reflection in the little mirror on the table shows us that these people are facing a window, through which comes the light which illumines them and all the details of the office.

With the death of Quinten Massys in 1530 the first period of Flemish painting comes to an end. The next generation of Flemings either practised their art in Italy or, like Jan Gossart, called Mabuse (*c.* 1472–1535), imported Italian fashions in painting.

Mabuse, who took his name from the town of Maubeuge, where he was born about 1472, was a Fleming before he naturalised his art. This we may see by studying the magnificent example of his first manner at the National Gallery. " The Adoration of the Magi," bought for the nation from the Countess of Carlisle in 1911, was painted by Mabuse before he visited Italy. In the architectural background we get a hint of the influence of Roger van der Weyden ; the thirty figures in their rather pompous costumes are stolid and almost stony in comparison with the grace of his later works.

Some ten years later Mabuse visited Italy in the train of the Duke of Burgundy, and in Florence Mabuse came under the influence of Leonardo da Vinci. That his first contact with the new naturalism did not have altogether happy results we know by the commonplace realism of his " Adam and Eve " at Hampton Court. Soon, however, the warm air of Italy won him to gentleness, and in his Italianised works it is as a portrait-painter that Mabuse excels. Of his many portraits in Great Britain, the most beautiful is the portrait of " Margaret Tudor " (the elder sister of Henry VIII) (see page 35), which now hangs in the Scottish National Gallery at Edinburgh.

THE REVIVAL OF SCULPTURE

Sculpture, which among the Greeks of the fifth century B.C. had reached a point of physical perfection never since surpassed, decayed with its sister art of painting after the fall of Rome. Statues became as stiff and mannered as the figures in Byzantine paintings. The first Gothic revival of the art took place in France. Nothing was accomplished in Italy from the twelfth to the fourteenth centuries equal to the contemporary statuary which adorns the cathedrals of Chartres, Bourges, Amiens, and Rheims. The revival in Italy began with Niccolo of Pisa (1205–78). At this time Pisa was a town politically important and prosperous in commerce. Its wealth attracted vendors of Greek and Roman antiques. Niccolo studied these classical marbles, and eventually abandoned his practice as an architect to devote himself wholly to sculpture. He broke away from Byzantinism, founded a new school, and proved to his fellow-craftsmen the advantage of study from Nature and the antique. He was followed by his son Giovanni and his pupil Andrea Pisano, and Orcagna felt his influence ; but with them ends the short story of Pisan art.

No better example of the patience and thoroughness of the mediæval artist could be found than Lorenzo Ghiberti (1378–1455), one of the greatest workers in bronze of his century. Ghiberti was painting frescoes at Rimini when he heard that the Merchant Guild of Florence was inviting Italian artists to compete for the making of the bronze doors for the Baptistery. He returned to Florence, and in the competition the exhibits of Ghiberti and Brunelleschi were pronounced equally good. The original bronze panels by both artists, illustrating " The Sacrifice of Abraham," are now in the National Museum, Florence. Brunelleschi withdrew, and in 1403 Ghiberti received the commission. These two gates became his life-work : he began them when he was twenty-five, and he was seventy-four when they were finished. The first gate, representing scenes from the New Testament, was set up in 1424 ; the second, still more wonderful, took longer. While Ghiberti was working at the first gate, Brunelleschi reduced the laws of perspective to a science ; and into the subjects from the Old Testament for the second gate Ghiberti introduced his newly acquired knowledge of perspective. Some panels contain as many as one hundred figures, which, said the artist, " I modelled upon different planes, so that those nearest the eye might appear larger, and those more remote smaller in proportion." The second gate was set up in 1452, and three years later Ghiberti died.

After his death Michael Angelo—never easy to please—viewed his works and pronounced them " fit to be the gates of Paradise."

A young companion of the architect Brunelleschi, who studied the antique with him at Rome and then returned to Florence, was Donatello (1386–1466). His. is one of

Photo : Anderson.

STATUE OF GENERAL GATTAMELATA AT PADUA, BY DONATELLO
(1386–1466).
One of the two finest equestrian statues in the world by the founder of Realism
in Sculpture.

the greatest names in the history of sculpture. He brought to great perfection the art of carving in low relief, and his many busts and statues have a vigour, humanity, and dramatic power which he was the first to introduce into sculpture. His relief, " The Charge to St. Peter," in the Victoria and Albert Museum, South Kensington, is almost an anticipation of the impressionism of Rodin in its

" JAN ARNOLFINI AND HIS WIFE," BY JAN VAN EYCK.

National Gallery, London.

This well-known picture, a favourite with all visitors to the National Gallery, is a splendid example both of Jan van Eyck's truthful and unflattering portraiture and also of his delight in rendering with scrupulous fidelity all the details of an interior. The reflection in the round mirror is itself a miniature within a picture.

suggestion of atmosphere and distance. Of his early period, when he was dominated by classic ideals, the bronze " David " at the Bargello, Florence, is considered the finest example. The first nude statue since Roman times

Photo : Anderson.

"THE ADORATION OF JESUS," BY HUGO VAN DER GOES
(*circa* 1435–1482).

Uffizi Gallery, Florence.

The obvious inconsistencies in this strangely original work should not blind us to its many fine qualities.   The adoring kings and angels are absurdly out of proportion, but the shepherds (on the right) are absolutely natural and true to life.   All are good, but best of all is the one, clearly the last arrival, who is breathlessly peering over the heads of the kneeling two at the marvel before them.   Admirable, again, is the figure of St. Joseph, on the left ; no courtly figure is he, but a sturdy, toil-worn peasant.   The true naturalism of the artist is also seen in the accurate painting of the architecture, the animals, and the still-life in the foreground.

thought out independently of its architectural surroundings, it is beautiful, both in its proportions and in its simple realism. The supreme masterpiece of his later years is the famous statue at Padua of the Condottiere Gattamelata on horseback. Majestic in its repose, yet pulsating with life, this work (see page 55) is one of the two great equestrian statues of the world, the other being the Colleoni Monument at Venice, begun about forty years later by Donatello's pupil Verrocchio, and completed by the Venetian sculptor Alessandro Leopardi.

III

THE WONDER OF THE RENAISSANCE

THE ART OF LEONARDO DA VINCI, MICHAEL ANGELO, AND RAPHAEL

§ I

"OCCASIONALLY," says the Italian historian Vasari, "Heaven bestows upon a single individual beauty, grace, and ability, so that, whatever he does, every action is so divine that he distances all other men, and clearly displays how his genius is the gift of God and not an acquirement of human art. Men saw this in Leonardo da Vinci, whose personal beauty and grace cannot be exaggerated, whose abilities were so extraordinary that he could readily solve every difficulty that presented itself."

His charming conversation won all hearts, we are told; with his right hand he could twist a horse-shoe as if it were made of lead, yet to the strength of a giant and the courage of a lion he added the gentleness of a dove. He was a lover of all animals, "whom he tamed with kindness and patience"; and like other great spirits whose souls are filled with poetry, he could not endure to see a caged bird. Often as he passed the place where birds were sold in Florence, Leonardo would stop, buy the birds, and restore them to liberty.

A painter and sculptor, the perfection of whose work outstripped that of all his predecessors, a scientist and inventor whose theories and discoveries were centuries ahead of his time, a practical engineer who could construct with equal ease and success an instrument of war or a monument of peace, an accomplished musician and composer, a deviser of masques and ballets, an experimental chemist, a skilful dissector, and author of the first standard book on Anatomy—is it surprising that this man should have been the wonder of his own and of all succeeding ages ?

Genius is wayward, and as a boy Leonardo—who was born in 1452—was a source of anxiety to his father, Ser Piero da Vinci, a man of good family who, like his father and grandfather, was a notary of Florence. At school, his masters said, he was capricious and fickle : " he began to learn many things and then gave them up " ; but it was observed that however many other things took his fancy from time to time, the boy never neglected drawing and modelling. His father took these drawings to his friend the artist, Andrea del Verrocchio, who, amazed at the talent they displayed, gladly consented to have Leonardo as his pupil.

One day his master received a commission from the friars of Vallombroso to paint a picture of " St. John Baptizing Christ," and having much work on hand Verrocchio asked Leonardo to help him finish the picture by painting one of the angels. When Leonardo had done this his angel surpassed all the other figures in beauty, so that his master was filled with admiration, yet also with despair that a mere boy should know more and paint better than he could himself. Chagrined, the older artist admitted his defeat ; he is said never to have touched a brush again, but to have devoted the rest of his life to sculpture.

From that moment the reputation of Leonardo was made, and the nobles and princes of Italy sought his services. In 1493 he was invited to Milan by the Duke Ludovico Sforza, who was captivated alike by the genius of the artist and the charm of his personality. While at Milan Leonardo painted his famous " Last Supper " (see page 69) for the Dominicans of Sta. Maria delle Grazie, choosing the moment when the Apostles are anxious to discover who would betray their Master.

Despite his marvellous facility, Leonardo was not a quick worker, and his procrastination in finishing this picture alarmed the Prior, who besought the Duke to reprimand the artist for " mooning about " instead of getting on with the work. When the Duke spoke to Leonardo the latter gently explained how necessary it was for artists to think things out before they began to paint. " Two heads remain to be done," he said. " I feel unable to conceive the beauty of the celestial grace that must have been incarnate in Our Lord. The other head which causes me thought is that of Judas. I do not think I can express the face of a man who could resolve to betray his Master, after having received so many benefits.

" But to save time," added Leonardo, " I will in this case seek no further, but for want of a better idea I will put in the head of the Prior."

The Duke laughed heartily and told the Prior to let Leonardo finish the work in peace.

More famous even than his " Last Supper," and happily in a far better state of preservation to-day, is Leonardo's portrait of " Mona Lisa," third wife of Francesco del Giocondo, a Florentine official. For centuries this portrait with the lustrous eyes and mysterious smile has been regarded as the supreme expression in art of the eternal enigma of womanhood. By a freak of fate the man who commissioned this portrait never had it, for it was still in the possession of the artist—by whom it was considered unfinished—when Leonardo left Italy for France on the invitation of King Francis. The King of France had met Leonardo at Milan, and had long wished to tempt him to his own Court. After innumerable disappointments in Italy, Leonardo in his old age sought refuge from Italian envy and ingratitude with the French King. Francis received him with every kindness and honour, and when the old man fell sick he frequently visited him.

One day the aged artist was seized with a paroxysm, and the kindly monarch, endeavouring to alleviate the pain, took his head into his arms. " Leonardo's divine spirit, then recognising that he could not enjoy a greater honour, expired in the king's arms." So Leonardo died, as Vasari relates, in 1519 ; and thus it came about that his world-famous portrait of " Mona Lisa " (see next page) is now in France's national museum, the Louvre.

"MONA LISA" (OR "LA JOCONDE"), BY LEONARDO DA VINCI
(1452–1519).

The Louvre, Paris.

The most famous painting in the world, this portrait has for centuries been considered the supreme embodiment of the eternal enigma of womanhood. The great Duke of Buckingham fell in love with it when Charles I sent him to France to act as escort to his bride-elect Henrietta Maria. Mona Lisa was the third wife of Francesco del Giocondo, a Florentine official, and Vasari relates that Leonardo hired musicians to sing and play while he painted her in order to preserve the intent expression of her face. Her mysterious smile is as famous and baffling as the Sphinx, and her right hand is supposed to be the most perfect hand ever painted.

§ 2

There is no one person in whom the spirit of the Renaissance—that is to say, the rebirth of ancient art and learning—is so completely summed up and expressed as in Leonardo da Vinci. Yet " The Martyrdom of St. Sebastian," by the brothers Antonio and Piero del Pollaiuolo (see page 64) again shows something quite modern in its feeling and expression. These two Florentines were contemporaries of Leonardo. Antonio (1432–98) was of humble origin. His father, who, as his surname shows, was a poulterer, apprenticed the boy to a goldsmith, with whom he soon made a reputation as the most skilful workman in the shop. In time he was able to open a shop of his own, and his reliefs and wax models were much admired by sculptors as well as by his patrons. Meanwhile his younger brother Piero, eleven years his junior, had been apprenticed to a painter, and in early middle age Antonio thought he would like to become a painter also. He had educated himself, learning all he could of anatomy and perspective ; and found no difficulty in the drawing, but the colouring was so different from anything he had done before that at first he despaired of success ; but firm in his resolve he put himself under his younger brother, and in a few months became an excellent painter.

Of all works painted by the two brothers the most famous is " The Martyrdom of St. Sebastian," now in the National Gallery.

The manysidedness, so characteristic of the artists of the Renaissance, which we have already found in Leonardo and Antonio Pollaiuolo, also distinguishes one of the most interesting of their contemporaries. Domenico Ghirlandaio (1449–94), who also was originally a goldsmith, owes his very name to a freak of fashion. He was the first to invent and make fashionable the head ornament worn by Florentine girls. Hence he became known as Ghirlandaio (the maker of garlands), not only because he was the original inventor but also we hear, because his were of

"THE MARTYRDOM OF ST. SEBASTIAN," BY ANTONIO AND PIERO
POLLAIUOLO (1432–1498 and 1443–1496).

National Gallery, London.

Antonio Pollaiuolo was a pioneer of Naturalism. For four centuries the figures
of the stooping cross-bowmen in the foreground of this picture have aroused
admiration by their extraordinary realism and sense of tension. " We can
almost hear them holding their breath for the effort " : this was written about
it 300 years ago, and we feel the same to-day.

Note also how the grouping of the figures forms a pyramid, of which the Saint is
the apex, and how the lines of the arrows contribute to the symmetry of the
composition. The landscape background, showing the valley of the Arno, with
Florence on the left, is the work of Piero.

such exceeding beauty that every girl wanted a garland from his shop.

Discontented with his trade, which gave comparatively small scope to his genius for design, Domenico began painting portraits of the people who came to his shop. These were so lifelike and so beautifully painted, that the fame of the artist soon spread, and he was inundated with orders for portraits, altar-pieces, and decorations for the palaces of noblemen. Pope Sixtus IV heard about him and sent to Florence, inviting him to come to Rome and join the band of famous artists who were already at work on what is now known as the Sistine Chapel.

His great work, " The Call of SS. Peter and Andrew," in the Sistine Chapel is a splendid example of the boldness of composition which he contributed to art ; but his small painting at the Louvre, " Portrait of an Old Man and his Grandchild," has a far wider celebrity. We present it (see page 67) not only as a specimen of Ghirlandaio's decorative arrangement and intimate feeling, but as an outstanding masterpiece of Christian art, Christian because the painter has here sought and found that beauty of *character* which was utterly beyond the range of the pagan artists who found beauty in *proportions*.

When we remember that Ghirlandaio began painting late, and was carried off by a fever at the comparatively early age of forty-four, we are astounded at the quantity and quality of the work he left behind. He was a man of immense energy and hated to be interrupted in his work. Once when his brother David bothered him on some domestic matter, he replied : " Leave me to work while you make provision, because now that I have begun to master my art I feel sorry that I am not employed to paint the entire circuit of the walls of Florence."

§ 3

Nine people out of ten, if asked to name the greatest artist who ever lived, would reply Michael Angelo Buona-rotti, who was born in 1475 at Castel Caprese, a small

5

town near Florence, of which his father was chief magistrate
The babe was put out to nurse with the wife of a marble-
worker, and in later days the great sculptor jokingly attributed his vocation to his foster-mother's milk. His father
had other ideas for him, and used a stick freely to impress
on the lad the advantages of a commercial career, but
Michael Angelo was obstinate and intractable. At last the
father gave way, and when the son was thirteen he apprenticed him to Ghirlandaio for three years. Long before his
apprenticeship was out, the boy had shown a preference for
sculpture. His talent in modelling was brought to the
notice of Lorenzo de' Medici, who nominated him for the
famous " Garden School " of sculpture which he had
founded under the direction of Donatello's chief assistant,
Bartoldo. The ruler of Florence, pleased with the progress
of his protégé took him into his household, and made him an
allowance of 500 ducats a month. This lasted till 1492,
when Lorenzo died, and the youth had to make his own way
in the world. Meanwhile a new influence came into his life.

In 1490, when Michael Angelo was a boy of fifteen,
Savonarola had begun to preach his impassioned sermons
in Florence. The whole city trembled at the terrible
voice, which hurled thunderbolts at the Pope himself. All
Florence was like a revival meeting ; people rushed about
the street weeping and shouting, wealthy citizens became
monks, high officials abdicated their positions.

Michael Angelo for the first time in his life was afraid,
afraid of the unknown horrors predicted for Florence. He
was miserable under the degenerate Piero de' Medici, a
stupid tyrant who wasted his time and his talent by com-
manding him to model a statue in snow ! One night a
poet friend of the sculptor dreamt that the dead Lorenzo
appeared to him and bade him warn Piero that soon he
would be driven from his house, never to return. He
told the Prinec, who laughed and had him well cudgelled ;
he told Michael Angelo, who believed and fled to Venice.

That was in October 1494. A month later Piero fled
in his turn, and Florence, with the support of Savonarola,
was declared a republic, owning no king but Jesus Christ.

Photo : W. A. Mansell & Co.

"PORTRAIT OF AN OLD MAN AND HIS GRANDCHILD,"
BY D. GHIRLANDAIO (1449-1494).

The Louvre, Paris.

One of the world's great masterpieces, this picture teaches us that true beauty resides in expression more than in regularity of features. The homely countenance of this good old man, despite his deformed nose, is transfigured by his expression of benevolence and affection ; in his own way he becomes as beautiful as the child gazing at him with love and perfect trust. Profoundly moving in its expression, this painting is equally masterly in its technique. Note the perfect balance in the placing of the heads and the way in which the child's hand provides the patch ot light needed in one corner to set off properly the view through a window which occupies the other.

Michael Angelo soon got over his superstitious terrors. That winter he spent at Bologna in learned circles, and forgetting Savonarola, he read Dante and Petrarch ; he was absorbed by the beauty of Nature and the dignity of the antique world. At the very time when his contemporaries at Florence were fanatically indulging in a religious revival, Michael Angelo seemed to assert his paganism by carving a " Sleeping Cupid " so full of Greek feeling that it was sold in Rome to the Cardinal San Giorgio as an antique by a Greek sculptor. When he discovered he had been cheated, the deceived collector was so delighted to think a living Italian could rival the dead Greeks that he sent for the young sculptor and took him under his protection. In 1496, while the Florentines were heaping pagan pictures, ornaments, and books on Savonarola's " Bonfire of Vanities," when his own brother, the monk Leonardo, was being prosecuted for his faith in the Friar, Michael Angelo in Rome seemed anxious to prove himself a pagan of pagans, producing a " Bacchus," an " Adonis," and the lovely " Cupid " (see page 77) which is now at South Kensington.

On May 23, 1498, the fickle populace of Florence turned against its idol. Savonarola was burnt to death at the stake. Still Michael Angelo appeared to take no notice. No mention of Savonarola or his martyrdom can be found in any of the sculptor's letters.

But in his own art he made his own comment. From 1498 to 1501 he worked feverishly, perhaps remorsefully, on a marble group the like of which had never before been seen : a Virgin whose haunting face is impressed with a " sorrow more beautiful than beauty's self," across whose knees is lying a Christ of such serene physical beauty and perfection that we say, " He is not dead but sleepeth."

This was Michael Angelo's confession to his Maker, the supreme " Pieta " at St. Peter's, Rome : a work of which the exquisite beauty is only equalled by its ineffable sadness. Botticelli, too, was more moved by the end of Savonarola than ever he had been by his preaching. But Botticelli was then an old man : Michael Angelo had but just turned

Photo : W. A. Mansell & Co.

"THE LAST SUPPER," BY LEONARDO DA VINCI (1452–1519)

Sta. Maria delle Grazie, Milan.

Verily I say unto you that one of you shall betray Me." This is the moment the artist has dramatically re-created. Judas (third on the Saviour's right) is guiltily withdrawing the hand extended to the dish, while behind his isolated figure Peter passionately consults the beloved disciple John. On the other side, beyond beckoning Thomas and the amazed James the Great, is the beautiful figure of Philip, whose gesture eloquently speaks to us, "Lord, Thou knowest I am not he!"

Leonardo's masterpiece has so stamped itself on the imagination of the world that we can no longer visualise the scene in any other fashion.

twenty-three and was only on the threshold of his career. Already his pagan days were over. Melancholy claimed him for her own, and never after let him go. In five years he had established his reputation as the greatest sculptor in the world, but then, as now, glory is not necessarily remunerative. His family believed he was making a fortune; and too proud to acknowledge his true poverty-stricken condition, he starved himself to give alms to his kindred. His own father pestered and abused him worst of all; his whole family bled him white, and then denounced him as being mean.

In 1501 he returned to Florence to make the famous statue of " David," which was to commemorate the deliverance of the city from her enemies. But no happiness awaited him in his native town. He was foolishly pitted against Leonardo da Vinci, and his envy and jealousy excited by tittle-tattlers. The two great men of the time, who ought to have been understanding friends and comrades, were forced into enmity. Michael Angelo grew morose and suspicious. One day as he was walking through the streets of Florence he saw Leonardo discussing a passage in Dante with a group of citizens. Meaning nothing but kindness, Leonardo hailed his rival and said to his friends, " Michael Angelo here will explain the verses of which you speak."

But the embittered sculptor scented an insult in the innocent remark and passionately retorted: " Explain them yourself, you who made the model of a bronze horse and who, incapable of casting it, left it unfinished—to your shame, be it said ! "

This allusion to his equestrian statue of Francesco Sforza, never finished, wounded Leonardo to the quick. Conscious of his fatal tendency to procrastinate, he reddened as Michael Angelo turned his back on him and strode away.

Unhappy in Florence, Michael Angelo was not sorry when in 1505 Pope Julius II called him back to Rome. Later he was to regret still more bitterly that he ever went. Julius desired a colossal mausoleum to be built for his remains, and the sculptor entered into the project with enthusiasm.

" VIRGIN ADORING THE INFANT CHRIST "
(ALBANI ALTAR-PIECE), BY PERUGINO
(1446–1523).

This central panel of the famous altar-piece in the Villa
Albani, Rome, is the most exquisite of all Perugino's
numerous paintings. It exhibits in equal perfection the
sweet gracefulness of his feminine types and the aerial
perspective which gives a sense of infinite distance to his
tender landscape backgrounds.

" PORTRAIT OF BALTHASAR CASTIGLIONE," BY RAPHAEL (1483–1520).

The Louvre, Paris.

This superbly handsome and lifelike portrait is Raphael's masterpiece in portraiture. Count Baldassare Castiglione was the intimate and lifelong friend of Raphael. He was himself a scholar and author of some repute : his book, *The Courtier*, gives a wonderful picture of the palace life at Urbino between 1504 and 1508.

"THE MADONNA OF SAN SISTO," BY RAPHAEL.

Dresden.

The **Sistine** Madonna is justly the most famous and most favoured of all Raphael's Madonnas ; for, though others may rival it in formal beauty, in no other does he reach the same **height** of spiritual expression. The Christ-child, so solemnly yet naturally gazing at the **infinite**, the slender, majestic, yet entirely human mother, are figures which, once we have seen them, haunt our memory for ever.

He spent eight months in the Carrara quarries selecting his marbles, and in December returned to Rome, where the blocks began to arrive. But a rival artist, Bramante, hinted to the Pope that it was unlucky to build your tomb in your own lifetime. The Pope hastily dropped the idea of the mausoleum, closed his door to Michael Angelo, who was left not only unpaid for his work and time, but in debt for the marbles he had obtained. The sculptor was driven out of the Vatican by a groom, and quivering with indignation the humiliated genius at once left Rome for Florence.

But no sooner was he in Florence than the Pope wanted him back at Rome. Eventually he got him back, and perhaps the eccentric, inconstant Pope meant kindly; but he reduced Michael Angelo to despair by demanding that the greatest sculptor in the world should spend his time painting the ceiling of the Sistine Chapel. Again the architect Bramante was the evil genius; he had prompted the command, believing the sculptor would fail ignominiously. What was meant for his dishonour became his greatest glory.

Michael Angelo never wanted to do the work. Already his young rival Raphael had commenced painting the " Stanze " of the Vatican with unparalleled success. The sculptor pleaded that this ceiling should be given to Raphael, but the Pope insisted and his will was law. On March 10, 1508 the distracted artist wrote : " To-day I, Michael Angelo, sculptor, began the painting of the chapel." The next year, on January 27, 1509, he wrote again : " This is not my profession. . . . I am uselessly wasting my time." To-day the whole world thinks otherwise.

Of all the palaces of art which Europe contains, there is not one more wonderful within, or with a meaner exterior, than the Sistine Chapel. The long barn-like structure, lit by twelve round-headed windows, was built over what was once the Library by Sixtus IV. His aim was to ornament the chapel with scenes from the world's history pointing to the coming of Christ. All the greatest artists of the preceding generation, Botticelli, Ghirlandaio, Piero di

"DELPHIC SYBIL," BY MICHAEL ANGELO (1475–1564).

Sistine Chapel, Rome.

The description of Michael Angelo as " a sculptor who painted " is aptly illustrated by this noble picture. The introduction of a pagan priestess into a Christian church may seem surprising, but at the time of the Renaissance ecclesiastics revered these Sibyls because one of them had prophesied : " A Child shall be born whose advent will bring peace to the world."

This was believed to be an inspired foretelling of the coming of Christ. Accordingly the Delphic Sibyl and her sisters could properly be included among these paintings, all of which point to the preparation of the world, from its earliest moments, for the revelation of Christianity.

75

Cosimo, and Perugino had been called upon to assist in the work, and after the death of Sixtus the completion of the Chapel occupied his nephew Count Giuliano Rovere, who succeeded him as Julius II.

Most artists who had received a papal commission of this magnitude began their work with an army of assistants. Bramante, with a show of giving his enemy every assistance, brought some experienced fresco-painters from Florence and erected a scaffolding whereby they might get at the ceiling. Furious and suspicious of everything and everybody, Michael Angelo began by declaring Bramante's scaffolding to be useless and by raising another. Next he got rid of his assistants. One morning he got there early, destroyed everything they had done, locked himself in, and refused to admit the Florentines.

During the next four years, working feverishly and in secret, the sculptor accomplished the mightiest series of paintings in the world. He had endless troubles and difficulties. The work was new to him, and he had to learn its technique as he went along. Hardly had he finished painting one panel, "The Deluge," when the surface became mouldy and he had to do it all over again. All this time his relatives badgered him for money; the Pope, irritated at his secrecy and seeming slowness, threatened to have him thrown from the top of his scaffolding, and at last, worn out, but still not content with his creations, Michael Angelo, after lying for four years on his back to paint this ceiling, once more stood erect and allowed the scaffolding to be taken down on All Saints' Day 1512.

His worst enemies were amazed at the greatness and magnitude of his achievement. Raphael, great enough himself to fear no rival, was the first to praise it, thanking God aloud that he had been born in the same century. No photographs can do justice to what Raphael and his contemporaries then saw. In default of the original, we can but show a single figure (see page 75), and let the imagination do the rest.

Michael Angelo divided the great oblong space of the ceiling into nine principal sections, or rather three groups

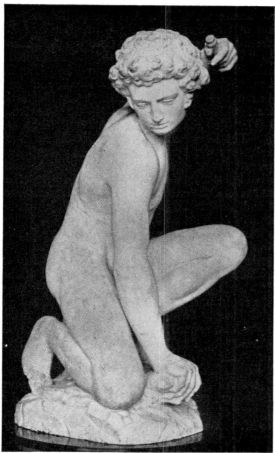

"CUPID," BY MICHAEL ANGELO.

This exquisite marble statue, now in the Victoria and Albert Museum, South Kensington, is an early work of the artist. It was executed in Rome when Michael Angelo was a young man of twenty-two, and reveals a perfection of form which hitherto his contemporaries had thought could only be realised in an antique.

of three scenes each. The first group, illustrating " The Creation of the World," consisted of (1) " God Dividing Light from Darkness," (2) " God Creating the Luminaries," and (3) " God Blessing the Earth." The second group, illustrating " The Fall of Man," showed (4) " The Creation of Adam," (5) " The Creation of Eve," and (6) " The Temptation and Fall." The last three, illustrating the uselessness of sacrifice under the old dispensation, represented (7) " The Sacrifice of Noah," (8) " The Deluge," and (9) " The Drunkenness of Noah." These nine panels were knit together by a connecting framework in which were placed single figures of Prophets, Sibyls, and other decorative figures, lunettes and triangles, so that the whole appeared as an elaborate architectural roof ornamented with reliefs and sculptured figures among which nine great pictures had been inserted.

The work was completed, but Michael Angelo at thirty-seven was an old man. His health was shattered. Working for months on end with his head thrown back had strained his neck and brought on painful swellings of the glands ; his sight was injured to such an extent that for long afterwards he could not read a book or letter unless he held it above his head. Then, when the old Pope, satisfied at last, might have rewarded the heroic artist, Julius died and was succeeded by Leo X, who had work for Raphael, but none for Michael Angelo.

The harassed sculptor went back to Florence, where he set to work on another masterpiece of sculpture, the " Tomb of Lorenzo de' Medici," with its beautiful recumbent figures of " Night " and " Morning," " Dawn " and " Twilight." Worse troubles were in store for him. Disgusted with all things, including himself, he threw himself into the revolution which convulsed Florence in 1527. Though no engineer like Leonardo, the republican revolutionaries put him in charge of the fortifications of the city. Distrustful of everybody, Michael Angelo feared that Malatesta Baglione, the general of the Florentine troops, might betray the city to the troops of the new Pope (Clement VII) ; his warning unheeded by the

" THE ANSIDEI MADONNA," BY RAPHAEL.

National Gallery, London.

This famous altar-piece, originally painted for the Ansidei family of Perugia, shows the Virgin and Child in the centre, with St. John the Baptist on one side and St. Nicolas of Bari on the other. In the eighteenth century the picture was purchased from the Church of S. Fiorenzo—where it had hung since 1506— by Lord Robert Spencer, who presented it to the third Duke of Marlborough. It was bought from the Marlborough collection at Blenheim for the National Gallery in 1885, at a cost of £70,000.

authorities, he feared the hostility of the powerful commander, and giving way to an attack of nerves he fled to
Venice for his life.   There he was safe and might have
gone to France, but an appeal to his honour brought him
back to Florence.   Once more he took his place in the
fighting line, and six months later Malatesta Baglione, as
he foresaw, betrayed the city to the Emperor.

Irony of fate!   The life of the wretched sculptor was
spared in order that he might work again for the glory of
those tyrants, the Medici, against whom he had fought.
In 1534, another Pope, Paul III, called him to Rome to
enter on a new project.   Again the sculptor was asked
to paint, to cover the immense wall at the entrance to the
Sistine Chapel with a fresco representing " The Last
Judgment."   He began the work when he was sixty-one,
and again shutting himself up, accomplished the task in a
little over five years.   It was no work for an old man of
nearly seventy, and the following year the sculptor had to
turn from painting to architecture ; by command of the
Pope he designed the mighty Dome which to all the world
to-day is the sign and symbol of the Eternal City.

Vasari, who visited the old man when he was eighty-
eight, gives a wonderful picture of Michael Angelo's last
years.   He lived like a poor man, ate hardly anything but a
little bread and drank but a little wine.   Unable to sleep,
he would get up at night to work with his chisel, and made
himself a paper helmet in which a candle was fixed, so that
he might have light to work without embarrassing his
hands.

On February 12, 1564, the old man spent the whole day
on his feet working at a " Pieta."   Two days afterwards
he was seized with fever, but with his usual obstinacy
refused to see a doctor or to go to bed.   On the 17th he
consented to be put to bed, and, fully conscious, dictated
his will, bequeathing " his soul to God and his body to the
earth."   About five o'clock on the following afternoon,
surrounded by his faithful servant and a few friends, the
worn-out genius breathed his last and found that rest which
had never been granted him in life.

" THE TRANSFIGURATION," BY RAPHAEL.

This picture at the Vatican, Raphael's last masterpiece, shows the transfiguration of Christ, floating over the Mount in clear air, between Moses and Elijah. Prostrate on the earth are Peter, James, and John, in varied attitudes. In the foreground an excited group gathers round the boy possessed of devils.

At the lying-in-state of Raphael, which followed the great artist's death, this picture—which he had painted for the Cardinal Giulio de' Medici—was placed at the head of the corpse in the Hall wherein Raphael had last worked.

§ 4

Happy the painter who has no history ! Life, so cruel to Michael Angelo, had nothing but kindness for his young contemporary, Raphael Sanzio. Born at Urbino in 1483, his way was smoothed for him from the moment (1504) that he left the workshop of his master Perugino to begin an independent career. Beautiful as an angel in person, sweet in disposition, charming in manner and conversation, Raphael was a favourite everywhere. After perfecting his art by study in Florence, he was invited to Rome in 1508 to undertake the decoration of the Stanze in the Vatican. These paintings at once established his reputation, and in 1511 he was appointed Chief Architect of St. Peter's, Surveyor and Guardian of the Ancient Monuments of Rome, and overwhelmed with commissions for mighty projects of painting which his gentle courtesy had not the determination to refuse.

He walked through Rome, in those years of his glory, amid a throng of assistants and admirers. Thus meeting him once, grim old Michael Angelo growled out, " You look like a General at the head of an army."

Laughing and quite unspoilt, Raphael wittily retorted : " And you, sir, like an executioner on the way to the scaffold."

As a portrait-painter his " Balthasar Castiglione " at the Louvre (see page 72), as a painter of altar-pieces his " Sistine Madonna " at Dresden (see page 73) and the " Ansidei Madonna " in the National Gallery (see page 79), have made Raphael familiar to all and loved by all. In 1520 he was working on his great " Transfiguration " in the Vatican, when a fever struck him down. On March 27 he laid down the brush that he was never to hold again, and on Good Friday, April 6, his birthday, he died as the sun went down, amid the tears of those who mourned not only the artist but the man. He had lived only thirty-seven years, but from that day to this not for one moment has the lustre of his name been dimmed.

" POPE JULIUS II," BY RAPHAEL.

Uffizi Gallery, Florence.

Giuliano da Rovere, afterwards Pope Julius II, was a nephew of Cardinal Francesco di Savona, who became Sixtus IV and began the erection of the world-famed chapel in the Vatican which bears his name. By his enlightened patronage of contemporary art, Julius II has secured an undying fame, which eclipses any reputation he once enjoyed for theological wisdom or political sagacity.

IV

THE ROAD TO VENICE

THE ART OF MANTEGNA, FRANCIA, CORREGGIO, BELLINI,
AND GIORGIONE

§ I

IT takes nine tailors to make a man. So runs the familiar saying, but one tailor of Padua in the fifteenth century sufficed to found a school of painting which has won immortal fame. In all the history of art no stranger figure exists than that of Francesco Squarcione, tailor and embroiderer of Padua. He had little to do with painting or painters till he was past forty, and yet this man was the master of 137 pupils and the "Father" of the glorious schools of Venice, Parma, Bologna, Lombardy, and Ferrara.

Here let us pause to explain that while the succession of painters known as the Florentine School were perfecting their art, as related in the last chapter, groups of artists had already begun to collect in other Italian cities. So far back as 1375, twelve years before the birth of Fra Angelico, a Florentine painter named Justus had settled in Padua ; and when Leonardo da Vinci was born in 1452, Padua was already famous as an art centre.

But to return to our tailor. To the University of Padua came, at one time or another, all the learned men of Italy. Nothing was heard in the streets but talk of ancient lore and the beauty of ancient art. The astute tailor soon found that a fragment of sculpture or a stone with a Greek inscription brought him more and better customers than the display of the latest fashions. Gradually the tailoring and embroidering became a side-line in his complicated business, and the shop of Squarcione gained much fame as a store-

"THE DOGE LEONARDO LOREDANO," BY GIOVANNI BELLINI
(1428–1516).

National Gallery, London.

All the pomp, prosperity, and splendour of the maritime State of Venice is summed up in this sumptuous portrait of her Chief Magistrate.

"Bellini," said Ruskin, "is the only artist who appears to me to have united, in equal and magnificient measures, justness of drawing, nobleness of colouring, and perfect manliness of treatment."

house of antique treasures of art. Artists came to him asking to be allowed to draw his fine old statues.

Squarcione had a keen eye to the main chance, and the power to discover and use the talents of others. Whether he himself ever painted is doubtful, but in 1441, when he was a man of forty-seven, he managed to qualify himself for admission to the Guild of Painters at Padua. His business instinct would not allow him to let slip a ready-made opportunity. When students sought to study his unrivalled collection of antique models, they found themselves bound as apprentices to Squarcione ; and henceforward — on the strength of *their* work — Squarcione blossomed into the proprietor of a flourishing art business.

In 1443 he was given the contract to decorate with paintings the Chapel of the Eremitani at Padua, and this contract he fulfilled for the most part by the hand of a boy of twelve, whom two years earlier Squarcione had adopted as his son and pupil. This boy was a nameless orphan, who acquired undying fame as Andrea Mantegna. He was only ten years old when, as the " son of Squarcione," he was admitted a member of the Padua Guild of Painters, and from this fact alone we can guess his extraordinary precocity. At the age of twelve Mantegna was employed on important paintings for the Chapel of the Eremitani, and it was the reputation of the pupil, rather than that of the master, which brought students in shoals to Padua.

Another great piece of good luck which befell Squarcione was the arrival in Padua of the Venetian painter Jacopo Bellini (*c.* 1400–71), whom the wily contractor inveigled into his business, and there is little room for doubt that Bellini was for many years the actual teacher of painting in the school of the Paduan contractor. Mantegna got his drawing from observing the Greek statues among Squarcione's antiques, but he learnt colouring from Bellini, who was his true master. But so precocious was the genius of Mantegna that at seventeen he had already formed his style and brought his natural talents to mature perfection. At this age he painted an altar-piece for St. Sophia at Padua, a picture which, as the sixteenth-century critic Vasari wrote, " might well be the production of a skilled veteran and not of a mere boy."

Success begets success, and at an early age Mantegna was able to set up for himself. Squarcione became still more furious when Mantegna married the daughter of Jacopo Bellini, who had now broken away from the firm and become a rival. Henceforward the old contractor blamed Mantegna's works as much as he had previously praised them, " saying they were bad, because he had imitated marble, a thing impossible in painting, since stones always possess a certain harshness and never have that softness peculiar to flesh and natural objects."

It is true that Mantegna's sense of form was severe and his figures often remind us of marble statues, but the envious carping of his old master in no wise injured his reputation. His fame spread throughout Italy, and Pope Innocent VIII invited him to Rome, where he was employed on painting the walls of the Belvedere. The payments for this work were not so regular as the painter thought they should have been, and one day he ventured to drop a hint to the Pope, who had come to look at Mantegna's paintings of the Virtues.

" What is that figure ? " asked the Pontiff.

" One much honoured here, your Holiness," said the artist pointedly ; " it is Prudence."

" You should associate Patience with her," replied the Pope, who understood the allusion, and later when the work was completed we are told Mantegna was " richly rewarded."

After painting in various Italian cities, Mantegna returned to Mantua, where he built himself a handsome house, and there in 1506, he died at the age of seventy-five. The peculiar qualities of his art, his austere draughtsmanship and compact design may be seen in many works in England, notably in " The Triumph of Julius Cæsar " at Hampton Court, and in his " Madonna and Child " and " Triumph of Scipio " in the National Gallery ; but the most perfect example of Mantegna's art is his great picture

"Parnassus," in the Louvre at Paris(see opposite page). Here, as the illustration shows, Mantegna is able to express all his love of Greek art in picturing the home of the Nine Muses, who dance in homage round Venus and Apollo, while Mercury, the Messenger of the Gods, awaits with Pegasus, the winged horse, to bear inspiration from this mythological heaven to the artists and poets of the earth.

§ 2

To enumerate all the artists who were influenced by Mantegna and the School of Squarcione would be to give a list of a hundred names, and to attempt a task beyond the scope of this Outline ; but brief mention must be made of one whose life, and particularly whose death, is of unusual and romantic interest. Francesco Francia (1450– 1517) was a goldsmith of Bologna who achieved great fame as an engraver of medallion portraits long before the example of Mantegna inspired him to become a painter also. Francia was one of the first artists to make prints from an engraved plate, and served literature by designing the famous italic type for the press of Aldus Manutius. As a painter, Francia began with portraits and proceeded to altar-pieces, in which he displayed a remarkable psychological insight. Both in ancient times and in modern his lunette of the Dead Christ in the lap of the Virgin has been regarded as a most beautiful work, poignant in the intensity of its expression. As the illustration on page 97 shows, this half-moon-shaped picture is the upper part of a famous altar-piece originally painted for the Church of St. Frediano at Lucca, and now in the National Gallery, London. The main picture below shows the Madonna and Child, with the following saints (from left to right) : St. Sebastian, St. Paul, St. Anne, St. Lawrence, and St. Benedict, while in front of the throne is the figure of the young St. John the Baptist ; and the wan, expressive face of the young Virgin seems to suggest that she is already forewarned of the tragedy commemorated by the picture above.

Francia was at the height of his reputation in Bologna

"PARNASSUS," BY MANTEGNA (1431-1506).

The Louvre, Paris.

The paganism of this picture illustrates the change that came over Italian art in the fifteenth century owing to that revival of interest in the achievements of Ancient Greece and Rome which is known as " The Renaissance."

Andrea Mantegna, who was devoted to Greek ideals, here pictures an imaginary scene on Mount Parnassus, the legendary home of the Nine Muses, personifications of the Fine Arts. On the mountain top stand Venus and Apollo, with Cupid trumpeting their praise, while around them the Muses dance. In the corner stands Mercury, the Messenger of the Gods, with Pegasus, the winged horse, waiting to bear inspiration from these divinities to the poets and artists of the earth. Note how the pyramidical design, helped by the horse's wing, gives dignity to the scene.

when the young Raphael was working in Rome. The two
artists never met, for Raphael was too busy to leave the
Vatican and Francia was too old to travel. But they heard
much of one another, and Francia, as the elder, offered to
help his junior in any way he could. He had never seen a
picture by Raphael, and longed to view some work by the
young man of whom everybody was talking. At last the
opportunity came. Raphael was commissioned to paint
a panel of " St. Cecilia " for a Bolognese chapel, St. Giovanni in Monte ; and when he had finished the painting
he sent it to Francia at Bologna with a courteous letter
begging the older artist to " correct any errors found in it,"
and then set it up on the altar for which it was intended.

When Francia drew the masterpiece from its case and
viewed it in a good light, he was filled with amazement and
with chagrin, so Vasari says, at his presumption in offering
to help so great a genius :

" Francia, half dead at the overwhelming power and
beauty of the picture, which he had to compare with his
own works lying around, though thoroughly discouraged,
took it to St. Giovanni in Monte, to the chapel where it
was to be. Returning home he took to his bed in an agony,
feeling that art could offer him no more, and died, some
suppose of grief and melancholy, due to his contemplation
of the living picture of Raphael."

That is the story told by Vasari, and though it may seem
incredible to us that any artist should be so fatally affected
by seeing the work of another, the fact that so strange a
cause of death was related in good faith reveals to us how
seriously art was taken in Italy in 1518.

§ 3

To appreciate all that Squarcione's school at Padua did
for Italian art, we must trace its influence into the second
and third generation. In addition to the sons of Bellini
—to whom we shall return—who were the real founders of
Venetian painting, the old contractor had among his
pupils Cosimo Tura (1420–95), who founded the School of

" THE CRUCIFIXION," BY ANTONELLO DA MESSINA (1430–79).

National Gallery, London.

This Sicilian artist, who went to Flanders for his training, was the first to introduce into Italy the Flemish method of painting in *oils*. We can see the influence of Flemish painting in his rather homely types, but the beautiful landscape with a city in the mid-distance is entirely Italian.

Ferrara. Tura had a pupil named Bianci, who founded a
school in Modena, and there had a pupil greater than any
of his predecessors, Antonio Allegri, known as Correggio,
from the place of his birth. Of the life of this great man
singularly little is known, and apart from his art it does not
seem to have been in any way eventful. Vasari tells us that
Correggio " was of a very timid disposition and, at a great
personal inconvenience, worked continually for the family
which depended on him. In art he was very melancholy,
enduring its labours, but he never allowed difficulties to
deter him, as we see in the great tribune of the Duomo of
Parma."

It is with Parma that the name of Correggio is always
associated, for his greatest works were executed there
between 1518 and 1530, and the Cathedral of Parma is
the monument of his genius. In its marvellous complexity and rich invention, his " Assumption of the Virgin "
there has no rival in the world. If his fluent and sure
drawing was derived from Mantegna, his mastery of light
and shade from Leonardo da Vinci, and his tremendous
forms and designs borrowed from the storehouse of Michael
Angelo, yet his marvellous colouring is entirely his own,
and it is as a colourist, above all, that Correggio is supreme.

" It is considered certain," wrote Vasari, " that there
never was a better colourist, nor any artist who imparted
more loveliness or relief to his things, so great was the soft
beauty of his flesh tints and the grace of his finish." Nearly
400 years have passed since these lines were written, but
no connoisseur of to-day would change a word in this
appreciation. The work of Correggio appeals to every
human being who is susceptible to the indefinable quality of
charm. Whether his subject be frankly pagan, as in " The
Education of Cupid " at the National Gallery (see page
opposite), or avowedly religious, as in his " St. Catherine "
at Hampton Court (see page 95), it is on the satisfaction
of the eye, and through the eye of all the senses, that
Correggio relies.

So modest was this great colourist, that no portrait of
himself by himself is known to exist. " He was content

" THE EDUCATION OF CUPID," BY CORREGGIO (1494–1534)

National Gallery, London.

" The soft beauty of his flesh tints and the grace of his finish," which won the admiration of this artist's contemporaries, still charm us to-day

In this lovely allegory Correggio shows us Mercury—the patron deity in Greek mythology of schools and colleges—teaching Cupid to spell out love, while Venus, the incarnation of feminine charm, looks on approvingly.

93

Photo : *Bruckmann.*

"GANYMEDE" BY CORREGGIO.
Pinakothek, Vienna.

Ganymede, according to an old Greek legend, was
a beautiful Trojan boy who was carried off from
Mt. Ida by an eagle to be Jupiter's cupbearer in
place of Hebe, who had excited the jealousy of Juno.

Correggio's unrivalled power of depicting bodies
floating in the air is beautifully displayed in this
painting.

with little," says Vasari, " and lived as a good Christian should." A modern critic, Mr. Berenson, has pronounced Correggio's paintings to be " hymns to the charm of femininity the like of which have never been known before or since in Christian Europe," yet from all accounts this artist's private life was singularly free from amours. Correggio was a model husband and father, and the only thing said against him by his Italian biographer is that he " was anxious to save, like everyone who is burdened with a family, and he thus became excessively miserly." This closeness is said to have brought about his premature death. " Payment of 60 crowns being made to him at Parma in farthings, which he wished to take to Correggio for his affairs, he set out with this burden on foot. Becoming overheated by the warmth of the sun, he took some water to

" ST. CATHERINE," BY CORREGGIO.

Hampton Court.

All the saints have their symbols, and St. Catherine of Siena is often represented with a book to denote her devotional nature. Correggio, whose art is always sweetly human rather than deeply spiritual, shows us the humanity rather than the saintliness of his subject. She might be a modern beauty immersed in a novel. As an exponent of feminine beauty Correggio ranks among the supreme artists of the world.

refresh himself, and caught a severe fever, which terminated his life in the fortieth year of his age."

§ 4

Soon after the death in 1470 9f Jacopo Bellini, there arrived in Venice a young Sicilian painter who, without being himself a great master, nevertheless changed the whole course of Italian painting. This was Antonello da Messina (1430–79), who, having seen at Naples in his youth a Flemish picture painted in oils, was so fascinated by the advantages of the new medium, that he went to Flanders and stayed there for some six years till he had thoroughly mastered the new process of painting. Then he returned to Italy, where he generously communicated his secrets to other artists, and so popularised in Italy the Flemish method of oil-painting. Antonello was a skilful painter, both of figures and landscape, as his " Crucifixion," reproduced on page 91, from the picture in the National Gallery, proves ; but unfortunately he died at the age of forty-nine, just when he had received commissions for a number of important paintings, and so we can only judge of his talent by the few small pictures and portraits which have survived.

Others reaped where Antonello had sown. Already Venetian painters had shown a certain independence in their art. In this maritime port, where sails were more plentiful than trees, pictures had long been painted on canvas, for wood that warps and plaster that scales and falls were ill suited to resist the damp that came from the canals. Van Eyck's method of oil-painting, introduced by Antonello, was soon found to be more damp-proof than the old method (*tempera*) of mixing pigments with yolk-of-egg, besides being lighter in weight and richer in colour.

Among the first to take advantage of the new method were the two sons of Bellini, who had soon followed their father to Venice, after his separation from Squarcione. Gentile, the elder, named after Gentile da Fabriano (Jacopo's first master), was born about 1429 ; his brother

Photo : *W. A. Mansell & Co.*

"THE FREDIANO ALTAR-PIECE," BY FRANCIA (*circa* 1450–1517).

National Gallery, London.

This altar-piece was commissioned by the Buonvisi Family for its chapel of St. Anne, in the Church of St. Frediano, Lucca. Francia managed to put his own wonderful feeling into the work, and the upper portion, a *Pieta* showing the Virgin and two angels weeping over the dead body of Christ, is of such tragic intensity that the most hardened sceptic can hardly gaze upon it unmoved.

7

Giovanni was a year or two younger. Both these sons far surpassed their father, and the younger outstripped the elder, but throughout their lives there was no jealousy between them.

" Although the brothers lived apart," says Vasari, " they bore such a respect for each other and for their father, that each one declared himself to be inferior to the other, thus seeking modestly to surpass the other no less in goodness and courtesy than in the excellence of art."

We are told that " the first works of Giovanni were some portraits which gave great satisfaction, especially that of the Doge Loredano." This last is the sumptuous painting, reproduced here (see page 85), now hanging in the National Gallery ; and from this noble portrait of the Head of the Venetian Republic may be obtained a just idea of Giovanni's power of characterisation and of the splendour of his colour when he was still at the outset of his great career. Impressed by the beauty of his portraits and of numerous altar-pieces which he painted for churches in Venetian territory, the nobles of the city desired this great painter, together with his brother Gentile, " to decorate the hall of the great council with paintings descriptive of the magnificence and greatness of their marvellous city." So, beginning with the brothers Bellini, and afterwards continued by painters of equal eminence, there came into being that unrivalled series of mural paintings in public buildings which makes Venice to-day the most wonderful art-city in the world.

Of all the altar-pieces painted by Giovanni Bellini, the most exquisite is the illustration " The Doge Barberigo Kneeling before the Infant Christ " (see page 101), a painting formerly in the Church of San Pietro at Murano, but now in the Accademia, Venice. This Madonna is one of the loveliest in all Italian art, serene, majestic, pensive, but altogether human and lovable.

Softness and gentleness always distinguish the work of Giovanni Bellini from that of his brother Gentile, who inclined more to the severity of his brother-in-law Mantegna. Good examples of Gentile Bellini may be seen

"CHRIST BEARING THE CROSS," by GIORGIONE (1477–1510).

Gardner Collection, Boston.

The most beautiful conception of Christ in art, this painting (now in an American collection) is either a study for or a fragment of a lost picture by Giorgione. Formerly the picture hung in a church in Venice, where, according to the sixteenth-century historian Vasari, its haunting loveliness worked miracles of faith among the multitudes who came to see it.

in the National Gallery, among them being an "Adoration of the Magi" and his portraits of "The Sultan
Mohammed II." The last has an interesting history.
Although paintings are prohibited by Mohammedan laws,
this Sultan saw some portraits by Giovanni Bellini in the
possession of the Venetian Ambassador, and, filled with
amazement and admiration, he earnestly desired to see the
man who could create such marvels. The Venetian Senate,
however, was disinclined to let Giovanni leave the city,
but allowed his brother Gentile to go in his stead. Gentile
arrived at Constantinople, where he "was received graciously and highly favoured," and after painting a number
of portraits, including one of the Sultan and one (by re-
quest) of himself, the Grand Turk was "convinced that the
artist had been assisted by some divine spirit." He wished
to reward the artist richly, and "asked him to name any
favour which he desired, and it would immediately be
granted."

Tactful and courteous, yet conscious that if he unduly
prolonged his stay in Turkey he might excite envy and
dangerous religious animosity, Gentile replied that he
"asked for nothing but a letter of recommendation to the
senate and government of his native Venice." Though
loath to let him go, the Sultan was as good as his word.
The letter was written "in the warmest possible terms,
after which he was dismissed with noble gifts and the honour
of knighthood."

So Gentile Bellini returned in honour to Venice, where
he lived till he was nearly eighty, when "he passed to the
other life," says Vasari, "and was honourably buried by his
brother in Santi Giovanni e Paolo in the year 1507." His
brother Giovanni survived him by some ten years and
continued, fine old patriarch that he was, painting portraits
till almost the end of his days. "At length," says our
historian, "when Giovanni had attained to the age of ninety
years, he passed from the troubles of this life, leaving an
everlasting name by the works which he produced in his
native Venice and elsewhere. He was buried in the same
church where he had previously laid his brother Gentile."

"THE DOGE BARBERIGO KNEELING BEFORE THE INFANT CHRIST," BY GIOVANNI BELLINI (*circa* 1430-1516).
Academia. Venice.

Serene, majestic, proud, yet pensive, this Madonna is one of the loveliest in all Italian art. Bellini has staged the scene with a magnificence worthy of Venice, whose semi-royal chief magistrate, the Doge Barberigo, kneels in adoration on the Virgin's right, supported by St. Dominic, while on her left stands an Archbishop who is possibly St. Augustin. Note how the pyramid form of the central group, rhythmically repeated in the mountains to the right and hinted at in the landscape to the left, has its severity softened by the varied attitudes of the two Saints.

§ 5

Justly famous by right of his own paintings, Giovanni is
also renowned as the master of some of the greatest painters
Venice ever saw, chief among his pupils being Giorgione and
Titian. The first was born at Castelfranco in 1470, and
was christened Giorgio, but " from his stature and the
greatness of his mind he was afterwards known as Giorgione,"
that is to say, " Great George." Though of peasant origin, contemporaries say he was " well bred and polished
all his life."   He was of a loving disposition and exceedingly
fond of the lute, " playing and singing divinely," and this
love of music became the new note which Giorgione definitely contributed to art, for not only did he frequently
introduce music as a subject in his pictures (*e.g.* " The
Concert " at Dresden, and the man playing a mandolin in
" The Golden Age " at the National Gallery, and the
" Fête Champêtre " or Musical Party in the Louvre), but
all his pictures, as Walter Pater wrote, " constantly aspire
to the condition of music."   By this it is meant that everything in a Giorgione is subordinated to beauty, and that
his first concern is to create *melody* of line and *harmony* of
colour.

The gentle nature of the artist, who found grace and
loveliness in all men and all things, can be traced in every
work of his that has survived the storms of time.   In his
great altar-piece " Madonna Enthroned, with St. Liberale
and St. Francis," for his native hill-town of Castelfranco,
painted before he was thirty, Giorgione charms us alike by
the rhythm and balance of the whole composition and by
the lovableness of his types.   The sweet simplicity of young
womanhood in the Virgin, the naturalness of the Child,
the knightliness of the soldier-saint Liberale, the welcoming
gesture of the nature-loving Saint who could preach to
birds and fishes and call them his brethren—all these things
are manifest in the illustration of this beautiful picture (see
opposite page).

It is a great misfortune that so many of Giorgione's

Photo : Anderson.

"THE MADONNA ENTHRONED, WITH SS. LIBERALE AND FRANCIS,"
BY GIORGIONE.

Castelfranco, Italy.

This, according to Ruskin, is "one of the two most perfect pictures in existence ; alone in the world as an imaginative representation of Christianity, with a monk and a soldier on either side."

Giorgione was only twenty-seven years of age when he painted this picture, which proves how early his astounding genius developed.

" PORTRAIT OF A YOUNG MAN," BY GIORGIONE.

Berlin Gallery.

Here, according to the great Italian art critic Morelli, " we have one of those rare portraits such as only Giorgione, and occasionally Titian, were capable of producing, highly suggestive, and exercising over the spectator an irresistible fascination."

Note the mysterious " VV " on the parapet. These letters are found in other portraits by Giorgione, and Dr. G. C. Williamson has suggested that they probably indicate the artist's signature, since Giorgione's name was spelt as " Zorzon " or " Zorzi " da Castelfranco by contemporary writers, and in old MSS. the capital Z is frequently made like a V.

"AN UNKNOWN MAN," BY GIORGIONE.

Querini-Stampalia Collection, Venice.

This unfinished portrait, probably of a member of the Querini family, is extraordinarily attractive in its colour-scheme of rich browns and reds. It represents a style of portraiture invented by Giorgione, which his pupil Titian afterwards adopted and developed.

paintings have been lost or destroyed in the course of
centuries. Barely a score are known for certain to exist
to-day, but among them are some of the most splendid

"ADRASTUS AND HYPSIPYLE," BY GIORGIONE.
Giovannelli Palace, Venice.

Nominally an illustration of the Greek legend how King Adrastus found Queen Hypsipyle
disguised as a nurse (after she had been driven out of Lemnos by a conspiracy), this
picture is famous as the first expression in art of a stormy landscape. It is a supreme
example of Giorgione's skill in pattern building : note how beautifully the broken columns,
almost in the centre of the foreground, balance not only the figure of the Queen, but also
the tall buildings beyond the bridge.

portraits in the world. His " Young Man " in the
Berlin Gallery (see page 104) and his " Unknown Man " in
the Querini-Stampalia Collection at Venice (page 105) are
presented here as examples of his power in portraiture.

Vasari tells us that Giorgione " did a picture of Christ bearing the Cross and a Jew dragging him along, which after a time was placed in the Church of St. Rocco, and now works miracles, as we see, through the devotion of the multitudes who visit it." We can form some idea of what the exceeding beauty of this painting must have been from the unforgettable head of " Christ Bearing the Cross," which still exists in the private collection of Mrs. Gardner, of Boston, U.S.A., and which is reproduced on page 99.

But, alas ! not a fragment has survived of the famous picture which Giorgione painted to prove the superiority of painting to sculpture. While Verrocchio was in Venice engaged upon the bronze horse of his splendid Colleone Monument, his admirers argued that sculpture, which presented so many aspects of a figure, was superior to painting. Giorgione maintained that a painting could show at a single glance all the aspects that a man can present, while sculpture can only do so if one walks about it, and thus he proved his contention :

" He painted a nude figure turning its shoulders ; at its feet was a limpid fount of water, the reflection from which showed the front. On one side was a burnished corselet, which had been taken off and gave a side view, because the shining metal reflected everything. On the other side was a mirror showing the other side of the figure."

The scarcity of Giorgione's work is partly explained by the fact that he died young. In 1510 he was deeply in love with a Venetian lady, who caught the plague, but " Giorgione, being ignorant of this, associated with her as usual, took the infection, and died soon after at the age of thirty-four, to the infinite grief of his friends, who loved him for his talents, and to the damage of the world which lost him. "

V

THE SPLENDOUR OF VENICE

§ I

WE never think of Titian as a young man ; to all of us
he is the Grand Old Man of Italian art, and there
is something patriarchal in his figure. He was, indeed,
very old when he died. Some would make out that he lived
to be ninety-nine, but there is considerable doubt whether
he was really as old as he pretended to be. The National
Gallery catalogue queries 1477 as the year of Titian's birth,
but few modern historians consider this to be accurate.
The date 1477 is only given by the artist in a begging letter
to King Philip of Spain, when it was to Titian's advantage
to make himself out to be older than he was, because he
was trying to squeeze money out of a rather tight-fisted
monarch on the score of his great age.

Vasari and other contemporary writers give 1489 as the
date of birth, but probably the nearest approach to the
truth is given in a letter (dated December 8, 1567) from the
Spanish Consul in Venice (Thomas de Cornoca), which
fixes the year of Titian's birth as 1482. This would make
Titian to have been ninety-four when he died.

Whether Titian lived to be ninety-four or, as Sir Herbert
Cook thinks, only eighty-nine, is a small matter compared
to the greater fact that he was born in the hill-town of
Cadore on a spur of the Alps, and spent his boyhood amid
solemn pine-woods and Alpine solitudes. Breathing the
keen mountain air, he grew up a young Hercules, deep-
chested, his features "sun-browned as if cast in bronze,"
his eyes clear, with an eagle glance bred of Alpine distances.

THE TAILOR," BY GIAMBATTISTA MORONI (*circa* 1520–1578).

National Gallery, London.

"A man's a man for a' that." Heralding the birth of democracy in art and the coming of a time when artists, no longer employed by nobles, could find nobility in the features of working-men, this picture is one of the world's great portraits and a splendid example of Venetian colour before its decadence.

So the young Titian (Tiziano Vecellio) came to Venice, a hardy mountaineer among the children of the plain, and all his art bears the impress of his origin. What we call the idealism of Titian is not the result of æsthetic reflection, but, as Muther has pointed out, " the natural point of view of a man who wandered upon the heights of life, never knew trivial care, nor even experienced sickness ; and therefore saw the world healthy and beautiful, in gleaming and majestic splendour."

By the early death of Giorgione in 1510, Titian was left without a rival in his own generation, and six years later (1516), when Bellini died, Titian was elected to succeed him as the official painter of Venice. Thenceforward his career was a royal progress. " All princes, learned men, and distinguished persons who came to Venice visited Titian," says Vasari, for " not only in his art was he great, but he was a nobleman in person." He lived in a splendid palace, where he received Royalty, and was able to give his beautiful daughter and his two sons every conceivable luxury, for Titian, says Vasari, " gained a fair amount of wealth, his labours having always been well paid."

Of the dramatic quality in Titian's art we have a splendid instance at the National Gallery in the " Bacchus and Ariadne " (see page 114), which, painted about 1520, is also a famous example of Venetian colour. Nobody before had ever given so dramatic and impassioned a rendering of Bacchus, the God of Wine, leaping from his chariot to console and cherish Ariadne, the beautiful maiden forsaken by her false lover Theseus. There is action not only in the drawing, in the spirited rendering of movement, but there is life also in the colour ; the amber, ruby, and sapphire of the flowing draperies sparkle, quiver, and radiate.

Whence came these qualities so new to Venetian painting ? They came from the great painter's memories of his birth-place, his boyhood's home beside the River Piave roaring down from storm-capped heights, from memories of the wind that swept through the tree-tops and rattled the rafters of the house. Familiar from childhood with the awe-inspiring, dramatic elements of Nature, Titian expressed her majesty and drama in his art.

Amid the wealth of pictorial beauty left by Titian it is difficult indeed to say which is his supreme masterpiece. According to Vasari, Titian's " Assumption of the Virgin " (see page 125) was held by his fellow-citizens to be " the best modern painting," and though it is no longer modern but an " old master," we cannot conceive a more impressive rendering of the subject than this picture, in which we almost hear the wind caused by the soaring ascent of the Virgin, her garments grandly swelling in the breeze by which the encircling cherubs waft her upwards.

Yet to this great painting of his mature years (1541) at least one of his earlier pictures is equal in beauty. To the transitional period in Titian's life, while the direct influence of Giorgione yet lingered, belongs the picture in the Borghese Gallery, Rome, known as " Sacred and Profane Love." But the title is only a makeshift. Nobody knows the true meaning of this picture of two lovely women, one lightly draped, the other in the full splendour of Venetian dress, seated on either side of a well in the midst of a smiling landscape. There is a tradition that the one represents " Heavenly Love," the other " Earthly Love " (see pages 118, 119), but on the other hand a passage in Vasari about another painting by Titian, now lost, gives countenance to the theory that these figures are personifications of Grace and Beauty, or more probably Grace and Truth. A third theory is that the picture illustrates a passage in some lost poem.

Titian's ideal of womanhood is seen not only in this picture, which inspired Mr. Arnold Bennett's novel with the same title, but in a number of exquisite portraits and figure paintings. According to Vasari, he painted mostly from his own imagination, and only used female models in case of necessity. Titian's types have little in common with the small, brown, black-eyed maidens we usually associate with Venice. They are nearer akin to the fair-haired Lombard women or the Dianas and Junos of his Alpine home. Further, it is the proud majesty of the

mature woman that Titian paints. His beautiful " Flora "
(see opposite page), in the Uffizi Gallery, Florence, does not
suggest spring-time but, as Dr. Muther has well said, " high
summer in its rich, mature splendour." Never old, but
never very young, Titian's " mighty women " seem to
" beam in an eternal, powerful beauty."

The same mature majesty characterises " The Magdalen "
(see page 117), to which Titian's contemporary Vasari pays
the following eloquent tribute : " Her hair falls about her
neck and shoulders, her head is raised, and the eyes are
fixed on Heaven, their redness and the tears still within
them giving evidence of her sorrow for the sins of her past
life. This picture, which is most beautiful, moves all who
behold it to compassion."

" He touched nothing that he did not adorn." So it
might be written of Titian, who ennobled all his sitters
with something of his own majesty. The supreme example
of his powers in this direction is the magnificent "Equestrian
Portrait of Charles V " (see page 115), now in the Prado at
Madrid. In 1530, when the Emperor Charles V was in
Bologna, Titian, by the intervention of his friend the poet
Pietro Aretino, was invited to that city and commissioned
to paint His Catholic Majesty in full armour. Vasari
tells us the Emperor was so delighted with this portrait that
he gave the artist a thousand gold crowns, declaring that he
would never have his portrait done by any other painter ;
and he kept his imperial word, frequently employing Titian
thereafter and always paying him a thousand crowns for
each portrait.

Never was money better spent. This Emperor of the
Holy Roman Empire and King of Spain still fires our
imagination, thanks to Titian. The historical truth about
Charles V is that he was a pale, scrofulous, emaciated man,
a prey to melancholy, full of hesitations and superstitious
fears ; so world-weary that in the end he abdicated from
his imperial position, and shut himself up in a monastery
where, with morbid satisfaction, surrounded by coffins and
ticking clocks, he constantly rehearsed his own funeral.
Titian shows us nothing of this. His wonderful imagination

" FLORA," BY TITIAN (*circa* 1482–1576).

Uffizi Gallery, Florence.

" The high summer of womanhood, in her rich, mature splendour." So a great critic
has described this beautiful example of Titian's idealised figure painting. The artist
only used models " in case of necessity," and this conception of Flora, the Goddess of
Spring, though so intensely alive that we feel she is real, probably only existed in the
imagination of the artist.

8

fastens on one great moment in the Emperor's life, the day when he was the victor at Augsburg. A Black Knight in steel armour, riding over the battlefield at daybreak, the Emperor in this painting becomes " the personification

Photo : W. A. Mansell & Co.

" BACCHUS AND ARIADNE," BY TITIAN.

National Gallery, London.

Bacchus, the God of Wine, leaps from his triumphal car to console and cherish the maiden Ariadne, who has been forsaken by her false lover. This painting is world-famous for the glory of its lovely, sparkling colour, and for an intensity of dramatic action unsurpassed in art.

of the coldness of a great general in battle, and of Destiny itself approaching, silent and unavoidable." Charles is here Napoleonic—but Napoleon had no Titian to immortalise his grandeur. Who would not pay a thousand crowns to be so transfigured for posterity ?

" CHARLES V," BY TITIAN.

Prado, Madrid.

" The personification of the coldness of a great general in battle, and of Destiny itself approaching, silent and unavoidable " : this is what the genius of Titian has made of this portrait.   Charles V was both King of Spain and Emperor of the Holy Roman Empire.

Titian has seized on one great moment in this monarch's life and pictured him riding at daybreak over the plain of Augsburg just before the battle in which his troops were victorious.

Still painting in his ninetieth year with unabated vigour, still able as a nonagenarian to play the host with undiminished magnificence to King Henry III of France, this grand old patriarch finally went down in 1576, like some battered but indomitable man-of-war, with his colours still proudly flying. Even then it was not of old age that he died ; he was a victim to the same pestilence which, sixty-six years earlier, had carried off his young fellow-pupil Giorgione. All Venice went into mourning when the greatest of her sons passed away, and the Senate set aside the decree that excluded victims of the plague from burial within church walls, so that Titian might be laid to rest in the Church of the Frari, within sight of his own picture of " The Assumption."

§ 2

The glowing mantle of Titian fell on the shoulders of Jacopo Robusti, nicknamed Tintoretto (the " Little Dyer ") from the calling of his father, Battista Robusti, who was a dyer, in Italian *tintore*. Tintoretto was born at Venice in 1518 and, having shown his precocious genius by covering the walls of his father's house with drawings and sketches, he was apprenticed as a pupil to Titian. Despite his prodigious capacity, for already the skill and speed of his workmanship were astonishing, he was not a satisfactory pupil. After some time Titian dismissed him, according to one account because he was jealous of his pupil, according to another because Tintoretto " would in no wise give obedience to commands." From all we know of Tintoretto's proud, wilful character the latter reason seems probable.

Left to himself, Tintoretto set up his own workshop, in which he nailed up the legend " The Design of Michael Angelo and the Colouring of Titian." Not only did he live up to his motto as regards his drawing and colour, but to these he added his own supreme understanding of light and shade ; and thus he was able to surpass Titian in the keenness of his literal yet romantic observation, and to outdo even Michael Angelo himself in the furious speed

"THE MAGDALEN," BY TITIAN.

Pitti Gallery, Florence.

" This picture. most beautiful, moves all who behold it to compassion,' writes Vasari,
a contemporary of Titian. " The eyes are fixed on Heaven, their redness and the tears
still within them giving evidence of her sorrow for the sins of her past life."

"SACRED AND PROFANE LOVE" (DETAIL), BY TITIAN.

Borghese Gallery, Rome.

According to tradition this figure is supposed to typify " Earthly Love," and the one opposite ' Heavenly Love " ; but since in the picture these two women are seated on either side of a well. others have interpreted them as Grace and Truth.

SACRED AND PROFANE LOVE " (DETAIL), BY TITIAN

Borghese Gallery, Rome.

Various conjectures have been made as to the meaning of these figures (see page 111), but the world is content to accept them as supreme examples of Titian's conception of feminine beauty.

119

and energy of his execution. Amazing stories are told of Tintoretto's activity. "This artist," remarks his contemporary Vasari, "always contrives by the most singular proceedings in the world to be constantly employed, seeing that when the good offices of his friends and other methods have failed to procure him any work of which there is question, he will nevertheless manage to obtain it, either by accepting it at a very low price, by doing it as a gift, or even by seizing on it by force."

An instance of this kind occurred when the Brotherhood of San Rocco decided to have the ceiling of their refectory painted with decorations. The four leading painters of Venice—Zucchero, Salviati, Veronese, and Tintoretto—were summoned to San Rocco and invited to submit designs for the project. It was announced that the commission would be given to the artist who produced the best design. "But while the other artists were giving themselves with all diligence to the preparation of their designs, Tintoretto made an exact measurement of the space for which the picture was required, and taking a large canvas, he painted it without saying a word to any one and, with his usual celerity, putting it up in the place destined to receive it.

"One morning, therefore, when the Brotherhood had assembled to see the designs and to determine the matter, they found that Tintoretto had entirely completed the work, nay, that he had fixed it in its place."

Naturally the three other artists were furious, and the head of the Brotherhood angrily inquired why Tintoretto had taken it on himself to complete the work when he had only been asked to submit a design in an open competition.

"This is my method of preparing designs," answered Tintoretto; "I do not know how to make them in any other manner. All designs and models for a work should be executed in this fashion, to the end that the persons interested may see what it is intended to offer them, and may not be deceived.

"If you do not think it proper to pay for the work and

remunerate me for my pains, then," the artist proudly added, " I will make you a present of it."

Thus, as Vasari relates, Tintoretto, " though not with opposition, contrived so to manage matters that the picture still retains its place."

Though he painted numerous portraits and altar-pieces, Tintoretto was essentially a decorative painter, and his mightiest achievements are on the walls and ceilings of the palaces and public buildings of Venice. His " Paradiso " in the Ducal Palace is the largest painting in the world, eighty-four feet wide by thirty-four feet high, and of this stupendous achievement and of most of his other great works no photograph can give any adequate idea. For this reason no attempt to reproduce them is made here. But fortunately the picture which is universally acknowledged to be Tintoretto's masterpiece is not on the same colossal scale. " The Miracle of St. Mark " (see page 129) is one of four large pictures painted by Tintoretto for the School of San Marco in Venice. It represents the Evangelist— who was the Patron Saint of Venice—appearing in the air and " delivering a man who was his votary from grievous torments, which an executioner is seen to be preparing for him : the irons which the tormentors are endeavouring to apply break short in their hands, and cannot be turned against that devout man."

The dramatic element in Titian's work is seen heightened and intensified in many of Tintoretto's paintings, but nowhere is it more splendidly manifest than in this impressive imagining of a supernatural event. Again we seem to hear the rush of air caused by the downward sweep of the Saint, from whom a celestial light irradiates. This great picture is not only an illustration of a saintly legend ; it had a symbolical meaning of great importance to Tintor etto's contemporaries. At this time political relations between Venice and Rome were strained. The Patriarch and Senate of Venice flattered themselves they were better Christians than the Romans, and were delighted to see in Tintoretto's masterpiece a picture in which they saw the Popes as the executioners of the Church, which is to be saved only by the fortunate interference of the Republic of St. Mark.

When Tintoretto died in 1594 there were no more great religious painters in Italy. Unlike Titian, who " had never received from Heaven aught but favour and felicity," and so throughout a long life looked out with ever joyous eyes, Tintoretto, notwithstanding his professional prosperity, was overshadowed by a spiritual gloom which finds expression in his mighty pictures. The works of his manhood and maturity show little of that serene joy in existence which glows from the canvases of Titian ; but in the fitful lighting of their sombre depths, in a constantly recurring hint of tragedy, they reveal a consciousness of stormy days to come, of perils for Church and State, which entitle us to see in Tintoretto a harbinger of the Reformation and the wars of religion.

§ 3

Working side by side first with Titian, afterwards with Tintoretto, was Paolo Cagliari, who, from Verona, the city of his birth, was known as Paul Veronese (1528–88). The whole splendour of Venice is revealed in his paintings, and his decorations in the Ducal Palace give immortality to the pageantry which characterised the Italy of his time.

When the Venetian Senate gave a festival in honour of King Henry III of France, the monarch was received (so history tells us) by two hundred of the fairest damsels in the city, dressed in white and covered with pearls and diamonds, " so that the King thought he had suddenly entered a realm of goddesses and fairies."

This is the realm we enter through a canvas by Veronese, whether his subject be professedly historical, as in " The Family of Darius before Alexander " in the National Gallery, or professedly religious, as in " The Marriage of Cana " (see opposite page) at Dresden. We have only to look at this painting with all its worldly pomp and ostentatious luxury to see how far art has travelled from the simple piety of the earlier Primitive Masters.

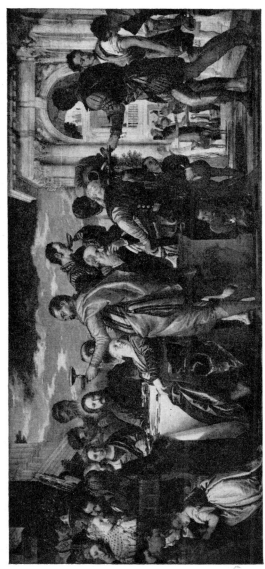

Photo : Alinari.

" THE MARRIAGE IN CANA," BY PAUL VERONESE (1528–88).

Dresden Gallery.

The luxurious pomp of a Venetian banquet is shown in this sixteenth-century painting, which is far removed from the simple piety of the earlier Italian masters. Veronese, whose opulent sense of colour and splendid design made him one of the great decorative painters of his day, was rebuked by the Inquisition for his worldly rendering of sacred subjects.

The monasteries were the chief employers of Veronese, as the eminent critic Mr. Berenson has pointed out : " His cheerfulness, and his frank and joyous worldliness— the qualities, in short, which we find in his huge pictures of feasts—seem to have been particularly welcome to those who were expected to make their meat and drink of the very opposite qualities. This is no small comment on the times, and shows how thorough had been the permeation of the spirit of the Renaissance when even the religious orders gave up their pretence to asceticism and piety."

A time came, however, when Veronese went too far even for the depraved ecclesiastics of his day. When he painted " The Last Supper "—now in the Louvre—in the style of " The Marriage at Cana," with the same glitter of crystal, silver, and jewels, the same sheen of silks and satins, the same multitude of serving men and attendants, the stricter clerics were scandalised. Information was laid against the painter, and on July 18, 1573, Paul Veronese was summoned before the tribunal of the Inquisition.

Exactly what happened then is not clearly known : while escaping banishment or severer punishment, the artist was sternly rebuked for his worldly treatment of religious subjects ; and though the reprimand appears to have had little permanent effect on his paintings, it is significant to note that his " Adoration of the Magi " in the National Gallery, which is dated 1573, is both in con- ception and in execution far more simple and respectful than are the majority of Veronese's pictures of sacred subjects.

The most beautiful picture by Veronese in the National Gallery, and one of the most haunting of all his works, is " St. Helena's Vision of the Cross " (see page 127), which is as reposeful as a piece of antique Greek sculpture and a superbly decorative example of the artist's skill as a maker of patterns. The curious will note in this work how cunningly the painter has arranged the figure to secure decorative balance and rhythm, how the right leg con- tinuing the line of the forearm repeats the diagonal of the cross, while the sharp horizontal of the cherub's wing

"THE ASSUMPTION OF THE VIRGIN," BY TITIAN.

Church of the Frari, Venice.

Titian's dramatic imagination, rich and powerful both in portraiture and in allegorical decorations for palaces, is here seen
applied with equal genius and deep feeling to the rendering of a
religious subject.

This picture, formerly in the Academy, Venice, but since the
war restored to its original position in the Church of the Frari at
Venice. was thought by Titian's contemporaries to be " the best
modern painting."

" THE PROTONOTARY APOSTOLIC JULIANO," BY LORENZO LOTTO
(1480-1556).

National Gallery, London.

" He looks out from his canvas as if begging for sympathy." So a modern American critic has written of this noble and dignified portrait by the most spiritual of all the great Venetian masters of the sixteenth century. Lotto was remarkable for his pious conservatism (see page 129), and would undertake the portraiture of no persons unless he respected their character.

"ST. HELENA'S VISION OF THE CROSS," BY PAUL VERONESE.

National Gallery, London.

Reposeful as a piece of antique Greek sculpture, this beautiful painting is also an illuminating example of the artist's skill in pattern-making. Note how the very angle of the Cross, seen by the Saint in her vision, is so arranged as to repeat the lines of her forearm and skirt, thus securing a symmetry which completes the rhythm and decorative aspect of the whole picture.

repeats the line of the window-sill. In these devices we recognise the hand of a master-craftsman.

§ 4

A greater than Veronese remains to be mentioned, a painter who was not only a consummate craftsman but also a profound thinker. This was Lorenzo Lotto (1480–1556) who, unlike his great contemporaries, was Venetian born. All the others—save Tintoretto, greatly his junior —came from the mainland : Giorgione from Castelfranco, Titian from Cadore, and Cagliari from Verona.

Few painters have lived so intense a life in the spirit as Lotto ; none has written so plainly as he his soul-history in his works. A true son of Venice, his youthful mind turned to Byzantium rather than to Rome for instruction and inspiration. To him Giorgione and Titian appeared as foreign intruders ; their worldliness shocked him, a follower of Savonarola. Lotto began by putting the Madonna back on a Byzantine throne in the apse of the church from which the painters of the Renaissance had taken her. Ploughing his lonely furrow at Venice he had his doubts, and in 1508 he journeyed south to see what Rome and Raphael had to teach him. What he saw there roused his reforming zeal, as it had that of Savonarola. Four years later (1512) he fled from metropolitan sinfulness and took refuge in the provincial tranquillity of Bergamo.

Here he possessed his soul in peace, and as though touched by the spirit of St. Francis he became reconciled to nature. No longer is the Madonna enthroned in church, but placed in the open country, where all existing things seem to praise the Creator in their beauty. Lotto became a pantheist and his message is the gospel of love. With his Venetian predecessors and contemporaries the Virgin is either soulful and humble, or aristocratic and proud ; Lotto paints her richly adorned, but imbues her countenance with a beneficent and tenderly maternal expression.

In portraiture Lotto is supreme even in a great epoch. When we look at his portrait in the National Gallery of

" The Protonotary Apostolic Juliano " (see page 126), noting through the window the wide and boundless land-scape traversed by a river which winds its way to the distant sea, noting also the exquisite Flemish-like painting of the still-life accessories, as well as the grave penetrating char-acterisation of the man, we cannot agree with Dr. Muther

Photo: Anderson.

" THE MIRACLE OF ST. MARK," BY TINTORETTO (1518–94).

Academy, Venice.

Tintoretto, the most famous pupil of Titian, illustrates in his dramatic picture the legend of how St. Mark, the patron saint of Venice, rescued a Christian slave from Pagan torturers.

that Lotto regards his sitters "unconcerned with their decorative appearance "; but we do heartily agree that Lotto shows us people " in their hours of introspection."

Why is it that Lotto, as a portrait-painter, strikes chords which, as Dr. Muther says, " are echoed in no other Italian work." The explanation is this : " Only those whom he loved and honoured were invited into his studio, and this circumstance alone differentiates his portraits from those of Raphael or Titian."

Though never such a great figure in his day as Giorgione, Titian, or Tintoretto, Lotto was not without influence on his contemporaries. One who felt it and gained by it greatly was a painter who came from Brescia to Venice, Giambattista Moroni (c. 1520–78). His "Portrait of a Tailor," which is reproduced on page 109, is full of human sympathy and almost perfect in craftsmanship. It is deservedly one of the most popular portraits in the National Gallery, and many of us feel almost equally drawn to Moroni's other great portrait at the National Gallery, "An Italian Nobleman" (see opposite page). Together they prove that, like Lotto, Moroni could extend his sympathies to sitters irrespective of their rank or position in life.

It is not easy to over-estimate the abundant excellence of portraiture in sixteenth-century Venice. Just as the wealth and power of her merchant-citizens were the source of the success of the republican State of Venice, so the luxury they were able to afford drew to the island-city of the Adriatic all the artistic talent born on the neighbouring mainland. Of the multitude of artists who during this century were adorning the public buildings and private palaces of Venice, only a few of the most celebrated can here be enumerated. Cima came from Conegliano to Venice in 1492, and worked there till 1516 or later, carrying on in his Madonnas the tradition of Giovanni Bellini. Vincenzo di Biagio, known as Catena, was born at Treviso about 1470 and died at Venice in 1531. He was greatly influenced by Giorgione, to whom was once ascribed the beautiful painting "A Warrior adoring the Infant Christ," which the National Gallery catalogue now gives definitely to Catena. Sebastiano del Piombo (c. 1485–1547), who about 1510 left Venice for Rome, where he was influenced by Raphael and Michael Angelo, has a special interest for us because his picture "The Raising of Lazarus" was the beginning of the National Gallery collection. It is still "Number 1." Palma Vecchio (1480–1528) was born near Bergamo, but came to Venice while still a student. In-

Photo : W. A. Mansell & Co.

" ITALIAN NOBLEMAN," BY MORONI (*circa* 1520–78).

National Gallery, London.

All things to all men, Moroni, the most accomplished disciple of Lorenzo Lotto, could depict an Italian nobleman with the same sympathetic skill and dignity that have made his " Portrait of a Tailor " one of the world masterpieces of portraiture.

fluenced first by Bellini and Giorgione, afterwards by Titian and Lotto, he very nearly reached the first rank, as his " Venus and Cupid," now in the Fitzwilliam Museum at Cambridge, amply proves.   He is called Vecchio (=Old) to distinguish him from a later painter Palma Giovine (1544–1628) or Young Palma.

Jacopo da Ponte (1510–92), called Bassano from his birthplace, is also splendidly represented in the National Gallery by " The Good Samaritan," a painting which used to belong to Sir Joshua Reynolds.   It is a magnificent example of vigour and muscular action.

In the art, as in the State of Venice, the spark of life lingered long.   So late as the eighteenth century, Longhi, Canaletto, and Guardi painted delightfully her canals and palaces and the life of her public places, while Giambattista Tiepolo (1696–1770), painting in the tradition of Veronese, earned for himself the proud title " the last of the Old Masters."

But with Tintoretto the last great word of Italy had been spoken, and when he died in 1594 it was left to the artists of other lands to take up the tale.

VI

THE DAWN OF THE REFORMATION

§ 1

SO far we have been following mainly the development of art in Italy, but that country had no monopoly of painting and sculpture during the Middle Ages. It was shown in the Second Chapter of this OUTLINE how a band of painters flourished on the banks of the Rhine during the fourteenth century.

Ever since the time of the Van Eycks paintings had been produced by natives of most of the great countries of Europe—even in England, where Odo the Goldsmith was employed by King Henry III to execute wall-paintings for the Palace of Westminster—but either because their work was not powerful enough to capture the imagination of Europe or, quite as probably, because they had no historians and biographers to trumpet their praises, the early artists of England, France, and Germany never acquired the fame won by their brethren of Italy and Flanders. With few exceptions their names, and in many cases their works, have been entirely lost.

> Full many a flower is born to blush unseen,
> And waste its sweetness on the desert air.

When all has been said, however, the fact remains that Italy was the centre of the world for mediæval Europe, and to it came all who were desirous of learning, culture, and advancement. In those times the painter born elsewhere made his way to Italy as naturally and inevitably as the artist of to-day makes his pilgrimage to Paris ; and in Italy the stranger artist was treated, not as a foreigner,

but as a provincial.   Looking at the political divisions of
Europe to-day, we are apt to forget that in the Middle
Ages the Christian nations of Europe were considered to
be one family.   Just as the Pope of Rome was the religious
Head of all Christendom, so in theory, if not in practice, its
secular Head was the Emperor of the Holy Roman Empire.
The capital of the Empire, again in theory, was Rome,
though in practice the Emperor was usually not very safe
outside his own kingdom in Germany.

When the Italian historian Vasari describes the great
German artist Albert Durer as a " Fleming," he is making
the same sort of mistake that a Londoner might make when
he was uncertain whether a west-countryman came from
Devon or Cornwall ; and just as some Londoners are so
narrow-minded that they cannot imagine any pre-eminent
greatness outside the metropolis, so Vasari in a patronising
way wrote of Durer :

Had this man, so nobly endowed by Nature, so assiduous and possessed of so many talents, been a native of Tuscany instead of Flanders,
had he been able to study the treasures of Rome and Florence as we
have done, he would have excelled us all, as he is now the best and most
esteemed among his own countrymen.

If Vasari thought this talented man had much to learn
from Italy, there were Italian artists who thought they had
something to learn from Durer.   Giovanni Bellini, whose
art has been described in Chapter IV, greatly admired
Durer's painting, and found his rendering of hair so marvellous that he thought the artist must have a special brush
for the purpose.   So when Durer visited Venice and in his
polite way offered to do anything in his power for Venetian
artists, Bellini begged to be given the brush with which he
painted hairs.   Durer picked up a handful of his brushes
and told Bellini to choose any one he wished.   " I mean the
brush with which you draw several hairs with one stroke,"
the Venetian explained.   Durer smiled and replied, " I
use no other than these, and to prove it you may watch me."
Then, taking up one of the same brushes, he drew " some
very long wavy tresses, such as women generally wear."

" KING HENRY VIII," BY HANS HOLBEIN

No previous period in English history lives so vividly in our imagination as the reign of Henry VIII. and it is due to the powers of Holbein that we are so familiar with the costumes and personalities of the time. This lifelike head, together with the elaborate costume, brilliantly displays the fine draughtsmanship of the artist.

135

Bellini looked on wonderingly, and afterwards confessed that had he not seen it nothing would have convinced him that such painting was possible.

Who was this Durer ?   Strangely enough, the artist who most fully revealed the spirit of awakening Germany was of Hungarian descent. His father, Albert Durer the Elder —whose portrait by his son hangs in the National Gallery, London—was born in Hungary. After travelling in the Netherlands for some time, he finally settled in Nuremberg, where his son was born on May 21, 1471. Albert the Younger had everything to foster the development of his gifts, his father was a goldsmith, and his grandfather also ; hence their removal to Nuremberg, a city which was in constant communication with Venice and had already begun to rival it in the arts and crafts of jewellery and metalwork. It is worth noticing that young Albert's god-father was the bookseller and expert printer Anton Koberger, and through him his godson probably became familiar with fine prints and engravings from his earliest years.

The father intended the son to succeed him in his craft, but as the latter tells us in his memoirs, " I was more inclined to painting, and this I confessed to my father. My father was not pleased," he adds with characteristic simplicity. Nevertheless young Durer got his way, and in 1486 was apprenticed to Michael Wohlgemut, a local artist then at the zenith of his fame. Wohlgemut had a large art school, which was the most important in Nuremberg, and here young Durer learnt to paint and also, possibly, to practise wood-engraving. But such a master had little to teach so brilliant a pupil, and after three years Durer the Elder wisely took his son away and sent him abroad for four years. Young Albert travelled in the south of Germany and probably paid his first visit to Venice during this period.

Returning to Nuremberg in 1494, Albert Durer—as we shall henceforth call him—married almost immediately Agnes Frei, daughter of a respected citizen. The young artist already had some reputation : in 1497 he painted the

Photo : Anderson.

"PORTRAIT OF THE PAINTER WHEN YOUNG," BY ALBERT DURER
(1471-1528).

Prado, Madrid.

Painted when the artist was only twenty-seven, this beautiful portrait of himself shows
the mature precision of a master in every detail. Note the wonderful painting of the
long wavy tresses, a feat which caused the Venetian artist Bellini to believe Durer had a
special brush for painting hair (see page 134).

portrait of his father, and in the following year the splendid portrait of himself which we reproduce. This comparatively early work, now at Madrid, shows all the characteristics of his later portraits; it has a simple dignity almost amounting to austerity, remarkable penetration into character, and in execution it shows perfect mastery of drawing and colouring.

In 1498 Albert Durer published a series of wood-engravings illustrating the Apocalypse, which greatly increased his reputation, for in these he was able to show not only the perfection of his drawing and design, but also the extraordinary power of his imagination. No design in this series is more famous than " The Four Horsemen of the Apocalypse " (see opposite page), which has recently become still more widely known by the popular novel of Ibanez and the film with the same title, both of which were directly inspired by Durer's masterpiece.

And I saw, and behold a white horse: and he that sat thereon had a bow: and there was given unto him a crown: and he came forth conquering and to conquer. . . . And another horse came forth, a red horse: and to him that sat thereon it was given to take peace from the earth, and that they should slay one another: and there was given to him a great sword. . . . And I saw, and behold a black horse; and he that sat thereon had a balance in his hand. And I heard as it were a voice saying, A measure of wheat for a penny . . . and behold a pale horse; and he that sat upon him, his name was Death.

These are the verses from Revelation (vi. 2–8) which Durer set himself to illustrate; and since it was executed in a period just previous to the Reformation, some critics have argued that its inner meaning is an attack on the Papacy. It is improbable, however, that Durer was at this time in any way actuated by religious bias; the series as a whole certainly attacks corruption, both lay and ecclesiastical, but in this woodcut, the most famous of the series, it is more likely that Durer confined himself strictly to his text. The Holy Roman Empire was in a chronic state of war, and Durer must have seen enough of fighting in his youth and early manhood to know who and what were the grim companions of conquest. The meaning of

"THE FOUR HORSEMEN OF THE APOCALYPSE."

FROM A WOOD-ENGRAVING BY DURER.

The four riders are Conquest, aiming afar with his arrow : War, with a drawn sword : Famine : and Death. Note the original conception of the third rider, whose rich costume and well-nourished body betray Durer's opinion of the War-Profiteer who fattens himself on the famine of others (see next page).

The most wonderful work of art ever inspired by the Book of Revelation (vi. 2–8), this magnificent design displays Durer's inventiveness as a decorative craftsman and the power and originality of his imagination. In our own day it has a peculiar fascination as revealing an Old Master's view of war.

this magnificent rushing design is clear ; it reveals Durer's view of War, war which sweeps mercilessly on, sparing neither man nor woman, priest nor layman, and inevitably accompanied by Famine, Pestilence, and Death.   The most subtle touch of satire is the third rider with the balances. In portraying Famine as this sleek, well-nourished, handsomely clothed man, Durer seems to hint that he is not ignorant of the existence of the War-Profiteer. The emaciated horse and its rider by his side tell their own tale.

It was by his engravings still more than by his paintings that Durer became famous, for the prints spread throughout Europe and created a great sensation.   But though invited to become a citizen of Venice or Antwerp by these municipalities, Durer remained loyal to his native city.   He continued to reside in Nuremberg.   After his father's death in 1502 his responsibilities increased, for now in addition to his own family Albert had to look after his mother and his younger brother Hans.

When commissions for portraits and altar-pieces were not forthcoming, Durer's wife used to hawk at fairs and gatherings her husband's prints illustrating episodes in the life of the Holy Family, and these wood and copper engravings not only brought in ready money by satisfying a popular demand, but they were the foundation of the artist's reputation as an engraver.   The success of these separate prints was immediate, and soon after the publication of the Apocalypse prints, Durer set to work on other sets of engravings, one of which was to illustrate the Passion of Our Lord and another the Life of the Virgin.

At the instigation and by the kindness of his friend, Wilibald Pirkheimer, who lent him the money for the journey, Durer in 1506 paid a visit to Venice, where he was commissioned by the German merchants to paint a panel for their chapel.   At first the painters of Venice were inclined to regard Albert Durer as a mere engraver who did not understand how to use colour, but the completion of this panel soon silenced hostile criticism and the work proved to be a veritable triumph for the painter.

LANDSCAPE DETAIL (FROM " THE RAPE OF AMYONE "), BY DURER.

Durer's love of Nature which found expression in his delicate yet vigorous drawing of trees, shrubs and clouds, is seen in this landscape.

141

In a letter to his friend Pirkheimer, Durer relates how the Doge and the Patriarch of Venice came to see his picture, and still more interesting is his account how the veteran Venetian painter Giovanni Bellini praised the picture in public and further proved his admiration for the work of the Northern painter. Bellini, Durer wrote, " wanted to have something of mine, and himself came and asked me to paint him something and he would pay well for it. All men tell me what an upright man he is, so that I am really friendly with him. He is very old, but is still the best painter of them all." It was at this time that the incident about the paint-brush already narrated occurred.

Altogether this visit to Venice was a success. It definitely established Durer's reputation as a painter, his small panels sold well, and later he went to Bologna, where he received a great ovation, but even the flattery of a Bolognese who declared he could " die happy " now he had seen Durer did not turn the artist's head, and he returned to Nuremberg the same modest, conscientious artist he had always been.

The succeeding years were very fertile in paintings, his principal productions being the " Crucifixion," now at Dresden, the " Adam " and " Eve," in which he tried to give his ideal of beauty of form, and the important altarpiece which he painted for the Frankfort merchant Jacob Heiler.

But the artist still found that painting did not bring him in so much profit as engraving, and after he had completed his great " Adoration of the Trinity " in 1511 he gave most of his time to engraving, continuing the first " Passion " series and the " Life of the Virgin." It was after the death of his mother in 1514 that he produced his famous print " Melancholia," a composition full of curious symbolism in which a seated female figure is shown brooding on the tragedies of existence.

Equally famous and still more difficult wholly to understand is the copper engraving known as " The Great Fortune " or " Nemesis " (see opposite page). It is supposed

"THE GREAT FORTUNE," BY DURER.

No work has roused more controversy than this famous design, in which Durer imaginatively shows " Fortune " or " Nemesis " with bridles in her left hand to curb the
" mad designs " of the proud.

If we are unable to admire the " goddess," we can all see the beauty of the landscape
beneath, and viewed from a distance or reversed the rhythmical disposition of the black
and white in this engraving makes it stand out as a fascinating pattern.

that this engraving was suggested by a passage in Poliziano's Latin poem, which may be thus translated :

There is a goddess who, aloft in the empty air, advances girdled about with a cloud. . . . She it is who crushes extravagant hopes, who threatens the proud, to whom is given to beat down the haughty spirit and the haughty step, and to confound over-great possessions. Her the men of old called Nemesis. . . . In her hand she bears bridles and a chalice, and smiles for ever with an awful smile, and stands resisting mad designs.

No work has aroused more controversy than this design ; some have regarded it as a splendid rendering of the physical attributes of mature womanhood, but others have pronounced the ugliness of the figure to be " perfectly repulsive," while others again have found it hard to reconcile the extreme realism of the woman's form with the fanciful imagination shown in her environment.

But however many opinions there may be as to the success of this engraving as an *illustration*, there is only one view about its merits as a *decoration*. Mr. T. Sturge Moore, himself an expert and gifted engraver, has well emphasised this point by reminding the readers of his book on Durer " that it is an engraving and not a woman that we are discussing : and that this engraving is extremely beautiful in arabesque and black and white pattern, rich, rhythmical and harmonious." If the experiment be made of turning the print upside down, so that attention is no longer concentrated on its meaning as an illustration, its extraordinary ingenuity and interest *as a pattern* will at once become apparent.

In 1518 Durer again resumed his activity as a painter : in that year he was summoned by the Emperor Maximilian to Augsburg, where he was employed in painting portraits of the emperor and of many of his nobles. In 1521 he visited the Netherlands and received much attention in Brussels and Antwerp ; though he drew and painted several portraits during his travels, he took up engraving again when he returned to Nuremberg. The series he then began is known as the " Second Passion " ; this set he did not live to complete. He died in 1528. Two years earlier he painted his celebrated " Four Apostles," which have a peculiar interest not only as Durer's last effort in picture-making, but also as an indication of the artist's attitude towards the Reformation.

It was in 1517 that Martin Luther sounded the tocsin for the Reformation by nailing his ninety-five theses on the nature of papal indulgences to the great door of the Church of Wittemberg. It was in the following year that Durer received kindness and attention from his imperial patron, the Catholic prince Maximilian I. The artist was in a difficult position, but though he took no definite side in the great controversy which ensued, his sympathy with the Reformers is shown in this picture by the fact that each of the four Apostles is holding and studying a Bible. It is significant to note that this painting was not a commission, but was painted by Durer to please himself and for presentation to the city of his birth. Here is the letter which accompanied the gift to the Council of Nuremberg :

Prudent, honourable, wise, dear Masters, I have been intending, for a long time past, to show my respect for your Wisdoms by the presentation of some humble picture of mine as a remembrance, but I have been prevented from so doing by the imperfection and insignificance of my works, for I felt that with such I could not stand well before your Wisdoms. Now, however, that I have just painted a panel upon which I have bestowed more trouble than on any other painting, I considered none more worthy to keep it as a remembrance than your Wisdoms.

Therefore, I present it to your Wisdoms with the humble and urgent prayer that you will favourably and graciously receive it, and will be and continue, as I have ever found you, my kind and dear Masters.

Thus shall I be diligent to serve your Wisdoms in all humility.

Possibly it was a remembrance of this picture in particular which prompted Luther, in his consolatory letter to the artist's friend Pirkheimer, to pen this memorable epitaph on Albert Durer :

It is well for a pious man to mourn the best of men, but you should call him happy, for Christ illuminated him and called him away in a good hour from the tempests and, possibly, yet more stormy times : so that he, who was worthy only to see the best, might not be compelled to see the worst.

10

§ 2

After Durer's death many carried on the tradition he had bequeathed to his country as an engraver—the prints of Aldegraver, Beham, and other followers are still treasured by collectors—but none of them won great fame in painting. Matthew Grunewald, Durer's contemporary, had a pupil Lucas Cranach (1472–1553), who was much esteemed by his fellow-citizens of Wittemberg and was appointed Court Painter to the Protestant prince Frederick of Saxony ; but we have only to look at the doll-faced " Portrait of a Young Lady " by him in the National Gallery to see how far Cranach's art fell below that of Durer.

Only one other painter of German origin beside Durer has so far succeeded in capturing the world's attention, namely Hans Holbein the Younger, who when Durer died in 1528 was a young man of thirty-one, painting in England. No more than twenty-six years separate the birth of Holbein from that of Durer, yet within the space of that one generation so great had been the revolution in men's minds that the two artists seem to belong to different ages. Holbein grew up during the greatest Wonder-Time in the world's history. We who have benefited by and taken for granted the astounding discoveries made during what is known as the Epoch of Maximilian (1493–1519), which approximates to the opening of the reign of our Henry VIII, find it difficult to realise the crash of old ideas and the bombardment of new ones which filled the world during this epoch :

That time [as Lord Bryce has told us]—a time of change and movement in every part of human life, a time when printing had become common, and books were no longer confined to the clergy, when drilled troops were replacing the feudal militia, when the use of gunpowder was changing the face of war—was especially marked by one event to which the history of the world offers no parallel before or since, the discovery of America. . . . The feeling of mysterious awe with which men had regarded the firm plain of the earth and her encircling ocean ever since the days of Homer vanished when astronomers and geographers taught them that she was an insignificant globe which, so far from being the centre of the universe, was itself swept round in the motion of one of the least of its countless systems.

Nothing but an appreciation of these historical facts can teach us rightly to comprehend the essential difference between the art of the two great German masters : for as the " feeling of mysterious awe " with which all his work, whether painted or engraved, is impregnated, makes Albert Durer the last and supreme expression of mediæ-valism, so an inner consciousness of man's insignificance and a frank recognition of material facts makes Holbein the first exponent in art of Modern Science.

The great Hans Holbein was the son of an artist of the same name, Hans Holbein the Elder, a poor and struggling painter of religious pictures in the flourishing city of Augsburg. Here Hans Holbein the Younger was born in 1497. There was never any doubt as to his calling, for he belonged to a family of painters. Not only his father, but his uncle and his brother were painters also. His father. who was chiefly influenced by the Flemish painter Roger van der Weyden (see Chapter II), had little to teach the son, and when he was seventeen or eighteen young Hans left his father's house in company with his elder brother Ambrosius, and began a foreign tour which eventually ended at Basle. Owing to the lack of any exact records and the constant confusion of the two Holbeins, father and son, the details of Holbein's early life are still a matter of conjecture and controversy. Some hold that the elder Holbein with his family moved from Augsburg to Lucerne about 1514, but the one thing certain is that young Holbein was at Basle in 1515, where he at once found work as a designer with the printer and publisher Frobenius. Through Frobenius he came to know Erasmus, who had recently left France and now graced Basle with his universal fame as a scholar ; and soon the young artist found plenty of employ-ment both as a book-illustrator and portraitist. One of the earliest and most loyal of his patrons was the Basle merchant Jacob Meyer, whose portrait and especially the splendid sketch for the same (see page 148) foreshadowed the future greatness of the artist as a portrait-painter. About 1516 or 1517 Holbein the Younger was in Lucerne, where he decorated a house, and it is conjectured that

" JACOB MEYER," BY HOLBEIN (1497–1543).
Basle.

Holbein's superlative merit as a draughtsman is seen in this early portrait study of one of his first patrons, the Burgomaster of Basle.   Note the union of delicacy and strength in the drawing of this head.   As a master of line Holbein in his own style has never been surpassed.

"PORTRAIT OF A YOUNG WOMAN," BY HOLBEIN.

Windsor Castle.

The Holbein drawings at Windsor are famous both in art and history, and it is largely through them that we are able to visualise so clearly the appearance and character of Henry VIII and his circle. This young woman was possibly one of Jane Seymour's maids-of-honour.

about this time he also travelled in Italy ; but there is no sure proof, and we can only guess at his movements till he reappears at Basle in 1519. Though but twenty-two, he is now a man and a master. In 1520 he became a citizen of Basle—a necessity if he wished to practise painting in that city—and about the same time he married a widow with two children.

He was a master, but a master of another order to Durer. Holbein was a pure professional painter, anxious to do a day's work and do it as well as he possibly could ; but he did not attempt to show how life should be lived or to penetrate its mysteries : he was content to paint what he saw, paint it truly and splendidly, but like the wise child of a sophisticated age he refrained from a futile endeavour to dig beneath the surface. Holbein can show you the character of a man, as in his portrait of Jacob Meyer ; but Durer would have tried to read his soul.

In 1521 he painted his masterly, though to many unattractive picture, " The Dead Man," horribly realistic some would say, yet in truth it is not morbid. For this outstretched corpse is painted with the calm detachment of a student of anatomy ; it is a manifestation of the sceptical, inquiring, but unmoved gaze of Science confronted with a Fact. In 1522 he painted " Two Saints " and a " Madonna," in the following year a " Portrait of Erasmus," in 1526 a " Venus " and a gay lady styled " Lais Corinthiaca," and in 1529 he painted a great " Madonna " for his friend Jacob Meyer.

The careful reader will have observed that no paintings are given above for the years 1523 to 1525, and indeed these were bad years for all painters. When Giulio de' Medici was elected Pope as Clement VII in 1523, he found, as a historian has said, " the world in confusion, a great movement going on in Germany, a great war just begun between the three most powerful Christian monarchs—a war to which he himself was pledged." Thinking the French would win, he sided with them. Two months after he had signed the treaty of alliance, Francis I of France was defeated and taken prisoner at Pavia, and the Emperor's troops—thousands of Protestants among them—headed for Rome. All the diplomatic wiles of the Pontiff were unavailing, and in May 1527 a horrified world beheld Christian troops, Germans, Spaniards, and Italians, engaged in the sack of Rome.

Basle, then a city of the Empire, though not exposed to the full force of the currents of war, was not untouched by these events, and Holbein, like a shrewd man of the world, began to look out for a shelter from the storm that was convulsing Europe. His native Germany was out of the question, for there paintings already in existence were being destroyed by zealots desirous of " purifying " Protestant churches. During this time of waiting, when commissions for pictures were scarce, Holbein began that series of wood-engravings which have done as much as any of his paintings to make his name illustrious.

No works of Holbein have held a more lasting place in the popular imagination than his little woodcuts illustrating " The Dance of Death." As remote in its origin as the " morality " play, this picturing of the fact that all living beings must die was probably in its beginning a monkish device to compel those who could not read to realise their inevitable fate. This lesson was driven home by the universality with which the theme was expounded. In the older prints of this subject the highest and lowest in the land were shown each dancing with a dead partner of the same rank and calling, a king dancing with a dead king, a bishop dancing with a dead bishop, a merchant with a dead merchant, a labourer with a dead labourer. Whoever you were you could not escape death, that was always dancing at your heels. This was the age-old theme to which Holbein gave new life, and if his version of the Dance of Death has eclipsed all other versions it is because Holbein was the first to present Death as an abstraction, common to all prints in the series, and because no other treatment of the theme has excelled his in the pictorial elements of design. Each of these prints is itself a perfect little picture —see how beautiful is the landscape with the setting sun in " The Husbandman " (see page 155). As for its value as preaching, Holbein's series serves a double purpose, emphasising by the skeleton that accompanies all alike, Pope, Cardinal, Miser, Husbandman, and what not, the equality as well as the universality of death.   Holbein's message is not only that " all flesh is grass " ; but also that under their skin " the colonel's lady and Judith O'Grady " are very much alike.

In 1526 Holbein found the haven for which he had been looking in England, an isle remote from the European storm-centre.   It is probable that he had become known through Erasmus to Sir Thomas More, and so was invited to come ; his painting of " The Household of Sir Thomas More " was one of the earliest and most important paintings executed by Holbein during his first stay in England. In 1528 he returned to Basle for three years, and having dispatched thence his gorgeous portrait of " George Gisze, Merchant of the Steelyard " (see opposite page) to show what he *could* do in portraiture, he returned to England in 1531.

This handsome and exceedingly ornate portrait of a young merchant in his counting-house was a deliberate show-piece which had exactly the effect the painter intended.   In troublous and uncertain times princes and great nobles were unreliable patrons ; at any moment they might be dethroned, killed, or executed.   Like a prudent man Holbein wished to establish a connection with a steadier, yet equally rich stratum of society, namely the great merchants.   Therefore he cleverly set his cap at the wealthy German merchants settled in London, and showed them in this portrait that he could make a merchant look as splendid and imposing as any king or nobleman.   He delivered his sample, and human vanity did the rest.   The German " Merchants of the Steelyard," as this Corporation was styled, flocked to his studio in London.   Three years later his first English patron, Sir Thomas More, was sent to the scaffold by Henry VIII because he declined to declare the nullity of that royal reprobate's first marriage with Catherine of Aragon.

To have been the friend of More was at this time no commendation to the favour of the Court ; nevertheless,

" PORTRAIT OF GEORGE GISZE," BY HOLBEIN.

Berlin.

There is no more popular element in any picture than the minute rendering of details which betokens a painter's industry and capacity.

This splendidly ornate portrait, in which the accessories are rendered with scrupulous care and brilliance, was a deliberate " show-piece " painted by the artist when he desired to obtain the patronage of " The Merchants of the Steelyard," the title of a Corporation of wealthy German merchants who settled and traded in London during the reign of Henry VIII.

Holbein was not the man to miss any opportunity of " getting on " for want of a little tact and diplomacy. Firmly based on the support of the German merchants, he tried another method of approach. Very soon we find him painting his splendid portrait of " Robert Cheseman, the King's Falconer " (see page 156), painting first the minor and then the greater courtiers, till at last, in 1536, he achieved what no doubt had been his aim from the first, and was appointed Court Painter to King Henry VIII.

Never did that sovereign do a wiser or a better thing for himself than when he made Holbein his painter. Not only did the artist present that king to posterity in a manner that mitigates our judgment of his cruelties, but he has made the whole history of that period live for us, as no previous period in English history lives, by his series of portraits and portrait drawings of the English Court. Mr. Ford Madox Hueffer has pointedly observed :

How comparatively cold we are left by the name, say, of Edward III, a great king surrounded by great men in a stirring period. No visual image comes to the mind's eye : at most we see, imaginatively, coins and the seals that depend from charters.

Mr. Hueffer truly argues that Henry VIII and his men would be just as lifeless without Holbein, and the way he has made them live in our imagination is a tribute not only to Holbein but also to the preserving power of art.

While preparing the way for his advancement in England, Holbein did not neglect the connection he already had on the Continent, and three years before his appointment as Court Painter he sought to widen and enhance his foreign custom by painting another show-piece : " The Ambassadors " (see page 157) was painted as deliberately to force an entry into diplomatic circles as the " George Gisze " had been to secure him the custom of the men of commerce. This remarkable group of Jean de Dinteville, Lord of Polisy, on the left, wearing the French Order of S. Michel, and of Georges de Selve, Bishop of Lavaur, in doctor's cap and gown, on the right, fascinates all beholders by the brilliance with which the accessories are painted, the globe,

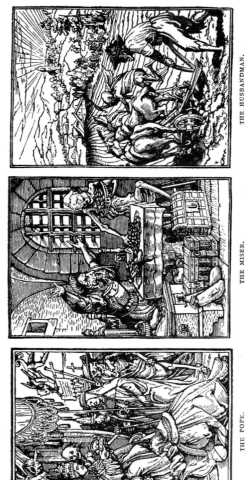

THE POPE. THE MISER. THE HUSBANDMAN.

FROM HOLBEIN'S "DANCE OF DEATH."

Like the old morality play *Everyman*, this ancient picture-sequence (see page 151) was intended to drive home the inescapable truth that "in the midst of life we are in death." With a pictorial pageantry unapproached in any previous or later rendering of the subject, Holbein here shows us Death dogging the footsteps of the Pope (and Cardinal), the Miser, and the Husbandman.

155

'ROBERT CHESEMAN, THE KING'S FALCONER," BY HOLBEIN.

The Hague.

By this simple and dignified portrait, both lifelike and decorative, of the King's Falconer, Holbein paved the way for his restoration to Court favour, after the execution of his first English patron, Sir Thomas More.

the turkey rug, the tiling, the mandoline, the astronomical instruments and in the foreground the anamorphosis (or distorted representation) of a human skull.   Many keen imaginations have set their wits to work to find an inner meaning to this curiously elongated death's-head, but the most plausible explanation is found in the fact that Holbein's own name means " skull " in his native language, and this device may consequently be regarded as a fanciful way of putting his seal or cipher on his work.   Another interpretation is that here, as in other portraits by Holbein,

Photo : W. A. Mansell & Co.

"THE AMBASSADORS," BY HOLBEIN.

National Gallery, London.

This famous picture of the Ambassadors Jean de Dinteville and the Bishop of Lavaur is another of Holbein's show-pieces, designed to maintain his Continental reputation and to attract the custom of foreign diplomats. The curiously distorted representation of a human skull in the foreground is an important element in the quadrilateral design and also a rebus on the name of the artist, " Holbein" meaning "skull."

the skull is introduced to reinforce the lesson of the " Dance of Death," that to this all must come. Whatever the painter's original idea may have been, his work is a complete success ; he painted it to create a sensation, and it has created a sensation for centuries. It may be added that this elongated skull completes the design, by paralleling the line from the one ambassador's hand (holding the dagger) to the head of the other ambassador.

THE " DUCHESS OF MILAN," BY HOLBEIN.
National Gallery, London.

The grace and sweetness of meditative maidenhood is
revealed with matchless beauty in this painting, which
is a portrait of a Princess of Denmark (afterwards Duchess
of Lorraine).

After the death
of Jane Seymour,
when Europe was
searched for mar-
riageable princesses
to console the royal
widower, Holbein
in February 1538
was sent to Brussels
to paint his match-
less portrait of King
Christian's daugh-
ter " Christina of
Denmark" (see
illustration on this
page), who, for-
tunately for her-
self, escaped Henry
VIII and afterwards
married the Duke
of Lorraine as her
second husband.
One of Holbein's
last works, this is by
many accounted his
greatest. Here he
has painted no
show-piece, but set
forth with divine
simplicity the grace
and dignity of me-
ditative girlhood.

From Brussels
Holbein went to
Burgundy, where
he painted other
portraits, and in
December of the
same year he re-

turned to London. Almost exactly five years later he caught the plague. In November 1543 Holbein died in London, a victim to the same disease that had already killed Giorgione in his youth and was destined, thirty-three years later, to carry off Titian in his old age.

Just as Durer and Holbein had no great forerunners, so they had no great successors, and Europe had to wait thirty-four years before another great master of art was born, outside Italy, in the person of Peter Paul Rubens.

VII

THE PRIDE OF FLANDERS

PAINTER, courtier, scholar, and diplomatist, Peter
Paul Rubens is one of the most picturesque figures
in European history. In origin he belonged to the upper
middle class, for though his grandfather had been a tanner
of Antwerp, his father John Rubens (1530–87) had taken
his degree at an Italian university and subsequently attained
considerable civic importance in Antwerp. At that time
Flanders was under Spanish rule, and trouble with the
authorities over political and religious matters drove the
Protestant John Rubens and his family into exile at
Cologne. There he became the intimate counsellor of
William the Silent, and unfortunately, too intimate with
his patron's wife, the Princess of Orange. Their love
affair was discovered and Dr. John Rubens was thrown into
prison, from which he was only released after the Prince
had divorced his wife. He did not long survive his imprisonment, and died at Cologne in 1587.

All this had its influence on young Peter Paul, who was
born at Siegen, Westphalia, in 1577, one year after the
death of Titian. Political complications had already
driven his father from Antwerp, and so the boy spent his
early childhood in exile. He was only ten years old when
his father died, and then his mother returned to Antwerp,
taking her three children with her, Blandina the eldest, a
young woman of twenty-three, Philippe a boy of thirteen,
and Peter Paul the youngest. By a curious coincidence,
just as only one year separated the birth of Peter Paul
Rubens from the death of Titian, so again one year divided

the death of John Rubens from that of Paul Veronese (1588), whose art his son was destined to develop and glorify.

After her daughter's marriage in 1590, the widow Rubens was able to say in a letter that both her sons were earning their living—so we know that their schooldays in Antwerp were short : Philippe obtained a place in the office of a town councillor of Brussels, while Peter Paul was Page of Honour to the Princess Margaret de Ligne-Aremberg. This gave the future diplomatist his first experience of court life ; but it was a short one, for already he felt art to be his true vocation, and in 1591 the lad of fourteen was allowed to begin his training as a painter in the studio of his cousin Tobias Verhaeght.

Here it may be well to recall that since the death of Mabuse in 1533 there had been no painter of the first rank in Flanders. Lucas da Heere (1534–84), a capable portrait-painter, though born at Ghent, worked chiefly in France and England. Returning to Flanders he could get little employment, and he died in poverty at Paris. A more successful portrait-painter, Antonio Moro (1519–78), better known as Sir Anthony More, also began his career in Ghent, but found more appreciation of his art in England and Spain. The most important of the immediate predecessors of Rubens were two families of artists, the Pourbus and the Breughels. Peter Pourbus (1510–84), a Bruges painter of portraits and religious subjects, had a son Frans Pourbus (1545–81), who settled in Antwerp. He in turn had a still more famous son, Frans Pourbus the Younger (1570–1622) who painted portraits not only in Antwerp but also at the Court of Henri IV in Paris. Young Pourbus, seven years older than Rubens, was one of the few of his contemporaries in Antwerp who not only never worked for Rubens but may have had some influence on his early style.

The founder of the Breughel family was Peter Breughel (c. 1525–69), whose dramatic " Adoration of the Magi " was secured for the National Gallery in 1929. Another interesting example of his forcible but primitive style, " Sacking a Village," is at Hampton Court. This painter had two sons, Peter, known as " Hell " Breughel [1] (1564–1638), because of his choice of subjects, and a younger, Jan, nicknamed " Velvet " Breughel (1568–1625), on account of the softness of his painting. The father made Brussels his headquarters, but the sons settled in Antwerp, where, notwithstanding his seniority, Jan Breughel eventually became an assistant to Rubens.

Rubens remained little more than six months with his cousin, who was a landscape artist. His next teacher, Adam van Noort, was a figure-painter, but it is unlikely he learnt much from this morose and often drunken boor. In 1596 he found a more congenial master in Otto Vaenius (1558–1629), who was a gentleman, a scholar, and a man of the world, though as a painter he was even duller and stiffer than his own master, the Venetian Zucchero (c. 1543–1616), well known in England by his numerous portraits of Queen Elizabeth. One thing that Vaenius did was to fire his pupil with enthusiasm for Italian art, and two years after he had come of age and had been admitted a member of the Guild of St. Luke, Peter Paul Rubens arrived in Venice. Here the admirable copies he made of paintings by Titian and Veronese attracted the attention of Vincenzo I, Duke of Mantua, into whose service Rubens almost immediately entered. With the Duke he was at Florence for the marriage of Marie de' Medici to Henri IV (by proxy), and in 1603—after he had visited Rome, Padua, and other Italian cities—Rubens was sent by Vincenzo I on a mission with presents of horses and pictures to Philip III of Spain.

Though not then entrusted with any work for the Spanish monarch, Rubens painted several pictures for his prime minister the Duke of Lerma before he returned to Italy. After working for his patron at Mantua, Rome, and Genoa, Rubens in 1608 was recalled to Antwerp by news of his mother's serious illness. Too late to see her alive when he reached his native city, the grief-stricken painter remained for several months in strict seclusion, when he was

---

[1] A characteristic example of " Hell " Breughel's work, " An Incantation Scene," may be seen in the Dyce Collection at the Victoria and Albert Museum, South Kensington.

Photo : W. A. Mansell & Co.

" LE CHAPEAU DE POIL," BY RUBENS.

National Gallery, London.

This smiling lady in the beaver hat (chapeau de poil) is Susanne Fourment, whose sister Helene became the second wife of the artist. Of the many portraits of women painted by Rubens this is the most famous, and it is a splendid example of his powers at their prime.

163

drawn by the rulers of Flanders, the Stadt-holders Albert
and Isabella, who, conscious of his growing reputation,
persuaded Rubens to leave the Mantuan service and become
their Court Painter. In accepting this position Rubens was
permitted to live at Antwerp instead of with the Court at
Brussels.

His brother Philippe had already married the daughter
of his chief, the Secretary of Antwerp, and it was probably
at their house that Rubens saw his sister-in-law's niece
Isabella, daughter of John Brant, whom he married in
1609. The following year the artist designed a palatial
residence in the Italian style, and had it built on the
thoroughfare now known as the *Rue de Rubens* : there he
took his young and beautiful wife, and there he settled
down to found the School of Antwerp. The ensuing ten
or twelve years were the most tranquil and probably the
happiest in the life of Rubens. An example of Rubens'
first manner is the portrait (see opposite page) of "Rubens
and his First Wife," painted when he was about thirty-
two and his newly married wife Isabella Brant little over
eighteen. During this period he executed the works on
which his fame most securely rests, notably his supreme
masterpiece, "The Descent from the Cross" (see page 169),
in Antwerp Cathedral. This work, executed in 1612,
marks the beginning of Rubens' second manner, just as his
"Elevation of the Cross," also in Antwerp and painted in
1609–10, concludes his first or Italian manner.

The late R. A. M. Stevenson, a most penetrating critic,
has pointed out how much more original and softer is the
later picture :

It started the Antwerp School, and beyond its ideal scarce any contemporary advanced. The forms are less muscular, the gestures less
exaggerated, the transitions suaver, the light and shade less contrasted
than in the first period, but the pigment is still solid, and the colours are
treated as large, unfused blocks of decorative effect.

The growth of Rubens was gradual, but the extraordinary
number of his collaborators makes the tracing of that
growth a task of infinite difficulty. Apart from other

"RUBENS AND HIS FIRST WIFE," BY RUBENS (1577–1640).

Pinakothek, Munich.

This portrait group of Rubens with his first wife Isabella Brant is a fine example of his early style of portraiture. Note the precision of drawing and wealth of detail which formed the foundation for the artist's later and more dashing style.

contemporary evidence, the letters of Rubens himself show the number of artists he employed to work from his designs. The truth is he established a picture-factory at Antwerp, and not only engaged assistants to help him carry out gigantic decorations for churches and palaces, but also farmed out commissions for easel-pictures, landscapes, and portraits. In addition to " Velvet " Breughel, his collaborators and pupils at one time or another included Snyders (1579–1657), Jordaens (1593–1678), Cornelius de Vos (1585–1651), Antony Van Dyck (1599–1641), David Teniers (1610–90), Jan Fyt (1609–61), and a score of others. A good example of the " team-work " accomplished in the Rubens studio is our illustration " Christ in the House of Martha and Mary " (see page 178). In this picture, now in the Irish National Gallery at Dublin, the figures are by Rubens, the landscape by " Velvet " Breughel, the architecture by Van Delen, and the accessories by Jan van Kessel. Yet all is so controlled by the master-hand that to any but an expert the whole appears to be the work of one man.

A story is told that the Dean of Malines Cathedral was furious when, having ordered a " Last Supper " from Rubens, a young man named Justus van Egmont came down to begin the work. Later on

the great man appeared with his fine calm presence and the urbane manner that was a bulwark against offence or misappreciation. As Rubens corrected the work, enlivened the colour or the action of the figures, and swept the whole composition with his unerring brushwork towards a beautiful unity of effect, the churchman acknowledged the wisdom of the master, and admitted that the money of the chapter had been safely invested.

Even the beautiful portrait of " Susanne Fourment " (see page 163), known as the " Chapeau de Poil," a canvas of 1620, which shows Rubens' second manner merging into his third—in which the pigment is less solid and the fusion of colour more subtle—even this work has been thought by some critics to be not altogether the work of Rubens. The late R. A. M. Stevenson considered that " the comparatively rude folds of the dress and the trivial details of the leather " betrayed another hand at work.

Photo. W. A. Mansell & Co.

"THE RAINBOW LANDSCAPE," BY RUBENS.
Wallace Collection, London,

This picture shows Rubens' attitude towards Nature, which he approached without awe and with the friendly arrogance of a strong man who respects strength.

The fame of the Flemish master had spread all over Europe, and in January 1622 Rubens was summoned to Paris by the Queen-Mother, Marie de' Medici, who wished him to decorate her favourite Luxembourg Palace. The great series of wall-paintings, which were the result of this commission, are now one of the glories of the Louvre. These pictures were designed to emphasise the greatness of the Medicis and the splendour resulting from the marriage of Marie de' Medici to King Henri IV of France. How cleverly Rubens fulfilled his double rôle of courtier and decorator may be seen by our illustration (page 173) of one of the most notable pictures in this series, "Henri IV Receiving the Portrait of Marie de' Medici." Here, in a wonderful blending of fable with reality, the artist idealises the King as monarch and lover, and turns a marriage dictated by reasons of state into a romantic love-match in which Cupid and all the deities of Olympus are deeply concerned.

Endowed by nature with a splendid presence, tactful in disposition and charming in manners, Rubens was a man to win the confidence of any Court. After the death of the Archduke Albert in 1621, his widow the Regent Isabella took Rubens into her inner counsels and employed him in semi-official visits to foreign courts. The great object of the rulers of Flanders was to keep England and Holland friendly with Spain and apart from France. One of the first missions which Rubens received was to secure a renewal of the treaty between Holland and Flanders, a task which took him to The Hague in 1623. It was at this time that he was ennobled by the King of Spain.

When visiting Paris the painter had made the acquaintance of the Duke of Buckingham, the virtual ruler of England under Charles I, and this nobleman had been greatly taken by the talents of the Fleming both as artist and diplomatist. It was Buckingham himself who suggested that Rubens should be sent to Spain in the summer of 1628 to ascertain the real feelings of Philip IV in the war which Buckingham planned against France through hatred of Richelieu, who had separated him from Anne of Austria.

Photo : Braun.

"THE DESCENT FROM THE CROSS," BY RUBENS.

Antwerp Cathedral.

Though temperamentally unfitted to be a religious painter, Rubens, by his splendid colour, flowing design, and naturalness of presentation, gives so fine a rendering of this awesome subject that it is counted to be his supreme masterpiece.

Rubens arrived at Madrid in the course of the summer, bringing with him eight pictures as a present to Philip ; but the assassination of Buckingham on September 2nd, 1628, changed the political aspect of affairs and enabled Rubens to give his whole attention to art. An important event in the history of painting was the meeting in Spain of Rubens, now fifty-two, with Velazquez, then a man of thirty ; the two became great friends, and we shall see, in the chapter on Spanish painting, that the younger man was considerably influenced by his elder.

Politically the great result of the Fleming's stay in Spain was that Philip IV consented to Rubens going as his official representative to King Charles I of England. The artist-diplomat arrived in London on May 25, 1629, and not only arranged the terms of peace between England and Spain but gave a new direction to English painting. Charles commissioned him to paint the ceiling which may still be seen in the Banqueting Saloon in Whitehall, now the United Services Museum, and many of his pictures were bought by the Royal Family and nobility of England.

The tact of the courtier, as well as the splendid powers of the painter, may be seen in our illustration (see opposite page) of a famous Rubens at the National Gallery, " The Blessings of Peace," which shows Minerva, goddess of Wisdom, pushing back War, while Peace receives Wealth and Happiness and their smiling children. This picture was presented to the English king by Rubens soon after his arrival in London as a delicate hint of the advantages to be derived from concluding peace with Spain.

It is said that while he was painting this picture in London an English courtier asked Rubens, " Does the Ambassador of his Catholic Majesty amuse himself with painting ? " " No," replied Rubens, " I amuse myself sometimes with being an ambassador."

On February 21, 1630, Charles I knighted the painter, and soon afterwards Sir Peter Paul Rubens returned to the Continent and again settled in Antwerp. Isabella Brant had been dead about four years, and in December Rubens married Helen Fourment, whom he must have known from

Photo: Hanfstaengl.

"THE BLESSINGS OF PEACE," BY RUBENS.

National Gallery, London.

When visiting England as Ambassador for Philip IV, Rubens presented this picture to Charles I, as a hint of the advantages to be derived if England made peace with Spain. It shows the Goddess of Wisdom pushing back War while Peace receives Wealth and Happiness and their smiling offspring.

childhood.   She was one of the seven daughters of Daniel
Fourment, a widower, who had married the sister of
Rubens's first wife.   Helen was only sixteen when she
married.

The last seven years of his life were devoted by Rubens
to domestic happiness and his art rather than to politics,
which he practically abandoned after 1633.   He had a fine
country estate near Malines, the Château de Steen, of
which we may see a picture in the National Gallery, and
there for the most part he lived quietly, happy with his
girl-wife and only troubled by attacks of gout.   During
these last years Rubens produced a quantity of fine pictures ;
in one year (1638), for example, he despatched a cargo of
112 pictures by himself and his pupils to the King of Spain.
The rapidity of the master's execution is well illustrated
by a story that, having received a repeat order from Philip
(*after* he had received the 112 pictures !), and being pressed
by the monarch's brother Ferdinand to deliver the new
pictures as quickly as possible, Rubens said he would do them
all with his own hand " to gain time " !

Among these new pictures, sent off in February 1639,
were " The Judgement of Paris " and " The Three Graces,"
both now at the Prado, and generally held to be the finest
as well as the latest of the painter's many pictures of these
subjects.   But still the King of Spain wanted more pictures
by Rubens.   Further commissions arrived, and in May
1640 the great master died in harness, working almost to the
last on four large canvases.

Excelling in every branch of painting, and prolific in
production, Rubens is a master of whose art only a brief
summary can be given.   A final word, however, must be
said on the landscapes which form a conspicuous feature
among his later works, and of which we possess so splendid
an example in " The Rainbow Landscape " (see page 167)
in the Wallace Collection.   The healthy and contented
sense of physical well-being, which radiates from every
landscape by Rubens, has been well expressed in a criticism
of this picture by Dr. Richard Muther : " The struggle of
the elements is past, everything glitters with moisture, and

" HENRI IV RECEIVING PORTRAIT OF MARIE DE' MEDICI,"
BY RUBENS.

The Louvre, Paris.

In this splendid decoration Rubens idealises a marriage made for reasons of state, and presents it as a romantic love match in which Cupid and all the deities of Olympus are deeply concerned.

the trees rejoice like fat children who have just had their breakfast."

It has been said that there are landscapes which soothe and calm our spirits, and landscapes which exhilarate. Those by Rubens come under the latter category. He was no mystic in his attitude towards Nature; he approached her without awe, with the friendly arrogance of a strong man who respects strength. Most of his landscapes were painted in the neighbourhood of his country seat, and in them we may trace not only the painter's love of the beauty in Nature, but something also of the landowner's pride in a handsome and well-ordered estate.

The heir of the great Venetians in his painted decorations, Rubens was a pioneer in all other directions. His portraits were the inspiration of Van Dyck and the English painters of the eighteenth century, his landscapes were the prelude to Hobbema and the " natural painters " of England and Holland; while in pictures like " Le Jardin d'Amour " and " The Dance of Villagers " he invented a new style of pastoral with small figures which Watteau and other later artists delightfully exploited.

§ 2

Of all the many followers of Rubens, the two most famous were Van Dyck and Jacob Jordaens (1593–1678), another exuberant Fleming, who though greatly influenced by Rubens was never actually his pupil. The " Riches of Autumn " (see page 177) in the Wallace Collection is a fine example of the bacchanalian opulence of Jordaens. The fruit, vegetables, and most of the foliage in this picture are painted by Frans Snyders (1579–1657), a noted painter of " still-life " who frequently collaborated with Rubens and other painters. The skill of Jordaens as a portrait-painter may be seen in his " Baron Waha de Linter of Namur " in the National Gallery, but though a capable and skilful painter of whatever was before him, Jordaens had no imagination and added little of his own to the art of Rubens.

" CORNELIUS VAN DER GEEST," BY VAN DYCK (1599–1641).
National Gallery, London.

How Van Dyck penetrated below externals to the mind and spirit of his sitter may be
seen in this wonderful rendering of a man's thought and character.

175

"CHARLES I," BY VAN DYCK.

National Gallery, London.

Nobody can withhold sympathy from this knightly figure, in which the artist portrays all the virtues of the royal martyr and none of his faults. After the execution of Charles I. this picture was sold by the Puritans and passed into the possession of the Elector of Bavaria, from whom it was purchased and brought back to England by the great Duke of Marlborough.

Antony Van Dyck, who was born at Antwerp in 1599, was supposed to have entered the studio of Rubens as a boy of thirteen, but recent research has shown he was originally

"THE RICHES OF AUTUMN," BY JORDAENS (1593–1678).
Wallace Collection, London.

This bacchanalian scene is a typical specimen of the exuberant art of Jordaens. The fruit and vegetables are painted by Snyders.

a pupil of Hendrick van Balen and did not enter the studio of Rubens till about 1618. He was the favourite as well as the most famous of his master's pupils, and yet temperamentally he was miles apart from Rubens. Where Rubens made all his sitters robust and lusty, Van Dyck made his refined and spiritual. From Rubens he learnt how to use his tools, but as soon as he had mastered them he obtained

"CHRIST IN THE HOUSE OF MARTHA AND MARY," BY RUBENS.
Irish National Gallery, Dublin.

This picture is an example of the co-operative painting carried on by Rubens when he established his "picture-factory" at Antwerp. The landscape is by Breughel, the architecture by Van Delen, the accessories by Jan van Kessel, and the figures by Rubens, who put the finishing touches which give unity to the whole.

widely different results. The English Ambassador at The Hague persuaded Van Dyck to visit England in 1620 when he was only just of age, but at that time he made only a short stay, and after his return to Antwerp Rubens urged him to visit Italy. It was good advice. The dreamy, poetic-looking youth, whose charming painting of himself at this time we may see in the National Portrait Gallery

"MARCHESA CATTANEO," BY VAN DYCK.
National Gallery, London.

The influence of Titian can be seen in this portrait of a Genoese noblewoman painted
during Van Dyck's second visit to Genoa after he had been studying the Venetian
painters.

London, was spiritually nearer akin to the Italian than to the Flemish painters. What he learnt from them, especially from Titian, may be seen in " The Artist as a Shepherd " in the Wallace Collection, painted about 1625–6, and from the still more splendid portraits in the National Gallery of the Marchese and Marchesa Cattaneo (see preceding page), both painted during the artist's second stay in Genoa.

Strengthened and polished by his knowledge of Italian art, Van Dyck returned to Antwerp, there to paint among many other fine things two of his outstanding achievements in portraiture, the paintings of Philippe Le Roy and his wife which now hang in the Wallace Collection. These portraits of the Governor of the Netherlands and his wife were painted in 1630 and 1631, when the artist was little over thirty years of age, and in the following year the young painter was invited by Charles I to visit England, where he became Sir Antony Van Dyck, Principal Painter in Ordinary to His Majesty.

His great equestrian portrait " Charles I on Horseback," which we reproduce (see page 176), passed through several hands before it found a permanent home in the National Gallery. When King Charles's art collection was sold by the Puritans in 1649, this picture passed into the collection of the Elector of Bavaria. Afterwards it was purchased at Munich by the great Duke of Marlborough, from whose descendant it was bought in 1885 for the National Gallery, the price given for this and Raphael's " Ansidei Madonna " being £87,500.

After he had established himself in England Van Dyck slightly altered his manner, creating a style of portraiture which was slavishly followed by his successors, Sir Peter Lely and Sir Godfrey Kneller.

To speak of the elegance of Van Dyck's portraits is to repeat a commonplace, but what the casual observer is apt to overlook is that this elegance penetrates below externals to the mind and spirit of the sitter. Of his powers in both directions an exquisite example is the portrait group of " Lords John and Bernard Stuart " (see opposite page), one of

" LORDS JOHN AND BERNARD STUART," BY VAN DYCK.

The most beautiful portrait group Van Dyck painted in England ; shows the refinement
of the artist's portraiture and his capacity as a psychologist.

181

Photo : W. A. Mansell & Co.

"PHILIPPE LE ROY," BY VAN DYCK.

Wallace Collection, London.

This portrait of the Governor of the Netherlands was executed in Antwerp when the painter was a little over thirty years of age.

the most beautiful pictures he ever painted in England, and a work which proves Van Dyck to have been not only a supremely fluent master of the brush, but also a profound and penetrating psychologist.

Had he lived longer no one can say what other master-pieces he might have achieved : but unfortunately, with all his other great qualities as a painter, Van Dyck lacked the health and strength of his master Rubens. How good-looking he was in his youth, we can see by the charming portrait of himself which hangs in the National Portrait Gallery, but this refined, almost girlish face suggests delicacy and weakness. Weak in a way, he was ; though not spoiled by success, he could not stand the social whirl and dissipation on which a Rubens could thrive. Very superstitious, he was a victim to quacks and spent much time and money in endeavouring to discover the phil-osopher's stone. It is said that his failure to find this precious fable of the alchemists preyed on his mind and contributed to his collapse in 1641, when, though no more than forty-two, his frail body was worn out with gout and excesses. On the death of Rubens in 1640 Van Dyck went over to Antwerp. It was his last journey, and soon after his return to London he joined his great compatriot among the ranks of the illustrious dead.

Van Dyck established a style in portraiture which succeed-ing generations of painters have endeavoured to imitate ; but none has surpassed, few have approached him, and when we look among his predecessors we have to go back to Botticelli before we find another poet-painter who with equal, though different, exquisiteness mirrored not merely the bodies but the very souls of humanity.

After Van Dyck's death, numerous imitators, both British and Flemish, endeavoured to copy his style of portraiture, but the next great impetus art was to receive after Rubens came, not from England nor from Flanders, but from Spain. It is to the country of Velazquez and Murillo, therefore, that we must next turn our attention.

VIII

SUNSHINE AND SHADOW IN SPAIN

THE ART OF EL GRECO, VELAZQUEZ, AND MURILLO

§ I

WHEN one thinks of Spain and art, the name of Velazquez jumps into the mind at once. Indeed, to most people, his is the only name in Spanish painting of outstanding importance. Looking back over the whole history of art in Spain, Velazquez's figure overshadows that of everyone who went before him and of all who have come after him. In a sense, he is the only great painter Spain has produced. He interpreted the life of his time in terms that appeal universally, and no art has had more influence than his on modern painters.

How art came to Spain must now briefly be related. Until the fifteenth century there was little painting in Spain, and then, owing to the political connection of Spain with the Netherlands, the influence was markedly Flemish. It will be remembered that Jan van Eyck (see Chapter II) visited Spain in 1428, and the brilliant reception he received there induced other Flemish artists to visit the peninsula. Later, when Naples and the Sicilies came under the dominion of the Spanish crown, Italian art set the fashion to Spanish painters and particularly, as we might expect, the art of Naples. The Neapolitan School owed its origin to Michael Angelo Amerigi, called Caravaggio (1569–1609) from his birthplace near Milan. Undaunted by the great achievements of the Italian painters who immediately preceded him, Caravaggio sought to form an independent style of his own based on a bold imitation of Nature. While he was working in Venice and Rome, this astute student of Nature saw his contemporaries falling into decadence

Photo : W. A. Mansell & Co.

" ST. JOHN AND THE LAMB," BY BARTOLOME ESTEBAN MURILLO
(1617–1682).

National Gallery, London.

Murillo was inspired by John the Baptist's words, quoted by the Apostle John :
" Behold the Lamb of God, which taketh away the sin of the world."

because they were artists imitating art. The seventeenth-century painters of Rome, Florence, and Venice degenerated into mere copyists of Titian, Tintoretto, Raphael, and Michael Angelo. Caravaggio saw their error, and perceiving that art based on art leads to decadence, he gave his whole attention to Nature and so became a pioneer of realism. By choice he elected to paint scenes taken from the ordinary life of his day, and " The Card Cheaters " (see opposite page) is an admirable example of the novelty both of his subject and of his treatment. The novelty in his treatment chiefly consisted of the use Caravaggio made of light and shade (technically known as *chiaroscuro*) to enforce the dramatic intensity of his pictures. He exaggerated his shadows, which were far too black to be scrupulously faithful to Nature, but by the emphasis he thus gave to his lights he produced original and arresting effects which undoubtedly had a powerful influence on the two greatest painters of the next generation. How widespread was his authority is proved by the extent to which he prepared the way for both Velazquez and Rembrandt.

After working in Milan, Venice, and Rome, Caravaggio settled in Naples, where among those influenced by his realism was the Spanish painter Josef Ribera (1588–1656). " The Dead Christ " in the National Gallery, London, is an example of Ribera's stern naturalism.

Through Ribera the influence of Caravaggio penetrated to Spain, but already that country had had its art sense profoundly stirred by a foreign artist who not merely visited Spain, as other artists had done, but made it his home. This was Domenico Theotocopuli, who from having been born at Candia, Crete, was universally called El Greco, that is to say " The Greek." El Greco (1545–1614), as we shall call him, went to Venice as a young man of twenty-five and worked there for a time under Titian. About 1575 he migrated to Spain and settled at Toledo, where he became affected by the great religious fervour which was then agitating the peninsula.

Art is the mirror of life, and a great part of the fascination of old pictures is that in them are reflected the great

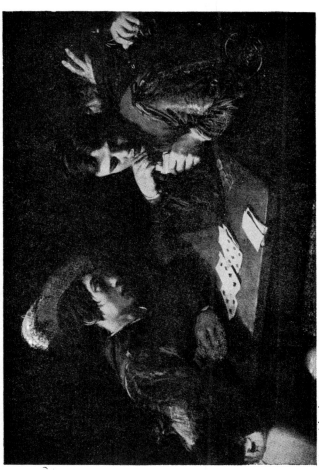

"THE CARD CHEATERS," BY CARAVAGGIO (1569–1609).
Dresden.

Life shrewdly seen and truly rendered furnishes the artist with themes as fascinating as any provided by history or legend. This Neapolitan painter, by giving dramatic intensity to scenes taken from the ordinary life of his day, became the founder of Naturalism in art, and his pictures are human documents of never-failing interest.

upheavals of history. We have seen how Florentine art was affected by the preaching first of St. Francis of Assisi and afterwards of Savonarola ; in Chapter VI it was shown how the Reformation influenced the last painting of Albert Durer and the whole outlook of Holbein. Now the most formidable antagonists that the Lutheran Reformers had to face, alike in action and in thought, were the Spaniards. The movement of the counter-Reformation originated and flourished in Spain. As the Spaniards in the Middle Ages had battled against the Moors till they won their land for Christianity, so they fought against the paganism of the Roman Church during the sixteenth century and strove with equal determination later against the Reformers, whom they regarded as heretics. The herald of this last battle was Ignatius Loyola, and he and his creation, the Order of the Jesuits, proved to be the most dangerous and powerful adversary of Protestantism.

El Greco's picture " Christ driving the Traders from the Temple," in the National Gallery, may be regarded as symbolising the purification of the Church by Loyola, but it is by his treatment infinitely more than by his choice of subject that El Greco expresses that vein of " convulsed mysticism " which was the peculiar attribute of Spanish Catholicism. El Greco as he grew older seemed to take delight in distorting natural forms. There is something savage, brutal even, in his art, and his deep earnestness gives grandeur to terrible things. The generally acknowledged masterpiece and most characteristic work by El Greco is his picture (see opposite page) in the church of San Tomé in Toledo, in which the members of a knightly order solemnly attend the funeral of Count Orgaz. The corpse is lowered into the ground by two saints, while Christ, Mary, martyrs, and angels hover in the air, and this " abrupt union of actual with transcendental "—as Dr. Muther puts it— together with the uncanny, slightly exaggerated forms found in parts of the picture, confess a touch of hysteria.

By a curious coincidence the tercentenary of El Greco was celebrated in 1914, at a moment when the whole of Europe was again in a turmoil and minds were full of

'THE BURIAL OF COUNT ORGAZ" (DETAIL), BY EL GRECO (1545–1614).
San Tomé, Toledo.

Reality and unreality intermingled in this picture (which shows a Spanish Count about to be buried in the presence of the members of a knightly order) reveal the heightened imagination of a painter whose art reflects the terrors of the Inquisition.

189

hatred and thoughts of violence. To a generation excited by war and rumours of war the suppressed violence in El Greco's pictures was irresistibly attractive. Some very advanced critics and ultra-progressive painters found in his neurotic temperament their ideal Old Master. El Greco was reputed to have held that colour was of far more importance than form or drawing, and if this belief was once regarded as " a curious anticipation of modern ideas," these " modern ideas " are themselves now out of date, drawing and design being now generally accepted as the foundation of all good art. El Greco's pictures are far from being formless. Historically and psychologically the paintings of El Greco are of the highest interest ; but they are a dangerous model for the art student.

Another foreign artist, who if he did not succeed in expressing the spirit of the time nevertheless influenced Spanish painting considerably, was Sir Anthony More, who, as mentioned in Chapter VII, visited Spain, and during his stay there, about 1551-2, set a style of portraiture which served as a model for Coello (1515-90) and other Spanish court-painters.

§ 2

These, then, were the principal influences alive in Spanish art when Diego de Silva y Velazquez was born at Seville in 1599. His family was not of Sevillian or even of Spanish origin, for his grandfather Diego Rodriguez de Silva came from Oporto, the home of the Silva family. The name which he made world-famous he took from his mother, Gernima Velazquez, who belonged to an old Seville family. His father Juan de Silva raised no objections when his son desired to study art, and when he was thirteen or fourteen Velazquez was placed in the studio of Francisco de Herrera (1576-1654), who showed something of the fanaticism of El Greco in the flashing eyes and majestic gestures of the saints in his religious pictures. Herrera is said to have been bad-tempered, and after enduring his roughness for about a year Velazquez changed masters and entered the studio of Francisco Pacheco (1571-1654). There he remained five years, and though his master had no great originality or power, he was probably a good teacher, for he was himself a careful draughtsman, a scholar, and the author of a book on painting. Presumably there was also another attraction, for on April 23, 1618, Velazquez married Pacheco's daughter Juana de Miranda. Henceforward Pacheco did everything he could to advance the interests of his son-in-law.

Within three years occurred the opportunity of a lifetime. Philip III died on March 31, 1621, and the young king Philip IV dismissed the Duke of Lerma and made Count Olivarez his prime minister. Now Olivarez, a son of the Governor of Seville, had lived in that city till 1615 and had made himself popular there as a patron of painters and poets. Several of his old protégés at Seville united to praise to the new minister the extraordinary talent of their young fellow-townsman. Velazquez went to Madrid and, after some vexatious delays, in 1623 Olivarez persuaded the young king to give Velazquez a sitting. He conquered at his first brush-stroke. The equestrian portrait he painted is now lost, but it pleased Philip so much that forthwith the painter of twenty-four was appointed Court Painter to a king of eighteen.

From the beginning Philip treated Velazquez in the most friendly manner. The king is said by a contemporary to have come to his studio " almost every day," by " those secret passages, hung with pictures, which led from the king's rooms to every part of the old Alcazar." The monotony of the stiff routine of the Court was broken in the autumn of 1628 by the arrival of Rubens, who, as stated in the last chapter, came to Madrid on a diplomatic mission, and for nine months was constantly with the king and Velazquez. According to Pacheco and others, Rubens thought highly of Velazquez, and delighted in his society, while his views of the king appears in a letter Rubens wrote to a friend :

He evidently takes quite a special pleasure in painting, and, in my opinion, this prince is endowed with the finest qualities. I already know him from personal intercourse, as I have a room in the palace, so that he almost daily visits me.

Philip IV appears to have been genuinely interested in painting, a result probably of his intimacy with Velazquez, and after Rubens's visit, and undoubtedly on his advice, the King permitted Velazquez to go to Italy with the great soldier and statesman Spinola, who was to be the Spanish governor of Milan and commander-in-chief in Italy. Velazquez arrived at Milan in the early autumn of 1629 and soon went to Venice, where he made a special study of the work of Tintoretto, who died, it will be remembered, five years before Velazquez was born. From Venice he went to Rome—missing Florence—and after some months there passed on to Naples, where he met Ribera, and returned to Madrid early in 1631. At Naples he painted Philip's sister, Mary of Hungary, and this portrait he brought back with him together with his painting " The Forge of Vulcan."

It is customary to divide the art of Velazquez into three periods, of which the first ends with this visit to Italy. Most critics agree that the finest and most typical painting of his first period is the bacchanalian scene known as " The Topers." In the strongly laid shadows of this painting we see the influence of Caravaggio, and while we admire the virile rendering of form and the well-balanced grouping of the figures, yet we feel that the scene, as R. A. M. Stevenson, the cousin of " R. L. S.," wrote in his classic book on Velazquez, " was never beheld as a whole vision in the mind's eye." The painter's complete mastery of his art was yet to come.

The time between his return to Madrid and his departure in 1649 for a second visit to Italy was the happiest period in the life both of Velazquez and of Philip. Daily the artist advanced in the mastery of his art and in the esteem of his sovereign. R. A. M. Stevenson has pointed out that :

Like Rembrandt, who never ceased to paint his own portrait, Velazquez studied one model, from youth to age, with unalterable patience and an ever-fresh inspiration. He could look at the king's well-known head with a renewed interest, as he went deeper into the mystery of eyesight, and became better informed as to the effects of real light.

Owing to fires and other accidents many of these portraits of Philip have been lost, but twenty-six exist to this day :

and they are all different. If we follow the development of the painter's art in these portraits of Philip IV—and nearly a dozen are in England—we shall see the slow transformation of a face, through a hard realism of feature and detail, to the soft, atmospheric impressionism of the final portraits. The bust portrait of " Philip IV : Old " in the National Gallery, London, is a superb example of the painter's last manner and of the way in which he could steep a whole canvas equally in a soft envelope of light.

What this continual painting of the same model did for Velazquez we can see from the portraits : it helped him to realise what every painter in the end must realise if he intends to excel, that it is not the subject but the treatment that makes the masterpiece. Velazquez found his fundamental inspiration, not in the novelty of a new subject, but in the ceaseless pursuit of seeing better and painting better something he had already seen. It is by the ultimate perfection of his rendering of the normal vision of man that Velazquez holds his supreme place among the very greatest masters of art. Other painters have expressed character, ideas, and beauty more poignantly, but nobody before or since has expressed *vision* so splendidly.

What this constant intercourse with a great artist did for Philip IV we can only imagine, but R. A. M. Stevenson again comes to our rescue by picturing in words how lonely is the lot of a king, and particularly in this period of a king of Spain :

To be a king of Spain, to preside at religious executions, to have a wife whom no man, even to save her life, might touch on pain of death, was to be a creature sorely in need of private liberty, and the solace of confidential intercourse. Philip IV seems to have been naturally kind, genial, and affable, and to have divided his leisure between the hunting-field and Velazquez's studio. The two, artist and king, grew old together, with like interests in horses, dogs, and paintings ; thawing when alone into that easy familiarity between master and old servant, freezing instantly in public into the stiff positions that their parts in life required. Painter to the king, when he was scarce twenty-five years old, Velazquez escaped most of the dangers and humiliations of professional portrait-painting, without losing its useful discipline of the eye, its rigorous test of the ever-present and exacting model.

13

It was when Velazquez was about forty that he was called upon to execute what proved to be one of the two supreme achievements of his art.   Olivarez had presented the King with a new palace, Buen Retiro, on the heights above the Prado, and the Court Painters, with Velazquez at their head, were commanded to set about its decoration.   For the decoration of this palace Velazquez produced his great historical picture " The Surrender of Breda " (see page 202) which is not only superb as a decoration but as moving in its sentiment as any picture artist ever painted.

The surrender of Breda, a fortified town twenty miles south-east of Dordrecht, was an incident in the memorable, and at first apparently hopeless, struggle which, beginning in 1568, lasted for eighty years and ended in the haughty Spaniards being compelled to recognise the independence of the Dutch Republic.   The capture of Breda was one of the last triumphs of Spanish arms before the tide turned against them.   This was the subject Velazquez chose for his contribution towards the decoration of Buen Retiro. Notwithstanding the armed crowd and multitude of uniforms, the noble bearing of the principal figures is the first thing that arrests attention.   The gestures of Spinola, the Spanish Commander, and of Justin, chief representative of the defeated Dutchmen and bearer of the key to the city, are poignant in expression, and what moves us most of all is the incomparable humanity of the scene.   There is no arrogance in the Spanish conqueror, who lays his hand consolingly, almost affectionately, on the shoulder of Justin ; in the Dutchman there is all the tragedy of defeat, but he is still dignified and does not cringe to the victor.   It is an ennobling presentment of a historic scene.

While admitting that " The Surrender of Breda " challenges the greatest masters on their own ground, rivalling the highest achievements of Titian, Tintoretto, and Veronese both in its dignity as illustration and in its beauty as decoration, yet Mr. Stevenson has affirmed that " it is not the complete expression of the Velazquez eyesight."   In a sense it is not ; it has not the amazing actuality of some of the painter's later works, but it may be

"EQUESTRIAN PORTRAIT OF DON BALTHASAR CARLOS," BY VELAZQUEZ
(1599–1660).
Prado, Madrid.

This quaint and rather pathetic little figure of King Philip's only son is one of the most adorable child portraits ever painted. Note how, with all its apparent naturalness, the artist has fitted horse and rider into a triangular pattern repeated in the landscapes in the distance.

Photo : Anderson.

"PHILIP IV AS A SPORTSMAN," BY VELAZQUEX.

Pardo, Madrid.

With unalterable patience and ever-fresh inspiration, Velazquez painted his King from youth to age. This portrait is an example of the artist's middle period and should be compared with his later " Æsop " (page 207) to show the painter's progress.

questioned whether it is desirable that it should have this quality. This painting, we must remember, was first and foremost a decoration painted to adorn a certain wall in a given apartment, and the experience of centuries has shown that ultra-realism does not produce the most effective forms of decoration, which need a certain deliberate convention to emphasise their beauty as patterns. In " The Surrender of Breda " Velazquez gives us the greatest amount of realism compatible with the success of the picture as a decoration : it fulfils its purpose to perfection, and than this no higher praise can be given.

Just about the time of this painting, Velazquez was introduced to a new sitter, the king's little son Balthasar Carlos. Of the many portraits he made of this prince none is more delightful than the one which shows him on horseback (see page 195). This quaint and rather pathetic little figure on his prancing steed, with the whole of Spain seemingly summed up and expressed in the landscape behind him, is the most adorable picture ever painted of a small boy. For all his pomp and importance (emphasised by the marshal's baton in his hand), the stern, set face— so like his father's—makes us feel sorry for him. He is very human ; we feel that he is a lonely child, and somehow the painter with prophetic insight seems to suggest that he has not long to live. Poor little Balthasar Carlos, born in 1629, did not live to be twenty. In 1646 he caught a cold at Saragossa and died. Thereafter Velazquez had no royal prince to paint, and Philip IV had to lavish all his domestic affection on a little princess, the Infanta Maria Teresa, who had been born in 1638. Soon after her arrival troubles came thick upon Spain. Olivarez mismanaged matters badly and was disgraced in 1643 ; and the same year those lances of Spain, hitherto invincible, which we see in " The Surrender of Breda," themselves suffered the agony of defeat and were utterly crumpled up and crushed at Rocroi by the great French commander Condé. Domestic griefs accompanied these public misfortunes, for two years before he lost his son, Philip lost his wife, the Queen Isabella.

In 1649 Velazquez again visited Italy, no longer the follower of an all-conquering army but the agent of a monarch whose power was waning. He landed at Genoa on January 2, and passing through Milan made for Venice, where he purchased several pictures for the King. This, indeed, was the principal object of his journey. From Venice he went to Rome, where he painted the splendid portrait of Innocent X which now hangs in the Doria Palace, Rome, and met several artists of note—among them being Salvator Rosa (1615–73), the Neapolitan painter of brigands and wild scenery, and Nicolas Poussin (1594–1665), the polished Frenchman, who in his classical subjects carried on the tradition of the great Renaissance and in his landscapes was a real pioneer.

In the summer of 1651 Velazquez returned to Madrid, where still further honours awaited him. He was made Marshal of the Palace, and as Philip IV had married again during his absence—married his own niece Mariana of Austria, a girl of fourteen—the new Marshal was kept busy organising festivities and tournaments for the amusement of the young Queen. By this second wife Philip had the Princess Margaret, born 1651, who is the central figure in the world-famous " Las Meninas." This picture (see page 201), in English " The Maids of Honour," marks the culmination of the third period of Velazquez and is the supreme achievement of his life.

Here, indeed, we have " the complete expression of the Velazquez eyesight," and great and glorious as " The Surrender of Breda " is, we are bound to confess that R. A. M. Stevenson was right in maintaining that this historical picture is not—like " The Maids of Honour "—" an absolutely unique thing in the history of art." Like so many of the greatest pictures in the world, " The Maids of Honour " originated in a spontaneous and unpremeditated flash of intense vision. The story generally accepted is that Velazquez was painting the king, who sat in the spot from which the spectator is supposed to see the picture of " Las Meninas." During a moment's rest the " Infanta " came in with her attendants, and the king was

Photo : Anderson.

" VIEW IN THE GARDEN OF THE VILLA MEDICI, ROME " BY VELAZQUEZ.
Prado, Madrid.

Painted during his first visit to Rome in 1630, this sketch from Nature shows how Velasquez
anticipated the open-air landscape painting of the nineteenth century.

struck with the group which fell together before his eyes.
Near him he saw the princess, her maids of honour Maria
Sarmiento and Isabel de Velasco (who is offering her water),
her dog, and her dwarfs Mari Barbola and Nicolasito
Pertusato ; a little farther on the left, Velazquez, who had

stepped back to look at his picture ; farther back on the right, a duenna and courtier talking ; while at the distant end of the gallery the king saw his queen and himself reflected in a mirror, and through the open door, Don Joseph Nieto drawing back a curtain.   The canvas shown in the picture would naturally be, as Stevenson maintains, the one on which Velazquez was painting the king's portrait.   Some, however, will have it to be the very canvas of " Las Meninas," which Velazquez was painting from a reflection in a mirror placed near to where the king had been sitting. R. A. M. Stevenson has justly pointed out that the perspective in the picture hardly seems to agree with this view, but rather makes Velazquez to have been working on the king's right hand.   It is not a matter of importance, and the story of the conception of the picture may easily have got mixed in the telling.   It is just possible that Velazquez was painting, or was about to paint, a portrait of the Infanta only, when the idea of the large picture suddenly occurred to him or to the king.   The canvas of " Las Meninas " is made of separate pieces sewn together, and one of these just contains the Infanta, with room for accessories or a subordinate figure.   However it originated, the picture was immediately recognised as a brilliant triumph, and tradition says the Red Cross of Santiago on the painter's breast was painted there by the king's own hand, as a promise of the honour that was to be conferred on him afterwards.

It is hard to conceive of a more beautiful piece of painting than this—so free and yet firm and so revealing.   When one stands before this canvas one is not concerned with any consideration of who it was painted by ; it fills the mind and suffices.   Like all of the great artists, Velazquez takes something out of life and sets it free.   The men and women in his finest pictures are released from what some one has called " mankind's little daily cage " ; and we are startled at the representation.   In this portrait group we have life stated so intensely that the ordinary life around us seems almost unreal.

The same intense and startling impression of life is given us by the paintings of single figures executed by Velazquez

Photo : Anderson.

"THE MAIDS OF HONOUR," BY VELAZQUEZ.

Prado, Madrid.

"An absolutely unique thing in the history of art." This intimate picture of the Spanish royal family (see page 198) is unparalleled for its brilliant actuality and its sense of light, space, and air. In no other painting in the world is the third dimension so perfectly expressed.

during his last years. If we compare the shabby but dignified philosopher " Æsop " (page 207)—a fine example of his late style—with " Philip IV as a Sportsman " (page 196), which is admittedly one of the best full-lengths

Photo: W. A. Mansell & Co.

"THE SURRENDER OF BREDA," BY VELAZQUEZ.

Prado, Madrid.

Incomparable in its humanity is this decorative commemoration of one of the last triumphs of Spanish arms in the Dutch war of in-ependence. Spinola, the Spanish conqueror, lays his hand almost a ectionately on the shoulders of Justin the Dutchman, who sadly, but with respectful dignity,

202

of his middle period, we shall begin to realise how far Velazquez travelled during the intervening years, not merely in the rendering of form but in the painting of light and air.

In 1659 Cardinal Mazarir sealed the reconciliation between France and Spain by arranging a marriage between the young Louis XIV and Maria Teresa of Spain. The meeting of the two courts on the frontier and the organising of the imposing ceremonies required, burdened the Marshal of the Palace with a multiplicity of work and anxiety. The wedding took place on June 7, but it was the last function Velazquez was able to perform. At sixty years of age the strain was too much for him, and a few weeks after he had returned to Madrid he collapsed and died on August 6, 1660.

In a sense it may be said that the most surprising adventures of Velazquez occurred after his death. By birth a hidalgo (*i.e.* a member of the lesser nobility), Velazquez was buried like a grandee. The entire court attended his funeral, and knights of all orders took part in the ceremonies. But after the generation that knew the man had passed away, the glory of the painter was strangely and unaccountably forgotten. For two hundred years, during which picture-lovers flocked to Italy and Italian artists became daily more famous, the name of Velazquez was seldom mentioned. Then, about fifty years ago, the sympathy of two or three great artists, notably Whistler in England and Manet in France, broke the spell of silence, and supported by a galaxy of writers, among whom was R. A. M. Stevenson —from whose great book *The Art of Velazquez* we have freely quoted — these enthusiasts made the light of Velazquez to shine before all men, so that to-day he is and evermore will be a star of the first magnitude in the firmament of Art.

§ 3

Contemporary with Velazquez, but influenced in his style of painting not so much by him as by Caravaggio, was the monastic painter Francisco Zurbaran (1598–1662), who, though born in the province of Estremadura, came to

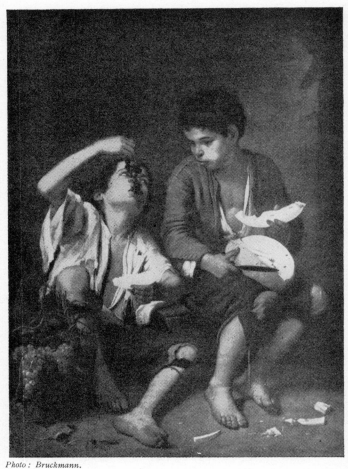

Photo : Bruckmann.

"THE MELON-EATERS," BY MURILLO (1617–82).

Munich.

Taken from life, this picture is an example of the painter's early style, and gives pleasure both by its warm humanity and by the realistic painting of the still-life accessories.

"THE IMMACULATE CONCEPTION," BY MURILLO.

The Louvre, Paris.

Innocence and sweetness characterise this ideal of the Virgin, whose upward gaze
seems to indicate, not longing, so much as naïve astonishment.   Compared with
El Greco's burial scene (page 189) this painting indicates a great change in the type
of religious presentation.

Seville when he was only sixteen and is generally regarded as a member of the School of Seville. He is chiefly famous for his religious pictures, and particularly for his monastic visions, among which "The Apotheosis of St. Thomas" in the Museum of Seville ranks as his masterpiece. His monks in white sheets often appear to be carved owing to the effect of high relief obtained by strong contrasts of light and shade, and the feeling of austerity and grandeur they display makes the paintings of Zurbaran illuminating documents of monastic life in Spain during the seventeenth century.

Among the immediate pupils of Velazquez were Juan Battista del Mazo (1600–67), who (in 1634) became his son-in-law and imitated his portraiture so cleverly that some of his paintings were at one time confounded with those by his master ; and one who became still more famous, Bartolome Esteban Murillo (1617–82). Also born at Seville, Murillo passed through a whole gamut of influences before he developed a distinct style of his own. When he was twenty-four he came to Madrid for a couple of years, and when he returned he did not forget the lessons of Velazquez. From this period date those popular pictures of beggar-boys and low-life subjects which were the first to bring him fame. "The Melon-Eaters" (see page 204) is a fine example of this side of Murillo's art. It charms the layman by its warm and graceful sympathy with life ; it delights the artist by the skill and taste shown in the painting of the accessories. The rind of the melon, the bloom of the grapes, the wicker of the woven baskets, all are depicted not only with great beauty of colour but with rare fidelity to the *textures* of the different objects.

Later in life Murillo altered his methods and employed a softer and more suave style, in which outlines are lost in the delicate fusion of graduated colours. The mysterious vaporous effect thus obtained was a variant of Correggio's famous "smoky" style (see Chapter IV), but has been distinguished from his by being technically described as *vaporoso*. Among the multitude of Murillo's religious paintings in this style the most famous is "The Immaculate

" .ESOP," BY VELAZQUEZ.

Prado, Madrid.

This incomparably real portrayal of a ragged philosopher is a
superb example of the last manner of Velazquez, when a sott
atmospheric impressionism has replaced the harder realism of his
earlier paintings.

Conception " (see page 205), now in the Louvre, which the French Government acquired in 1852 for the sum of £23,440. The change in the type of religious presentation is marked if we compare this painting with the frenzy of El Greco or the dramatic action displayed in a Titian or a Tintoretto. The storm and strife of the Reformation and counter-Reformation is passing away, and the enervation of the once combative Spain finds expression in a soft serenity that dreams of an ideal world. Not tragedy nor power, but innocence and sweetness characterise this vision of Mary, whose eyes, as a modern critic has pointed out, are not filled with inspiration and longing, but " astonished as those of a child gazing upon the splendour of the candles of a Christmas-tree."

Murillo was very famous in his lifetime, and the sweet sentimentality of his paintings appealed so strongly to the eighteenth and nineteenth century that for nearly two hundred years after his death he was considered the foremost of Spanish painters. To-day at least three Spanish painters, Velazquez, Goya, and El Greco, are rated more highly. Senhor A. de Beruete y Moret, the learned director of the Prado Museum at Madrid, has stated that

> The art of Murillo is of less interest than formerly, owing to present-day preferences, which seek spirituality in art, a force, and even a restlessness which we do not find in the work of this artist. . . . His conceptions are beautiful, but superficial. There is in them no more skilful groundwork, dramatic impulse, nor exaltation than appears at first sight. To comprehend and enjoy them it is not necessary to think ; their contemplation leaves the beholder tranquil, they do not possess the power to distract, they have no warmth, nor that distinction which makes a work unique.

Historically the art of Murillo must be regarded as a sign of the decadence of Spain, and it was not till a century later that the country gave birth to another great artist ; then the agony of the Wars of Succession found expression through the grim, satirical powers of Goya, whose work will be considered when we come to the art of the Napoleonic period.

The political power and prosperity of Spain rose to its

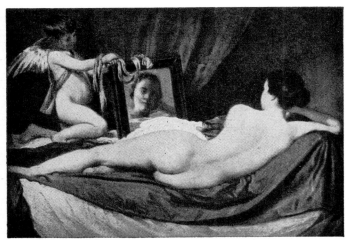

VENUS AND CUPID," BY VELAZQUEZ

This superb example of the last manner of Velazquez, unique among all his great works for its refined and natural rendering of a classical subject, was for many years in an English private collection. In 1906 it was exhibited at Messrs. Agnew's gallery and was on the eve of being sold to America, when the National Art Collections Fund by indefatigable exertions raised the sum of £45,000. and in the New Year of 1907 secured the picture for the National Gallery London.

zenith between the reigns of Philip II and Philip IV, and flowered in the paintings of El Greco and Velazquez. But as the power of Spain weakened and her prosperity dwindled, so also did the glory of her art begin to wane. It is not without significance that all the great painters of Spain, Murillo included, were born before 1648, the year in which the humbled Spanish empire was compelled to recognise the independence of the Netherlands by the Peace of Munster. Immediately after Velazquez we must look for the great masters of the seventeenth century, not in decaying Spain, but in Holland, victorious and independent, the country of Hals and Rembrandt.

14

IX

HOW ART ROSE WITH THE DUTCH
REPUBLIC

THE WORK OF FRANS HALS AND REMBRANDT

§ 1

SHORTLY before the Spanish army began its seven
months' siege of Haarlem in the winter of 1572–3, a
burgher of that city named Pieter Hals made his escape
with his wife and family, and found shelter in Antwerp.
Well for the world that he did so, for had he taken part
in the heroic defence of his native city he might have been
killed in the general butchery that followed when the
Spaniards at last took the town ; and then one of the
world's greatest painters would never have been born.

Of the life of his son comparatively little is known, but it
is tolerably certain that Frans Hals was born at Antwerp in
1580, that is to say, about five years after El Greco's arrival
in Spain. Exactly when the Hals family returned to
Haarlem is not known, but since the younger son, Dirk
Hals (1591–1656), is reputed to have been born in Haarlem,
it may be conjectured that the Hals family returned some
time between 1590 and 1600. By the latter date Frans
Hals was certainly working in Haarlem, and there he
remained all his life.

The police records of Haarlem show that on February 20,
1616, Frans Hals was summoned for maltreating his wife
(Anneke Hermans), was severely reprimanded, and dismissed on the undertaking that he would eschew drunken
company and reform. On this one fact, which is indisputable, gossip has built up a legend that Hals was a man
of imperfect morals and a continuous and habitual drunkard.
But, as Mr. Gerald S. Davies has pointed out, drunkenness

210

"THE LAUGHING CAVALIER," BY FRANS HALS

"One of the most irresistible things ever painted" is the smile of this unknown young officer. "He looks out at you with an air of supreme contempt at one moment, of supreme good-nature at another," says the Rev. G. S. Davis, Master of Charterhouse; "but the expression is full of changefulness, full of that electric current which plays over the human face and tells you while you look at it at one moment what to expect from the next."

is not only a moral but a physical matter, and it is physically impossible that a confirmed inebriate should have had a hand steady enough to paint the pictures Hals painted when he was sixty and older.

We must admit an ugly passage in the painter's life—though, as a Scottish critic once observed, we do not know what provocation Hals' wife gave him !—and we must conclude that his first marriage was miserable. The poor woman died soon after the police-court case—though not, it would seem, as the result of her husband's misconduct —and a year later Hals married again. His second wife became the mother of many children, surviving her husband after fifty years of married life, and since she never had occasion to take him to the police court, we may reasonably conclude that Hals was *not* an habitual wife-beater.

He appears to have been a jovial and very human being, fond of a glass in good company, and now and then, perhaps, taking one too many ; a real Bohemian, as his paintings of gipsies and strolling players attest ; but he was not a social outcast, or he would not have been constantly employed by respectable citizens and important corporations, nor would he at the age of sixty-four have been appointed a director of the Guild of St. Lucas, which protected the interests of the artists and craftsmen of Haarlem.

Yet towards the end of his life, when his honourable position cannot be assailed, he was in sad financial difficulties. At one time he supplemented his income by teaching, and Adriaen Brouwer (1605–38) and A. J. van Ostade (1610–85) were among his pupils ; but this connection did not last, and in 1652 he was distrained upon for debt by his baker, Jan Ykess. Ten years later his distress was such that he had to apply to the Municipal Council for aid, and was given the sum of 150 florins ; two years later he had to apply again, and this time (1664) the Council voted the old man a yearly pension of 200 gulden. That year Hals, now eighty-four years of age, painted his last two pictures, portraits of the " Managers of the Almshouses at Haarlem," and in 1666 he died, and was buried on September 7 in the choir of the Church of St. Bavon.

" NURSE AND CHILD," BY FRANS HALS (1580–1666).

Berlin.

Look well at the face of this babe and you will see it " just beginning to ripple all over with the laugher that will come in a minute." The picture shows the artist's power to seize a fleeting expression, and the keen eye and steady hand needed to paint the elaborate details of lace and embroidery.

Properly to appreciate the art of Frans Hals, there is one thing we must never forget, namely, that all the work of his maturity was done during the excitement of war. It was a war which must have thrilled every Dutchman through and through, for it was waged to defend hearth and home and to deliver the fatherland from a foreign yoke ; it was a war in which one of the smallest nations in Europe had the hardihood to challenge the mightiest empire of the time. It began in 1568, about twelve years before Hals was born, and as he grew up the apparent hopelessness of the conflict disappeared, and the gaiety and elation of victory in sight began to sparkle in his paintings. When Hals first painted the officers of the St. Joris' Shooting Guild in 1616 the issue was still doubtful ; when he painted the last of his great series of military groups in 1639, again of the " Officers of St. Joris' Shooting Guild," the ultimate triumph of Holland was a foregone conclusion. In the earliest group many of the faces appear anxious and worried, but see how happy they all are even in the " Reunion of the Officers of the Guild of Archers of St. Adriaen " (pages 216–217), a picture painted in 1633. These stout fellows bear their fortune with varying demeanours ; some are smiling and jovial, some are grave and stern, one or two are evidently elated, one or two are thoughtful, but *all are confident.* In no countenance can a trace of doubt be felt, and their freedom from anxiety finds its parallel in the flowing brush of the painter, equally confident and unerring.

If in the intoxication of victory, coming and assured, some of the soldier-patriots of Holland became boisterous in their exuberance, who will blame them ? And who will blame Hals if in this great and exhilarating period his art also becomes boisterous and exuberant ?

It was nearly a quarter of a century before the final victory and the Spanish acknowledgment of Holland's independence, when Frans Hals about 1624 painted that portrait of an officer known all over the world as " The Laughing Cavalier " (see page 211). The treatment and the subject are in complete unity, for the swagger of the brushwork is in harmony with the swaggering pose of the officer. Mr. Davies, the Master of Charterhouse, has commented on the extraordinary mobility of feature in the expression of this portrait—how at one moment the face of the cavalier seems provocatively disdainful, at another full of amused good-humour. Another brilliant example of the unrivalled power of Hals to catch a fleeting expression will be found in his later painting, " Nurse and Child " (see page 213), a work which with its wonderfully elaborate and intricate detail no alcoholic hand could possibly have painted. Look well at this babe with its odd little old face, and you will see it " just beginning to ripple all over with the laughter that will come in a minute." Mr. Davies thinks Hals must have learnt the knack of this from watching his own children in his own home, and surely we may say with conviction that the man who could paint babies with so penetrating an eye was a good father.

Splendid as these two paintings are, good as the portraits by Hals in the National Gallery, London, yet to know Hals to the uttermost it is necessary to visit his home-town of Haarlem and to see there the series of great portrait-groups he painted of the Guilds, the " Archers of St. George " (Joris) and the " Archers of Saint Adriaen." These shooting guilds may be roughly described as equivalent to our own Honourable Artillery Company when it was first instituted.

It is in these paintings of the citizen-soldiers of his own city that Hals displays his highest gifts both as a decorator and as a painter of actuality. The figures are so real that we who look at them seem to be one of the company ; but though the arrangement appears so natural our eyes are always gladdened by a beauty of pattern, a flow of line, and a balancing of masses which testify to the painter's science of design. There is nothing with which we can compare them save " The Surrender of Breda," and in making this comparison we must not forget that if Velazquez was his contemporary he was also by nearly twenty years the junior of Hals. It is easy to count up the qualities lacking in the art of Frans Hals, who had neither the grave dignity and mastery of light that Velazquez possessed nor

Photo : Hanfstaengl.

" REUNION OF THE OFFICERS OF THE GUILD OF ARCHERS OF ST. ADRIAEN," BY FRANS HALS.

Haarlem.

Very similar to our own Honourable Artillery Company when it was first instituted, these Guilds of Dutch citizen-soldiers played a gallant part in the eighty years' struggle with Spain which ended in the independence of the Dutch Republic.

" REUNION OF THE OFFICERS OF THE GUILD OF ARCHERS OF
ST. ADRIAEN," BY FRANS HALS.

Haarlem.

In these vivacious portrait groups Hals, with his confident and flowing brush strokes,
expresses the exuberance of his own nature and of his country in the hour of approaching
victory.

the scenic splendour of Rubens, nor the thought of his contemporary Rembrandt; but a painter, like a man, must be judged by what he is—not by what he is not—and Hals keeps his place among the great masters by his own peculiar gifts as an exuberant, and indeed an inspired, portrayer of the bravery of Holland in her greatest hour.

§ 2

There is this initial difference between Hals and Rembrandt, that whereas Hals passed the greater part of his working life during a time of war, Rembrandt attained his maturity and executed most of his greatest works after the conclusion of peace. Hals lived in and depicted a life of action, when men must be up and doing and there was no time to think; Rembrandt's middle years and old age were spent in an age of comparative peace and quiet, when Holland had the leisure to think and to meditate not only on the greatness of her political achievements but on the problems of life. Hals expressed the gallantry of Holland in action; Rembrandt, the profundity of her thought.

One ought not to lay too much stress on a mere coincidence, yet when we remember the philosophical temper of his art it seems peculiarly appropriate that Rembrandt should have been born in the university town of Leyden, the headquarters of Dutch philosophy and learning. He came into the world on July 15, 1607, being the fifth and youngest son of Hermon Gerritzoon van Rijn, a prosperous miller who possessed a mill, several fields, and other property. The parents were ambitious for their youngest son and sent him to school " to learn the Latin tongue to prepare himself for the Academy of Leyden, so that in the fulness of time he might serve the city and the Republic with his knowledge."

The boy, however, did not take kindly to book-learning, but was for ever drawing and designing. At school Rembrandt is said to have been one of the idle pupils who " during their writing lessons, when they ought to be writing, scrawl figures of vessels and animals all over the

"THE ARTIST AND HIS FIRST WIFE," BY REMBRANDT (1607–69).
Dresden.

In this early picture Rembrandt shows himself feast-making with his bride. It is almost the only riotously joyful self-portrait painted by an artist whose life was full of sorrow.

margins of their books." He was at the University in 1620, but it soon became clear to his father that it was unprofitable for Rembrandt to continue his studies there. His aptitude for art was unmistakable, and accordingly he was apprenticed first to Jacob van Swanenburch, and afterwards to Pieter Lastman, of Amsterdam, a fashionable portrait-painter of the day.

Six months were enough to satiate this earnest young student with the smooth and flattering trivialities of a fashionable merchant of likenesses, and in 1624 he returned to Leyden to study and practise painting by himself. One of the earliest of his known and dated pictures is " St. Paul in Prison," painted in 1627, and now at Stuttgart. This picture shows the precise rendering of detail characteristic of his early style, but also anticipates the light effect of his later work by the way in which the light is concentrated on the head of the apostle. That the painter had already attracted some attention is clear from the fact that in the following year Gerard Dou, a promising boy of fifteen, was placed with him as a pupil.

About 1631 Rembrandt removed from Leyden to Amsterdam, an important step taken no doubt owing to the increasing number of portrait commissions he received from the rich merchants of this flourishing city. He had also made some reputation for himself as an etcher, and in 1632 Hendrik van Uylenburg, who had previously published some of his etchings, commissioned Rembrandt to paint a portrait of Saskia van Uylenburg, a young cousin of the printseller. The acquaintance thus begun soon ripened into love, and the form and face of this dainty little patrician, an orphan who had lost both her parents, suddenly becomes the prevailing theme both in the painted and etched work of Rembrandt. The attraction was mutual, and though her relatives disapproved of the attachment, considering the painter not good enough for a well-dowered young lady of quality, yet love won the day, and Rembrandt and Saskia were married in 1634. The veiled hostility shown by his bride's relations led the painter to relieve his feelings by painting a series of pictures illustrating the life of Samson,

Photo : W. A. Mansell & Co.

"THE ARTIST'S SON, TITUS," BY REMBRANDT.
Wallace Collection, London.

In this portrait of his only son we see a superb example of Rembrandt's later style which should be compared with his earlier portrait group on page 219. The features here are built up boldly by patches of light and shade, and the portrait has a consequent softness and richness as compared with the earlier work.

Photo : Bruckmann.

" HENDRICKJE STOFFELS," BY REMBRANDT.

Kaiser Friedrich Museum, Berlin.

First his maidservant and then his second wife, Hendrickje was a loyal helpmate to Rembrandt. By her own efforts she practically supported him during his worst financial crisis, and she was a devoted mother to Titus, his son by his first wife.

in which Saskia is the Delilah, the artist Samson, and the Philistines, of course, are his wife's relatives. These paintings not only express the artist's defiance of family pride, but also his attitude towards the world at large, and his recurring amazement at his having won for himself so sweet a maid. The joyous picture (see page 219) of himself with Saskia on his knee, shows Rembrandt at the zenith of his happiness. Still popular as a painter, his portraits were sought after, he had a crowd of pupils, and a charming wife who brought him a moderate fortune. The young couple felt that the world was their own, and behaved like children in their utter disregard of the value of money. Rembrandt kept on buying new jewels and fine stuffs with which to deck his beloved and paint her in a new guise : he bought the works of other artists and beautiful objects of all kinds, wishing to create a fairy world around a fairy wife. But soon all this luxurious beauty was overshadowed by sorrow. Two children died one after the other, and in 1642 Saskia herself died after giving birth to the boy Titus.

Rembrandt had had his fun, and now came the time to pay. Already money was beginning to be scarce, and his popularity as a portrait-painter was beginning to wane. In the year Saskia died Rembrandt had completed his great picture, the " Sortie " or " Night Watch " (see page 226), which though to-day the most popular of all his works and universally ranked among his greatest achievements, almost destroyed the contemporary reputation of the painter and began that decline of his fortunes which ended in his bankruptcy.

The subject of this picture is explicitly stated in an inscription on the back of an old copy of it in water-colour which is in a private collection in Holland : " The young Laird of Purmerlandt (Frans Banning Cocq) in his capacity as Captain gives to his Lieutenant, the Laird of Vlaerdingen, the command to march out his burgher-company." This amply justifies the more correct title of " The Sortie," but the purpose and hour of this " going out " of a company of civic militia are not easy to define. In the eighteenth century it was assumed to be a nocturnal watch turning out on its rounds by artificial light, hence the French name for the picture " Ronde de Nuit, ' which has been anglicised as " The Night Watch." But as Prof. Baldwin Brown of Edinburgh University justly pointed out, the time is " certainly the day and not the night. The shadow of the captain's outstretched hand and arm is thrown by the sun upon the yellow dress of the second in command, and it is easy to see by the relative positions of object and shadow that the sun is still pretty high in the heavens."

Before we too hastily condemn those who condemned this splendid picture, we must put ourselves in their position. To see what Captain Banning Cocq and his friends expected we should turn back and look at Hals' portrait group of the Guild of Archers. They expected to be painted like that, and Rembrandt painted them like this ! In point of fact, Rembrandt did not paint *them*, he painted the *scene*. Hals shows a collection of individual officers, each of whom is clearly seen and recognisable. Rembrandt shows a patrol many of whose members are lost in shadow and unable to be identified. As a picture Rembrandt's work has splendid qualities of drama, lighting, and movement which we cannot find in the Hals ; but Captain Banning Cocq and his friends did not want to see these qualities, they wanted to see themselves. Rembrandt had painted a great picture, but he had dealt a heavy blow to human vanity, and his contemporaries could not forgive him.

It must be admitted that Rembrandt was wilful and wayward. He would go his own way, and he was only justi-fied by the greatness of his genius. He was, as Dr. Muther has said, " the first artist who, in the modern sense, did not execute commissions, but expressed his own thoughts. The emotions which moved his inmost being were the only things which he expressed on canvas. He does not seem to think that anyone is listening to him, but only speaks with himself; he is anxious, not to be understood by others, but only to express his moods and feelings."

An interesting example of the liberties Rembrandt took with his nominal subject will be found in the Wallace Collection. The picture now known as " The Centurion

"SIX'S BRIDGE," BY REMBRANDT (1645).

Etched for a wager while a servant was fetching mustard, forgotten for lunch, from a neighbouring village, this delightful little landscape shows the delicacy of Rembrandt's handling and the swift sureness of his drawing.

15

Photo : W. A. Mansell & Co.
"THE NIGHT WATCH," OR "THE SORTIE," BY REMBRANDT

Amsterdam.

"Turn out the guard!" This dramatic rendering of a company of militia about to march displeased the officers who had commissioned the painting because Rembrandt had painted a *scene* mysterious in its light and shadow. The officers wanted a collection of recognisable likenesses. Now acknowledged as a great masterpiece, the picture ruined Rembrandt's practice as a portrait-painter.

Cornelius" used to be called "The Unmerciful Servant," and commentators explained that the figure in the turban and red robe was Christ, and enlarged on the displeasure shown in his face and the guilt and fear of the Unrighteous Servant, whom they took to be the central of the three figures to the right. Then a mezzotint by James Ward, published in 1800, was discovered, and in this reproduction the correct title was given. The red-robed figure proved to be Cornelius, in no way "displeased," while the remain-

Photo : Braun.

"THE 'LANSDOWNE' MILL," BY REMBRANDT.

In his appreciation of the veil of beauty which atmosphere casts over a scene, as well as in his capacity to find strangeness in the familiar and beauty in the commonplace, Rembrandt anticipated the romantic landscapes of the nineteenth century.   A few years ago this picture was sold for £100,000 by Lord Landsowne to an American collector, Mr. J. E. Widener.

ing three figures are " two of his household servants, and a devout soldier of them that waited on him continually " (Acts x. 7).   This widely-spread error shows how easy it is to misread pictures if they are approached with preconceived ideas.   The misunderstanding, of course, has been brought about by Rembrandt's fondness for oriental splendour, which led him to put a Roman centurion in Asiatic costume ! It is not " correct " in the way that Alma-Tadema's classical scenes are ; but real greatness in art does not depend on accuracy of antiquarian details—however praiseworthy this may be—but on largeness of conception, noble design, and splendid colour.

Overwhelmed by his domestic sorrows — he lost his old mother two years before Saskia died—neglected by his former patrons, Rembrandt turned to Nature for consolation. He wandered about the countryside recording all he saw. Practically all his landscapes were painted between 1640 and 1652. Many of his most beautiful landscape etchings were also executed during this period. The most famous of them all, " The Three Trees " (see page 231), was done in 1643. It shows a view of Amsterdam from a slight eminence outside the town, and a storm-cloud and its shadow are used to intensify the brilliance of the light and the dramatic aspect of this mood of Nature. This is landscape in the grand style; but its homelier, more intimate note appealed equally to the artist. A lovely example of the picturesque corner portrayed for its own intrinsic beauty is the etching executed in 1645 known as " Six's Bridge " (see page 225). Tradition relates that this plate was etched against time for a wager at the country house of Rembrandt's most loyal friend, Jan Six, while the servant was fetching the mustard, that had been forgotten for a meal, from a neighbouring village. There is nothing impossible in the story, for Rembrandt is known to have been an impetuous and rapid worker on occasion ; but if this little masterpiece was done in haste, we must not forget that it was also done with " the knowledge of a lifetime."

Even while Saskia was alive Rembrandt was in want of ready money, and when on his mother's death in 1640 he inherited a half-share of a mill, he hastened to have it transferred to his brother Wilhelm and his nephew. Though he lost money by the transaction, he probably gained his end in keeping all the mill in the family instead of a share going to his creditors. Then in 1647 he became involved in lawsuits with Saskia's family, who objected to Rembrandt's connection with his servant Hendrickje Stoffels, and wished to prevent Rembrandt from being trustee for his and Saskia's son Titus. These lawsuits, which lasted till after 1653, and ended in Saskia's relatives obtaining the trusteeship but not the custody of Titus, greatly contributed to Rembrandt's difficulties.

FRANCOISE VAN WASSERHOVEN, BY REMBRANDT.
National Gallery, London.

This noble rendering of the dignity of age teaches us that while physical beauty may be only " skin-deep " and quickly fade, beauty of character endures while life lasts.

His marriage with Hendrickje Stoffels, a woman of humble birth, was another cause of offence to aristocratic patrons ; all the same, it was a wise action. This devoted woman mothered Titus with loving and unremitting care ; she made great efforts to stem the tide of ill-fortune, and when the crash came and Rembrandt was made bankrupt in 1656, she loyally shared her husband's troubles and used her wits to rebuild their fortunes. As soon as Titus was old enough she combined with him in keeping an old curiosity shop, starting, one imagines, with some relics of the treasures Rembrandt had amassed for Saskia. Money, or the want of it, however, was not a thing which could profoundly trouble a philosophic dreamer like Rembrandt. If he had it, he spent it royally ; if he had it not, he went without. Only a year after his bankruptcy he achieved one of the world's masterpieces of portraiture, " The Artist's Son Titus " (see page 221), in the Wallace Collection. If you look at the Pellicorne portraits, also in the Wallace Collection, you will obtain a fair idea of Rembrandt's ordinary professional style in 1632-4, when his painting was still popular. But how thin and shallow these early portraits seem beside this haunting and passionate portrait of the son he loved so dearly. Turning to the " Titus " after these early works, we see how far Rembrandt has travelled. Three or four years later he painted the wonderful " Portrait of Françoise van Wasserhoven " (see preceding page), in the National Gallery, one of the most reverent, sympathetic, and intimate studies of old age ever painted.

Throughout his life Rembrandt was a keen student of human nature, and no painter has ever penetrated further than he did into the inner lives of the men and women he painted. His wonderful insight into character made him the greatest psychologist in portraiture the world has yet seen, and since he searched faces above all for the marks of life's experience which they bore, old people—who had had the longest experience—were inevitably subjects peculiarly dear to him and subjects which he interpreted with consummate mastery. His own face he painted over and

Photo: W. A. Mansell & Co.

"THE THREE TREES," ETCHING BY REMBRANDT

Though we see to the left a distant view of Amsterdam, this masterly etching is not merely a transcription of something seen, but a dramatic rendering of a mood of Nature. Its grandeur is unequalled in etching and has rarely been approached in painting.

Photo: W. A. Mansell & Co.

"CHRIST WITH THE SICK AROUND HIM, RECEIVING LITTLE CHILDREN,"
ETCHING BY REMBRANDT.

The most famous of Rembrandt's etchings, this is popularly known as the "Hundred Guilder Print," from the price it once realised at auction early in the eighteenth century. No work shows more splendidly Rembrandt's command of the etcher's art and his deep insight into manifold phases of human character and emotion.

232

over again, and if we study the sequence of his self-por-
traiture from early manhood to ripe old age, we see not only
the gradual development of his technical powers but also
the steady advance made by Rembrandt in expressing with
poignant intensity the thoughts and emotions of humanity.

Of Rembrandt's technique Sir John Everett Millais
wrote : " In his first period Rembrandt was very careful and
minute in detail, and there is evidence of stippling in his
flesh paintings ; but in the fullness of his power all appearance of such manipulation and minuteness vanished in the
breadth and facility of his brush, though the advantage of
his early manner remained. . . . I have closely examined
his pictures in the National Gallery, and have actually
seen beneath the grand veil of breadth, the early work that
his art conceals from untrained eyes—the whole science of
painting." Among his contemporaries the minute detail
in the work of his earlier period was far more admired than
the " veil of breadth " which he cast over his later paintings,
and it was long before people who admired his early portraits
could be persuaded that his later paintings were not only
equally good, but vastly superior both in workmanship and
expression.

Gradually among the discerning few the outstanding
excellence of Rembrandt's portraiture was again acknowledged, and in 1661 he received a commission for another
official portrait group. He was asked to paint a portrait
group of five officials of the Clothmakers' Company, and
staging them on the dais on which they presided over a
meeting, Rembrandt produced the wonder-work known
as " The Syndics." Avoiding the dangers of " The Sortie,"
Rembrandt places all five figures in a clear light and yet gives
them the unity of a scene taken from life.

Alas ! this fresh artistic triumph was dearly paid for by
more domestic misfortunes. Soon after this work was
completed, Hendrickje the loyal helpmate died. Titus,
now grown up, married his cousin, and after less than a
year of married life he also died. Now, indeed, Rembrandt
was alone in the world, and though a posthumous daughter
to Titus was born in 1669, the artist, now in his sixty-third

"THE BLINDNESS OF TOBIT," ETCHING BY REMBRANDT.

Never has the pathos of a blind man's groping been more movingly
expressed than in this etching.

year, was too worn out to struggle much longer against
" the slings and arrows of outrageous fortune." He lived
long enough to see his little granddaughter Titia christened
after her father, and then, crushed by the accumulated
sorrows of a lifetime, passed to his long rest on October 4,
1669. To all appearance the illness and death of the
greatest man Holland ever produced passed unnoticed,
and only the bare fact of his burial in the Westerkerk,
Amsterdam, is attested by an official entry.

X

DUTCH PAINTING IN THE SEVENTEENTH CENTURY

THE ART OF CUYP, DOU, HOBBEMA, DE HOOCH, POTTER, MAES, RUISDAEL, VAN DE VELDE, AND VERMEER OF DELFT

§ I

WE saw in the last chapter how, after a long struggle, the yoke of the Spaniards was broken, and the independence of the Dutch Republic was established in 1648 by the Peace of Münster. This event is commemorated by Terborch's picture (in the National Gallery) of the signing of the Treaty ; in this it will be noticed that the Protestant Dutch delegates (on our left) raise their hands to affirm, while the Roman Catholic plenipotentiaries of Spain lay their hands on the Gospels to take the oath. Careful and exact both in the portraiture of those present and in the painting of every little detail, this moderate-sized picture expresses the sober spirit in which Holland celebrated her victory.

While of considerable historic interest, this picture is not a supreme masterpiece of art ; it is not so effective as the same painter's "Portrait of a Gentleman," a small full-length figure which also hangs in the National Gallery. Historical subjects did not call forth the highest powers of the painters of the Netherlands. The art of Holland was neither an ecclesiastical nor a state art : it was a domestic art which produced pictures, not for churches or public buildings, but for the private homes of citizens. So wonderful was the artistic activity inspired by the wave of patriotism which swept through Holland, that the name of these so-called " Little Masters " is truly legion, and no attempt can be made in this OUTLINE to mention each by name. Only a few representative artists can be selected for individual notice.

Chronologically, the first place among the Little Masters is claimed by Adrian Brouwer (1605–38), whose " Boor Asleep " is one of the most precious Dutch pictures in the Wallace Collection. It is still a matter of dispute whether Brouwer was born in Holland or Flanders, but he certainly spent his youth in Haarlem, where he studied under Frans Hals. Afterwards he worked both in Amsterdam and Antwerp. How highly Brouwer was esteemed by other painters of his time is shown by the fact that Rubens possessed seventeen of his pictures, while even Rembrandt, in spite of his financial difficulties, managed to collect and retain eight Brouwers. A humorous vividness of vision, concise and vigorous drawing, and an enamel-like beauty of colour are the distinctive qualities of his art.

Apart from the landscape-painters—whom we must consider subsequently—most of the Dutch painters of the home descended (artistically) either from Hals or from Rembrandt. Gerard Dou (1613–75), one of Rembrandt's many pupils, was the most successful painter financially of his day. He made his fortune by never progressing beyond the first manner of his master and by painting with a careful literalness which demanded no exercise of the beholder's imagination. "The Poulterer's Shop" (see page 245) is a typical example of Dou's minutely finished style. It has always been popular because it is much easier to recognise industry than to understand inspiration, and in rendering this everyday incident in a shopping expedition Dou has spared no pains to render each detail with laborious fidelity.

How even in the rendering of detail there is all the difference in the world between the Letter of Exactitude and the Spirit of Truth may be seen when we compare the pictures of Dou with those of similar scenes by Terborch, De Hoogh, or Vermeer. Each one of these three exquisite painters has an eye for detail as keen as that possessed by Dou, but they all have far more ability than Dou possessed to subordinate details to the unity of the whole. The eldest of these three masters, Gerard Terborch or Terburg

"HEAD OF A YOUNG GIRL," BY JAN VERMEER OF DELFT.

The Hague.

" The Perfect Painter " is the name Mr. E. V. Lucas has recently given to this artist,
who, long numbered among the " Little Masters " of seventeenth-century Holland, is
now recognised to have been probably the greatest colourist who ever lived. This head
is his masterpiece in portraiture.

(1617–81), has already been mentioned. As a young man he studied at Haarlem, where he was probably influenced by Hals and Brouwer, but Terborch did not found his style only on what he found within the borders of Holland. He was more a man-of-the-world than most of his artist contemporaries. He visited England, Germany, France, Italy, and Spain, and in the last country he certainly studied the paintings of Velazquez, who was only eighteen years his senior. Like Velazquez, but unlike most of his fellows in Holland, Terborch was aristocratic in the temper of his art, so that his pictures as a rule show us a higher strata of Dutch society than that depicted by the majority of Dutch artists.

Here it may be well to pause in order to emphasise the fact that these Dutch painters were preoccupied with rendering the *manners* of their time. This characteristic, which gives their work a lasting historical value, has caused their little pictures of courtyards, interiors, tavern scenes, conversations, toilet-scenes, and the like to be known as " genre " painting, from the French word *genre* (*i.e.* manner or style). A few, like Terborch, show us the manner of dress and living of the upper classes ; others show us the middle classes, and still more concern themselves with the manners of the peasants and lower classes. Among these last the best known is Jan Steen (1626–79), who is often amusingly satirical in his outlook ; other painters of a similar style were Adrian van Ostade (1610–85) and the Fleming David Teniers (1610–90).

These painters may amuse us for the moment, but they do not hold us spellbound as some of the others do. The greatest rival of Terborch was Peter de Hooch or de Hoogh (1629–77), who was only twelve years his junior. De Hooch's figures may not be so aristocratic as those of Terborch, but they are seen as finely and have their being in the same clear light which both these masters observed and rendered so lovingly. This passion for the rendering of light began to show itself in the paintings of Brouwer ; it becomes still more marked in the work of Terborch, and it approaches perfection in the pictures of De Hooch. His

"THE PEARL NECKLACE," BY VERMEER.

Berlin.

In this picture of a lady looking in a mirror to see how her necklace suits her, we are fascinated by the artist's rendering of light, which softly illumines every object in the scene. Vermeer, who has been described by Mr. E. V. Lucas as " The Perfect Painter," was neglected for two hundred years after his death, but to-day he is one of the most popular of the Old Masters and universally recognised to be one of the greatest colourists in art.

chief interest, as the late Sir Walter Armstrong remarked, " is always absorbed by the one problem, that of capturing and bottling the sunlight." How supremely well he succeeded in his object is shown by our illustration of " A Girl Reading " (see page 247), a masterpiece of interior

Photo : W. A. Mansell & Co.

"THE MILL," BY JACOB VAN RUISDAEL 1628–82).

Amsterdam.

" His grave and solemn mind gives to the simplest and most commonplace of landscapes a look of sad importance, which is almost like a reproach of lightmindedness to any other man's work which happens to hang alongside."

illumination, in which every object is not only perfectly rendered but keeps its proper distance within the room owing to the painter's delicately exact notation of the relative degrees of lighting.

In his youth, as Armstrong has pointed out, De Hooch liked the broadest daylight, but with advancing years he preferred " merely to suggest the outside sun, as it creeps

"INTERIOR OF A DUTCH HOUSE," BY DE HOOCH.
National Gallery, London.

The artist's joy in painting sunlight is delightfully expressed in his brilliantly lit interior. The figure standing before the fireplace is an afterthought added to improve the design of the grouping after the picture had been finished, and that is why the black and white tiling of the floor can be seen through the woman's skirt. (See page 242.)

down tiled passages, through red curtains and half-open shutters." An interesting example of De Hooch's earlier period when he chose the broadest daylight for his scene is the " Interior of a Dutch House " (see preceding page). Nothing could be more brilliant or more faithful to Nature than the bright sunlight which streams down on the group near the window. It is instructive to observe here that the standing figure by the fireplace was an afterthought, put in by the artist to improve his design. This woman forms the apex of a triangle of which the wall with the windows forms the base. We know that she was an afterthought because the artist had already painted the black-and-white tiled floor right up to the fireplace before he began the figure, and that is why we can still see the tiling through the woman's skirt. This correction would not have been visible to De Hooch's contemporaries, but it is a peculiar property of oil paint that an under-painting, invisible when the paint is fresh, will in time work its way up to the surface. Since De Hooch was a consummate craftsman whose handling of pigment approached perfection, the fact that even he has been unable to disguise a correction is a useful lesson to a living painter that he must get his picture right from the start, or otherwise, however clever he may be, his errors will be found out after his death. In De Hooch's interior, this emergence of what it was endeavoured to hide is too trivial and unimportant to affect seriously the beauty and merit of the painting.

§ 2

Jan van der Meer, commonly known as Vermeer of Delft (1632–75), is one of the Old Masters whom modern research has rescued from unmerited neglect. Houbraken, a historian who wrote only forty years after his death, does not even mention him, and for two centuries his name was almost forgotten and his paintings were sold as works by De Hooch, Terborch, Metsu, or even Rembrandt. Then in the middle of the nineteenth century a French exile named Thoré spent three years (1858–60) studying records

Photo : Hanfstaengl.

"RIVER SCENE" BY ALBERT CUYP (1620–91).
National Gallery, London.

The glowing light and golden colour of Cuyp's skies have placed him in the front rank of those painters who "set the sun in the heavens." In this picture we see how effectively he uses cows as dark spots which bring out the luminosity of the sky and lend enchantment to the distant horizon.

243

and archives in Holland and patiently searching out
Vermeer's paintings. Since Thoré published his account
of his studies, the fame of Vermeer has rapidly spread and
increased. To-day he is one of the most costly and one of
the most popular of the old masters.

Photo : Bruckmann.

" VIEW OF DELFT," BY VERMEER ((1632-75).
The Hague.

The loveliest view of a town in art, this picture is exquisite in its quality of light and sense
of airiness. Nothing could be more natural, more true to the thing seen.

Of his private life very little is known. Vermeer was
three years younger than De Hooch, and fifteen years
younger than Terborch. We know that as soon as he came
of age in 1653 he married Catherine Bolenes and by her had
eight children. He was evidently esteemed in his native
city, for in 1662 and again in 1670 he was elected one of the
principal officers of the Guild of St. Luke of Delft. But

"THE POULTERER'S SHOP," BY GERARD DOU (1613–75).

National Gallery, London.

A typical example of the precise, minutely finished style of this artist, a pupil of Rembrandt, who made his fortune by imitating the first manner of his master. Though Dou lacked imagination and dramatic grandeur, his faithful rendering of everyday incidents makes him a valuable chronicler of the manners of his time.

245

fame is one thing and fortune is another. When Vermeer died in 1675 he had nothing to leave his wife and family but twenty-six unsold pictures. If these were put into the market to-day they might fetch anything *over* a quarter of a million pounds—not a penny less—but there were no American millionaires in the seventeenth century ; so poor Vermeer was judged to have died insolvent and his widow's affairs had to be put in the hands of a liquidator, who happened to be the naturalist Leeuwenhoek.

To explain in words the incomparable charm of Vermeer's painting is as simple and as difficult as to explain the beauty of light. The illumination in his pictures is as perfect as it is in the best works of De Hooch ; and if the pictures of Vermeer are still more beautiful than those of De Hooch it is because Vermeer was a still finer and more subtle colourist. He was, indeed, one of the greatest colourists the world has ever known. He excelled in all subjects. His " Head of a Young Girl " (see page 237) is one of the loveliest portraits in the world. This young girl is not strikingly beautiful in herself. She has a sweet face, and Vermeer has brought out the sweetness of her disposition and the charm of her youth ; but he has done more than this : by the loveliness of his colour—particularly by the contrast of the blue and lemon-yellow of which he was so fond—Vermeer has made her a joy for ever. Colour of this lyrical beauty sings its own sweet song.

Vermeer's " View of Delft " (see page 244), also at The Hague, is the loveliest street scene or town view in art. It has the crystal purity of colour and limpid atmosphere of Delft itself, which a living writer has described as " the cleanest city in Europe, looking as if all the houses were thoroughly scrubbed down and polished each day before sunrise." Nothing could be more natural, more true to the thing seen, than this painting, yet nothing could be more perfect in every quality that goes to the making of a work of art.

These two pictures are exceptional even among the paintings of Vermeer, and when we come to consider his more numerous paintings of small figures in interiors, the

"A GIRL READING," BY DE HOOCH (1629-77).

Munich.

Whatever his subject, de Hooch was absorbed by one problem, that of " capturing and bottling the sunlight." Compare this masterpiece of illumination with Dou's picture on page 245, and it will be seen how Dou's details appear hard and unsympathetic, while every object in de Hooch's interior is soft and atmospheric owing to the greater subtlety of his lighting.

richness he offers us makes selection embarrassing. It would be perilous to say " The Pearl Necklace " (see page 239) is better than " The Milkmaid " or other pictures one could mention ; but it is certainly one of the best and shows how Vermeer could compete with De Hooch in " bottling sunlight " and beat that master even at his own favourite game.

Vermeer's art undoubtedly affected his contemporaries, those of his own age as well as those who were his juniors. Gabriel Metsu (1630–67) sometimes comes near to Vermeer, and the colour of " The Letter Writer Surprised " in the Wallace Collection has a tenderness which is apt to make even a Terborch look a little hard. Metsu knows how to set his stage decoratively ; his pictures are always sprightly ; but his observation is less subtle, and his research into light and shade is not carried to the point of perfection reached by De Hooch and Vermeer.

Nicolas Maes (1632–93), another pupil of Rembrandt, though less gifted than Metsu, used to be thought of chiefly as a portrait-painter, but is now much esteemed for the anecdotal pictures he painted in his youth. " The Idle Servant " (see page 255) is an amusing example of his work in this style, and shows both his own powers of observation and what he learnt from Rembrandt in the way of using lighting to enhance a dramatic effect. But if we look critically at the picture, say at the cat stealing the plucked bird, or at the whole area of the tiled floor, we shall have to admit that in drawing Maes was inferior to Dou, and in illumination far inferior to De Hooch or Vermeer. All these subject pictures were painted between 1655 and 1665, after which date circumstances drove Maes into " pot-boiling " portraiture.

§ 3

We have seen now with what variety and perfection the Dutch artists painted their national hearthside : and next we must consider how they painted their homeland. Midway between the genre painters and the landscape-painters stands Aart van der Neer (1603–77), who forms a bridge,

Photo : W. A. Mansell & Co.

"THE AVENUE," BY HOBBEMA (1638-1709).

National Gallery, London.

The most popular landscape in the National Gallery, this masterpiece expresses the joy and thankfulness we all feel for bright weather and fresh country air. For all his genius Hobbema could not earn his living by painting, and at thirty he had to take a smallposition in the Civil Service.

249

as it were, between the two groups. Born three years before Rembrandt, he, like Jan van Goyen (1596–1656), is one of the early pioneers of landscape painting, yet by the little figures in his landscapes he tells us a great deal of the life of Holland. Thus his " Skating Scene " (see page 253) in the Wallace Collection has been ranked by the famous Dr. Bode as " among the most perfect landscape delineations of winter," but it is also a charming picture of manners, giving us a glimpse of the life on the ice in seventeenth-century Holland.

Towards the end of his life Aart van der Neer deteriorated as other " Little Masters " did also ; in addition to painting, he kept a tavern, and possibly business losses in the wine-trade drove him to do inferior but more immediately saleable work during his last years. Nearly all his best work was done before 1665, when he was not dependent on painting for a livelihood, but a happy amateur who could paint what he liked. He was one of the first artists to attempt painting night scenes, but though the novelty of his moonlit views attracted attention his winter landscapes in daylight are usually considered to be his best work.

Agriculture has always been an important industry in Holland, and the local artists who catered so well for the needs of the citizen did not forget to make an appeal also to the farmers. Of many who made a speciality of painting cattle, Paul Potter (1625–54) is the most celebrated, though he died in his twenty-ninth year. His big picture " The Bull " (see opposite page) is a favourite show-piece at The Hague, where guides—most conservative critics—wax enthusiastic about its accuracy. Courageous people, however, have been known to confess that they find its precise statement of fact a little dull, though few dare to be so severe as Dr. Muther, who once described Potter's cattle as " essentially Dutch, for they know neither passions, nor struggles, nor movement, but chew the cud phlegmatically or lie down in comfortable repose."

Cattle also figure largely in the paintings of Albert Cuyp (1620–91), who is splendidly represented in English collections. Cuyp was no mere animal-painter : his principal interest lay neither in the beast nor in the earth, but above in the mighty vault of the heavens. He does not so much set out to paint cattle as to *use* cattle, and we may see in his " River Scene " (page 243) how effectively cows can be used as dark spots which bring out by contrast the luminosity of the sky, and as prominent objects in the foreground which emphasise the great stretch of flat landscape which reaches

Photo : Bruckmann.

"THE BULL," BY PAUL POTTER (1625–54).
The Hague.

One of the earliest and most celebrated cattle-pictures in the world, Potter's " Bull " is a show-piece which delights farmers to-day as it did in the seventeenth century

out to the horizon. The glowing light and golden colour of Cuyp have placed him among the great sky-painters of the world, and his work has for centuries been an example and an incentive to British landscape painting.

Apart from all other Dutch painters of landscape — seeming, indeed, to belong to another race — stands the austere and majestic figure of Jacob van Ruisdael (1628–82). Though he took all Nature for his province, and in his youth painted her more peaceful aspects, we instinctively associate his sublime spirit with holy spots " both savage and enchanted." It is difficult to think of him as eight years younger than Cuyp, for so serious and austere is his vision that we can hardly believe Ruisdael was ever young.   Even

Photo: W. A. Mansell & Co.

THE SHORE AT SCHEVENINGEN," BY RUISDAEL.
National Gallery, London.

Scheveningen to-day is a fashionable watering-place, but this beautiful picture shows it as it was 250 years ago, when the majesty of Nature was undisturbed by the villadom of Man.

when he paints a simple seaside scene like " The Shore at Scheveningen " (see above) he gives dramatic intensity to the scene by the rolling clouds in the sky which seem to repeat the restlessness of the agitated waves.   Again, in his famous painting of " The Mill " (see page 240), for all the stillness of the scene, we feel that this is the calm before the storm—as, indeed, the sky betokens.   Grandly designed as this painting is, it is one of the quietest works of the artist, who, though infinitely varied in his choice of subject, delighted especially in painting waterfalls, cascades, and

Photo: W. A. Mansell & Co.

" A SKATING SCENE," BY VAN DER NEER (1603–77).
Wallace Collection, London.

One of the " most perfect landscape delineations of winter," this picture also illustrates the life of Holland in times of frost when the canals and rivers become highways for the traffic of the country.

rocky cliffs. Ruisdael, says a gifted American painter, Mr. John La Farge,

is as different from Cuyp as shadow is from sunshine ; and his grave and solemn mind gives to the simplest and most commonplace of land-scapes a look of sad importance, which is almost like a reproach of light-mindedness to any other man's work which happens to hang alongside.

Meindert Hobbema (1638–1709) was Ruisdael's pupil and friend, but as different in temperament from his master as a man could well be. Ruisdael approaches Nature with the devoutness of a worshipper approaching a shrine; Hobbema, with the unconscious ease of a man entering his own home. He painted the same subjects over and over again, but he painted them so naturally, so freshly and convincingly, that they take us straight back to Nature, not to the pictures of another artist. In the humbleness and sincerity of his naturalism he expresses everybody's feeling of delight and thankfulness in sunny weather and fresh country air. "The Avenue" (see page 249) is probably the best beloved landscape in the National Gallery, London, and this and other works by Hobbema have had a profound and far-reaching effect on British landscape. Out of his smiling and friendly art grew our Norwich school of landscape. Gainsborough acknowledged his worth by word and deed, and the last sentence ever uttered by John Crome was, "Oh, Hobbema, my dear Hobbema, how I have loved you!" It is sad to think that this simple, honest, and most easily understood painter, a man of genius who has given happiness to millions for six generations, fared so poorly in his profession of painting that when he was thirty he sought another means of livelihood. He sought and obtained a small position in the wine-customs, and thus made himself independent of picture-buyers and dealers. He saw his master, the great painter Ruisdael, battling with poverty and becoming no more prosperous as the years rolled on, so Hobbema wisely determined to look elsewhere for his bread-and-butter and make landscape painting his hobby and pastime. It is significant to note that his supreme masterpiece, "The Avenue," was painted some years after he had become a civil servant, and when, without having to think of what the buyer might or might not like, he could indulge to the full his feeling for the pattern in landscape and his sense of beauty in the elements of Nature.

It must be admitted that if Holland had a galaxy of artistic talent during the seventeenth century she did little to encourage genius. As so often happens in modern times, the mediocre painters made the best income, while the men of genius starved. This state of affairs is not satis-

Photo : W. A. Mansell & Co.

"THE IDLE SERVANT," BY NICOLAS MAES (1632–93)
National Gallery, London.

An amusing example of this artist's powers of humorous observation. Maes was a pupil
of Rembrandt and enjoyed a considerable vogue as a portrait-painter, though his
drawing was not equal to Dou's, and his illumination is far less perfect than that of
de Hooch or Vermeer.

factory, but it is not inexplicable. The men who prospered and made money were, as a rule, painters like Gerard Dou, who painted every feather on a bird, every scale of a fish, the shine of a copper pan, and the lustre of an earthenware pot. These were things within the range of everybody's observation and interest, and demanded no imagination, no culture. Therefore the painters of pots and pans, of insects, fruit and flowers, all prospered, while great artists like Rembrandt, Hals, Vermeer, and Ruisdael, who concentrated their attention on higher things, were neglected. Anybody could understand a picture of a cat stealing a fish, but to appreciate the beauty of pearly light stealing through high windows to lighten an apartment, presupposes some sense of poetry in the mind of the beholder.

§ 4

All classifications of so individual a thing as art are bound to be artificial and imperfect ; but just as we may say that the genre-painters of Holland depicted the life of the city, and the landscape-painters the life of the country, so a third group of artists mirrored another phase of national activity in constituting themselves painters of shipping and the sea. Holland, as England once knew to her cost, was, and still is, a great maritime nation, and her sea-captains and shipowners inevitably set up a demand for pictures of the element on which they triumphed and prospered. Moreover, this low-lying land was at the mercy of the sea, which was only kept back by the dykes, so that every Dutchman may be said to have had a personal interest in the ocean. One of the earliest painters of sea-pieces with shipping was Hendrik Dubbels (1620–76), who was the master of a more famous sea-painter, Ludolf Bakhuizen (1631–1708). Bakhuizen is as much a painter of shipping as of the sea, and in addition to being a picture-painter he was a naval architect who made constructive drawings of ships for the Russian Tsar Peter the Great. There is a great deal of spirit in his sea-pieces, particularly in his tempestuous subjects, but his storms, as John Ruskin pointed out, were storms that belonged to melodrama rather than to Nature.

We do not feel, however, that there is anything theatrical in the marines of his far greater contemporary, Willem van de Velde the Younger (1633–1707), who belonged to a

Photo : W. A. Mansell & Co.

"A GALE," BY WILLEM VAN DE VELDE (1633–1707).

National Gallery, London.

" It was in Holland that marine painting first began to play an important part, for the sea was both the glory and the menace of this low-lying naval power." By a strange freak of fortune Van de Velde, born in the country of De Ruyter, came to England in later life as marine painter to Charles II. He died at Greenwich after his own countryman, William of Orange, had ascended the throne of England.

famous family of artists settled in Amsterdam. Some critics hold that the younger Van de Velde is at his best when depicting shipping in a calm, and assuredly he has painted the stillness of the sea with a beauty and true dignity which go straight to the heart of every sailor. But there are pictures also in which Van de Velde has portrayed crashing waters under a charged sky, and if he rarely essayed

17

to express the terrors of a great storm, yet he succeeds perfectly in conveying the excitement and somewhat perilous exhilaration of a stiff breeze. An example of his powers in this direction is " A Gale " (see preceding page), in which we see the waves washing over a fishing-smack in the foreground, while farther on a frigate proudly approaches with bellying sails, and still farther in the distance a second frigate rides out the gale at anchor beneath the dark clouded sky. This gale is not awe-inspiring, as it might have been had Ruisdael painted it, but it is a picture that instinctively makes us square our chests and brace ourselves to meet the wind. Both the Willem van de Veldes, the father and the son who soon surpassed him in accomplishment, came over to London in 1677 and entered the service of Charles II. Willem van de Velde the Younger died at Greenwich, and owing to his long sojourn in England his pictures are plentiful in our public galleries, where they have served as models for Turner and other British sea-painters.

Painting, so flourishing in Holland at the beginning of the seventeenth century, was dead or dying when the next century dawned. The rapid rise of art to the eminence attained by Rembrandt was followed by an equally rapid decadence, so that in the early years of the eighteenth century Dutch painting, while maintaining a creditable level of craftsmanship, had sunk to the meticulous and un-inspired painting of fruit, flowers, and the odd collections of inanimate objects known as " still-life." In the Nether-lands the vein of Rubens was now exhausted, and his true heir appeared in France in the person of that strangely attractive painter, Antoine Watteau.

XI

THE RISE OF FRENCH PAINTING

THE ART OF WATTEAU, CHARDIN, BOUCHER, FRAGONARD
AND GREUZE

§ 1

COMING events in the world of politics cast their
shadows before them on the field of art, and as
soon as we begin to study closely the national painting of
France during the seventeenth and succeeding century,
we become conscious of two streams of tradition, one democratic and derived from the Low Countries, the other
aristocratic and inspired by Italy.

These two French schools of painting, which mirror
respectively the life of the nobles and the life of the peasants,
give us warning of that sharp division of the classes which
were afterwards to meet and mingle in the clash and conflict
of the French Revolution.

The seventeenth century, which in its beginning and
middle period had seen art flourishing in Holland with the
rise of the Dutch Republic, witnessed towards its close the
shifting of political interest from Holland to France, and
the rapid growth and development of a group of artists who
added to the glory of the court of Louis XIV. Although
France had given birth to artists of considerable distinction
long before the end of the seventeenth century, it was not
till the reign of the Grand Monarch that she evolved a
distinct national style of her own.

The earlier French painters were almost wholly under
the influence first of Flanders and then of Italy. Thus
Jean Clouet, who in 1516 was appointed Court Painter
to King François I, was the son of a Brussels artist, and both
he and his son François Clouet (c. 1510–72), who succeeded

259

" HEAD OF A GIRL LOOKING UP," BY GREUZE.

National Gallery, London.

A beautiful example of one of the many fanciful portraits of his lovely but erring wife by which this artist has attained world-wide fame and popularity.

eventually he was able to deflect his fellow-countrymen from Italian ideals and revivify French painting with the vigorous realism of Rubens. His worship of the great Fleming, to whom he felt himself related by ties of race as well as artistic sympathy, never degenerated into servile imitation : " by means of a gradually widening realism," says the distinguished French critic M. Camille Mauclair, Watteau " arrived at the point of preserving in his small canvasses all Rubens' admirable breadth, while achieving a masterly originality of grouping." A superb example of Watteau's powers in this respect is his exquisite " Lady at her Toilet " (see page 266) in the Wallace Collection. Here a theme, in which Rubens could hardly have avoided a certain coarseness, becomes a model of grace and refinement.

Once again the jealousy of a senior threatened Watteau's progress. Watteau showed his master a realistic painting of soldiers on the march, and Audran, who naturally did not want to lose so talented an assistant, advised him not to paint realistic pictures lest he should lose his skill as a decorator. But Watteau, determined to devote himself to original work, was now diplomat enough to avoid a quarrel, and desirous of leaving Audran courteously, he informed him that he must return to Valenciennes to visit his family. At Valenciennes the young artist continued his studies of nature and contemporary life, and he painted a series of military pictures illustrating camp-life, marches, and outpost duty. But after staying there long enough to justify his visit, he returned to Paris, where he was now not altogether unknown.

At this time his great desire was to win the Prix de Rome and to visit Italy, and with this object he competed in 1709, the subject set by the Academy being " David granting Abigail Nabal's Pardon." The prize, however, was won by a student named Grison, Watteau being placed second and thus losing his opportunity of visiting Rome.

Still desirous of studying in Italy, and still hopeful that the Academy might help him to accomplish his desire, Watteau three years later contrived to get two of his military pictures hung in a room through which Academicians were

Photo: W. A. Mansell & Co.

"LADY AT HER TOILET," BY WATTEAU.

Wallace Collection, London.

Unique as the "Venus" of Velazquez, this picture is held by many to be the most beautiful Watteau ever painted. Though almost directly inspired by the figure paintings of Rubens, which Watteau studied at the Luxembourg, this charming little painting is exquisite in its grace and refinement.

266

in the habit of passing. Several admired the " vigorous colouring, and a certain harmony which made them appear the work of an old master," and one Academician, de la Fosse by name, made inquiries as to the painter. It was then discovered that this young painter, already twenty-nine, was so modest that all he wanted from the Academy was its influence with the King that he might receive a small grant to enable him to study in Italy.

Attracted by his talent and modesty, M. de la Fosse sought an interview with Watteau which had the most surprising results. With a rare generosity the Academician told the young man that he had no need to seek instruction in Italy, that he undervalued his own ability, and the Academicians believed he was already capable of doing them honour ; in short, he had only to take the proper steps to be accepted a member of their society. The young artist did as he was told, and was immediately received as a member of the French Academy.

In all the long and memorable history of the Academy of France no incident similar to this has ever been recorded. That a young artist, without friends or fortune, who had failed to win the Prix de Rome and humbly begged for help in his studies, should spontaneously and unanimously be elected an Academician, is a miracle without precedent or sequel in the history of all Academies. This unique event was the turning-point in Watteau's career, and henceforward his fame was assured and he was able to earn his living in comfort.

It was on August 28, 1717, that Watteau was definitely admitted to the Academy. All successful candidates are required to deposit a diploma work after their election, and it was for this purpose that Watteau eventually painted his famous masterpiece, " L'Embarquement pour Cythère," which is now in the Louvre. In this poetically conceived picture, which shows a crowd of gallant youths and fair maidens about to embark for the legendary isle of perfect love, Watteau revealed a science of colour harmony which was one hundred and fifty years ahead of his day. He had already excited the admiration of his contemporaries by a method of painting which was as successful as it was original. He would cover his canvas copiously and, to all appearance, vaguely with a thick layer of pigment, and on this he would proceed, so to speak, to *chisel* out his detail. Figures, sky, and landscape background were then built up by a series of minute touches, which gave his pictures a peculiarly vibrating and scintillating effect. His division of tones and his wonderful orchestration of complementary colours make Watteau a forerunner of the prismatic colouring of the more scientific painters of the nineteenth century.

Unfortunately he was not destined to enjoy long the fame and fortune which now awaited him. The privation and hardship of his early manhood had undermined his always frail constitution and left him a prey to phthisis.

As if he knew the end was approaching, he worked feverishly during his last years. For a time he lived with a wealthy collector named Crozat, for whose dining-room he painted a set of "The Four Seasons." Though very comfortable at M. Crozat's house, which was filled with precious things and with paintings and drawings by old masters he admired, a desire for more complete independence led Watteau to leave it and live with his friend Vleughels, who afterwards became Principal of the Academy at Rome. In 1718 he left Vleughels, and shut himself up in a small apartment alone with his dreams and his illness, displaying then that craving for solitude which is said to be one of the symptoms of phthisis. Later somebody having spoken well of England, he suddenly had an almost morbid longing to cross the Channel.

In 1719 he came to London, where he painted and had some success, till the climate made him ill and unable to work. He returned to France more exhausted and weaker in health than he had ever been before, but slightly recovered during a six months' stay with his friend, the art-dealer Gersaint, for whom he painted a sign, an exquisitely finished interior with figures, in the short space of eight mornings—he was still so weak that he could only paint half the day. Then, hoping that he might recover his strength in the country, a house at Nogent was lent to him, but there his health rapidly declined and he gave himself up to religion, his last picture being a Crucifixion for the curate of the parish.   Still pathetically hopeful that change of air might do him good, he begged his friend Gersaint to make arrangements for him to journey to Valenciennes. But while waiting for strength to move to his native town the end came, and on July 18, 1721, he died suddenly in Gersaint's arms.   He was only thirty-seven years old.

The real sweetness and generosity of Watteau's nature is well illustrated by a touching incident during the last months of his life.   His pupil Jean Pater (1696–1736) had offended him, as Lancret had also done, by imitating his own style and subjects too closely, and in a fit of ill-temper he dismissed him from his studio.   But during his last illness Watteau remembered how he had suffered in his youth from the jealousy of his seniors, and he reproached himself with having been unjust as well as unkind to Pater. He besought his friend Gersaint to persuade Pater to return to him, and when the latter arrived the dying man spent a month giving Pater all the help and guidance that he could in order to atone for his former injustice.

Pater, though possessed of less individuality than Lancret, was in many respects the best of Watteau's followers, and, like his master, he also died young.   He was haunted by a fear that he would become old and helpless before he had saved enough to live upon, and he worked so incessantly and feverishly to gain his independence that eventually his health broke down and he died in harness at forty.

Lancret, who lived on till 1743, continued Watteau's Italian comedy manner, and had considerable success with his theatrical portraits, two of which are in the Wallace Collection.   He is seen at his best in the portrait of an actress known as " La Belle Grecque " (see page 276), which has a vivacious charm of its own and is full of life. The pose of the figure is particularly happy and conveys admirably a sense of movement.   But while they could imitate more or less cleverly the superficial appearance of Watteau's pictures, neither Lancret nor Pater were able to give their paintings that undercurrent of pathos which lifts Watteau's work high above the trivial.

Only a very superficial observer of Watteau's pictures would accuse him of being a painter of frivolities, a chronicler of picnics. Watteau lived in an artificial age, and being a true artist he could not help reflecting something of its artificiality. The French Court life of his day had the splendour of autumn leaves about to fall. Watteau, himself a dainty rose with canker in the bud, shows us the hectic charm of a civilisation already being consumed by mortal malady; but his honesty and intellectual insight prevented him from pretending that the happiness of his puppets was anything more than a passing moment of self-deception. His pictures haunt us, not because of their gaiety, but by reason of their gentle, uncomplaining melancholy; and the late Sir Frederick Wedmore penetrated to the secret of Watteau when he laid stress on " the reflective pathos, the poignant melancholy, which are among the most appealing gifts of him who was accounted the master of the frivolous, of the monotonously gay. "

Watteau is unique in his qualities of drawing and colour. There have been many painters who were great draughts-men, and a number of painters who have been great colourists; but those who were supreme both in drawing and colour we can count on the fingers of one hand. Watteau is among them. If we look at the little figures in a typical Watteau like " The Conversation " (see page 263), we perceive that the drawing rivals that of Raphael in its per-fection of form and that of Rembrandt in its expressiveness. Watteau's powers of drawing may be studied still further in his chalk drawings in the British Museum Print Room.

As for his paint, hardly among his predecessors will you find anything so exquisite in colour and so jewel-like in quality. The brightness of his palette, and the little touches with which he laid on his colour, make his pictures vibrate and sing as those of no other artist had done before. Watteau was not only a great master; he was one of those pioneer artists whose original research and brilliant achievements have given a new impetus to the art of painting.

"THE SWING," BY FRAGONARD (1732–1806).

Wallace Collection, London.

In this picture we have an example of that affectation of rustic simplicity which thinly veiled the real sensual character of Court life at Versailles. After squandering his great artistic gifts on pandering to the taste of a depraved nobility, the greatest decorator of his age lived to see his patrons sent to the guillotine and though the painter himself escaped the worst terrors of the French Revolution he died in poverty.

271

" THE PANCAKE-MAKER," BY CHARDIN (1699-1779).

Hunterian Museum, Glasgow

Unmoved by the affectations of his age and the artificialities of the French Court, this great artist painted humble scenes of domesticity with a penetration that divined their innermost truths and with a perfection of workmanship that invested them with beauty.

§ 2

While Watteau was laying the foundations for the romantic and impressionist painting of modern France, another group of French figure-painters were evolving a national " grand style " for French portraiture. This new style first made its appearance when Largillière began painting Louis XIV and his family, and a typical example of it may be found in the Wallace Collection.

Nicolas Largillière (1656–1746), who was nearly thirty years older than Watteau, was born in Paris, but worked for many years in London, where he was an assistant to Sir Peter Lely and a great favourite with King Charles II. But unlike his master Lely—who rivalled the Vicar of Bray in keeping in with both sides—Largillière was a Royalist through and through, and like the fallen Stuarts he returned to France and made Paris his home during the latter part of his life. His drawing is accurate but rather hard, his colour harmonious and lighter in hue than that of his predecessors Mignard and Le Brun, and his great canvas at the Wallace Collection of Louis XIV with the Dauphin, the Duc de Bourgogne, the infant Duc d'Anjou (afterwards Louis XV), and Madame de Maintenon, shows how magnificently he could stage and present a royal group.

Among his contemporaries were Hyacinth Rigaud (1659–1743), and his pupil Jean Baptiste Oudry (1686–1755), who won much fame as superintendent of the royal tapestry manufactories of the Gobelins and Beauvais ; but his most famous successor was Jean Marc Nattier (1685–1766), a Parisian-born, who became one of the favourite portrait-painters at the Court of Louis XV. Nattier commenced his career as a historical painter, and only took up portraiture in 1720 after he had lost all his savings through the speculations of John Law, the Scottish financier and adventurer. His paintings are also a little hard, but they are light and gay in colour and remarkably stately in their grouping and arrangement.

18

Another Paris-born artist acquired still wider fame. This was François Boucher (1703–70), who gained the first prize at the Academy when he was only twenty years old and afterwards studied in Rome. " No one," wrote the late Lady Dilke of this artist, " ever attacked a greater variety of styles ; his drawings—often extremely good—are to be met with in every important collection. Innumerable were his easel pictures, his mural decorations, his designs for tapestries at Beauvais or the Gobelins, his scene paintings for Versailles and the Opera."

No artist more completely illustrates and represents French taste in the eighteenth century than François Boucher, who was indeed the leader of fashion in this direction, and by his creative genius brought a new note into European painting. He introduced a lighter and gayer scheme of colour into tapestries and decorative paintings, pale blues and pinks being predominant in his colour-schemes. He designed many paintings and decorations for the famous Madame de Pompadour, and the sweet colour now generally known as *rose du Barry* was invented by Boucher and was originally called *Rose Pompadour.*

To do justice to the French portraiture of the late seventeenth and early eighteenth centuries, we must remember the ornate gilt furniture of the period with which they were surrounded. Portraits like Nattier's " Mademoiselle de Clermont " and Boucher's " Marquise de Pompadour " (see opposite page)—both of which are in the Wallace Collection—must not be judged as easel paintings, but as items in an elaborate scheme of interior decoration. There is nothing like them in the history of portraiture, just as there never was a Court exactly like that of the " Grand Monarch " or of his immediate successors. These portraits reconvey to us all the splendours of Versailles, its luxury and its heartlessness. They are the quintessence of aristocratic feeling, so full of culture that there is little room for humanity. The pride they express ends by alienating our sympathy, for they are the most pompous pictures the world has ever seen.

MARQUISE DE POMPADOUR, BY BOUCHER (1703–1770).

Wallace Collection, London.

This notorious favourite of the King of France possessed an unerring instinct for beauty, and during the twenty years of her reign she exerted a great and, on the whole, a beneficial influence on the arts. "Her death in 1764," says Lady Dilke, "deprived the great group of artists employed by the Crown of a court of appeal whose decisions were ruled by a taste finished to the point of genius."

PORTRAIT OF AN ACTRESS (" LA BELLE GRECQUE "), BY LANCRET
(1690–1743).

Wallace Collection, London.

This superb portrait of an actress shows that in one quality, that of dramatic force.
Lancret surpassed his master Watteau. We can almost hear this graceful creature recite
her lines, and her gesture is eloquent of the point she has turned to make.

§ 3

Side by side with these aristocratic painters whose art reflected the temper of the French Court, we find now and then an artist of genius who expresses the life and feelings of the people. The greatest of these was Jean Baptiste Simeon Chardin (1699–1779), who was also born in Paris. Though he worked for a time under the Court painter Van Loo at Fontainebleau, and was elected a member of the Academy in 1728, Chardin was never a favourite with the nobles of France, nor did he make any effort to pander to their taste. His pictures, like those of his predecessors the brothers Le Nain, were " tainted with democracy," and the intense humanity of Chardin links him to his great contemporary on the other side of the Channel, William Hogarth.

Though Chardin, as Lady Dilke once said, " treated subjects of the humblest and most unpretentious class, he brought to their rendering, not only deep feeling and a penetration which divines the innermost truths of the simplest forms of life, but a perfection of workmanship by which everything he handled was clothed with beauty."

Like the Persian poet, Chardin could compose a song about a loaf of bread and a glass of red wine—as his beautiful still-life in the National Gallery, London, proved—while " The Pancake-Maker " (see page 272) shows what beauty and tenderness he could find in the kitchen.

Amid all the artificiality of the gaudy Court of Versailles, Chardin stands out as the supreme interpreter of the sweetness and sane beauty of domesticity. He was a poet with the unspoilt heart of a child who could reveal to us the loveliness in the common things of life.

How strong a character Chardin must have been to resist the current of the time and adhere unswervingly to his simple democratic ideals we realise when we contemplate the talent and career of Jean Honoré Fragonard (1732–1806), who was for a time his pupil. We have only to look at Fragonard's charming domestic scene, " The Happy Mother," in the National Gallery, London, to see that this artist also might have been a painter of the people. He shows us here the home of a blacksmith, whose forge is seen in the background, while in the centre the young mother with her three children sits at a table, and beyond another woman rocks a cradle.

For good or ill Fragonard chose another path, and after he had gained from Chardin a knowledge of sound craftsmanship which he never afterwards lost, he chose a more fashionable master and became the pupil of Boucher. In 1752, at the age of twenty, he won the Prix de Rome, and in 1756 he went for four years to Italy, where he made a particular study of the decorative paintings of " The Last of the Venetians," namely, Giovanni Battista Tiepolo (1696–1769). He returned to Paris in 1761 and almost immediately became a favourite with the French nobility.

In Fragonard, wrote Lady Dilke, " Boucher found his true heir. The style of Court fashions and customs, highly artificial even in the affectation of nature and simplicity. the temper of society, purely sensual in spite of pretensions to sentiment, gave birth to innumerable fictions which took their place in the commerce of ordinary life. Eternal youth, perpetual pleasure, and all the wanton graces, their insincere airs masked by a voluptuous charm, came into seeming—a bright deceitful vision which cheated and allured all eyes. . . . The hours float by in waves of laughter, and the scent of flowers which breathe of endless summer fills the air. Existence in the gardens of Fragonard is pleasure ; its penalties and pains are ignored, just as sickness and sorrow were then ignored in actual life."

Highly typical of the period and of the manner in which Fragonard catered for the taste of his patrons is his picture " The Swing " (see page 271), painted to order and exhibiting all the characteristics which Lady Dilke has so brilliantly analysed in the passage quoted. The workmanship is beautiful, the drawing and colour are alike charming, but these displays of so-called " gallantry " are detestable to many people, and through it all we are conscious of the insincerity of a clever and highly gifted painter.

Pictures which Fragonard painted purely to please

GIRL WITH DOVES," BY GREUZE (1725-1805).
Wallace Collection, London.

Though she appears the incarnation of sweet innocence and simplicity, the original of this portrait broke Greuze's heart by her infidelities and eventually robbed him of his savings. She was the daughter of a Paris bookseller. The artist married her in haste, and by his paintings made her a reigning beauty of her day.

himself, like " The Happy Mother " and the " Lady Carving
her Name," a tiny canvas which cost Lord Hertford £1400
in 1865, are less typical of Fragonard, but often pleasanter to
gaze upon than his commissions and elaborate decorations.
But even in these subjects Fragonard is always frolicsome
and playful where Chardin was serious and earnest, and it is
impossible to escape the conclusion that Fragonard's was
essentially a shallow nature.   For all his cleverness he paid
the penalty of his insincerity ; he outlived his popularity
and ultimately died in dire poverty.   In 1806 the times had
changed : Napoleon and the French Revolution had swept
away the frivolities of Versailles.

§ 4

Contemporary with Fragonard was a painter who,
though never the equal of Chardin as a craftsman, nevertheless approached him in the democratic temper of his
art.   Jean Baptiste Greuze (1725–1805), who was born near
Macon and came to Paris in 1746, suddenly acquired fame
and popularity when he was thirty by exhibiting at the
Salon of 1755 his picture " A Father Explaining the Bible
to his Family."   This familiar scene, with its everyday
details and its personages taken from humble life, made an
immediate appeal to the bourgeois, who found in it those
new ideas of simplicity and morality which Jean Jacques
Rousseau had spread among the middle classes.   Lady
Dilke, who evidently suspected the moral sincerity of
Greuze, pronounced his pictures to be " stained by
artificiality."   His pictures were rendered attractive, she
argued, by " a vein of wanton suggestion which found
an echo in the dainty disorder in which his heroines are
dressed."

There are some strange parallels between the life of
Greuze and that of Watteau, who died four years before
his birth.   Greuze's father was also a carpenter, and he
also opposed his son's determination to become an artist.
Greuze also began his career in extreme poverty, but
fortunately he had a more robust constitution and with-

MLLE. SOPHIE ARNOULD, BY GREUZE.
Wallace Collection, London.

No artist owes so much of his fame to the beauty of his models as Greuze did, but it must be admitted that he knew how to present them to advantage and to paint them with a rare tenderness and atmospheric softness. He also, like Fragonard, outlived his popularity and died in poverty.

stood hardship better than Watteau. Greuze's father whipped him when he caught him drawing, and Greuze also ran away to Paris with another painter, and he, too, when he got there found that nobody wanted to

Photo : T. & R. Annan.

"LADY MAKING TEA," BY CHARDIN.

Hunterian Museum, Glasgow.

Revealing a power of observation and justness of lighting which rivals the exquisite work of the best Dutch Masters, this painted fragment of everyday life also shows a grace and subtle refinement which is characteristic of France. Its beauty is as indisputable as its truth.

give him any employment. Both men were close on thirty before the turning-point came, Watteau by his election to the Academy, and Greuze by the exhibition of his picture at the Salon. But there the parallel ends, and the close of Greuze's life is more like that of Fragonard. For he also outlived his popularity and died in poverty.

It seems extraordinary that Greuze, the most popular of painters at all times, should have fared so badly at the end of his life. We cannot account for it by saying that Greuze could not accommodate himself to the change of taste brought about by the French Revolution, for throughout his career he was distinctly a bourgeois rather than an aristocratic painter. No, we must seek another explanation.

The miserable truth is that the seemingly sweet and innocent little person, who looks out at us continually from those pictures of girls' heads which have brought the painter his greatest posthumous fame, was the cause of her immortaliser's wretched end. To look at all the portraits of her which hang in the Wallace Collection, or at the one entitled " Girl Looking Up " (see page 260), which is in the National Gallery, is to find it difficult to believe that the original was an arrant little baggage. Yet some people, who profess to be judges of character, say that the Greuze girl is not so innocent as she pretends to be.

The historic truth is that she was the daughter of an old bookseller on the Quai des Augustins, Paris, and Greuze is said to have married her to save her reputation. He married Anne Gabriel in haste, and he repented at his leisure. Owing to her husband's constant exposition of her charms, Madame Greuze became one of the noted beauties of the day, and though her husband was devoted to her and gave her crazily everything he could that she wanted, the ungrateful little hussy repaid him by robbing him not only of his peace of mind but of large sums of money that he had saved.

It is easy to be wise after the event, and Mr. John Rivers in his book on *Greuze and his Models* maintains that every feature of Anne Gabriel " announced a hasty, passionate, and rather voluptuous nature " ; nevertheless we are inclined, as human beings ourselves liable to error, to give our sympathy to Greuze and praise him for a generous and chivalrous action rather than to condemn him for having made an imprudent marriage. Though he painted other beautiful women, it is by his various fanciful portraits of his erring wife that Greuze has obtained his world-wide popularity, and there is hardly another instance in art of a painter who has achieved so great a fame by his exposition of the physical charms of a single model.

XII

ENGLISH MASTERS OF THE EIGHTEENTH CENTURY

THE ART OF HOGARTH, RICHARD WILSON, AND SIR JOSHUA
REYNOLDS

§ I

IN all the annals of British Art there is no more illustrious
name than that of William Hogarth. Not only was
he, as Mr. E. V. Lucas has pointed out, " the first great
national British painter, the first man to look at the English
life around him like an Englishman and paint it without
affectation or foreign influence, but he was the first to make
pictures popular. Hogarth's engravings from his own
works produced a love of art that has steadily increased
ever since. During Hogarth's day thousands of houses that
had had no pictures before acquired that picture habit
which many years later Alderman Boydell and his team of
engravers were to do so much to foster and establish."

That is where Hogarth differs from the French democratic painters, from Chardin and Greuze, mentioned in
the last chapter ; he was an engraver as well as a painter,
and so was one of the first artists in Europe to devote talent
of the highest order to providing art for the masses as
well as the classes. People who could not afford to buy
oil-paintings could buy engravings, and it was by his
engravings that Hogarth first acquired fame.

William Hogarth was born in Bartholomew Close, Smith-
field, on November 10, 1697. He was the son of a schoolmaster and printer's reader, who was apparently a man
of some education and had the intelligence to recognise
his son's talent for drawing, and to place no obstacle in his
path. At an early age young Hogarth was apprenticed to

a silversmith near Leicester Fields (now Leicester Square), for whom he chased tankards and salvers, and two years after his father's death in 1718 he felt sufficiently confident in his powers to set up as an engraver on his own account. Meanwhile he had taken every opportunity of improving his drawing, and had attended classes at the art academy of Sir James Thornhill (1676–1734), a portrait-painter and decorative artist much in favour with Queen Anne. He was especially renowned for his ceilings, and the Painted Hall at Greenwich is a famous example of Thornhill's art.

Hogarth did not get on very well with Thornhill and his method of tuition, which consisted principally of giving his pupils pictures to copy. This did not suit a youth so enamoured of life as Hogarth, who had a habit of making notes on his thumb-nail of faces and expressions and enlarging them afterwards on paper. In this way he trained his memory to carry the exact proportions and characteristics of what he had seen, so that his drawings, even done from memory, were extraordinarily vivacious and full of life. " Copying," Hogarth once said, " is like pouring water out of one vessel into another." He preferred to draw his own water, and this sturdy determination to see life for himself set him on the road to greatness. Previous English artists had not done this ; they had looked at life through another man's spectacles, and their pictures were more or less good imitations of the manner of Van Dyck, Lely, and Kneller.

Nevertheless he continued for a long time to frequent Thornhill's academy, the real attraction being not the master's tuition but his pretty daughter Jane. In the end Hogarth eloped with Miss Thornhill, whom he married without her father's consent and very much against his will. At the time the match was considered a *mésalliance*, for Thornhill was a Member of Parliament and a knight, whereas Hogarth had as yet acquired little fame and had rather scandalised society by bringing out in 1724 a set of engravings, " The Talk of the Town," in which he satirised the tendency of fashionable London to lionise foreign singers.

"THE AGE OF INNOCENCE," BY SIR JOSHUA REYNOLDS.

National Gallery, London.

This delightful portrait of his little grand-niece, Theophila Gwatkin aged six, while showing in its harmonious arrangement all Sir Joshua's mastery of the " grand style," also reveals the tenderness of his emotions and his reverent affection for the innocence of childhood.

Four years later, however, the tide was turned in Hogarth's favour when Mr. Gay lashed the same fashionable folly in *The Beggar's Opera*, which, produced at the Lincoln's Inn Fields Theatre in January 1728, proved to be as great a popular success then as it has been in our own day. Hogarth was naturally attracted to a piece that revealed a spirit so akin to his own, and he painted several pictures of its scenes, one of which is now in the Tate Gallery. His genial, bohemian temperament delighted in the society of actors and writers, and Hogarth's association with the company of *The Beggar's Opera* indirectly led him to take up portrait-painting. One of his earliest portraits is " Lavinia Fenton as *Polly Peachum*," the gay young actress who created the part and became Duchess of Bolton.

This portrait—as indeed are all of Hogarth's—is a wonderful achievement. It has nothing of the manner of Lely or Kneller or any of his predecessors ; it is fresh, original, unmannered, and sets life itself before us. To some extent, perhaps, he was influenced by Dutch painting, which has the same quality of honesty, but in the main he was " without a school, and without a precedent." Unlike the portrait-painters who preceded and those who immediately succeeded him, Hogarth does not show us people of rank and fashion. His portraits are usually of people in his own class or lower, his relatives, actors and actresses, his servants. Hogarth was too truthful in his painting and not obsequious enough in his manner to be a favourite with society, and it was only occasionally that a member of the aristocracy had the courage to sit to him. Simon Fraser, Lord Lovat, did, and the magnificent little full-length in the National Portrait Gallery shows how vividly Hogarth grasped and expressed his character.

Still more amazing as an example of Hogarth's vivid characterisation and vivacity of expression is " The Shrimp Girl " (see page 289). It is only a sketch, mostly in greys with a few touches of other colours, but there is no work in the National Gallery more abounding with life. These portraits, painted with joy for the painter's satisfaction,

" THE SHRIMP GIRL," BY HOGARTH (1637–1764).
National Gallery, London.

" Life more abundant in her face you see."

Though hardly more than a sketch in its lightness of handling and reticence of colour, this is the most famous of all Hogarth's portraits for its amazing vitality and actuality.

19

never produced an income. He made his living by other pictures, and especially by his engravings, which had a wide sale and made his name a household word. The series of pictorial dramas which he invented brought him both fame and fortune, and after " The Rake's Progress "

Photo : W. A. Mansell & Co.

"MARRIAGE A LA MODE," BY HOGARTH.

SCENE I. THE MARRIAGE CONTRACT.

National Gallery, London.

The first scene in Hogarth's celebrated picture-drama. Note how the young lawyer (" Silvertongue ") is already beginning to court the bride, while her prospective husband admires himself in the mirror.

and other sets had firmly established Hogarth in popular favour, Sir James Thornhill became reconciled to his son-in-law, whom he now saw o be capable of earning a good living.

Narrative pictures were not a new thing in the history of art ; the reliefs of Trajan's Column at Rome tell the story of the Emperor's Dacian campaigns, and we saw in the first chapter how Giotto and other early Italian painters recounted Bible stories and the lives of the saints in a series of pictures. But no painter before Hogarth had invented the story as well as illustrating it. Without any text familiar to the public, Hogarth by paint and engraving told

"MARRIAGE A LA MODE," BY HOGARTH.

SCENE II. SHORTLY AFTER MARRIAGE.

National Gallery, London.

The mutual boredom resulting from a " marriage of convenience " is the moral Hogarth points in this morning scene, adorned with a wealth of exquisitely painted details.

new and original stories of his own time, and told them so clearly that they were universally understood. Sometimes these stories were almost wholly humorous, as in " The Election " series, but more often they had a serious intention and amusing incidents were introduced only by way of light relief.

To regard Hogarth as a satirist first is wrong : he was

more than that : he was a great moralist. For though no
man more severely scourged the folly of his time, Hogarth
taught his lessons not only by exposing the ridiculous, but
also by revealing the tragedy of wrong and the beauty
of goodness. Among his many inventions none more

Photo : W. A. Mansell & Co.

"MARRIAGE A LA MODE," BY HOGARTH.

Scene III. The Visit to the Quack Doctor.

National Gallery, London.

The harsh faces of the quack and his companion and the gay unconcern of the Earl are
contrasted with the rigid figure of the little girl, the victim of his profligacy, in this third
scene, which shows how the married couple are drifting apart.

beautifully display his method than the " Marriage à la
Mode " series which we reproduce (pages 290–295) from
the original paintings at the National Gallery; and though
each one of these pictures tells its own story clearly, it may
be helpful to summarise the action of each scene, and
add the illuminating comments made by the great critic
Hazlitt :

Scene I. The Marriage Contract

In a splendid apartment the father of the bridegroom points to his pedigree, while the rich alderman, father of the bride, studies the marriage settlement. " The three figures of the young nobleman, his intended bride, and her inamorato, the Lawyer, show how much Hogarth excelled in the power of giving soft and effeminate expression. . . . Nothing,"

Photo : W. A. Mansell & Co.

'MARRIAGE A LA MODE," BY HOGARTH.

Scene IV.—The Countess's Dressing-room.

National Gallery, London.

Hogarth's powers as a satirist find their fullest expression in this mocking picture of a polite company enduring an exhibition of " culture."

writes Hazlitt, " can be more finely managed than the differences of character in these delicate personages."

Scene II. Shortly after Marriage

Note the delicious touch of satire in the four pictures of saints which adorn the walls of a worldly interior. An old steward, shocked at the way things are going, is leaving with a bundle of bills and one receipt. The wife sits yawning at breakfast, while the card-tables and the candles, still burning, in the room seen beyond, show how the husband, lazing in his chair, had spent the night. "The figure, face, and attitude of the husband are inimitable," says Hazlitt. "Hogarth has with great skill contrasted the pale countenance of the husband with the yellow-whitish colour of the marble mantelpiece behind him, in such a manner as to preserve the fleshy tone of the former. The airy splendour of the

Photo: W. A. Mansell & Co.

"MARRIAGE A LA MODE," BY HOGARTH.

SCENE V. THE DUEL AND DEATH OF THE EARL.

National Gallery, London.

The tragedy culminates in the Earl's discovery of his wife's unfaithfulness and his death at the hands of the lover, who is escaping through the window.

view of the room in this picture is probably not exceeded in any of the productions of the Flemish school."

SCENE III. THE VISIT TO THE QUACK DOCTOR

The peer, with a cane in one hand and a box of pills in the other, rallies the sardonically smiling quack for having deceived him. "The young girl," says Hazlitt, "who is represented as the victim of fashionable profligacy, is unquestionably one of the artist's *chefs-d'œuvre.* The exquisite delicacy of the painting is only surpassed by the felicity and subtlety of the conception. Nothing can be more striking than the contrast between the extreme softness of her person and the hardened indifference of her character."²

SCENE IV. THE COUNTESS'S DRESSING-ROOM

The gradations of ridiculous affectation in the Music Scene are finely

Photo : W. A. Mansell & Co.

" MARRIAGE A LA MODE," BY HOGARTH.
SCENE VI. THE DEATH OF THE COUNTESS.
National Gallery, London.

The last act showing the suicide of the Countess, while her father seems more intent on securing her rings than on consoling the orphan daughter, whom a nurse holds up to the dying mother.

imagined and preserved. The preposterous, overstrained admiration of the Lady of Quality, the sentimental, insipid, impatient delight of the Man, with his hair in paper, and sipping his tea, the pert, smirking, conceited, half-distorted approbation of the figure next to him, the transition to the total insensibility of the round face in profile, and then to the wonder of the negro boy at the rapture of his mistress, form a perfect whole. The sanguine complexion and flame-coloured hair of the female virtuoso throw an additional light on the character. . . . The gross, bloated appearance of the Italian Singer is well relieved by the hard features of the instrumental performer behind him, which might be carved of wood. The negro boy holding the chocolate, both in expression, colour, and execution, is a masterpiece. The gay, lively, derision of the other negro boy, playing with the Actæon, is an ingenious contrast to the profound amazement of the first.

Scene V. The Duel and Death of the Earl

" Silvertongue," the young lawyer whom in the last scene we saw passing a masquerade ticket to the Countess, has now been found out. The Earl, who surprised him with his wife, has fought a duel and is dying as the result, while the young lawyer escapes through a window as the Watch enters.

Scene VI. The Death of the Countess

A bottle of poison on the floor shows that the Countess's death is self-sought, while the paper near it, with the words, " Counsellor Silver- tongue's Last Dying Speech," reveals the end of another leading character in the drama. While the father absent-mindedly draws the rings from the fingers of his dying daughter, the half-starved dog ravenously snatch- ing the meat from the table suggests with subtlety the straitened resources of the household as a result of previous prodigal expenditure.

While the merited success of his prints and subject- pictures made Hogarth a very prosperous man, he pre- served his simple character to the last, and on one occasion he walked home in the rain, completely forgetting that now he had his own coach, which was waiting for him. He had a town house at 30 Leicester Square (now rebuilt) and a country house at Chiswick, now a Hogarth Museum, and when he died in 1764 he was buried in Chiswick Church- yard.

§ 2

The greatest of Hogarth's contemporaries, the link indeed between him and Sir Joshua Reynolds, was the artist known as " The Father of British Landscape," Richard Wilson. His is one of the saddest stories in British Art, for, though acknowledged to be one of the most eminent men of his day, and attaining a modest measure of success in middle life, Fortune, through no fault of his own, turned her back on him, and his later years were spent in the direst poverty.

Richard Wilson was born at Penegoes in Montgomery-shire on August 1, 1714, the day Queen Anne died and George I ascended the throne. His father was a clergyman of limited means, but his mother was well connected, and one of her well-off relatives took sufficient interest in young Richard's talent for drawing to have him sent to London to learn painting. Though it is by his landscapes that Wilson acquired lasting fame, he began life as a portrait-painter ; one of his earlier portraits of himself is in the National Portrait Gallery, while a very much later portrait, in the Diploma Gallery of the Royal Academy, we reproduce (page 299). This magnificent work, which speaks for itself, is enough to prove that even in portrait-painting Wilson had, among his immediate predecessors, no equal saving Hogarth.

Like Hogarth, Wilson was of a sturdy, independent dis-position, little inclined to truckle to the conceit of fashion-able sitters or to flatter their vanity, and consequently he was not the man to make it the staff of his professional practice, though in 1748 he had acquired a considerable eminence in this branch of art. In this year he was com-missioned to paint a group of the Prince of Wales and Duke of York with their tutor—a portion of which now hangs in the National Portrait Gallery—and with the money earned by this and other commissions he decided in the following year to carry out a long-cherished wish to visit Italy.

Hitherto there has been a general belief that Wilson did not attempt landscape painting till he found himself in Italy, but it has recently been ascertained [1] that he un-questionably painted landscapes before he left England.

In Italy Wilson devoted more and more of his time to landscape till he finally established himself in Rome as a landscape-painter, only doing an occasional portrait. His beautiful pictures of Italian landscapes, in which dignity of design was combined with atmospheric truth and loveliness of colour, soon gained him a great reputation in that city, and his landscapes were bought by the Earl of Pembroke, the Earl of Thanet, the Earl of Essex, Lord Bolingbroke,

[1] Cf. *Richard Wilson and Farington*, by Frank Rutter, 1923.

Lord Dartmouth, and other Englishmen of high rank who were visiting Italy. Consequently, when he returned to England in 1756, his reputation preceded him and he enjoyed a considerable measure of success when he first established himself in London at Covent Garden. But unfortunately for Wilson, the taste of the eighteenth century was severely classical, and after the first novelty of his Italian

By courtesy of Capt. Richard Ford.

"ITALIAN LANDSCAPE," BY RICHARD WILSON (1714–1782.)

A beautiful example of Wilson's poetic rendering of Italian scenery, and of his power to render the glow in the sky and the limpid atmosphere in a spacious landscape.   Note also the dignity and harmony of the carefully balanced composition.

landscapes wore off, only one or two enlightened patrons, like Sir Richard Ford, were capable of appreciating the originality and beauty of the landscapes he painted in England. Thanks to the discrimination of Sir Richard and Lady Ford, the best collection in the world of landscapes by Richard Wilson is still in the possession of the family, and by the courtesy of Captain Richard Ford we are permitted to reproduce two fine examples in these pages.

Photo : W. A. Mansell & Co.

"PORTRAIT OF THE ARTIST," BY RICHARD WILSON.

Diploma Gallery, Royal Academy.

A noble and dignified portrait of himself by the artist, who won lasting fame as " The Father of British Landscape."   Owing to an ill-timed jest, Wilson lost Court favour, and his later years were spent in pitiful poverty and privation.

It is only in the Ford Collection that the full measure of Wilson's greatness can be seen, for while the splendour of the flaming sunset sky in " The Tiber, with Rome in the Distance " reveals how Wilson showed the way to Turner, the sweet simplicity and *natural* beauty of " The Thames near Twickenham " (page 308) proves him also to have been the artistic ancestor of Constable.

Wilson's English landscapes went begging in his own day. His memorandum-book, preserved in the Victoria and Albert Museum, South Kensington, shows how he sent them out on approval and often had them returned. As his fortunes dwindled, Wilson despairingly set about painting replicas of the Italian landscapes which he had found more saleable, and these repetitions of his Italian scenes have done much harm to his reputation in succeeding years, for the later Italian pictures do not always attain the quality of the first version when the painter was freshly inspired by the original scenery.

Nevertheless, with the help of one or two unaffected lovers of art and Nature, who bought his English landscapes, and more who bought repetitions of his Italian scenes, and with the fees of his pupils—among whom was the diarist, Joseph Farington, R.A.—Wilson managed for some years to make a tolerable living, and when the Royal Academy was established in 1768, George III—who in his boyhood had had his portrait done by this landscape-painter— nominated Richard Wilson as one of the founder-members of the Academy. At the Academy exhibitions Wilson exhibited with credit, if without much commercial success, and nothing serious happened till 1776, when he sent a picture of " Sion House from Kew Gardens," which the King thought of buying.

Unfortunately he sent Lord Bute to bargain with the artist, and this canny nobleman thought the price asked, sixty guineas, was " too dear." " Tell His Majesty," said Wilson roguishly, " that he may pay for it by instalments." Had an Irish peer been the intermediary he might have seen the joke and have made Wilson's fortune, but Lord Bute belonged to a race that is reputed to take money very

"MRS. SIDDONS AS THE TRAGIC MUSE," BY SIR JOSHUA
REYNOLDS (1723–92).

Dulwich Gallery.

The most famous example of " the grand style " introduced by Sir Joshua
into English portraiture : the great actress is shown as a queen of tragedy
seated on her throne. As he put his signature at the bottom of the painted
skirt, Sir Joshua, in his courtly manner, told the sitter he would go down
to posterity on the hem of her garment.

Photo : W. A. Mansell & Co.

"THE INFANT SAMUEL," BY SIR JOSHUA REYNOLDS.
National Gallery, London.

Sir Joshua once told Hannah More that he was mortified to be asked by even his more enlightened sitters for information as to " who " Samuel was !

seriously, and to be not too quick at grasping the English sense of humour. He was shocked and scandalised, deeming the answer insulting to royalty.

The harmless gibe cost Wilson what little Court favour he had, and proved to be his ruin. Fortunately, before this disastrous retort had been made, he had secured the Librarianship of the Royal Academy, and the salary of this post, fifty pounds a year, was all Wilson had to live on during his later years. His few patrons fell away from him, his brother Academicians—most of whom had been rather jealous—now shunned him, and he lived in a miserable garret in Tottenham Street, Tottenham Court Road, existing chiefly on bread and porter. He had always been fond of the last—" though not to excess," said Beechey, R.A., who knew him intimately—and want of nourishment rather than excess of liquor wrought sad changes in his countenance, so that he became known as " red-nosed Dick."

Just before the end he had a year or two of quiet and comfort, for he left London and made his home with his relatives in Wales, where he died, at Llanberis, in 1782. Wilson did not altogether abandon portrait-painting when he returned from Italy, and in addition o the noble portrait of himself, there is in the Academy's Diploma Gallery a very beautiful full-length of the young artist Mortimer, whom he painted about the same time. A splendid portrait of Peg Woffington, very rich in colour, which hangs in the Garrick Club, is another example of Wilson's portraiture after his return from Italy.

Richard Wilson was the first English artist to show his countrymen not only the beauty of Nature but the beauty of their own country. He should not be judged by such large pictures as " Niobe " and " The Villa of Mæcenas," which he painted " to order," but rather — so far as the National Gallery is concerned — by his exquisite " Italian Coast Scene " (No. 2646) and " On the Wye," which together show how beautifully and truly Wilson rendered the characteristic scenery of the two countries he so deeply loved.

§ 3

When Richard Wilson was already learning the business of portrait-painting in London, Joshua Reynolds was a little boy of six. He also was the son of a clergyman, the Rev. Samuel Reynolds of Plympton Earl, near Plymouth, where Joshua, the seventh son, was born on July 16, 1723. Sir Godfrey Kneller died the same year.

Nature and Fortune were both kind to Reynolds : the first endowed him with courtly manners as well as talent, the second gave him opportunities to use these to the best advantage. Doubtless Reynolds would have made his way to the front, by one path if not by another, but it was a piece of good luck for him when Commodore Keppel of the *Centurion* put in at Plymouth for repairs, and met the young painter at the house of Lord Mount-Edgcumbe. Keppel took a liking to the painter and offered him a free passage on his ship to the Mediterranean. Reynolds gladly accepted, and after a long stay with Keppel at Minorca, went on to Rome, where he gave himself up to that worship of Michael Angelo that he retained all his life. His well-known deafness dates from this early period, and was the result of a cold which he caught while copying at the Vatican.

From Rome, Reynolds went to Florence, Venice, and other Italian cities, returning to England in 1753, and then he settled in London, never to leave it again except for a holiday. His youngest sister Frances kept house for him, and he never married ; like Michael Angelo, the object of his worship, Reynolds said he was " wedded to his art." After living for a time at 104 St. Martin's Lane, and then at 5 Great Newport Street, he made his permanent home at 47 Leicester Square, and Messrs. Puttick & Simpson used to hold their auctions in the room that was once his studio.

Reynolds did not capture the town at the first assault ; the deep richness of the colouring he had adopted from the Venetian masters, and the atmospheric contours of his forms, did not appeal to connoisseurs accustomed to the lighter colour and harder outlines of Kneller ; but supported by the influence of Lord Mount-Edgcumbe and

"MRS. HOARE AND HER INFANT SON," BY SIR JOSHUA REYNOLDS.
Wallace Collection, London.

Unsurpassed as a decorative example of the typically British " open-air portrait," this picture is also a supremely beautiful expression of the tenderness of a mother's affection.

Admiral Keppel, he gradually became acknowledged as the head of his profession. When the Royal Academy was founded, his appointment as President met with universal approbation, for it was felt that no painter could fill the office so well. Reynolds, as Mr. E. V. Lucas points out, " was sought not only for his brush, but also for his company ; and though he did not court high society, he was sensible of the advantages it gave him. Other and finer intellects also welcomed him—such as Dr. Johnson, Burke, and Goldsmith—and his house became a centre of good talk."

Reynolds was not only a great painter, but a great gentleman, for long before the King knighted him in 1769, five days before the opening of the first Academy exhibition, he had shown court and society " that a painter could be a wise man and a considerable man as well."

The story of Sir Joshua's life is not dramatic ; it is the placid, smoothly running story of his art, of well-chosen friendships, of kindly actions, occasional displays of professional jealousy—for he was human and not an angel—and of a happy domestic life. When his brother-in-law Mr. Palmer died in 1770, Sir Joshua adopted his daughter Theophila, then thirteen, and later her sister Mary Palmer also came to live with him, so that though a bachelor Reynolds was not without young people in his house. Both his nieces remained with him till they married, and it was Theophila's daughter, little Theophila Gwatkin, who was the original of one of Reynolds's most charming and popular paintings, " The Age of Innocence " (see page 287).

His grand-niece was six years old when Reynolds, in 1788, painted her portrait, a work which in conception and in every touch proclaims that it was " a labour of love." Indeed, nowhere do the simplicity, the benevolence, and the affectionate nature of the man shine out more beautifully than in his paintings of children. Splendid and decorative in its colour-scheme and open-air setting, his " Mrs. Richard Hoare with her Infant Son " (see preceding page) in the Wallace Collection has the same winning simplicity of intention ; for it is much more than a mere portrait, it is a grave and tender expression of a mother's love.

Photo: *W. A. Mansell & Co.*

"MISS EMILY POTT AS *THAIS*," BY SIR J. REYNOLDS.

Sir Joshua's dramatic power is finely displayed in the arresting pose of the figure in this theatrical portrait. "Thais" was an Athenian beauty who accompanied Alexander the Great on his expedition to Asia. After his death she was claimed by Ptolemy, to whom she bore three children.

307

The other side of Sir Joshua's art, " the grand manner," is seen in the famous " Mrs Siddons as the Tragic Muse " (see page 301) and in " Miss Emily Pott as *Thais* " (preceding page). This was the side most admired by his contemporaries, and we must admit that Reynolds had a rare power of dramatic presentation, which found its happiest outlet when he was dealing with contemporary subjects. " The

Photo : W. A. Mansell & Co.

" THE THAMES NEAR TWICKENHAM " BY RICHARD WILSON.

Capt. Ford's Collection.

Perfect in its rendering of the light in the sky and on the water, this wonderful landscape anticipates Constable in the absolute fidelity with which it mirrors the sweet natural beauty of English scenery.

Tragic Muse " is something of a wreck to-day, because in his desire to emulate the deep, rich colouring of the Venetians, Reynolds made use of bitumen, a pigment which gives brilliant immediate results but never dries, and in time trickles down a canvas in channels, ruining its surface. This pigment, which liquefies like asphalt when the sun is hot, is chiefly responsible for the poor condition to-day of many paintings by Reynolds, and it must be admitted that as a *craftsman* he was not so particular a. Wilson and Hogarth, who were more careful in their choice of pigments.

When Sir Joshua was sixty-six he lost the sight of his left eye, and from this calamity and the dread of losing the other, which was threatened, he never recovered. For three years he lingered on, seeing his friends and bearing his infirmity with fortitude, but the will to live was gone when he could no longer practise his art with assurance. He died on February 23, 1792, and was buried in state at St. Paul's Cathedral.

"I know of no man who has passed through life with more observation than Reynolds," said Dr. Johnson ; " when Reynolds tells me anything, I consider myself as possessed of an idea the more." Sir Joshua himself was distinguished by his literary abilities, and his " Discourses on Painting," which formed his yearly addresses to the students of the Royal Academy, are treasured and read to-day both for their literary merit and their instructive art teaching.

XIII

EIGHTEENTH-CENTURY BRITISH PORTRAITURE

THE ART OF GAINSBOROUGH, ROMNEY, RAEBURN, HOPPNER, AND LAWRENCE

§ 1

SHORTLY before little Joshua Reynolds celebrated his fourth birthday in the West of England, there was born in the Eastern Counties a babe destined to become his greatest rival in life and death. Thomas Gainsborough was born in 1727 at Sudbury, in Suffolk. He was one of a large family, his father being a wool manufacturer and clothier of moderate means, while his mother was a woman of education, the sister of a schoolmaster and herself a skilful painter of flowers. Thomas inherited his mother's love of Nature and her talent for art, and spent his boyhood rambling about the countryside and sketching the scenery round Sudbury. His gift for catching a likeness revealed itself early. One day, having seen a man robbing an orchard, he made a quick sketch of him, with the result that the robber was recognised from Gainsborough's drawing and arrested. The boy's faculty for copying, however, was not always exercised in the interests of law and order; and on another occasion, when he desired to play truant, he forged his father's handwriting in a letter to the schoolmaster, asking for a day's holiday. The ruse succeeded, but was subsequently found out, and seeing clearly that the boy would work at nothing bu his drawing and his sketching, the father wisely sent his son at the age of fifteen to London to study art under the French engraver Henri Gravelot. Young Gainsborough also studied at the St. Martin's Lane Academy, and later became the pupil of the portrait-painter Francis Hayman (1708–76), with whom he con-

"PORTRAIT OF MRS. SIDDONS," BY THOMAS GAINSBOROUGH.

National Gallery, London.

The most popular of all Gainsborough's portraits of women, this picture represents the celebrated actress, Sarah Kemble, afterwards Mrs. Siddons, in her prime. She was the daughter of an actor and the sister of John Philip Kemble. The painting was in the possession of the great actress till the day of her death, and Mrs. Jameson relates that once she found Mrs. Siddons, when she was seventy, seated besides this portrait, and " the likeness was still remarkable."

tinued nearly four years.   In 1745 he returned to his native
town of Sudbury, where he began practice as a portrait-
painter and occasionally painted a small landscape for his
own pleasure.

Unlike Reynolds, who was " wedded :o his art," Gainsborough married when he was only nineteen. He fell in
love with Margaret Burr, a beautiful girl of eighteen, who
fortunately possessed an income of £200 a year of her own,
and as no obstacles were raised to their wedding he boy-
and-girl couple settled down at Ipswich, where Gainsborough soon acquired a considerable local reputation as a
portrait-painter. Here his two daughters were born and
the painter led a happy domestic life, sketching in the
country between the intervals of his professional portraiture and spending his evenings playing the violin—for
he was devoted to music—either in his own home or in the
houses of some of his friends.

In 1760 he was tempted to leave this simple life at
Ipswich and moved to Bath, a fashionable centre to which
everyone who was anyone in London society came sooner
or later.   From a professional point of view this move was
the beginning of Gainsborough's fortune, for the fashionable
world soon flocked to the studio of this " new man " who
made his sitters look so august and distinguished, and the
modest provincial, who had begun painting three-quarter
lengths at five guineas apiece, now asked eight guineas, and
was soon able to increase his figure to something nearer
London prices.   But while his fortune waxed, his happiness
waned, and having now secured the entry into the fashionable world, Gainsborough began to pay attention to other
ladies and so excite his wife's jealousy. His home life was
no longer simple or happy, and as time went on his private
troubles increased, for both Mrs. Gainsborough and his
two daughters became subject to mental derangement.   To
the world, however, he continued to show a cheerful face,
and his sprightly conversation and humour made Gainsborough a welcome favourite in all society.

In time the fame of the Bath painter spread to London,
where Gainsborough occasionally exhibited at the Society

of Artists, but though in 1768 he was chosen as one of the foundation members of the Royal Academy, he did not immediately leave Bath.   He came there when he was thirty-three ; and it was not till he was forty-seven that he was persuaded to move to London.   In 1774 he took a part of Schomberg House in Pall Mall, and his success was immediate.   " The King sent for him and Duchesses besieged his studio."   Society was rent in twain, divided into a Reynolds faction and a Gainsborough faction, and under these circumstances it is not altogether surprising that Sir Joshua's jealousy did not allow him to be quite fair to his rival, whose power of securing a likeness he once formally denied.

Many stories are told of the rivalry between the two painters, and they have mostly increased with the telling in the course of years.   As an example of the growth of legends, we may cite the widely circulated story that Reynolds at an Academy banquet once proposed the health of " Mr. Gainsborough, the greatest landscape-painter of the day " whereupon Richard Wilson is said to have retorted, " Ay, and the greatest portrait-painter, too."

The original version of this incident is told by Thomas Wright in his *Life of Richard Wilson*, published in 1824, and here we learn that the dialogue took place, not at an Academy banquet, but at the Turk's Head in Gerrard Street, shortly after Gainsborough had arrived in London from Bath.   Meeting Richard Wilson there, Reynolds in a bantering spirit said, " Have you heard, sir, that our greatest landscape-painter has come to Town ? "

" Nay, Sir Joshua," retorted Wilson, " you mean our greatest portrait-painter."   Thus what was originally a piece of good-humoured chaff between two great artists has been twisted by inaccurate repetition into a display of maliciousness on both sides.

Nevertheless it must be admitted that here was a decided coolness between Reynolds and Gainsborough, and this was natural enough, for not only were the two men competitors for the patronage of Society, they were also temperament-ally too far apart to understand one another completely.

" With Reynolds," Sir Walter Armstrong has said, " deliberation counted for much ; Gainsborough's good things are impromptu." The seriousness and slight pomposity of Reynolds could not mix easily with the free-and-easy gaiety of Gainsborough. To Gainsborough, Reynolds seemed something of a pedant ; to Reynolds, Gainsborough appeared rather a frivolous person. For many years neither missed many opportunities of getting a " dig " at the other.

In his discourse to the Academy students in 1778, Reynolds observed that blue should not be massed together in a picture, whereupon Gainsborough proceeded subsequently to paint his famous " Blue Boy " and, by his brilliant success with the boy's blue dress, put Reynolds in the wrong. It is highly probable that the blues which figure so prominently in his beautiful portrait of " Mrs. Siddons " (see page 311) are another expression of Gainsborough's disapproval of Sir Joshua's dogmatic teaching. We have only to compare this Gainsborough portrait with Reynolds's painting of the same actress as " The Tragic Muse " to realise the difference between the two artists. Reynolds painted his picture in 1783, Gainsborough his in 1784, when Mrs. Siddons was twenty-eight ; but, though actually a year younger, everyone will agree that the actress looks years older in Sir Joshua's picture. Reynolds emphasised the intellectual qualities of the great tragedienne, his endeavour was to show the sublimity of her mind ; Gainsborough was content to show the charm and vivacity of her person, and that is why Mrs. Siddons looks younger in his portrait. Another temperamental difference between the two artists is shown in their hobbies ; while Sir Joshua was interested in Literature and delighted in conversing with the learned, Gainsborough's ruling passion was Music. He was not only a good musician himself but was completely carried away by the playing of others. Once when a talented amateur, a Colonel Hamilton, was playing the violin at his house, Gainsborough called out, " Go on, go on, and I will give you the picture of ' The Boy at the Stile ' which you have so often wished to buy of me." The

MISS HAVERFIELD, BY GAINSBOROUGH (1727–88).

Wallace Collection, London.

The most charming of all Gainsborough's portraits of children, this picture admirably
illustrates the lightness of his touch. This little lady is as exquisite and fragile as the
flower growing at her feet.

315

"THE MARKET CART," BY GAINSBOROUGH.
National Gallery, London.

This artist confessed once that he painted "portraits for money, landscapes for love."
His delight in the simple happiness of country life is eloquently expressed in this masterly
rendering of a typical scene in rural England.

Colonel " went on " and eventually returned home with the coveted picture as his reward. This love of music makes itself felt in Gainsborough's pictures, which are lyrical, the paintings of an artist who sings, while those of Reynolds are more philosophical, the pictures of a man who thinks in paint.

Of all the English eighteenth-century portraitists Gainsborough is the lightest and airiest, and in freshness of colour and in gracefulness without affectation his portraits more than rival those of Reynolds. His " Miss Haverfield " (see page 315) is more of a little lady than any of Sir Joshua's children, and though her gentility may not be accounted a virtue, and while we must admit that Reynolds's " Age of Innocence " has more psychological profundity, yet we cannot find another portrait in the world which excels this Gainsborough in rendering the flower-like charm of childhood.

Though by his portraits Gainsborough acquired so considerable a fortune that he could afford to have country houses at Richmond and in Hampshire as well as his town house, his landscapes rarely found buyers, and remained " admired and unsold till they stood ranged in long lines from his hall to his painting-room." At his death his house was filled with his own landscapes. The end came with some suddenness. A pain in the neck, to which he had paid little attention, turned out to be due to a cancer, and when the physicians pronounced his case hopeless, he settled his affairs with composure and prepared to meet death. He was particularly anxious to be reconciled with Sir Joshua and begged him to visit him on his death-bed. When Reynolds came an affecting reconciliation took place : " We are all going to Heaven," said Gainsborough, " and Vandyck is of the party." Thomas Gainsborough died on August 2, 1788, and by his own desire was buried as privately as possible in Kew Churchyard. Sir Joshua Reynolds was one of the pall bearers, and in his presidential address to the Academy in the following year he paid an eloquent tribute to the memory of his former rival.

§ 2

The third great English portrait-painter of the eighteenth century was George Romney, who never exhibited at the Royal Academy, and all his life was hostile to that institution and to its president, Sir Joshua Reynolds. Romney was born at Dalton-in-Furness, Lancashire, in 1734, when Reynolds was a boy of eleven and Gainsborough a child of seven. He was one of eleven children, and his father was a man of many occupations—farmer, builder, cabinet-maker, and dealer—and little prosperous in anything he undertook. George Romney consequently had his education neglected : at eleven years old he was helping his father in the workshop, and there he displayed precocious ability in drawing portraits of the workmen and other people. When he was twenty he made the acquaintance of a vagabond artist named Christopher Steele, who journeyed from place to place making portraits, and in 1755 this man secured Romney as his pupil and took him with him on his travels. In the following year Romney fell ill with a fever and was tenderly nursed by his landlady's daughter, a domestic servant named Mary Abbott, and being a highly-strung romantic youth Romney married this girl in the first burst of his gratitude, and later found her utterly unsuited to be his mate. Steele meanwhile had settled at York and summoned Romney to join him there as soon as he was well enough, and since he was not earning enough to keep a wife Mrs. Romney had to go back to service when her husband rejoined the man to whom he was apprenticed.

There was little good that Steele, a mediocre artist and a loose liver, could teach Romney, and their association was more profitable to the older than the younger man, and after a year or two in bondage at York, Romney managed to purchase his freedom, and he then made a home for his wife at Kendal. With this town as his headquarters, he rambled about the Lake Country painting heads at £2 2s. each and small full-lengths at £6 6s., till in 1762 he had at last managed to save a hundred pounds.

Romney was now twenty-eight, and he felt that if ever

'THE PARSON'S DAUGHTER," BY ROMNEY (1734–1802,
National Gallery, London.

Known throughout the world by the title under which the picture was first exhibited,
this pensive beauty, whose powdered auburn hair is bound up with green ribbon, is still
an enigma whose identity has never been discovered. The charm of her person and the
delicacy of the painting have combined to make this Romney's masterpiece.

he was to make his fortune by his art he must seek it in
London. So giving £70 to his wife, with the remaining
£30 he came to the capital, where he at once competed for
a prize offered by the Society of Arts for an historical picture
on " The Death of Wolfe." Romney was at first awarded
a prize of fifty guineas for his version of this theme, but
later the judges reversed their verdict and awarded the

fifty guineas to John Hamilton Mortimer (1741–79), a young friend of Richard Wilson and Reynolds, and gave Romney only a consolation prize of twenty-five guineas. Romney, not unnaturally, believed this reversal of the first judgment to be the result of favouritism, and to the end of his life he thought that it had been brought about by Reynolds, who had been actuated by fear of a rival. In 1766 Romney again gained a premium for his " Death of King Edward " from the Society of Arts, to which he was now admitted a member, and henceforward he exhibited regularly at the Society's exhibitions, but always held aloof from the Academy. In 1767 he paid a visit to his wife and two daughters at Kendal, and returning alone to London soon established himself in public favour, and in the early 'seventies he was making over   thousand a year by his profession. He thought the time had now come when he should visit Italy, and in March 1773 he set off for that country in the company of a brother artist, Ozias Humphrey (1742–1810), who afterwards became a famous miniature-painter. At Rome, Romney separated himself from his fellow traveller and led a hermit's life, shunning the society of his compatriots, and giving his whole time to work and study. In 1775 he made his way back to England via Venice and Parma, studying with advantage the work of Correggio in the latter city, and reaching London in the month of July. Greatly improved now in his colouring and confident in his increased knowledge and power, Romney boldly took the house and studio of Francis Cotes, R.A. (1725–70), who had been one of the chief of the older portrait-painters, at 32 Cavendish Square, and there seriously entered into competition with Reynolds. Gainsborough, it will be remembered, did not come to London till 1779, so that Romney, though the younger man, was the first formidable rival that Reynolds had to endure. Charging £15 15s. for a head life-size, Romney soon found himself surrounded by sitters, and Reynolds was alarmed at the way in which his practice for a time was diminished by the painter to whom he contemptuously referred as " the man in Cavendish Square." Later Romney had so

Photo : W. A. Mansell & Co.

LADY HAMILTON, BY ROMNEY.

National Gallery, London.

For nearly five years Romney neglected wealthy sitters in order that he might devote himself without interruption to portraying, in various guises, the inexhaustable fascina--tion of the wonderful woman known to history as " Nelson's enchantress."

many commissions that he was able to put up his prices, but even so he received only about 80 guineas for the full-length portraits which now fetch many thousands of pounds when they are sold by auction at Christie's. When Reynolds died he left a fortune of £80,000 earned by his brush, and though Romney was not successful to this extent he made a good living, his income in the year 1785 being £3635.

But Romney was never a mere money-grubber, and when at the age of forty-eight he first met his most famous sitter, the dazzlingly beautiful Emma Lyon, known to history as Lady Hamilton, he was so fascinated by her extraordinary personality, that time after time he refused all kinds of wealthy sitters in order that he might continue uninterruptedly to paint the lovely Emma. In 1782 the future Lady Hamilton was a mere girl of twenty or twenty-one, living under the protection of Charles Greville, who four years later—when he was in money difficulties—heartlessly handed her over to his uncle, Sir William Hamilton, who treated her more kindly and honourably. For five years Romney painted this fascinating creature continually in a variety of characters, and though gossip soon busied itself making scandal out of their relations, there is no evidence that the painter's affection for her was anything but platonic. Of his many paintings of her we reproduce one of the most charming, the " Lady Hamilton " (see preceding page) in the National Portrait Gallery.

In the art of George Romney there is a peculiar feminine quality which gives an extraordinary winsomeness, almost a pathos, to his paintings of frail women. There is a paternal tenderness rather than the passion of a lover in his paintings of Emma Hamilton and of another famous beauty, Mrs. Robinson, known as " Perdita " (see page 327). Romney's beautiful portrait of the last in the Wallace Collection was done while this gifted actress was under the protection of the Prince of Wales, afterwards George IV. But that royal rascal soon tired of her, and at the age of twenty-four she had already been abandoned by " the first gentleman in Europe." When he sent her away the Prince gave her a bond for £20,000 ; but he never paid it, and " Perdita " Robinson died in 1800, poor and paralysed.

Nobody has yet discovered who was the original of Romney's most famous masterpiece, " The Parson's Daughter " (see page 319), but we may imagine that this beautiful creature, with a gentle melancholy behind her smile, was also one of the frail sisterhood to which both Lady Hamilton and Mrs. Robinson belonged. The extraordinary sweetness and simplicity of Romney's portraiture of women has the same tender reverence for the sex that we find in *The Vicar of Wakefield*, and the peculiar winningness of Romney is perhaps best described by placing him as the Goldsmith of English painting.

Though he never brought his wife and family to London —where it is probable that they would have felt ill at ease in a sphere to which they were not accustomed—Romney supported them in comfort, and when after years of hard work in London his health broke down, he went back to his wife at Kendal. She received him without reproaches, and under her affectionate care the tired, worn-out genius " sank gently into second childhood and the grave." He died at Kendal on November 15, 1802.

§ 3

The greatest portrait-painter that Scotland has ever produced, Sir Henry Raeburn, R.A., belonged to a younger generation than any of the artists whose lives we have so far recounted. Raeburn was born at Stockbridge, a suburb of Edinburgh, on March 4, 1756, and so was thirty-three years younger than Reynolds, twenty-nine years younger than Gainsborough, and twenty-two years younger than Romney. His father, a well-to-do manufacturer, died when young Henry was six, and his elder brother then looked after him, had him educated at Heriot's School—where he showed his leaning by making caricatures of his masters and school-fellows—and apprenticed him at the age of fifteen to an Edinburgh goldsmith. There he also began to paint miniatures, and these gradually attracted attention

SIR JOHN SINCLAIR, BY RAEBURN

This Highland Chieftian in the tartan of his clan is one of the most superb male portraits ever painted. In truth, distinction. and dignity without haughtiness, Raeburn's masterpiece surpasses the elegance of Vandyck and rivals the supreme achievements of Velazquez.

till Raeburn broadened out into oil portraits and land-scapes.

Like Gainsborough, he loved to ramble about the country-side sketching, and in one of his open-air sketches he intro-duced the figure of a charming young lady whom he had seen crossing the meadow. Some time later this young lady presented herself at Raeburn's studio to have her portrait painted. She was the widow of a wealthy French-man, Count Leslie, but herself a Scottish girl, her maiden name having been Ann Edgar. During their sittings the artist and his model fell deeply in love with each other ; there was no one to hinder their union, so they were quickly married, and at the age of twenty-two young Raeburn found himself the possessor of a charming wife, a fine house at Edinburgh, and a comfortable income which made " pot-boiling " unnecessary.

Under these happy circumstances he rapidly came to the front as a portrait-painter. About 1785 he visited London and called on Sir Joshua Reynolds, who, himself now almost an Old Master, showed the young artist every possible kindness and gave him much good advice. Reynolds urged him to visit Rome and " saturate " himself in Michael Angelo, generously offering to lend him money for the journey. This, however, Raeburn did not need, but he followed the advice of the veteran, and went to Rome, where he remained for nearly two years and greatly strengthened his art. In 1787 he returned to Edinburgh, and soon after, inheriting some property from his brother, he built himself the splendid studio and picture gallery in York Place, which still stands and is known as " Raeburn House."

From this time on till the day of his death in 1823, the career of Raeburn was an unbroken sequence of happiness and success. Acting, it is said, on the advice of Lawrence, he wisely preferred to be the best painter in Edinburgh rather than one of several good painters in London. But though he never resided in England, he exhibited regularly at the Academy from 1792 to the year of his death ; he was elected an Associate in 1812 and made a full Academician three years later. He was knighted when George IV visited

Edinburgh in 1822 and soon afterwards appointed His Majesty's Limner for Scotland.

Raeburn was probably wise to remain in Scotland, for it is by no means certain that the rugged truthfulness which was the chief characteristic of his portraiture would have pleased London society. He was the most vigorous of all the eighteenth-century British portrait-painters, and none of them succeeded so well as he did in setting on canvas the splendid figure of a man. Though he has left us many noble and dignified paintings of women, Raeburn is held to have excelled himself in male portraiture, and his master-piece, " Sir John Sinclair " (see page 324), can hold its own for vitality, solidity, and dignity with any painted man in existence.

Raeburn was one of the most methodical and industrious of all the world's great portrait-painters. He rose at seven, breakfasted at eight, entered his studio at nine, and worked there till five in the afternoon. It is said that he spent more time looking at his sitters than in painting them, for he would search the countenance before him till he had pene-trated to the character of the person, and then beginning with forehead, chin, nose, and mouth, he would paint away rapidly, never making any preliminary drawing, and never using a mahl-stick to support his brush. His method was free and vigorous, and the results he obtained by it preserved the freedom and vigour of his process.

Though money is not everything in art, it is a rough-and-ready index to the estimation in which a painter is held, and therefore it may be mentioned here that the sale-room record for a British portrait was made in 1911 by a Raeburn, which fetched 22,300 guineas at Christie's.

§ 4

Within the space of this OUTLINE it is not possible to enumerate all the talented painters who made England during the eighteenth century the most prolific country in Europe for the production of notable works of art. The wealth of the country and the patronage extended to art

Photo : W. A. Mansell & Co.

MRS. MARY ROBINSON, BY ROMNEY.

Wallace Collection, London.

Famous as " Perdita," this beautiful actress was at one time loved by the Prince of Wales ,afterwards George IV, but though a reigning beauty in her day her vogue did not last, and she died in 1800 poor and paralysed.

by the Court and Society brought painters from all over the world to London, and in addition to the native-born artists many foreign painters settled in London, among them being the two American historical painters, John Singleton Copley (1737–1815) and Benjamin West (1738–1820), who succeeded Reynolds as President of the Royal Academy.

In portraiture, however, the true heir of Reynolds was John Hoppner (1758–1810), who, though born at White-chapel, was from childhood brought in touch with the high personages he was afterwards to paint. His mother was employed at Court, and his father—though there is some mystery about his birth—is said to have been a surgeon. George III was certainly interested in the boy when he was a chorister at the Chapel Royal, and perceiving his aptitude for art he made the lad a small allowance, and in 1765 got him admitted as a student to the Academy schools. There Hoppner gained the gold medal in 1782, and later when he settled at 18 Charles Street, St. James's Square—close to Carlton House—he at once had the favour of the Court. He painted Mrs. Jordan for the Prince of Wales, and the three princesses for the King, and soon became the fashion. Though too much influenced by Reynolds to be considered a very original artist, and too hard as a rule in his colour and not strong enough in his drawing to be considered that great man's equal, Hoppner has nevertheless left us many charming portraits, among which "The Countess of Oxford" (see opposite page) is usually considered to be his master-work. In this thoughtful head we see that Hoppner, like Reynolds, was also a scholar and a thinker, and he not only had great intelligence but the capacity to express his thoughts clearly and well. He was associated with Gifford of the *Quarterly Review*, to the first numbers of which he contributed some brilliant articles, which do credit to his powers of literary expression, to his artistic judgment, and to his goodness of heart, but, owing to his intimate relationship with this famous Whig periodical and its editor, he gradually lost the favour of the Court, which was given to the Tory party and its protégé, Thomas Lawrence.

"THE ARTIST AND HER DAUGHTER," BY E. L. VIGÉE LEBRUN
(1755–1842).

The Louvre, Paris.

One of the first woman-painters to reach high distinction in her art, Mme Elizabeth Louise Vigée Lebrun painted Queen Marie Antoinette in her youth and lived late into the nineteenth century. She married very young, and this charming portrait of herself and her daughter was painted shortly before the outbreak of the French Revolution.

22

" Exhibition of Youth " in the Place Dauphine, which was open for only *two hours*.

At the last Salon held under the old monarchy in 1789 only 350 pictures were exhibited : in 1791 the National Assembly decreed that an exhibition open to all artists, French and foreign, should be held in the Louvre, and the number of pictures shown was 794. In the year of the Terror (1793) the number of exhibits exceeded 1000 : in 1795 the number of pictures shown increased to 3048. These figures tell their own story, and show that the first thing the French Revolution did for art was to give painters a fuller liberty to display their work to the public. Further, notwithstanding the exhausted state of the finances, the Revolutionary Government encouraged artists by distributing annual prizes to a total value of 442,000 francs, and began the systematic organisation of public museums. On the 27th July 1793 the Convention decreed that a museum should be opened in the Louvre, and that art treasures collected from the royal palaces, from monasteries, and from the houses of aristocrats who had fled the country should be placed there. At the same time a sum of 100,000 francs was voted for the further purchase of works of art.

While in some parts of the country an ignorant and savage mob ruthlessly destroyed many precious monuments, libraries, and art treasures, the leaders of the Revolution throughout showed a special solicitude not only for contemporary art but also for the monuments of the past. Yet while the Revolution did everything it could to foster contemporary art, and to preserve and popularise the best art of the past, it could not produce one really great master of painting or sculpture. Now, if ever, we might expect to find a realism and a rude, savage strength in art ; yet the typical painting of the French revolutionary period is cold and correct, and its chief defect is its bloodlessness. While in England the taste, as we have seen, was all for a happy Romanticism in art, the taste of revolutionary France was for a stern Classicism. A nation aspiring to recover the lost virtues of antiquity was naturally disposed to find its ideal art in the antique, and just as politically its eye was on republican Rome rather than on Athens, so its Classicism in art was Roman rather than Greek. The man who gave a new direction to French painting was Jacques Louis David (1748–1825), who, curiously enough, was a distant relative of Boucher, and, for a time, worked under that master, whose art in later years he cordially detested. Later he became the pupil of Vien (1716–1809), whom he accompanied to Rome when Vien was appointed director of the French Academy in that city. In Rome David became absorbed in the study of the antique ; and began painting pictures of classical subjects, which were well received when exhibited in Paris. During the Revolution David became an enthusiastic supporter of Robespierre, and though he was in danger for a time after the fall of Robespierre, he escaped the perils at the end of the Terror by wisely devoting himself to art and eschewing politics. When the Directory created the Institute of France on the ruins of the old monarchical academies, David was appointed one of the two original members of the Fine Arts section and charged with the delicate mission of selecting the other members.

Henceforward David was omnipotent in French art. Like so many other revolutionaries, he was completely carried away by the genius of the First Consul, who seemed to him the right Cæsar for the new Romans. One morning, after Bonaparte had given him a sitting for a head, David spoke enthusiastically of the General to his pupils. " He is a man to whom altars would have been erected in ancient times ; yes, my friends, Bonaparte is my hero." But the portrait of his hero was never completed, and only the head remains to-day, for Napoleon disliked long sittings and did not care for exact likenesses. What he demanded from an artist was a picture to rouse the admiration of the people, and to satisfy this demand David painted " Bonaparte crossing the Alps," " Napoleon distributing the Eagles to his Army," and similar pictures which, though correct and precise in drawing, seem cold, strained, and dull to-day.

The best works of David are not his official pictures, but some of his portraits, which have more force and life.

" DONA ISABEL CORBO DE PORCEL," BY GOYA (1746–1828).

National Gallery, London.

Unrivalled as a satirist when painting people he disliked, Goya could also render marvellously, as we see here, the ethereal charm of a Spanish beauty of aristocratic lineage. At a time when all artistic Europe was in raptures over the " antique," Goya anchored his art to Nature and became the greatest painter of his age.

The most celebrated of these portraits is his " Madame
Recamier " (see page 345), now in the Louvre, though the
painter himself did not regard it as more than an unfinished sketch which he once threatened to destroy. The
sitter greatly displeased David by leaving him when the
portrait was half finished and going to his pupil Gerard
(1770–1837), who had suddenly become the fashion, to have
another portrait of herself painted by him. A few years
later Madame Recamier, tired of Gerard's flattering portraiture, came back to David and begged him to go on with
his picture. " Madame," he replied, " artists are as
capricious as women. Suffer me to keep your picture in
the state where *we* left it."

After Waterloo and the restoration of the Bourbons,
David, who had taken so prominent a part in the Revolution,
was exiled from France in 1816, and not being allowed to
go to Rome as he wished, he settled in Brussels, where he
continued painting classical pictures, now chiefly of Greek
subjects, till he died in 1825. Even in exile David was still
regarded as the head of his school, and few painters of so
moderate a talent have so profoundly influenced the art
of Europe. He completely crushed for the time being the
ideals of Watteau and his school and of Boucher—" cursed
Boucher," " that Boucher of ridiculous memory "—as he
called him ; and as a good republican he delighted other
republicans by maintaining that the art of the last three
Louis represented " the most complete decadence of taste
and an epoch of corruption." To David and his pupils
Europe owes that revival of classical subjects which was a
feature of nineteenth-century painting in all north-western
Europe, and France owes him in addition that tradition of
fine drawing which has characterised her art for the last
century.

§ 2

Most attractive of all the portraitists of this period is
the woman artist Madame Elizabeth Louise Vigée Lebrun
(1755–1842). Her father, a portrait-painter himself, died
when she was only twelve years old, and his daughter carried

on his practice almost at once, for when she was only fifteen she was already painting portraits with success and talent. While still young she married Lebrun, a prosperous and enterprising picture-dealer, who managed her affairs well, and whose stock of Old Masters afforded the young artist many models which she studied with good results. In 1783 Vigée Lebrun was admitted to the French Academy, and during the last years of the French monarchy she was a favourite at Court and painted several portraits of Marie Antoinette and her children. In 1789, alarmed at the way things were going in France, she went to Italy, where she was received with enthusiasm and made a member of the Academies of Rome, Parma, and Bologna. Thence she went to Vienna, where she stayed three years, and subsequently visiting Prague, Dresden, Berlin, and St. Petersburg, she only returned to France in 1801. Thus she escaped the Revolution altogether and saw little of the Empire, for about the time of the Peace of Amiens she came to England, where she stayed three years, and then visited Holland and Switzerland, finally returning to France in 1809.

Entirely untouched by the Revolution and by the wave of Classicism which followed it, Mme. Vigée Lebrun was a cosmopolitan artist whose art belonged to no particular country, and whose style had more in common with English Romanticism than with the asceticism then in vogue in France. Among all her portraits none is more charming than the many she painted of herself, and of these the best known and most popular is the winning " Portrait of the Artist and her Daughter " (see page 337) at the Louvre. Though in time she belongs to the revolutionary era, Mme. Lebrun is, as regards her art, a survival of the old aristocratic portrait-painters of monarchical France.

§ 3

How great was the influence of David on the painters of his generation is revealed by the tragic story of Antoine Jean Gros (1771–1835), who killed himself because he

"THE MAJA NUDE," BY GOYA.

The Prado, Madrid.

This unconventional portrait of a Duchess, said to have had a weakness for the artist, is one of the most famous paintings of the nude. A companion picture exists in which the Duchess is shown in the same attitude, only clothed, and the story goes that this second picture was painted for the Duke, and the one illustrated for the artist's own pleasure

343

thought he was bringing disgrace on the tradition of his master. Gros entered David's studio in 1785, and though he was unsuccessful when he tried for the Prix de Rome in 1792, in the following year his master helped him to get a passport for Italy, and so Gros got as far as Genoa, where in 1796 he made the acquaintance of Josephine, afterwards Empress. Josephine carried him off to Milan and presented him to Bonaparte, who took a liking to the young man, attached him to his staff, and allowed him to paint that wonderful portrait, now in the Louvre, of " Napoleon at Arcole " (see page 346), which is the most haunting and poetic of all the many portraits of the Emperor.

Thenceforward the career of Gros was outwardly a series of triumphs. Owing to his experiences in Italy—where, in 1799, he was besieged with the French army at Genoa— he had a closer acquaintance with the realities of war than any of his artist contemporaries.

In Genoa and elsewhere Gros had made a particular study of the work of Rubens and Vandyck, and in his canvases he now endeavoured to emulate the opulent colour of the Flemish School. Consequently his battle-pictures were so informed with knowledge and inspired by feeling and fine colour that they aroused high enthusiasm in Paris. When his picture " Les Pestiférés de Jaffa " was shown in the Salon of 1804, all the young artists of the day combined to hang a wreath on the frame in honour of the life, truth, and colour in the work of Gros.

Already there was a beginning of a reaction in Paris against the ascetic Classicism of David, and while Gros, as an old pupil of that master, still commanded the respect of the classicists, his spirited renderings of contemporary events pleased the younger generation who were later to give birth to the Romanticists. Thus, for a time, Gros pleased both camps in painting, and his position was unimpaired when Napoleon fell and the Bourbons were restored. In 1816 he was made a member of the Institute, he was commissioned to decorate the cupola of the Panthéon, and in 1824, on the completion of this work, he was created a Baron.

Meanwhile David, exiled in Brussels, was uneasy about

the style of his former pupil, whom, on leaving Paris, he had left in charge of the Classical Movement. From Brussels he wrote constantly to Gros, begging him to cease painting " these futile subjects and circumstantial pictures " and to devote his talent to " fine historical pictures." By this David meant, not those paintings of the battles of

Photo : W. A. Mansell & Co.

MME. RECAMIER, BY DAVID (1748-1825).

The Louvre, Paris.

Reputed to be the most brilliant conversationalist of her age, Mme. Recamier was famous for her " salons," which were attended by all the most eminent men of the Directory and First Empire. This refined and sympathetic portrait shows the most gracious and human side of a painter who was fanatical in his adoration of Greek and Roman art. Even the furniture in this picture is said to have been made from classical models designed by David.

Aboukir, Eylau, the Pyramids, etc., which *were* fine historical pictures, but paintings depicting some incident in the history of Greece or Rome. These alone, according to David, were the fit themes for a noble art, and he could not accept the rendering of events of his own times as true historical pictures. Unfortunately Gros, in his unbounded veneration for his old master, took David very

Photo : W. A. Mansell & Co.

"BONAPARTE AT ARCOLE," BY BARON GROS (1771–1835).

The Louvre, Paris.

A poetic portrait of the young Napoleon, as he was at the beginning of his Italian campaign, by an artist who finally committed suicide because he was unable to paint in accordance with his ideals.

seriously. He saw with alarm that the younger generation of painters were departing from the classical tradition and heading for Romanticism, and he blamed himself for leading them astray.

In the very year when he was made a Baron, his fellow-pupil, Girodet (1767–1824), died, and at the funeral of this follower of David, Gros lamented the loss of a great classic artist, saying : " For myself, not only have I not enough authority to direct the school, but I must accuse myself of being one of the first who set the bad example others have followed."

Conscience-stricken at falling away from his master's ideals, and particularly so when David died in the following year, Baron Gros now did violence to his own talent by forcing himself to paint subjects of which David would have approved. While the truth of his war pictures had shocked the Classic School, the artificiality of his new classical pictures roused the mocking laughter of the young and increasingly powerful Romantic School. His " Hercules and Diomed " in the Salon of 1835 was openly sneered at ; the younger critics treated him as a " dead man," till, wearied out and depressed by the disgrace and shame which he thought he had brought on the school of David, poor Baron Gros, on the 25th June 1835, lay down on his face in three feet of water at Meudon, where on the following day two boatmen discovered his body.

That leadership of the Classic School, for which Baron Gros, both by his art and his temperament, was utterly unfitted, was eventually assumed with honour and credit by his junior, Jean Dominique Auguste Ingres (1780–1867). A pupil of David and the winner of the Prix de Rome in 1801, Ingres was not at first regarded as a " safe " classic by the purists of that school. To these pedants, who worshipped hardly any art between the antique and Raphael, Ingres was suspicious because of his loudly proclaimed admiration of the Italian Primitives. On his way to Rome, Ingres had stopped at Pisa to study the frescoes by Benozzo Gozzoli and his contemporaries in the Campo Santo. " We ought to copy these men on our knees," said the young enthusiast, and his words were repeated to David, who regarded them as ominous.

Though he gained the prize in 1801, Ingres was not sent to Rome till 1806, and then he remained in Italy for nearly eighteen years. These were years of quiet, fruitful labour, during which the artist, in his own words, was " drawing to learn and painting to live," and by living abroad he escaped all that contemporary drama of victories and disasters, of changes of dynasties and changes of opinion, that was going on during this period in his own country. Nevertheless, from Italy he sent pictures now and again to Paris, where they attracted attention in the Salons, though they were criticised by the followers of David. When he exhibited in 1819 his " Paola and Francesca di Rimini " (see page 351), the work was pronounced to be " Gothic " in tendency, and in this small historical painting we can recognise the influence of the Primitives whom Ingres admired for the purity and precision of their drawing.

When Ingres returned to Paris in 1824 the battle between the Classicists and the Romanticists was in full swing, and with Girodet dead, David in exile and dying, and Gros incompetent, the former were glad to welcome the support of Ingres, and soon made him the chief of their party. Ingres was amazed and enchanted at his sudden popularity and the honours now thrust upon him. He was speedily elected to the Institute, and later was made a Grand Officer of the Legion of Honour and a Senator. The full story of the war between the Classicists and Romanticists must be reserved for a later chapter, but it may be said at once that Ingres threw himself heart and soul into the championship of the classics by precept and example.

But where Ingres differed from his predecessor David was, that with him it was the treatment rather than the subject which was all-important. A fanatic for drawing from the first, he held strong and peculiar views on Colour. " A thing well drawn is always well enough painted," he said ; and his own use of colour was merely to emphasise the drawing in his pictures. " Rubens and Vandyck," he argued, " may please the eye, but they deceive it—they

"CHARLES IV ON HORSEBACK," BY GOYA.

The Prado, Madrid.

Uncompromisingly truthful even in the portrayal of Royalty, Goya shows the King of Spain, who was a puppet in the hands of his dissolute wife, as " a monument of serene and complacent stupidity."

belong to a bad school of Colour, the School of Falsehood."
From his early Roman days Ingres had shown himself to be
a faultless draughtsman of the human figure, and his drawings and paintings of nudes are the works on which his fame
most surely rests to-day. The most celebrated, and perhaps
the most beautiful, of his works, " La Source " (see page
354), has an interesting history, for, though begun as a
study in 1824, it was not till 1856, when the artist was
seventy-six, that he turned it into a picture. One of the
most precious gems of painting in the Louvre, this picture
preserves the freshness of a young man's fancy, while it is
executed with the knowledge of a lifetime. " It is a fragment of Nature, and it is a vision," is the comment of a great
French critic on this picture.

If Ingres was the greatest artist the classical movement
produced in France, yet he belongs too much to the nineteenth century to be considered a true product of the
revolutionary and Napoleonic period. Indeed, the greatest
Continental artist of that period was not a Frenchman, and
it is to Spain that we must turn to find a man of outstanding genius whose protean art fully expresses the surging
thoughts and feelings of this time of changes.

§ 4

The life-story of Goya is as full of storm and stress as
that of his unhappy country, which between 1788 and 1815
saw more misery and more changes of government than
any other country in battle-scarred Europe. Under the
rule of Charles IV and his depraved consort, Queen Maria
Louisa, Spain was in a miserable condition ; its Court was a
frivolous, shallow imitation of Versailles, and its monarchy
and government were even more rotten and more corrupt
than those of France under Louis XVI. A young lieutenant
of the Guards, Manuel Godoy, was made Prime Minister
because he was the Queen's favourite lover, and the King was
a puppet in the hands of this Spanish Messalina. Public
offices were openly sold to the highest bidder, and eighteen
thousand priests drained the purse of the people and stifled

PAOLO AND FRANCESCA DI RIMINI," BY INGRES (1780–1867).
Chantilly.

An early example of the painting of this master, showing the delicacy and precision of his line and the extent to which he was first influenced by the work of the Italian primitives. While Paolo is embracing Francesca, her husband, Malatesta, is seen in the background drawing his sword to slay his brother Paolo.

351

their intellects. Art seemed dead and past the hope of revival till Goya came to Madrid.

Francisco José de Goya y Lucientes was born on March 30, 1746, that is to say, twelve years after Romney, and ten years before Raeburn. He was the son of a peasant in a village in Aragon, and legend relates that, like Giotto, he was found drawing sheep by an amateur who recognised the boy's talent and sent him in his fourteenth year as pupil to a painter in Saragossa. There the boy grew up strong, handsome, wild, and passionate, continually involved in love affairs and quarrels. In one of the last, three men were left wounded and bleeding, and as a result of this midnight affray Goya had to leave the city hurriedly.

In 1766 he was in Madrid, and there his adventurous disposition soon got him into trouble. He was wounded in some love quarrel, placed under police supervision, and chafing at this restraint he escaped from the city with a band of bull-fighters and sailed to Italy. At the end of the 'sixties he was in Rome, where he appears to have been much more interested in the teeming life of the people than in the antiquities of the city. Here again his amorousness got him into trouble, for it is said that one night he made his way into a nunnery, was nearly captured, and only escaped the gallows by a headlong flight from the city.

In 1771 he returned to Saragossa and found shelter in a monastery, where he seems to have reformed his manner of living, for four years later this scapegrace adventurer, the hero of a hundred fights, reappeared in Madrid as a respectable citizen, married to the sister of Bayen, a painter of good standing. Through his brother-in-law he got to know people of a better class, and he was finally introduced to the Court and permitted to paint the portrait of Charles III.

Goya's pictures of this period reflect the manners of the Spanish Court, for pictures like " The Swing " and " Blind Man's Buff " at Madrid are obviously imitations of Watteau and his school, as the Spanish Court imitated the artificiality of Versailles, only Goya, a cynic from his youth, does not give his figures the daintiness of the Frenchmen.

With almost brutal realism he depicts the rouge on the women's cheeks and the pencilling of their eyebrows, and seems to take a delight in unmasking their falseness and dissipation. While he was intelligent enough to perceive the rottenness of Spanish society, Goya was no moralist himself and lived the life of his time. Countless stories are told of his relations with women of high society, and Goya is said to have been the terror of all their husbands. In this connection one inevitably thinks of his famous double picture at Madrid, " The Maja Nude " (see page 343) and " The Maja Clothed," the latter being an almost exact reproduction of the former with the garments added, and these are so filmy, so expressive of the limbs underneath, that the second picture has justly been said to reveal a woman " naked in spite of her dress." The story runs that the lady was the Duchess of Alva, and that when the Duke desired to see Goya's work, the painter hurriedly produced the clothed portrait and concealed the other.

When Charles IV came to the throne Goya became still more firmly established in Court favour, though he produced the most impudent portraits of royalty that have ever been painted. Nowhere can we find a more pitiless exposure of serene stupidity than his " Charles IV on Horseback " (see page 349). " He sits there, asthmatic and fat, upon his fat asthmatic horse . . . like a Moloch," says Dr. Muther, " an evil god who has battened upon the life-blood of his people." When he painted the Queen Maria Louisa, Goya portrayed her as the brazen old courtesan she was ; he shows up the Crown Prince as a sly, spiteful, hypocritical meddler, and the favourite minister Godoy as a nincompoop and a panderer. When the French novelist Gautier first saw Goya's large portrait group of the Spanish Royal Family and its favourites, his comment was, " A grocer's family who have won the big lottery prize " ; and that is exactly the impression the picture gives us, a collection of stupid, ill-bred people who owe their fine clothes and position to no talent or merit of their own but to sheer luck. It is amazing that this daring satirist of royalty should have gone unpunished and

23

" LA SOURCE," BY INGRES.

The Louvre, Paris.

Begun as a study in 1824, this exquisite work, the painter's
masterpiece, was taken up again in 1856 and completed
when Ingres was seventy-six. It is unrivalled as a happy
blending of truth to Nature with ideal beauty.

"JOAN OF ARC AT RHEIMS," BY INGRES.

The Louvre. Paris.

The faultless drawing in this picture admirably illustrates the point of view of the artist who said, " A thing well drawn is always well enough painted."

355

unreproved, but the King and his family circle were themselves too stupid to realise that the artist was holding them all up to the ridicule of the world.

As, while outwardly a courtier, he insidiously undermined the pretences of the Spanish monarchy, so while appearing to respect the observances of Catholicism, Goya surreptitiously attacked the Church which was blinding the eyes of the people. In 1797 he began to produce a series of engravings which, under the title of " Caprices," pretended to be nothing more than flights of fancy, but which were in reality biting satires on the social, political, and ecclesiastical conditions of his age. He drew devout women with rolling eyes worshipping a scarecrow, priests drawling out the Litany with obvious indifference, and in one fantastic plate—which he had the audacity to dedicate to the King !—he showed a corpse rising from the grave and writing with its dead finger the word *Nada*, i.e. " Nothingness." It was tantamount to saying that the hope of immortality held out to the people was only a blind to make them endure want and misery without murmuring, while kings and priests grew fat at their expense. If the Court and high ecclesiastics were too stupid to comprehend Goya's message, the people understood, for the revolutionary era was at hand.

A more subtle example of Goya's anti-clerical tendency is the little picture in the National Gallery, " The Bewitched " (see page 358), in which, while professing to do no more than paint a stage scene from a popular comedy of the time, the artist shows us a priest frightened by demons in forms of a goat and jackasses.

Like most of the intellectual men in Spain, Goya had at first welcomed the coming of Napoleon, for anything seemed to promise a hope of better things than the old regime. But, later, the piteous spectacle of his country in the throes of warfare seemed to rouse the patriot in him, and he began to champion its rights in a series of the most moving paintings and engravings. In 1810 he began to execute a series of engravings entitled " The Disasters of War," which were absolutely a new thing in art. Hitherto

Photo : *Anderson.*   " A MILITARY EXECUTION IN 1808," BY GOYA.

The Prado, Madrid.

In this tragic picture of the execution of Spanish volunteers by Napoleon's soldiery, Goya reveals his sympathy with the patriots and his horror at the brutality of warfare. Goya was the first artist to attack Militarism.

357

"THE BEWITCHED," BY GOYA.

National Gallery, London.

A priest, frightened by demons in the form of jackasses, hurriedly pours oil into a lamp held by a goat. In this painting of a scene from a comic play, the artist satirises the Spanish clergy of his time and hints his opinion of the value of the "light" they profess to throw on the unknown.

Photo : *Anderson*.

"THE BULL-FIGHT", BY GOYA.

Accad. S. Fernando, Madrid.

The artist who painted all conceivable aspects of Spanish life, could not ignore this national institution, and in his paintings of bull-fights Goya displays a professional knowledge of the sport which he gained in his youth, when he ran away once with a band of bull-fighters.

artists, with few exceptions, had shown only the imposing side of war, its panoply and splendour, its daring and heroism. Goya was the first artist to make a deliberate and systematic impeachment of Militarism. Not only did he refuse to glorify the old adage that "it is sweet and decorous to die for one's country," but he persistently showed all the blood and misery with which military glory was bought. In his engravings of the war he shows the unchaining of the "human beast," and his prints of the torturing of prisoners and the shooting of deserters are ghastly in their revelation of raging madness and the distortions of death agonies.

In his paintings also Goya told the terrible story of the tragedies which ensued when the Spanish volunteers took up arms against Napoleon's soldiery. There is no more awful war picture in the world than Goya's painting of an incident in 1808 (see page 357), in which we see the gleam of the gun-barrels, and poor wretches who have been condemned by court-martial falling forward prone before the musket-fire of the troops. The despair of the condemned, and the cold-blooded energy of the executioners are appalling.

Yet while he lamented the sufferings of the patriots during the Peninsular War, Goya could not rejoice at the restoration of the Bourbons after the fall of Napoleon. For when King Ferdinand returned to Madrid in 1814, Goya saw that all hope of liberalism and freedom of thought had vanished, and that the powers of darkness, which for the time had been scared away, again settled on the land and obscured truth, progress, and enlightenment. The last "disaster of the war" was the resettlement of the Bourbons, who had "learnt nothing and forgotten nothing," on the throne of Spain, and Goya with his old fearlessness expressed his view of the matter in his engraving "The Death of Truth," in which he showed the naked figure of Truth suffering martyrdom at the hands of the priests.

We might expect that this outspoken work would have proved too much even for the most stupid, priest-ridden Court to swallow, but nothing that Goya could do ever brought home to royalty what the artist really thought of them and their government. King Ferdinand confirmed Goya's appointment as Court Painter, and even persuaded him to paint a portrait of him in the purple mantle of empire, but now the artist himself was too old and too sick at heart to play the hypocrite at Court and paint grandees with his tongue in his cheek. Gradually Goya withdrew from public life and established himself in a simple country house on the outskirts of Madrid. His wife and son were both dead, since 1791 he had himself been afflicted with deafness, and in this villa the lonely painter lived out his life in company with his art. His last protest against the tendencies of the time were some small paintings of the interiors of prisons and torture-chambers, in which he reminds us that the Inquisition had again raised its head under King Ferdinand. Among his last works were scenes of bull-fights, of the details of which Goya, in his youth, had acquired a professional knowledge. Greatly as all humanitarians must detest this horrid sport, its colour and movement appeal to the artistic sense, and the decorative aspect of the scene is the dominant note in Goya's renderings of this subject.

After nine years of this lonely life Goya seems to have felt himself no longer very secure in Spain. Perhaps he feared that the clerics would in the end perceive his purpose and have their revenge on him. At all events, in 1824 he sought and obtained leave of absence for six weeks to visit the sulphur springs of Plombières in Lorraine on account of his gout. But this appears to have been merely an excuse to get out of Spain, for he never went to Plombières, but after visiting Paris, settled at Bordeaux, where, on April 16, 1828, he died as the result of a stroke of apoplexy. In his last years he was not only stone deaf but half blind, and consequently his creative work in France was small, but one engraving remains to show that the old cynic never swerved from his faith and still had hope for the future. " Lux ex tenebris " is the pregnant title of this work of his old age, and in it he shows us a shaft of light falling on a dark spot of earth (Spain ?) and scaring away from it owls, ravens—and priests !

XV

THE RISE OF LANDSCAPE PAINTING

§ I

THE greatest difference between the art of the nine-teenth and that of the preceding centuries is the increasing importance attached to natural scenery. The Old Masters were not altogether inattentive to inanimate Nature, but it did not occur to them that scenery alone could be a sufficient subject for a picture. In the East, as we shall see in a later chapter, Nature had always pre-occupied the minds of the finest artists, and in China landscape was regarded as the highest branch of art ; but in Europe men thought otherwise, and it was only slowly that landscape crept forward from the background and gradually occupied the whole of the picture.

The artist who is usually considered to have been the father of modern landscape painting was a Frenchman, or rather a Lorrainer, Claude Gellée (1600–82), born near Mirecourt on the Moselle, who at an early age went to Rome, where he remained practically for the rest of his life. Claude's interest was entirely in Nature, and parti-cularly in the illumination of Nature. He was the first artist who " set the sun in the heavens," and he devoted his whole attention to portraying the beauty of light ; but though his aerial effects are unequalled to this day, and though his pictures were approved and collected in his own day by the King of Spain, Pope Urban VIII, and by many influential Cardinals, yet the appreciation of pure landscape was so limited then that Claude rarely dared to

" THE FIGHTING *TEMERAIRE* TOWED TO HER LAST BERTH," BY J. M. W. TURNER, R.A.

National Gallery, London.

The *Temeraire* fought at Trafalgar in 1805, and was broken up in 1838. With poetic imagination Turner visualises her last voyage, the old man-of-war looking almost ghostly in the silvery light of the moon, while the sun is setting on the tug that tows her home.

leave figures out of his pictures, and was obliged to choose subjects which were not simply landscapes but gave him an excuse for painting landscapes.

Nobody to-day pays very much attention to the little figures in Claude's " Marriage of Isaac and Rebecca " (see page 371) at the National Gallery. We are not disposed to ask which is Isaac and which Rebecca, or to try to discover what all these figures are doing, because to us the beauty of the landscape is an all-sufficient reason for the picture's existence. Our whole attention is given to the beautiful painting of the trees and the lovely view that lies between them, to the golden glow of the sky, to the flat surface of the water with its reflected light, and to the exquisite gradations of the tones by which the master has conveyed to us the atmosphere of the scene and the vastness of the distance he depicts.

Similarly, in his " Embarkation of the Queen of Sheba " (see page 369), we are at once conscious that the glorious rendering of the sun in the sky and of its rays on the rippled surface of the sea constitute the principal interest of the picture ; this was what primarily interested the painter, and his buildings, shipping, and people are only so many accessories with which he frames and presents to us his noble vision of light. But to Claude's contemporaries these titles and the figures which justified them had far more importance than they have to us, and it was by professing to paint subjects which the taste of his day deemed elevating and ennobling that Claude was able to enjoy prosperity and paint the landscapes which are truly noble.

Another Frenchman, also a contemporary of Claude, Nicolas Poussin (1594–1665), must be regarded as a pioneer of landscape painting, though he was also a figure painter of great ability who upheld the classic style of the antique in his Biblical and pagan figure subjects. Poussin also worked chiefly at Rome, and, having no son, adopted his wife's younger brother, Gaspar Dughet, who became known as Gaspar Poussin (1613–75), and under his brother-in-law's tuition developed into an excellent landscape painter.

For a little while, before his health was ruined by drink, he was in easy circumstances, for his paintings of domestic scenes and farm life were exceedingly popular, and he was better known to the people than any of his august contemporaries. All his principal works were engraved, and these coloured prints after Morland's pictures found their

Photo : W. A. Mansell & Co.

"THE EMBARKATION OF THE QUEEN OF SHEBA," BY CLAUDE
National Gallery, London.

One of the earliest and one of the grandest endeavours to paint the actual source of light, this picture has for two centuries been an inspiration to landscape painters by the beauty of its sky and the sunlight shining on the water.

way into many humble homes. It is probable that his well-known painting at the National Gallery, " The Interior of a Stable " (see page 366), was painted about 1791, which would nearly coincide with the period of Morland's greatest prosperity. The stable is said to be that of the White Lion Inn at Paddington, where Morland once had as many as eight horses, but partly owing to his drinking habits and partly owing to his unbusinesslike methods his prosperity soon dwindled.

Notwithstanding his dissipation—and a day rarely passed in which he was not drunk—he was not idle, for Morland was the author of four thousand pictures and of a still greater number of drawings.   But his intemperance and his dependence on dealers gradually impoverished his art, and the man who had a genuine love and understanding of country life, and ought to have been one of the world's greatest rustic painters, sank into " pot-boiling," painting what the dealers wanted instead of what he wanted to do himself.   His terms were four guineas a day — and his drink ! Morland had got into the state when he " didn't care," though in his sober moments he must have seen the irony and impropriety of a man of his character painting Hogarthian moralities like " The Fruits of Early Industry," " The Effects of Extravagance and Idleness," and so forth. Indeed, these in his own day were Morland's most popular works, and though some of them show the degeneration of his drawing, and his carelessness in their " woolly " rendering of form, even to the end a little painting more carefully handled and jewel-like in colour will now and again show what a great painter he might have been.   His last miserable years, 1800-4, were spent in a debtor's prison, yet even here, with a brandy-bottle always handy, he was still industrious, and for one dealer alone during this period he painted one hundred and ninety-two pictures.   At the early age of forty-one George Morland died, completely wrecked, the victim of his own want of education and of roguish employers.

§ 3

The establishment of landscape in the popular estimation as a branch of art, equal to the highest achievements of portraiture or historical painting, was finally achieved by Turner, the greatest glory of British art.   Joseph Mallord William Turner was born, appropriately enough, on Shakespeare's birthday, April 23, 1775 ; appropriately, because he was destined to become the Shakespeare of English painting. He was the son of a London hairdresser in humble circumstances, who lived and had his shop at 26 Maiden Lane, Covent Garden.   As a boy he showed ability as a draughtsman and colourist, and his father exhibited some of the lad's drawings in his shop, where now and

Photo : W. A. Mansell & Co.

"THE MARRIAGE OF ISAAC AND REBECCA." BY CLAUDE.
National Gallery, London.

When this picture was painted in 1648, the beauties of natural scenery were so slightly appreciated that it was politic for an artist to put in figures and pretend he was illustrating a story from the Bible even when, as here, his whole interest was in a lovely landscape.

again they found a purchaser.   One or two artists who went to the elder Turner to be shaved noticed his son's drawings, and urged the father to give his son a proper artistic training.   So at the age of eleven young Turner was sent to the Soho Academy and had lessons from Thomas Malton, who grounded him well in perspective, and also from Edward Dayes ; and in 1789, when he was fourteen, he was admitted to the school of the Royal Academy.

Meanwhile he was managing to support himself by selling a few sketches now and then, by putting in backgrounds for architects who wanted nice drawings to show their clients, and by colouring prints for engravers. While tinting prints for John Raphael Smith (1752–1812), the mezzotinter, who made a fortune by engraving the work of Morland, Turner met the brilliant water-colourist, Girtin, with whom he made friends, and Girtin introduced him to the friendly house of Dr. Thomas Monro, at 8 Adelphi Terrace. Here the two young men and other students were welcome every evening, for Monro was an enthusiastic connoisseur who had a studio fitted up for his protégés to work in; he gave them oyster suppers, a few shillings for pocket-money when they had nothing of their own, and free medical attendance if they became ill.

In 1797 Turner exhibited his first oil picture, a study of moonlight, at the Royal Academy, but most of the views he painted at this time were in water-colour. In 1792 he was commissioned to make a series of topographical drawings for a magazine, and this enabled him to make the first of those sketching tours which ever afterwards were a feature of his artistic life and to which we owe his enormous range of subject. In the following year he opened his own studio in Hand Court, Maiden Lane, where he exhibited and sold the drawings he had made on his tours.

Turner never had any difficulty in making a living, and we may account for his success where so many other landscape artists had failed by the fact that he established his reputation in water-colour before he proceeded to oils. From the time of Richard Wilson there had always been a demand for topographical drawings in water-colours, and Wilson's contemporary, Paul Sandby, R.A. (1725–1809), the " father of water-colour art," was one of the first to popularise landscape by going about the country and sketching gentlemen's mansions and parks. Landowners were pleased to purchase his and other artists' water-colours of views on their estates, and their pride in their own property was gradually converted by these artists into a real appreciation of the beauties of Nature.

At Dr. Monro's house Turner met John Robert Cozens (1752–99), a most poetic painter in water-colours and the son of a water-colour artist, Alexander Cozens, who died in 1786 ; and while Turner owed most to his diligent study of Nature, he always owned his obligation to Cozens, who was indeed his immediate predecessor in water-colour and the first to produce those atmospheric effects which Turner rivalled and excelled.

In 1799, at the age of twenty-four, Turner was elected an Associate of the Royal Academy, and henceforward, surer of himself and his public, he eschewed the merely topographical imitation of landscape for a nobler art. He looked beyond the mere details to a larger treatment of Nature, seizing all the poetry of sunshine, and the mists of morn and eve, with the grandeur of storm and the glow of sunset. In feeling his way to this period of his first style Turner looked not only to Nature but also to the example of his great predecessors, Claude, Richard Wilson, and the Dutch painters of the seventeenth century. The influence of the Dutch School, and particularly of Van de Velde, is apparent in many of these early works, even in " Calais Pier " (see page 367), which, painted in 1803, was held by Ruskin to be " the first which bears the sign manual and sign mental of Turner's colossal power." Already, however, Turner had improved on Van de Velde, who was never able to interpret weather so truly and vigorously as it is painted in the rolling sea and windy sky of this stimulating sea-piece.

The year before this picture was painted, Turner was elected R.A. (1802), and during the succeeding years he spent much time in travelling, visiting France, Switzerland, Italy, and the Rhine, and producing innumerable water-colours, as well as some of his finest oil-paintings.

That splendour of the sky, which was to be the peculiar glory of Turner, is first indicated in his " Sun rising through Vapour," painted in 1807, and it was possibly because this was the first picture in which he was able to obtain the effect after which he strove most earnestly that he was so attached to this picture. He sold it, but twenty years later, at the De Tabley sale of 1827, he bought it back for £514 10s.

"CROSSING THE BROOK," BY TURNER
National Gallery, London.

Painted in 1815, this beautiful picture illustates the second manner of Turner, and in its classical arrangement shows how he was influenced by Richard Wilson. The river seen in the middle distance is the Tamar, which divides Devonshire from Cornwall, and looking towards Plymouth and Mount Edgcumbe we see Calstock Church beyond Poulston Bridge. Thus, though idealised by the painter's imagination, the scene is founded on fact.

in order that he might bequeath this to the nation, together with his " Dido Building Carthage " (see page 368) on condition they should be hung in perpetuity beside Claude's " Marriage of Isaac and Rebecca " and " Embarkation of the Queen of Sheba." Conscious of his own powers and confident in the verdict of posterity, Turner was jealous of other painters' fame, and he was enraged at the way in which English connoisseurs extolled the pictures of Claude while they neglected his own works.

The pictures already mentioned, together with the lovely " Crossing the Brook " (see opposite page), a view near Weir Head, Tamar, looking towards Plymouth and Mount Edgcumbe, also painted in 1815, may be regarded as the chief masterpieces in oils of Turner's first period. After 1820 a great change was manifest in his manner of painting. In the early paintings dark predominated, with a very limited portion of light, and he painted solidly throughout with a vigorous and full brush ; but his later works are based on a light ground with a small proportion of dark, and using opaque touches of the purest orange, blue, purple, and other powerful colours, Turner obtained infinitely delicate gradations which produced a splendid and harmonious effect. This new manner is first seen in his " Bay of Baiæ," painted in 1823, and six years later, in 1829, it is revealed in all its glory in one of Turner's most beautiful and poetical works, " Ulysses Deriding Polyphemus," in which, as Redgrave has said, " while in no way gaudy, it seems impossible to surpass the power of colour which he has attained, or the terrible beauty in which he has clothed his poetic conception." In this glorious picture, " a work almost without a parallel in art," the nominal subject has little more power over us to-day than it has in the Claudes. Turner's painting attracts us primarily, not as an illustration to a familiar story from Homer, but as a glowing piece of colour, a magnificently decorative transcription of a flaming sunrise. And with all this the picture is a " magic casement " through which our imagination looks out on a world of romance, for in this colour is all the intoxication of triumph, of final victory after perils escaped ; and though

Turner himself probably did not know it, and few who look upon his masterpiece are conscious of the fact, this picture subconsciously expresses the elation, the pride, and even the touch of insolence, that all England felt after her victorious issue from the Napoleonic wars.

As Turner altered his style of oil-painting, so also he revolutionised his practice in water-colour. Originally, in common with the older members of the Early English Water-colour School, Turner began a drawing by laying in the gradations of light and shade with grey or some other neutral tint, and afterwards represented the hue of each object by tinting it with colour ; but this he found resulted in a certain heaviness of aspect. Accordingly, in his later water-colours he proceeded to treat the whole surface of his drawing as colour, using at once the pigments by which the scene might most properly be represented. By delicate hatchings he achieved wonderful qualities of broken hues, air tints, and atmosphere, so that the view when finished glowed and sparkled with the brilliance of Nature's own colours. This method of putting on the colour direct, without any under-painting of the subject in light and shade, has been to a great extent the foundation of modern painting.

Determined to outshine his fellows, Turner had a habit, dreaded by other artists, of coming to the Academy on Varnishing Day armed with his paint-box, and putting a brilliant touch or two on his own canvas when necessary to heighten its effect if its brilliance happened to be in any way challenged by that of a neighbouring picture. The brightness of the yellows and reds in his " Fighting Temeraire being Towed to her Last Berth " (see page 363) is said to be due to after-touches put on to " kill " a highly coloured painting by Geddes which hung near it in the Academy of 1839. Towards another landscape painter Turner was merciless, but he had respect and kindly feeling for Sir Thomas Lawrence, and on one occasion he darkened a landscape of his with lamp-black because it injured the effect of pictures by Lawrence on either side.

As he grew older, and particularly after his visit to

"ULYSSES DERIDING POLYPHEMUS," BY TURNER.

National Gallery, London.

Never in the history of art had the flaming splendour of a sunrise been so gloriously depicted in vivid colours as when Turner painted this picture in 1829.

Venice in 1832, Turner became more and more ambitious
of realising to the uttermost the fugitive radiances of dawn
and sunset.   Light, or rather the colour of light, became
the objective of his painting, to the exclusion of almost
everything else, and few of his contemporaries could follow
him as he devoted his brush more and more to depicting the
pageant of the heavens.   His work when exhibited was
severely criticised and held up to ridicule and mirth by
Thackeray and other wits ;   he was regarded as a madman
and accused, as other artists after him have been, of " flinging a pot of paint in the public's face."   Even " The Fighting Temeraire," which seems to us so poetic to-day in its
contrast of moonlight with sunlight, to match the contrast
between the sailing-ship that was passing away and the
steamer that heralded the future, even this work was
deemed to be exaggerated and extravagant, and to most
of the admirers of his earlier pictures paintings like " The
Approach to Venice " were utterly incomprehensible.

Fortunately, Turner was now independent of patrons and
could paint as he liked.   During the earlier part of his career
he had amassed a considerable fortune, a great part of
which was derived from the engravings of his works, for he
was a good business man, able to drive a close bargain with
publishers, and clever enough to retain an interest in his
works.   He had commenced im 1808 the series of etchings
known as the " Liber Studiorum," and the excellence of
these plates—now of great rarity and value—had led to
his employment as an illustrator, and his fame was greatly
increased and extended by the beautiful work he did for
books like Rogers' *Italy* and *Poems, The Rivers of France,
Southern Coast Scenery*, etc.   He had a fine studio at what
is now 23 Queen Anne Street, and he also owned a house
at Twickenham, where he lived with his father, who had
retired from business and made his home with his son from
about 1807 till his death in 1829.   Here, with his father and
an old housekeeper, Turner led a retired life ;   but though
habitually taciturn and reserved, he could be jovial at
a convivial gathering of artists which he now and then
attended.

In 1840, when Turner was sixty-five, he met a young man of twenty-one, fresh from Oxford, who, from the time he first saw the illustrations to Rogers' *Italy*, had worshipped the genius of Turner, and was destined to become his persistent and most eloquent champion. This was John Ruskin, who, in 1843—the year in which Turner painted " The Approach to Venice "— published the first volume of his *Modern Painters*, an epoch-making book, the real subject of which was the superiority of Turner to all painters past and present. Henceforward, however others might laugh at and ridicule his magical colour visions, Turner now had an enthusiastic defender whose opinion yearly became more authoritative and more widely respected. It is no exaggeration to say that to the constant eulogy of Ruskin is due in no small measure the universal esteem in which Turner is held to-day.

Though he never married, Turner had a natural liking for a quiet domestic existence, and after his father's death he began to lead a double life.   Under the assumed name of Booth he formed a connection with a woman who kept a house at 119 Cheyne Walk, where he had been accustomed occasionally to lodge, and " Puggy " or " Admiral " Booth became a well-known character in Chelsea, where he was reputed to be a retired mariner of eccentric disposition, fond of his glass, and never tired of watching the sun.   On the roof of the house in Cheyne Walk there was a gallery, and here " Mr. Booth " would sit for hours at dawn and sunset.   The secret of his double existence was not discovered till the day before his death, for he had been accustomed to absent himself from Queen Anne Street for long intervals and therefore was not missed.   Suddenly those who knew him as Turner learnt that the great artist was lying dead in a little house at Chelsea, where his last illness had seized him, and where he died on December 19, 1851.   The body was removed to the house in Queen Anne Street, and afterwards buried in the crypt of St. Paul's Cathedral.

Turner left a fortune of £140,000, and after making a number of small annuities left the bulk of it for the benefit of art and artists; but his will, drawn by himself, was so vague and unskilfully framed that, after four years' litigation, a compromise was arranged on the advice of the Lord Chancellor.   The Royal Academy received £20,000, which it set aside as the Turner Fund for the relief of poor artists not members of their body, and the National Gallery acquired the magnificent gift of 362 oil-paintings, 135 finished water-colours, 1757 studies in colour, and thousands of drawings and sketches.   The task of sifting, arranging, and cataloguing the water-colours and sketches which Turner bequeathed to the nation was rightly placed in the sympathetic hands of his great advocate, John Ruskin.

The life of Turner, as we have seen, was full of strangeness and contradictions, and it is possible he may have inherited some of his eccentricities from his mother, a woman of fierce temper, who eventually became insane. There was little correspondence between his art and his life, for, as Mr. E. V. Lucas has justly said : " Turner's works are marvels of loveliness and grandeur ; Turner was grubby, miserly, jealous, and squalid in his tastes.   He saw visions and glorified even what was already glorious ; and he deliberately chose to live in houses thick with grime, and often to consort with inferior persons."   The evidence before us compels us to believe that he was really happier as " Puggy Booth " with a few cronies in a Chelsea bar-parlour than as " the famous Mr. Turner " in the company of his patron, Lord Egremont, or in the hospitable mansion of Mr. Fawkes of Farnley Hall.

§ 4

Jealous as he was of other painters, there was one of his contemporaries for whose art Turner had nothing but admiration.   " Had Girtin lived," he once said, " I should have starved," and he roundly admitted that painter's " White House in Chelsea " to be better than anything of his own up to that time.   Thomas Girtin was born in 1773 at Southwark, where his father was a rope manu-facturer, and, like Turner, he was for a time the pupil of

Dayes. But for his short life—for he died in 1802 at the early age of twenty-seven—he would probably have rivalled Turner as a painter in oils, and though his career was cut short he lived long enough to make himself one of the greatest of our painters in water-colours. In this medium his style was bold and vigorous, and by suppressing irrelevant detail he gave a sense of grandeur to the scenes he depicted. His chief sketching-ground was the northern counties, and particularly its cathedral cities, and his favourite

Photo : W. A. Mansell & Co.

"THE TRENT, NEAR BURTON," BY DE WINT (1784–1849).
South Kensington Museum, London.

Dutch by descent, though born in England, De Wint was at his best in painting flat stretches of river scenery under a placid luminous sky. This water-colour of a hayfield with a hay-barge on the river is a happy example of his rural idylls.

subjects were the ruins of our old abbeys and castles, and the hilly scenery of the north. The water-colour at South Kensington of " Kirkstall Abbey " (see page 383) is a fine example of his power to present his subject with truth and majesty.

A younger fellow-student with Turner and Girtin in the hospitable house of Dr. Monro was another artist who achieved fame chiefly as a painter in water-colours. This was Peter De Wint, born at Stone in Staffordshire in 1784. His father was a Dutch physician belonging to an old and respected Amsterdam family who settled in England. Peter,

NATURE," BY LAWRENCE.

After the Engraving by G. T. Doo.

In the title of this charming study of two children, Sir Thomas Lawrence, P.R.A. pays his tribute to the Nature worship which distinguished the opening years of the nineteenth century.

"KIRKSTALL ABBEY," BY GIRTIN (1773–1803).

South Kensington Museum, London.

A masterly example of the water-colour art of this short-lived painter of whom Turner said, "Had Girtin lived, I should have starved."

his fourth son, was originally intended for the medical profession, but was allowed to follow art, and placed with the engraver, John Raphael Smith, in 1802. Five years later he was admitted to the Royal Academy School, and the same year (1807) he exhibited at the Academy for the first time, sending three landscapes, and thereafter he exhibited there occasionally till 1828. But his reputation was principally made by the drawings he contributed to the Water-colour Society, of which he was elected an Associate in 1810 and was long one of the chief ornaments.

De Wint loved to paint direct from Nature, and was never so happy as when in the fields. His subjects are principally chosen in the eastern and northern counties, and though often tempted to extend his studies to the Continent, the love of England and English scenery was so strong that, except for one visit to Normandy, he never left these shores. He formed a style of his own, notable for the simplicity and breadth of his light and shade, and the fresh limpidity of his colour. He was a great purist in technique and objected to the use of Chinese white and body colour, which he thought tended to give a heavy effect to a drawing. He excelled in river scenes, and " The Trent near Burton " (see page 381), in the Victoria and Albert Museum, South Kensington, is a beautiful example of his tender and faithful rendering of a typical English scene.

While De Wint excelled in painting the placid aspects of landscapes, his contemporary, David Cox, was at his best on a windy day or in stormy weather. Cox was the son of a blacksmith and was born at Deritend, a suburb of Birmingham, on April 29, 1783. During his school-days he had an accident and broke his leg, and this misfortune proved to be his good fortune, for having been given a box of colours with which to amuse himself while he was laid up, young David made such good use of the paints that his parents perceived the bent of his genius, and when he was well again apprenticed him to a painter. David Cox received his first tuition from an artist who painted miniatures for lockets, but when his master committed suicide young Cox went to the other extreme of painting, and at the age of seventeen he became an assistant scene-painter at the Birmingham Theatre. It is said that he even took a small part now and then at this theatre, which was then managed by the father of Macready.

Photo : W. A Mansell & Co.

A WINDY DAY," BY DAVID COX (1783–1859).
National Gallery. London.

Among all the remarkable landscape artists of his day, David Cox was notable for the freedom of his handling and his vigorous rendering of weather. In this picture we can almost feel the wind that is blowing across the common in the face of the woman with her dog.

From Birmingham David Cox went to London to paint scenery—at four shillings a square yard !—in the Surrey Theatre, varying this work with sepia drawings, which he sold to a dealer at two guineas a dozen for school copies. Meanwhile he made every endeavour to improve his art and took lessons from John Varley (1778–1842), an artist of refined accomplishment, who was one of the founders of

25

the Water-colour Society in 1804. Varley, who had had his own struggles before he made a position for himself as one of the best water-colourists of his time, liked Cox so much and thought so highly of his talent that he would not allow the young man to pay him for his lessons.

Under Varley's tuition Cox rapidly improved his art and his circumstances ; he was able to quit the theatre and earn money in his turn by giving lessons, and in 1805 he made his first visit to Wales, where he discovered Bettws-y-Coed, ever after to be his Mecca. On his return he exhibited his Welsh water-colours, which attracted some attention, and in 1808 he married and settled down in a little house on Dulwich Common. Here he gave lessons to pupils and polished his own art by the diligent study of the surrounding scenery, learning to render the varied effects of Nature and the aspects of morning, noon, and twilight. In 1813 he was elected a member of the Water-colour Society and became one of the principal contributors to its exhibitions.

In 1829 he made a tour on the Continent, choosing his subjects on the coasts and in the market-places of Antwerp and Brussels, and the crowded bridges of Paris, but he liked best the scenery of his own country, particularly the mountainous country of Wales and Scotland, whose gloomy passes he painted with great effect and grandeur. He also painted many views of the Thames and of the country round London, but till he was past fifty he worked exclusively in water-colours.

In 1839, however, when he was fifty-six, Cox became acquainted with a young Bristol painter, William James Müller (1812–45), who had just returned from a long journey through Greece and Egypt. Müller was himself a very brilliant colourist and a skilful painter in oils ; the man and his work made a deep impression on Cox, who studied Müller and watched him at work, and henceforward devoted himself more to oils than to water-colours. About 1841 Cox left London and settled at Greenfield House, Harborne, near Birmingham, and there, with an annual excursion of some weeks to his beloved Bettws-y-Coed, he lived till the day of his death on June 7, 1859.   During these later years Cox gave himself chiefly to oil-painting ; his best pictures were seldom seen in London during his own lifetime, and when shown were not generally appreciated.   It was only after his death that his merit as an oil-painter became widely recognised.

Whether in oil or in water-colour the work of David Cox is distinguished by its light, its vigour, and its spaciousness.   His picture " A Windy Day " (see page 385), also known as " Crossing the Common," is a happy example of the scene and weather he excelled in rendering.

XVI

NATURAL LANDSCAPE

§ 1

UNQUESTIONABLY the two greatest English painters of landscape, and probably the two greatest English painters of any kind, were Turner and Constable, who were born within a year of one another. Turner, as we saw in the last chapter, amassed a large fortune ; Constable, on the other hand, could hardly earn a bare living, and not until 1814, when the artist was thirty-eight, did he sell a picture to any but his own personal friends.

How was it that, from a worldly point of view, Constable failed where Turner succeeded ? The explanation is to be found in the totally different character of the landscapes painted by these two artists. Turner, as Claude had done before him, made frequent use of nominal subjects as an excuse for his pictures of Nature ; there was a dramatic element in his art which appealed to the popular imagination, and even when, as in many of his later works, people found difficulty in apprehending the elements of his style, they were insensibly affected by the splendour of his colour and brought to admit that these pictures, if difficult to understand, were paintings in the " grand style."

Constable never made use of fictitious subjects and titles as an excuse for painting landscapes. His works were wholly free from any dramatic or foreign interest, and following the example of the Dutch landscape painters of the seventeenth century, he whole-heartedly devoted himself to painting the simple, homely beauty of the scenery in his native land. He modestly confessed that he thought there was room for a " natural painter," and by this he meant a painter who would devote himself to painting as truly as he could the beauty of Nature without importing into his pictures any extraneous reference to Homeric legend or to events in the past or present.

His landscapes were long unappreciated because they appealed to a pure love of Nature which was not fully awake in the artist's lifetime. " My art," said Constable a little bitterly in his middle years, " flatters nobody by imitation, it courts nobody by smoothness, tickles nobody by petiteness, it is without either fal-de-lal or fiddle-de-dee ; how can I then hope to be popular ? "

John Constable was born on June 11, 1776, nearly fourteen months, to be precise, after the birth of Turner. He was the son of a miller who owned watermills at Flatford and Dedham and two windmills at East Bergholt in Suffolk. It was at the mill house in East Bergholt that John Constable was born, and here he passed the greater part of his youth. His father wished him to enter the Church, but Constable had no inclination in this direction, and after he had finished his education in the local school, at the age of eighteen he assisted his father in the mill at East Bergholt which figures in so many of his landscapes.

Meanwhile his love of Nature and art was encouraged by a great amateur who happened to have his seat in the neighbouring county of Essex and was quick to recognise the talent of young Constable. Sir George Beaumont (1753–1827) was something of a painter himself, he had been a pupil of Richard Wilson ; and he was an enthusiastic patron of art and artists. He had peculiar ideas about colour, and his well-known saying that " a good picture, like a good fiddle, should be brown," was not helpful to a painter like Constable, who saw the lovely greens in Nature and painted them as he saw them ; but at this time Constable was a beginner, and the friendly encouragement and advice of Beaumont decided Constable's career.

One of the best things about Sir George Beaumont, to whose zeal and generosity we owe in large measure the establishment of the National Gallery, was his unremitting

"FLATFORD MILL," BY JOHN CONSTABLE, R.A.

National Gallery, London.

At a time when fashionable opinion held that " a good picture, like a good fiddle, should be brown," Constable dared to paint Nature truly in her own colours and became the pioneer of " natural " landscape painting.

efforts to make England appreciate the genius of her own artists. As a young man he had waggishly shown up the ignorance of the public and its ridiculous passion for foreign artists by advertising in the newspapers that a wonderful German had arrived in Bond Street who could take likenesses by a new method of heating the mirror in which the sitter looked, and for ever fixing and preserving the reflection! On the next day a crowd of fashionable folk flocked to Bond Street, only to be laughed at by the practical joker and his friends.

Sir George Beaumont not only encouraged young Constable to go on with his sketching, but lent him works which might serve as models for his practice. Among these were two water-colours by Thomas Girtin, which Constable always maintained set his feet firmly in the right road, and also Claude's " Landscape with the Angel appearing to Hagar," a work Beaumont so loved that he took it about with him wherever he travelled. In 1826 he gave this with fifteen other pictures to the nation, but finding he could not live without it he asked for it back till his death, which occurred in the following year. This Claude is now in the National Gallery.

The opinion of this artist-baronet naturally carried weight with Constable's father, and as a result of his influence John Constable was permitted to go to London in 1795 to study art. Here he was encouraged by Joseph Farington, R.A. (1747–1821), who communicated to him some of the precepts he had himself derived from his master Richard Wilson, and in 1799 Constable, through Farington's influence, was admitted to the Royal Academy Schools. Although the first painting Constable exhibited at the Academy was a landscape, shown in 1802, he began his professional career as a portrait painter, which was then the only profitable branch of art. But after painting some portraits and altar-pieces for Brantham in 1804 and for Nayland in 1809, he came to devote himself more or less exclusively to landscape, which was the true bent of his genius. He felt he could paint his own places best, he delighted in the flats of Dedham, with its trees and slow river " escaping from milldams, over willows, old rotten planks, slimy posts, and brickwork " ; and so he finally settled down as the painter of the rural scenery among which he had been born. In 1803 he had written, " I feel now, more than ever, a decided conviction that I shall some time or other make some good pictures ; pictures that shall be valuable to posterity, if I do not reap the benefit of them."

These words were prophetic, and for some years almost the only patrons the young artist had were a kindly uncle and his friend Archdeacon Fisher, the nephew and chaplain of the Bishop of Salisbury. Had Constable been content to be a merely topographical artist as Farington and most of the older water-colourists were, he would probably have found it easier to sell his works and make a respectable income ; but from the first it was his desire not merely to paint " portraits of places," but to give a true and full impression of Nature, to paint light, dews, breezes, bloom, and freshness. The multitude of his sketches—of which a fine collection may be seen in the Victoria and Albert Museum, South Kensington—show how earnestly and assiduously he studied Nature in all her aspects to attain this end, and though a love of Nature and of truth is discernible even in his earliest works, it was only gradually that Constable acquired the breadth and freedom which distinguish his later works.

If we compare even so beautiful an example of his early style as " Boat-building near Flatford Mill " (see page 396), painted in 1815, with " The Hay Wain " (see page 409), painted in 1821, we at once perceive the tremendous advance made by the artist in the intervening six years. It is not altogether without significance to note that the greatest strides forward in his art were made during the early years of his married life, and it may not unreasonably be surmised that the happiness of his private life and domestic contentment compensated Constable for public neglect and helped to give him increased confidence in his own powers.

It was in 1816 that he married Maria Bicknell, with whom

"THE CORNFIELD," BY JOHN CONSTABLE, R.A. (1776–1837)

National Gallery, London.

Though much admired by the discerning when it was first exhibited at the Academy in 1826, this brilliant example of Constable's genius remained unsold till after the artist's death, when a number of his admirers clubbed together to buy the picture from his executors and presented it to the nation. The church in the distance is Stratford St. Mary, Suffolk.

he had been in love since 1811, and the correspondence between the two during these five years—several letters of which still exist—shows the simple nature of the writers and the complete trust each had in the other. The marriage was delayed owing to the long opposition of Constable's father, and eventually it took place against his wishes, but there was no serious breach between father and son, and neither Constable senior nor Mr. Bicknell, who was also very comfortably off, allowed the young couple to be in actual want. Two years before his marriage Constable had for the first time sold two landscapes to total strangers, but as yet he had no real success, and the young couple set up house modestly at 76 Charlotte Street, Fitzroy Square.

In 1819, when Constable was forty-three, he exhibited at the Academy a large landscape, " View on the River Stour," which was keenly appreciated by his brother artists and resulted in his being elected an Associate, and in the following year his love of Nature led him to take a house at Hampstead.

When " The Hay Wain " was exhibited at the Royal Academy in 1821 it attracted comparatively little attention, but three years later it was sold to a French collector, who sent it to the Paris Salon of 1824, where it created a veritable sensation. Constable was awarded a gold medal, and his picture had an immediate and lasting effect on French art. His pure and brilliant colour was a revelation and an inspiration to French painters, and under the glamour of " The Hay Wain " Delacroix, the leader of the French Romanticists, obtained leave to retouch his " Massacre of Scio " in the same exhibition. In a fortnight he repainted it throughout, using the strongest, purest, and most vivid colours he could find, and henceforward not only were Delacroix's ideas of colour and landscape revolutionised by Constable's masterpiece, but a whole school of French landscape painters arose, as we shall see in a later chapter, whose art was to a great extent based on the example and practice of Constable.

It was in France, then, that Constable had his first real

success, and Frenchmen were the first in large numbers fully to appreciate his genius. It is a piece of great good luck that " The Hay Wain " ever came back to England, but fortunately it was recovered by a British collector, George Young, and at his sale in 1866 it was purchased by the late Henry Vaughan, who in 1886 gave it to the National Gallery.

In 1825 Constable, now possessing a European reputa-

STUDY FOR THE LEAPING HORSE," BY CONSTABLE
South Kensington Museum, London.

This magnificent six-foot sketch, painted direct from Nature in 1825, gives the essence of Constable's fresh, naturalistic art.

tion though still neglected in his own country, sent to the Academy his famous picture " The Leaping Horse," which is generally considered to be his central master-work, though many shrewd judges consider that the essence of his fresh, naturalistic art is still more brilliantly displayed in the big preparatory six-foot sketch of the same subject (see above), now in the Victoria and Albert Museum. It was Constable's habit to make these large preparatory sketches for pictures of special importance, and the great difference between the sketch and the picture is that the former was done in the open, directly from Nature, while the latter was worked up in the studio. Consequently the sketch always contains a freshness and vigour, something

Photo : W. A. Mansell & Co.

"BOAT-BUILDING NEAR FLATFORD MILL," BY CONSTABLE.
South Kensington Museum, London.

This peaceful scene, painted in 1815, is a perfect example of Constable's early style before he had acquired the vigour and freedom which distinguish his later works.

of which is lost in the picture, though this last sometimes has refinements of design not to be found in the sketch.

For example, in the " Sketch for the Leaping Horse," the bent willow is to the right of the horse and its rider, as it doubtless was in the scene that Constable actually beheld ; but in the picture of " The Leaping Horse " in the Diploma Gallery of the Royal Academy, the tree is shifted to the other side of the horse and rider, more to our left, in order to improve the design and emphasise the rhythm of the diagonal accents from the big tree on our left to the water-weeds in the opposite lower corner. This transposition of the willow-tree is exceedingly instructive, for it proves that Constable did not, as some have maintained, simply paint " snapshots " of Nature ; he understood the science of picture-making as well as any artist, and while desirous above all of presenting the *general* truth of the scene before him, he did not scruple to alter the position of one particular tree or other object if thereby he thought he could improve the composition of his picture.

Constable was now fifty, but still he was only an A.R.A. Neither " The Leaping Horse " nor " The Cornfield " (see page 393), which he exhibited in 1826, moved his brother artists to make him an Academician, and though " The Cornfield " attracted a good deal of attention and was one of the first pictures to make Constable talked about in London, it did not sell, but remained in his possession to the day of his death. There would seem to be no denying that to the end a number of Academicians were unable to appreciate the genius of Constable, and after the death of Joseph Farington in 1821 he had no keen admirer with influence within their ranks. The story is told that one year, after he had at last been elected R.A. in 1829, Constable submitted one of his works labelled with another name to the Academy jury. When the majority had voted for its rejection, Constable admitted his authorship and quietly remarked, " There, gentlemen, I always thought you did not like my style of painting."

When official recognition came it was " too late," as Constable sadly said. Fortunately he was not in want, for in 1828 his wife's father had died and left Constable the sum of £20,000. " This," wrote Constable, " I will settle on my wife and children, and I shall then be able to stand before a six-foot canvas with a mind at ease, thank God ! " From this exclamation it would certainly appear as if the painter himself took more pleasure in his six-foot sketch than in painting a picture from it for the market.

Any pleasure he might have experienced in his election to the Academy as a full member in 1829 was counteracted by his grief at the loss of his wife, who had just previously died. It was the thought of this faithful companion and helper that prompted Constable to say his election as R.A. was " too late."

Though it would be a gross exaggeration to say that Constable ever obtained anything like popularity in his own lifetime, his landscapes after 1831 began to be known to a wider public by virtue of the mezzotints of some of his best paintings by David Lucas (1802–81). Lucas was an engraver of genius, who brilliantly translated into black-and-white the beauties of Constable's light and shadow, but when he first approached the artist for permission to engrave his work Constable was dismally despondent about the project. " The painter himself is totally unpopular," he said, " and will be so on this side of the grave. The subjects are nothing but art, and the buyers are wholly ignorant of that." Nevertheless Lucas persisted with his mezzotints, which did much to spread the fame of Constable, and these engravings are now eagerly sought for at high prices by collectors.

Though never becoming actually despondent or em-bittered, Constable naturally craved for the appreciation which he felt he deserved, and in the endeavour to court notice he even went so far as to advertise in the news-papers :

" Mr. Constable's Gallery of Landscapes, by his own hand, is to be seen *gratis* daily, by an application at his residence."

But few except other artists applied, and as he grew older his house became fuller and fuller of unsold pictures. After his sixtieth birthday, in 1836, his health became uncertain, and on March 30, 1837, he died suddenly in his house at Hampstead. Almost immediately after his death the world awoke to his genius, and in the same year a number of gentlemen who admired his work clubbed together and bought from the executors his picture " The Cornfield," which they presented to the nation. Strangely enough this artist, who was so little known during his own lifetime, has since his death become a familiar personality, thanks to the pious solicitude of his friend, the genre-painter C. R. Leslie (1794–1859), whose *Memoirs of John Constable, R.A.* is one of the best biographies of a painter ever written. It is a classic which, for the intimate insight it gives us into the character of the man, may be compared

Photo : W A. Mansell & Co.

"SALISBURY CATHEDRAL," BY CONSTABLE.
South Kensington Museum, London.

One of Constable's earliest patrons and most constant friends was the Rev. John Fisher, nephew and chaplain to the Bishop of Salisbury. Owing to this friendship the artist painted several pictures of the Cathedral, among which this painting is notable for the brilliance and beauty of its lighting.

with Boswell's *Johnson.* All who met Constable were attracted by his simple, kindly, affectionate nature, and perhaps the most touching tribute to his memory was paid by a London cab-driver who, when he heard that he would never drive Constable again, told Leslie he was " as sorry as if he had been my own father—he was as nice a man as that, sir."

Leslie had always been a firm believer in the genius of Constable, and wrote of his works : " I cannot but think that they will attain for him, when his merits are fully acknowledged, the praise of having been the most genuine painter of English landscape that has yet lived." Subsequent generations have corroborated Leslie's opinion, and another genre-painter, Sir J. D. Linton, who was born three years after Constable's death, has testified to the genius of Constable and to the effect of his painting. " His art," wrote Linton, " has had the widest and most lasting influence both at home and abroad. . . . Although Turner is accepted as the greatest master of landscape painting, and his work has not been without very great influence, Constable's robust and massive manner has affected the modern schools more universally."

While we admire Turner we love Constable the more dearly, perhaps because his art is so essentially English. Never did a landscape painter travel less than Constable in search of a subject. While Turner toured all over Europe, Constable opened his door and found beauty waiting to be painted. With exceptions so few that they do not bulk largely in his work, all Constable's landscapes are drawn either from his birthplace, that is to say the borders of Essex and Suffolk about the Stour, now known as " the Constable country," or at Hampstead, where his house yet stands. The hill with a clump of firs on it, close to the Spaniard's, is to this day spoken of as " Constable's Knoll." His only other sketching ground of real importance was Salisbury, whither he was doubtless drawn by his friendship with the Rev. John Fisher. Of his many paintings of Salisbury Cathedral, one of the most beautiful is the painting (see preceding page) in the South Kensington Museum, from which we see that had his bent been that way Constable could have painted architectural subjects as truly and beautifully as he did landscapes.

It was the supreme distinction of Constable to destroy Beaumont's fallacy that a " brown " landscape was a " good " landscape, and to paint all the greenness in Nature. He loved to paint the glitter of light on trees after rain,

and the little touches of white paint with which he achieved
the effect of their sparkle were jocularly alluded to as
" Constable's snow." No painter before him had painted
with so much truth the actual colour of Nature's lighting,
and since Constable the true colour of Nature in light and

Photo : W. A. Mansell & Co.

"WHERRIES ON THE YARE," BY JOHN SELL COTMAN (1782–1842).
National Gallery, London.

So little was the genius of Cotman appreciated in his own day that this beautiful painting
was sold at Norwich in 1834 for eighteen hillings !

shadow has increasingly become the preoccupation of the
" natural " landscape painter.

§ 2

Constable was not the first nor was he the last English
painter whose art was appreciated in France long before
his talent was duly recognised in his own country, and it
may be argued that his triumph at Paris in 1824 was to
some extent anticipated by the warm welcome which he
26

Parisians had already given to his young compatriot Richard Parkes Bonington. The father of Bonington was an extraordinary man who had originally succeeded his father as governor of the Nottingham county gaol, but he lost this appointment through his irregularities and then set up as a portrait painter, while his wife kept a school which was the real mainstay of the family. His son Richard was born at Arnold, a village near Nottingham, on October 25, 1801, and at an early age showed a talent for drawing which made him another infant prodigy, like Lawrence.

Meanwhile his father's love of low company, intemperate habits, and violent political opinions had broken up his wife's school, and about the time of the fall of Napoleon the family fled to France, first to Calais and then to Paris. Henceforward Richard Parkes Bonington, though still a boy, was the chief breadwinner for the family. In 1816 he obtained permission to copy pictures at the Louvre, where he was said to be the youngest student on record, and he also worked in the studio of Baron Gros, where his improvement was so rapid that his master soon told him he had nothing more to learn from him, and advised him to go out into the world and paint from Nature on his own account. This advice Bonington took, travelling extensively in France and also visiting Italy in 1822. His oil-paintings and water-colours, which were exceedingly rich in colour and full of vitality, were quickly appreciated and the reputation of Bonington rapidly increased in Paris. In 1824, when Constable received his gold medal, another gold medal was also awarded to Bonington for the two coast scenes which he had sent to the Salon.

Though he had visited England now and again, Bonington was quite unknown here till 1826, when he exhibited at the British Institution two views on the French coast which surprised the English painters and at once gave him a name among his own countrymen. In the following year he exhibited another marine subject at the Academy, and in 1828—though still residing in Paris—he sent to the Academy a view on the Grand Canal, Venice, and a small historical painting of " Henri III of France." Though but twenty-seven years of age, Bonington for some time had been greatly esteemed in France, and now commissions flowed upon him from England also. Anxious to fulfil them, the artist worked feverishly during the hot summer, and after a long day sketching under a scorching sun in Paris he was attacked by brain fever, followed by a severe illness. When his health had slightly improved he came over to London for medical advice, but it was too late. He had fallen into galloping consumption, and the brilliant promise of his career was cut short by his death on September 23, 1828. He was buried in the vaults of St. James's Church, Pentonville.

The early deaths of Girtin and Bonington were the two greatest blows British art had received, and had they lived it seems probable that Bonington might have gone even further than Girtin. His range for his years was remarkably wide, and he was as skilful in painting figures as he was in landscapes and marine subjects. His art was picturesque, romantic, and often dramatic, while he had an opulent sense of colour and was able to imbue his figure paintings with a wonderful sense of life. In the Louvre, Paris, where the artist studied as a boy, the examples of Bonington's art are more numerous and important than those at the National Gallery, London, which possesses two only, a Normandy landscape, bequeathed by Mr. George Salting, and " The Column of St. Mark, Venice " (see page 407). Happily Bonington's work is well represented in the Wallace Collection, where there are ten of his paintings and twenty-four water-colours, among the former being the picture of " Henri IV and the Spanish Ambassador," which so long ago as 1870 fetched the considerable price of £3,320 in a sale at Paris.

§ 3

Another great landscape painter who during his lifetime never took the place in the world that his genius warranted was John Crome, frequently called " Old Crome," to distinguish him from his son, who also became a painter.

Photo : W. A. Mansell & Co.

A WINDMILL ON MOUSEHOLD HEATH," BY JOHN CROME (1768–1821).
National Gallery, London.

Founder of the Norwich School, Crome devoted his life to painting the beauties of the country round his birthplace, and never attempted to establish himself in London. His feeling for light, air, and space are splendidly revealed in this noble landscape.

Crome, who was born at Norwich on December 21, 1769, was the son of a poor weaver and began life as an errand-boy, carrying bottles of medicine for a doctor, but when he was about fourteen or fifteen his love of art led him to apprentice himself to a house and sign painter. While following his trade during his apprenticeship, Crome took every opportunity of sketching the picturesque scenery which surrounds his native city. He was very, very poor, but he persevered and his perseverance gained him friends.

Chief among these friends was Mr. Thomas Harvey, of Catton in Norfolk, who possessed a fine picture gallery and encouraged Crome to study and make copies of the pictures he had collected. Mr. Harvey's collection included landscapes by Richard Wilson — by whom Crome was greatly influenced—Gainsborough's "Cottage Door," and many fine examples of the Dutch painters of the seventeenth century, notably Hobbema, for whose art Crome then conceived a passionate admiration which lasted all his life. Mr. Harvey not only introduced Crome to other Norwich amateurs, but also obtained him some pupils to whom he taught drawing, though at this time the artist was only an awkward, uninformed country lad, whose deficiencies of education were to some extent compensated for by his great gifts and his natural shrewdness.

Meanwhile Crome had formed an intimate friendship with a lad of his own class, Robert Ladbrooke (1770–1842), then a printer's apprentice, but also ambitious to become an artist. After living together for some two years, Crome and Ladbrooke married sisters, and abandoning their original trades they established themselves in partnership as artists, Ladbrooke painting portraits at five shillings apiece, and Crome selling his landscapes for what they would fetch—which was not always as much as five shillings ! But for Crome's practice as a drawing-master he could hardly have kept himself, let alone a family, in these early years, but gradually he acquired a local reputation and his landscapes found occasional purchasers, though at pitifully low prices.

In February 1803 Crome gathered round him the artists

of his native city for their mutual improvement, and from this beginning arose the Norwich Society of Artists, founded in 1805. The Society held annual exhibitions to which Crome was a large contributor, for he rarely sent his pictures to London for exhibition and consequently was little known there. Crome's pupils and associates, among whom the most distinguished were John Sell Cotman, James Stark (1794–1859), George Vincent, and his eldest son John Bernay Crome, formed what is known as the " Norwich School." The inspiration of this school was derived chiefly from Crome, but also from the Dutch painters by whom he was influenced.

The Norwich School prospered exceedingly, more so than any other body of provincial artists has ever done in England, and their success was due not only to the excellence of their own work but also to the fact that they laboured in a field well prepared to receive art. It will have been observed how many of the great English landscape painters belonged to the Eastern Counties—Gainsborough and Constable were both Suffolk men—and the extent to which the art of all of them was influenced by the art of Holland. The explanation is to be found in the intimate trade relations which had existed for centuries between East Anglia and the Netherlands. Owing to this commercial intercourse numbers of Dutch and Flemish pictures found their way into East Anglian homes, and while London during the eighteenth century worshipped Italian art almost to the exclusion of all other, well-to-do people in Norfolk and Suffolk took a keener delight in the homelier art of the Dutch and Flemish Schools. Thus at the very time that Constable was being neglected in London, John Crome was enjoying esteem and wide popularity in Norfolk.

It is true that Crome never made a fortune ; to the end his lessons brought him in more money than his paintings, for any of which fifty pounds was a long and rarely attained price ; but Crome did sell his pictures and in time became quite comfortably off. In 1801 he moved into a big house in Gildengate Street, he kept two horses, and managed before his death to acquire many good pictures and to

Photo : W. A. Mansell & Co.

"THE COLUMN OF ST. MARK'S, VENICE," BY R. P. BONINGTON (1802–28).

National Gallery, London.

Though he died when he was only twenty-six, this artist greatly influenced his contemporaries by his rich colour and romantic feeling. Had he lived he would undoubtedly have been one of the greatest artists of his time.

The view shown is of the Piazetta at Venice, with the column supporting the winged lion of St. Mark and the companion column, on the right, which is crowned by a statue of St. Theodore, the first patron saint of Venice.

form a library. Norwich was proud of her distinguished painter, and a special seat was always reserved for him in the parlour of the old inn in the market-place, where in his later years he was treated as an oracle, revered by all.

Under these circumstances we can understand why Crome continued to reside in his native Norwich and was never tempted to settle in London. In 1806 he exhibited for the first time at the Royal Academy, but between then and 1818 he only sent thirteen pictures in all to be exhibited there. He visited London occasionally, twice he went to Cumberland, in 1802 and 1806, once to Weymouth, and in 1814 he made a tour in France and Belgium, but his chief subjects were almost exclusively local. He was perfectly satisfied with the lanes, heaths, and river-banks surrounding Norwich, without wishing to journey further afield. In his great tree picture, " The Poringland Oak," he rivalled his own idol Hobbema ; in " Moon Rise on the Yare," he surpassed the moonlight paintings of Van der Neer, by whom it was inspired ; while his masterpiece, " Mousehold Heath," at the National Gallery, will always rank Crome amongst the grandest of landscape painters. Asked by his son why he had painted this last subject, Crome made the memorable reply : " For air and space."

In addition to his oil-paintings Crome executed a few water-colours and also a number of etchings. In 1834 a series of thirty-one of his etchings was published under the title of " Norfolk Picturesque Scenery."

While out sketching in his fifty-third year he caught a chill, and after a few days' illness died on April 22, 1821. On the day before he died he addressed to his son the words so often quoted : " John, my boy, paint, but paint only for fame ; and if your subject is only a pigsty, dignify it." The art of Old Crome is indeed a perpetual reminder that a masterpiece of painting is due far more to the treatment than to the subject, and nobody knew better than the Norwich master how to give dignity to the humblest subject by its stately presentation in a well-balanced composition.

Though his landscape art is limited in comparison with that of Turner and Constable, within his own self-imposed limits Crome is second to none. He did not set out, like Turner, to mirror the blazing glories of dawn and sunset, nor did he, like Constable, hold himself ready to paint Nature and weather in every aspect : Crome waited for the quieter moods of Nature in his own homeland, and he painted these to perfection.

Photo : W. A. Mansell & Co.

"THE HAY WAIN," BY CONSTABLE.

National Gallery, London.

Almost unnoticed when shown at the Academy in 1821, this picture created a sensation when it was exhibited in the Paris Salon of 1824. Constable was awarded a Gold Medal, and his example led French artists to adopt a new and truer style of landscape painting.

§ 4

The Norwich School owes its fame to two stars of the first magnitude, Crome and Cotman, and to a host of lesser luminaries. John Sell Cotman was fourteen years younger than Crome, and though also born at Norwich, on June 11, 1782, he did not, like Crome, acquire his art education in his native city. Cotman from the first was in a very different position. He was the son of a well-to-do draper, received

Photo: W. A. Mansell & Co.

"GRETA BRIDGE," BY COTMAN.

British Museum, London.

The artist's masterpiece in water-colour, majestic in design, splendidly strong and massive in its drawing, and rich and harmonious in colour.

410

a good education at the Norwich Grammar School, and was intended to enter his father's shop ; but when his bent for art clearly declared itself his father was sensible enough to allow his son to make it his vocation and sent him to London.

Cotman remained in London from 1800 to 1806, and probably the most fruitful part of the education he received there was his association with the group of artists who

"BRIGHTON BEACH WITH COLLIERS." BY CONSTABLE.
South Kensington Museum, London.

The vigour and freedom of the artist's later style is seen in this thickly painted sketch of Brighton on a breezy day.

frequented the house of Dr. Thomas Monro, who has already been mentioned in this OUTLINE as the friend of Turner and Girtin. In Dr. Monro's house at 8 Adelphi Terrace, Cotman made the acquaintance of and worked with all the most brilliant young artists of the day, and in addition to the studies he made there under these stimulating circumstances he joined a sketching club which Girtin had founded.

To Girtin, who was not only an inspiring genius but also a most generous and affectionate friend, Cotman probably owed most at this stage of his career, and it must have been a great shock to him when Girtin died at the early age of twenty-seven. After Girtin's death in November 1802 London was not the same place to Cotman, and though as a young struggling artist he could hardly complain of want of success — for he had exhibited no fewer than thirty paintings at the Royal Academy between 1800 and 1806— he made up his mind to return to his native city.

In London Cotman had applied himself especially to architectural subjects, and it is possible that even in these early days he was influenced in this direction by the gifted West Country artist, Samuel Prout (1783–1852), who excelled in water-colours of these subjects, and was living in London from 1802 to 1804 ; but when he returned to Norwich in 1806 or 1807, Cotman at first set himself up as a portrait painter. Gradually, however, under the influence of Crome—who was thirty-nine when Cotman was twenty-five — he devoted himself more and more to landscape. He became a member of the Norwich Society of Artists and was for a time its secretary.

Cotman was a prolific worker at this time, and to the Society's exhibition in 1808 he contributed no fewer than sixty-seven works. In 1809 he married, and soon afterwards removed to Yarmouth, where he added to his means by teaching drawing as well as painting in oils and water-colours, and also etching. In 1811 he commenced a publi-cation by subscription of his " Architectural Etchings," and having made a number of topographical tours throughout the country, he published in 1816 his " Specimens of Norman and Gothic Architecture, Norfolk Churches," etc. He formed a useful association with Dawson Turner, the Norfolk antiquary, for whose antiquarian publications Cotman drew and etched the illustrations, and during the next three years (1817–19) he made annual expeditions into Normandy with this writer, whose *Architectural Antiquities of Normandy*, illustrated by Cotman, was published in 1822. All the time that he was engaged on drawings for these and other publications Cotman was exhibiting oil-paintings and water-colours both in Norwich and in London, but though several of these found purchasers the prices were so low that, notwithstanding his immense industry, Cotman could not have supported his wife and family if, in addition to all his other activities, he had not continued to give drawing lessons.

In 1825, when he was again living in Norwich, Cotman was elected an Associate of the Water-colour Society in

Photo : W. A. Mansell & Co.   Reproduced by permission of the Corporation of Manchester.

"THE HIRELING SHEPHERD," BY W. HOLMAN HUNT (1827–1910).
Manchester Art Gallery.

One of the three founders of the Pre-Raphaelite Brotherhood, Holman Hunt was throughout his life the most faithful adherent to that accurate observation of Nature which was its early ideal.

London, and from that year was a constant contributor to the Society's exhibitions ; but though his work was known and respected both in London and Norwich, the genius of Cotman was never recognised in his lifetime nor indeed for many years after his death. The struggle to make a living began to tell on his nerves and health, and it was in the hope of giving him some ease by assuring him a regular income that his steadfast friend Dawson Turner, the antiquary, succeeded in getting Cotman appointed in 1834 as drawing-master at King's College School, then in the Strand. Removing to London in view of this appointment, Cotman settled himself at 42 Hunter Street, Brunswick Square, but the change seemed to do him more harm than good. His health gradually declined, and the nervous depression to which he was a victim became more and more severe till in the end his mind became slightly unhinged. His eldest son, Miles Edward Cotman (1811–58), a water-colourist of moderate ability, succeeded him as drawing-master at King's College School, and on July 28, 1842, John Sell Cotman died and was quietly buried in the churchyard of St. John's Wood Chapel, close to Lord's Cricket Ground. How little Cotman was appreciated then was made painfully evident when his remaining oil-paintings and water-colours were sold at Christie's in the following year. Works for which collectors would now gladly pay hundred of pounds hardly realised as many shillings in 1843, and the highest price for a painting by him then obtained was £8 15s. ; the highest price given for a Cotman water-colour was £6.

To discover exactly why an artist, afterwards recognised to be a genius, is not appreciated in his own lifetime, is never an easy task, but it is certain that many of his contemporaries considered Cotman's work to be " unfinished " because it had that vigorous breadth which now wins our admiration. Whether we look at an oil-painting like his " Wherries on the Yare " (see page 401), or a masterly water-colour like the " Greta Bridge " (see page 410) at the British Museum, we cannot fail to be impressed by the grandeur which the artist has given to his rendering of the scene by his subordination of detail and suppression of all that is irrelevant.

Cotman took a big view of Nature, and the breadth and simplicity of his masses materially help to give his pictures, whether in oil or water-colour, a monumental majesty unsurpassed even by his great contemporaries.

XVII

THE PRE-RAPHAELITES

THE ART OF FORD MADOX BROWN, ROSSETTI, HOLMAN HUNT,
MILLAIS, AND BURNE-JONES

§ 1

AMONG the pupils of John Sell Cotman when he was a drawing-master at King's College School was a strange, foreign-looking boy, the son of an Italian poet and patriot living in exile in London. This boy was Dante Gabriel Rossetti, who afterwards combined with Millais and Holman Hunt to found the Pre-Raphaelite Brotherhood. Innumerable books have been written in which it has been sought to show that first one and then another of these three young men was the real motive-power in the founding of a new style of painting; but the fact remains that it was not till all three came together in 1848 that any revolution was effected, and it was the peculiar and diverse gifts which each brought to the common stock which made their union so formidable and enabled them eventually to triumph over opposition and hostile criticism.

Rossetti, according to Ruskin, was " the chief intellectual force " in the association ; his fire, enthusiasm, and poetic feeling were valuable assets, but technically he was the least accomplished of the three. He had ideas, but at first he was weak in translating them into drawing and painting, and he shirked the drudgery of the discipline necessary to perfect his powers of expression. Millais, on the other hand, was not remarkable for original ideas, but he had brilliant powers of eye and hand ; he was a precocious genius in technique to whom the problems of drawing and painting presented no difficulty. Holman Hunt had neither the facility of Millais nor the impatience of Rossetti, but he had a high seriousness of purpose and a determined perseverance which held the others steadily together and chained their endeavours to lofty ideals.

Before considering what " Pre-Raphaelitism " was, and what it ultimately became, it will be helpful to glance briefly at the origin of its three founders. William Holman Hunt, the eldest of the trio, was born in Wood Street, Cheapside, on April 2, 1827. His father, the manager of a city warehouse, opposed his wish to be an artist and placed him at the age of twelve in the office of an estate agent. His employer encouraged young Hunt's artistic leanings, and the father reluctantly allowed the boy to spend his salary on lessons from a portrait painter. In 1843 Hunt was at last allowed to devote himself to art, but entirely at his own risk, and the sixteen-year-old boy bravely struggled along, studying half the week at the British Museum and supporting himself by painting portraits on the other three days. Eventually he was admitted as a probationer to the Academy Schools, where he soon made friends with his junior, Millais, and while studying still managed to earn a bare living.

The youngest of the three was John Everett Millais, who was born at Southampton in 1829. He came from a Norman family settled in Jersey, and his early childhood was spent in that island, at Le Quaihouse, near St. Heliers. His father was a popular, gifted man with some artistic talent, who delighted in and encouraged the precocious ability his son soon showed in drawing. In 1837 his parents came to live in Gower Street, London, and on the advice of the Irish artist Sir Martin Archer Shee (1769–1850), who was then President of the Royal Academy, young Millais was sent to Henry Sass's art school in Bloomsbury. Here his progress was so phenomenal that when he was only nine years old he won the silver medal of the Society of Arts. Two years later he was admitted to the Royal Academy Schools as the youngest student who ever worked there, and " The Child," as he was then called, was already considered to be a marvel of precocity whose achievements rivalled those of the youthful Lawrence.

"THE ORDER OF RELEASE, 1746," BY SIR JOHN EVERETT MILLAIS
Tate Gallery, London.

This brilliant and pathetic painting of a Highlander, wounded in the '45 Rebellion and unexpectedly delivered from prison, his wife having brought an order for his release, won for the artist his A.R.A. in 1853.

The woman is a portrait of Mrs. John Ruskin, who afterwards became Lady Millais.

27

When he was twelve years old he painted his first picture in oils, and in 1845, when he was sixteen, he was able to earn £100 a year by painting in backgrounds for a dealer and selling him some of his sketches. In the following year he exhibited " Pizarro seizing the Inca of Peru," a large painting of remarkable maturity now in the Victoria and Albert Museum, South Kensington, and in the next year, 1847, he was awarded a gold medal for his " Young Men of the Tribe of Benjamin seizing their Brides." In neither of these pictures do we perceive any tendency of the artist to revolutionise the style of painting then in vogue ; both of them are more or less in the manner of William Etty (1787–1849), whose art, like that of Sir Joshua Reynolds, was chiefly based on the Venetian masters and whose colour was rich, but heavy and dark. At the Academy Schools Millais had already made the acquaintance of Holman Hunt, but though the two young students may have been discontented with the pictorial ideals of the time, and may have discussed aims and methods in private, they did not show any signs of a new faith in their works till after they had made the acquaintance of Rossetti.

After leaving King's College School, Rossetti studied art at Cary's Academy in Bloomsbury, and though he was not able to gain admittance into the life-class, he worked in the Antique School of the Royal Academy in 1845 and 1846. Born in London in 1828, Dante Gabriel Rossetti was a year younger than Holman Hunt, and a year older than Millais, but though so near their own age, he was from an art-master's point of view far below them, so that he was kept drawing from casts of antique statues when they were already drawing and painting live human beings. This was dull work for Rossetti, who was passionately interested in life, and he looked around to see where he might obtain more congenial tuition. He had been greatly attracted by a picture he had seen in an exhibition, " Our Lady of Saturday Night," and he went to the painter, Ford Madox Brown, and besought him to accept him as a pupil. After some demur Brown consented, but when Rossetti, though allowed brushes and colours, found that his new master's method of tuition consisted in setting him to paint studies of still life, his impatience at discipline soon overcame him ; and declaring that he was tired of painting " pots and pans," when his head was full of exciting pictures of romantic women and knightly men, he broke away from Brown after an apprenticeship that only lasted some four months.

Ford Madox Brown (1821–93) was never a member of the Pre-Raphaelite Brotherhood, but he was so much in sympathy with their aims and his art was so nearly related to their own, that some brief account of him must be included in any review of this phase of English painting. Madox Brown was six years the senior of Holman Hunt. He was born in Calais at a time when David and the Classicists had imposed a new artistic ideal on France, and when he began to paint about 1835 this classical ideal was being attacked by a new romantic movement to which Madox Brown was attracted. He was from his childhood, therefore, conversant with Continental art movements— as the majority of English painters were not — and after studying at Bruges, Ghent, and Antwerp, where he was the pupil of the Belgian historical and romantic painter, Baron Wappers, he worked for three years in Paris. His desire then was to become a painter of large historical pictures, and in 1844 he came to England in order to enter a competition for the commission to paint decorations for Westminster Hall. In this he was unsuccessful, and in the following year he went to Rome, where he became acquainted with two curious German painters named Cornelius and Overbeck. These artists were leading semi-monastic lives, and in so far as they deliberately cultivated the devotional frame of mind of the Italian masters who preceded Raphael, they were the first " Pre-Raphaelites." Cornelius and Overbeck, who were both devout Catholics, worked in cells, and like the mediæval monastic painters, they prepared themselves for their work by scourging, vigil, and fasting. In order that their work might be free from all taint of " fleshliness," they avoided the use to human models. It is not likely that their dry

"THE LAST OF ENGLAND," BY FORD MADOX BROWN (1821–1893).
Birmingham Art Gallery.

Though an older artist, Madox Brown was influenced by the "Brotherhood," and the picture—which shows emigrants taking their last look at the "old country"—is "Pre-Raphaelite" in its exact rendering of details and in its serious thoughtfulness of expression.

and rather affected painting influenced Madox Brown to any great extent, but they doubtlessly opened his eyes to the excellencies of the earlier Italian painters, and showed him that there was more than one way of looking at Nature.

It cannot be too strongly emphasised that for the connoisseurs of the eighteenth and early nineteenth centuries, the " Old Masters " began where in the opinion of to-day they end. We look upon Raphael, Michael Angelo, and Leonardo da Vinci as the *end* of a great school of painters ; but our forefathers were inclined to regard them as the *beginning* of a great school. Their successors, men like Annibale Carracci (1560–1609), Domenichino (1581–1641), and Carlo Maratti (1625–1713), were at one time esteemed as Masters, though to-day we recognise that their art was decadent and debased. Cornelius and Overbeck were perfectly right in preferring the painters before Raphael to those who followed him, but they made the deadly error of merely imitating the pictures of the Italian Primitives, instead of going, as they had done, direct to Nature. Thus the German painters made exactly the same mistake as the late Italian painters had done, and their art was sterile also for the same reason, because it was " soup of the soup," art based wholly on preceding art.

The effect of the early Christian painters on Ford Madox Brown was to cause him, not to imitate their work slavishly, but to look at Nature for himself, as they did. When he did look he perceived that Nature was far brighter than it appeared to be in the pictures of his British contemporaries. Since the time of Reynolds, Sir George Beaumont's dictum that a good picture must be a brown picture had been the general opinion, and though certain landscape painters rebelled against this doctrine as we have seen, no English figure painters made any serious stand against it till Ford Madox Brown and the Pre-Raphaelites began to exhibit.

How had this cult in brown pictures arisen ? The explanation is very simple. Painters had observed that the pictures by the recognised great masters, Rembrandt, Titian, Tintoretto, etc., were usually brown in tone, but this brownness was often due, not only to the pigments originally used by the masters, but also to the grime of centuries, to the " tone of time." Seeking to be praised as " Old Masters " in their own lifetime, painters used artificial means to make their pictures look brown, and were in the habit of painting on a brown bituminous ground in order to give to their pictures a fictitious quality of golden-brown light and " Rembrandtesque " shadow. For Madox Brown reversed the general practice of his day by painting his pictures on a white ground, and immediately his colour became brighter and truer to Nature.

By the time he was back in England in 1846, Madox Brown had come independently to very much the same conclusions that Hunt and Millais were now whispering to one another, and he had begun to adopt a method of painting very similar to that subsequently practised by the Brotherhood, to whom we must now return.

§ 2

Unknown to one another, Rossetti and Holman Hunt both had a passion for the poetry of Keats, and it was this that first really brought them together. It was in 1848 that Rossetti persuaded Madox Brown to have him as a pupil, and to the Academy of that year Hunt had sent a painting inspired by a poem of Keats. In the memoirs which he wrote in his old age, Mr. Hunt gave an account of how he met the younger artist in a picture gallery and what ensued :

Rossetti came up to me [he wrote] loudly declaring that my picture of " The Eve of St. Agnes " was the best in the collection. . . . Rossetti frankly proposed to me to come and see him. Before this I had been only on nodding terms with him in the schools, to which he came but rarely and irregularly. He had always attracted there a following of clamorous students who, like Millais's throng, were rewarded with original sketches. Rossetti's subjects were of a different class from Millais, not of newly culled facts, but of knights rescuing ladies. A few days more and Rossetti was in my studio.

The upshot of these meetings was that Rossetti left Madox Brown and shared a studio with Holman Hunt, under whose guidance he began painting his first picture,

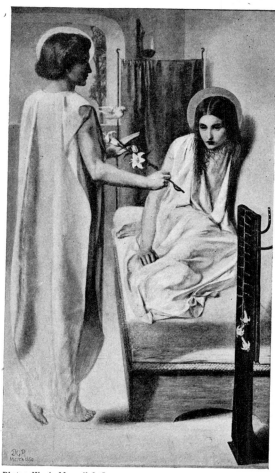

"THE ANNUNCIATION," BY D. G. ROSSETTI (1828–1882).

Tate Gallery, London.

In this, his second attempt to paint a picture, the poetic nature of the artist finds exquisite expression in his haunting conception of wistful, meditative maidenhood. His sister, Christina Rossetti, the poetess, posed for the figure of the Virgin.

" The Girlhood of the Virgin " (see opposite page). Intimacy with Hunt naturally led to intimacy with his friend Millais, and it is said that the immediate occasion of the founding of the Brotherhood was an evening spent by the three friends in the house of Millais's parents looking at engravings of the early Italian wall-paintings in the Campo Santo at Pisa. According to Mr. Hunt, it was Rossetti who insisted that their union should be a close one, and that it should be styled a " Brotherhood." The term " Pre-Raphaelite " originated as a nickname, somebody exclaiming when they had expressed a preference for the painters before Raphael to those who succeeded him, " Why, then you must be pre-Raphaelites." The title was adopted as an official label which fitly conveyed their aims. These aims were to paint Nature with minute fidelity and to regain the intense sincerity of the early Italian painters, but undoubtedly Rossetti held that the latter also implied intense poetic expression.

Thus the Pre-Raphaelite Brotherhood was established, and in addition to the three founders, membership was extended to Dante Gabriel's brother, W. M. Rossetti, and to three of their friends, Woolner, a sculptor, James Collinson, and F. G. Stephens. James Collinson was probably elected on the strength of his picture, " The Charity Boy's Debut," in the Academy of 1847, and would doubtless have been a more important figure had he not ceased exhibiting after 1870 and retired to a monastery. His most important picture, " St. Elizabeth of Hungary," painted in 1851, is now in the Johannesburg Gallery. William Rossetti and Stephens soon abandoned painting ; both became art critics, and their eloquent and enthusiastic articles did much to convert the public to an appreciation of the work of the other Brothers.

It is no unusual thing for art students or young artists to form themselves into clubs and societies, to hold regular meetings, and to discuss their aims, methods, and ideals ; but so often the talk leads to nothing. In the case of Millais and Hunt it led to a revolution of their painting ; in the case of Rossetti it led to something approaching a

"GIRLHOOD OF THE VIRGIN," BY DANTE GABRIEL ROSSETTI.

Lady Jekyll's Collection.

The first picture ever painted by Rossetti, who under the guidance of Holman Hunt here shows an exactitude in the painting of details which he never **surpassed** later.   The artist's mother sat for St. Anne and his sister Christina for the Virgin.

masterpiece at the first effort. In 1848 Millais had exhibited " Cymon and Iphigenia," another painting in the style of Etty ; in 1849 he exhibited " Lorenzo and Isabella," now at Liverpool, and but for the conclaves of the brethren and the stimulating encouragement of comradeship he could never in one year have leapt the gulf which separates the two pictures. Holman Hunt's " Rienzi "

" CHRIST IN THE HOUSE OF HIS PARENTS," BY SIR JOHN EVERETT MILLAIS (1829–1896).

Tate Gallery, London.

Dreadfully abused as " mean, odious, revolting, and repulsive " when it was first shown at the Academy in 1850—Charles Dickens joining in the attack—this picture is now generally considered to be the painter's noblest masterpiece. John Ruskin was the first great writer to praise it, and his eulogy turned the tide of public opinion.

was an equally sensational advance on his " St. Agnes's Eve," but in many respects the most remarkable achievement of all was Rossetti's " Girlhood of Mary Virgin." Finely painted as " Lorenzo and Isabella " is, it has not the touching simplicity of Rossetti's first painting; it is more imitative, a skilful exercise in the manner of the early Italian masters. It was immensely clever, but it was not quite what the Pre-Raphaelite Brotherhood set out to do.

Rossetti's maiden effort may appear childish in places when compared with the accomplishment of the Millais, but it is a much better example of true Pre-Raphaelitism in its absolutely honest and unconventional attempt to render what the painter saw. Mr. Hunt has told us that

Photo: *W. A. Mansell & Co.*

OPHELIA," BY MILLAIS.

Tate Gallery, London.

Painted on the Ewell, near Kingston, this picture is famous for the precise study of Nature shown in the foreground and background. The figure was painted in his studio from Miss Siddal, who had to lie in a bath of water; one day Millais forgot to fill the lamps which kept the water warm, with the result that this beautiful and gifted woman, afterwards Mrs. Rossetti, contracted a serious illness which eventually shortened her life.

every detail in this picture was painted directly from life under his supervision, and it says much for his patient influence that in the first year of the Brotherhood its most romantic member should have painted the most naturalistic picture.

The trouble with Rossetti, owing to his teeming, poetic imagination, had been that he had always wanted to paint things " out of his head " at a time when his hand and eye needed to be educated by an endeavour to paint truly what was before him. With infinite tact Holman Hunt let him set to work on a romantic subject, the choice of his heart, but he took care that every detail in this imaginative scene should be painted truly and carefully from facts.   In Madox Brown's studio Rossetti had rebelled at painting so prosaic an object as a pot ; Holman Hunt led him to paint the same object with delight because it held the symbolical lily needed by his subject. For the first time in his life Rossetti became passionately interested in *things*, because he had been made to see that they helped him to express his ideas. He borrowed big books from his father, and window curtains from his parents' house in Charlotte Street.   His sister Christina sat for the Virgin, and his mother for St. Anne. He borrowed a child's nightgown and painted that on a small lay-figure, which probably explains why the figure of the little angel is not so convincing as the head ; but when we remember that Rossetti was painting every object in the picture for the very first time we are compelled to stop fault-finding to marvel at the wonder of his achievement.

" Rienzi " and " Lorenzo and Isabella " were exhibited in the Academy of 1849 ; " The Girlhood of Mary Virgin " in the Hyde Park Gallery known as the " Free Exhibition " ; but somewhat to the disappointment of their authors they attracted very little public attention. Even the " P.R.B." after Rossetti's signature on his picture appears to have escaped comment. Undismayed, if a trifle disappointed, the young revolutionaries set about more vigorous propaganda by means of new pictures, and a periodical, *The Germ*, in which they could ventilate their opinions and doctrines.

It was with the idea of writing a journal for this magazine that during the summer Hunt and Rossetti made a tour in France and Belgium, and this journal was duly written, though later it was considered too personal to be published in *The Germ*. In their judgments of the pictures they was abroad the young artists were terribly severe. Van

Photo : W. A. Mansell & Co.

Reproduced by permission of the Corporation of Birmingham.

THE BLIND GIRL," BY MILLAIS.

Birmingham Art Gallery.

One of the last paintings in which Millais strictly adhered to the principles of the Pre-Raphaelite Brotherhood, this picture moves us equally by the pathetic tenderness of its subject and by the beautiful precision of its rendering of Nature.

Eyck and the early Flemings they admired intensely, but the works of the later painters from Rembrandt to Rubens were dismissed in two words as " filthy slosh."

After what they had seen abroad they held more firmly than ever before that it was not enough for a picture to be correctly drawn and well painted, it must also enshrine a worthy idea. In accordance with this doctrine, now added to the rules of the Brotherhood, Hunt, Millais, and Rossetti all chose serious subjects for the pictures they intended to exhibit in 1850. Hunt painted " An Early Christian Missionary escaping from Druids," Millais his famous " Christ in the House of His Parents " (see page 426), and Rossetti " The Annunciation " (see page 423), or " Ecce Ancilla Domini " as it was originally called. Curiously enough Rossetti, who in the previous year had been the most, was now the least Pre-Raphaelite of the three. His strangely beautiful work is not a vision of things seen, but a reverie, the romantic rendering of a mood. Again his sister Christina sat for the Virgin, and Thomas Woolner posed for the head of the Archangel.

Millais, on the other hand, had now thoroughly grasped the principle of Pre-Raphaelitism, and no longer giving a clever imitation of an Italian Primitive, he outdid Hunt himself in the thoroughness with which each detail in his picture was studied from Nature. In order to get absolute truth, Millais took his canvas to a carpenter's shop to paint the details ; he painted the figure of Joseph from the carpenter because that was, he said, " the only way to get the development of the muscles right." He was not able to get sheep, but he purchased two sheep's heads from a butcher and painted the flock from them ; and it will be observed that the sheep in the picture only show their heads, the bodies being tactfully concealed by wickerwork.

By the time the Academy of 1850 opened the existence and doctrines of the Brotherhood had become more widely known, and this year there was no opportunity to complain of any want of public attention. The three pictures aroused a storm of criticism which fell with particular fury on the head of Millais. The true meaning of " Pre-

Raphaelite " was not very well understood, and the popular view was that a group of young painters had set themselves up to be " better than Raphael " and deserved to be trounced for their vanity and impudence. And trounced they were. " Their ambition," wrote one newspaper critic, " is an unhealthy thirst which seeks notoriety by means of mere conceit. Abruptness, singularity, uncouthness, are the counters by which they play the game."

The title " The Carpenter's Shop," by which Millais's picture is now generally known, was contemptuously applied to it by enemies of the Pre-Raphaelite movement. The artist originally exhibited it at the Academy with no other title than an extract from Zachariah (xiii. 6) :

And one shall say unto Him, What are these wounds in Thine hands ? Then He shall answer, Those with which I was wounded in the house of My friends.

The very humanity which endears the picture to us to-day and makes it irresistibly winning was at that time a cause of offence. Millais was accused of dragging down the Saviour to " the lowest of human levels, to the level of craving human pity and assistance." The picture was described as " a pictorial blasphemy " from which right-minded people would " recoil with disgust and loathing." Even Charles Dickens took part in the general attack, and denounced the picture in *Household Words* as follows :

In the foreground of the carpenter's shop is a hideous, wry-necked, blubbering red-haired boy in a nightgown, who appears to have received a poke in the hand from the stick of another boy with whom he had been playing in an adjacent gutter, and to be holding it up for the contemplation of a kneeling woman so horrible in her ugliness that (supposing it were possible for a human creature to exist for a moment with that dislocated throat) she would stand out from the rest of the company as a monster in the vilest cabaret in France, or the lowest gin-shop in England.

Since the famous novelist's abuse was directed far more at the persons than the painting, it is interesting to recall that the " blubbering boy " was little Noel Humphreys, the son of an architect, while the " monster horrible in ugliness " was Mrs. Henry Hodgkinson. Not one of the

" THE BELOVED," BY D. G. ROSSETTI.

Tate Gallery, London.

" My beloved is mine and I am his." This poetical concèption of the Bride in the Song of Solomon was commissioned by Mr. George Rae in 1863 and painted by Rossetti in 1865.

people in the picture was painted from a professional model, and though the body of St. Joseph is that of the carpenter the head is a portrait of the father of Millais.

This shower of vituperation affected the fortunes of the brethren, and Woolner, who had unsuccessfully competed for a commission to execute a Wordsworth Memorial, abandoned sculpture for a time and set sail for the gold-diggings in Australia. There eventually he returned to sculpture, and in later years he had a modest success in Australia and England with his portrait busts. Holman Hunt, who could not lean on his parents, as Millais and Rossetti could, had a desperate struggle with poverty, and was compelled to take on the job of washing and restoring the wall paintings by Rigaud (1659–1743) at Trinity House. Stephens was employed with Hunt on this work, and William Rossetti got a place in the Inland Revenue Office. Millais, though the most abused, was the best off of the band, for a dealer named Farrer had the courage to pay him £150 for his picture and showed his faith in the artist by pasting all the adverse criticisms on the back of the canvas. Late in the year a purchaser was found also for the picture by Hunt, who then abandoned his restoration, and set to work on his splendid picture " Two Gentlemen of Verona," now in the Birmingham Art Gallery. Millais at the same time began painting his " Woodman's Daughter," and in these pictures the artists obtained a greater brilliancy of colour than they had yet secured by painting upon a *wet* white ground. They prided themselves on having rediscovered one of the secrets of the early Italian masters, and later on Hunt communicated the " secret " to Madox Brown, whose pictures certainly gained much in luminosity and brightness of colour immediately after 1851.

Rossetti had begun an oil-painting of a subject from one of Browning's poems, but he did not get it finished, so that Millais and Hunt alone had to sustain the renewed attack which was made when their pictures were exhibited in the Academy of 1851. In addition to " The Woodman's Daughter," Millais exhibited " Mariana, or the Moated

28

Grange " and " The Return of the Dove to the Ark," and again he and Hunt were told that their paintings were " offensive and absurd productions," displaying nothing but " puerility," " uppishness," and " morbid infatuation." This year, however, they were not without defenders. William Rossetti had begun his career as an art critic and upheld Pre-Raphaelite aims and ideals in the columns of the *Spectator*. Still more important were two letters of chivalrous and whole-hearted appreciation which appeared in *The Times*, signed by " An Oxford Graduate," and everybody knew that the writer was the great John Ruskin. In the same year appeared a new volume of *Modern Painters*, in which Ruskin wrote of Millais and Holman Hunt :

> Their works are, in finish of drawing and splendour of colour, the best work in the Royal Academy, and I have great hope that they may become the foundation of a more earnest and able school of art than we have seen for centuries.

It is difficult to exaggerate the revulsion of feeling produced by Ruskin's pronouncements, for at that time he was almost a dictator of taste in England. Slowly the tide began to turn in favour of the brethren, but it was very nearly too late for Hunt. His picture returned to him unsold from the Academy, he was absolutely penniless and had nothing to tide him over until better times ; indeed, he was on the point of abandoning painting and seeking his fortune as a sheep-farmer in Australia when Millais and his parents came to the rescue. Millais had made a little money and, with his parents' consent, he gave it to his comrade in order that he might make one more attempt. This generous help bound the two " Brothers " still more closely together, and they spent the late summer and early autumn in the country near Surbiton, searching the backwaters of the Thames to find just the right background for the picture of " Ophelia " (see page 427), which Millais had decided to paint, and studying the meadows for the scene of Hunt's crucial picture " The Hireling Shepherd " (see page 413). But Hunt did not have to wait till this, perhaps his most perfect picture, was finished and exhibited before learning that the tide was turning ; for while he and Millais were painting in the fields a letter was brought them announcing that the Liverpool Academy had awarded a prize of £50 to the painter of " Two Gentlemen of Verona."

" The Hireling Shepherd " embodies the essence of Pre-Raphaelitism and indicates its high-water mark. In the

Photo : W. A. Mansell & Co.   Reproduced by permission of the Corporation of Birmingham.

THE TRIUMPH OF THE INNOCENTS," BY W. HOLMAN HUNT.
Walker Art Gallery, Liverpool.

Rigidly faithful all his life to Pre-Raphaelite principles, Mr. Holman Hunt visited Palestine twice in order that he might be able to paint sacred subjects with literal truth to Syrian landscape. With poetic imagination the artist depicts the flight into Egypt as a royal progress in which " only the Child's eyes are open to see the children whose wakening souls are His retinue."

heedless shepherd, who dallies with a coquettish beauty while a wolf is worrying his sheep, a worthy moral lesson is inculcated ; while its bright, jewel-like colour reveals the minute fidelity with which Nature has been painted. When it was shown in the Academy of 1852 the battle was nearly over, for though there was still considerable opposition, the Pre-Raphaelite picture had now become an accepted type of painting, and other Academy exhibitors

"KING COPHETUA AND THE BEGGAR-MAID,"
BY SIR EDWARD BURNE-JONES (1833–1898).

Tate Gallery, London:

In this dreamlike picture of the King about to lay his
jewelled crown at the feet of the begger-maid, we may
trace the mediæval romanticism of Rossetti refined by the
spirituality of a Celtic mystic.

436

were beginning to change their practice and paint in a similar style.

The battle was won, but the Brotherhood was beginning to break up ; Woolner was in Australia, Collinson thinking about retiring to a monastery, William Rossetti and Stephens had definitely become writers, and worse still Dante Gabriel Rossetti was beginning to drift away. From 1850 to 1853 Rossetti produced no large picture, he was steeping himself in Dantesque literature and his mind was more occupied with poetry ; now and again he produced some lovely little water-colours, Ruskin, who had become his principal patron, encouraging him in this direction with his purse as well as his praise. In 1853— the year in which he painted " The Order of Release " (see page 417) — Millais was elected A.R.A., and in the following year Holman Hunt, who had just painted and sold for £400 " The Light of the World," set sail for Palestine in order that he might be able to paint incidents from the life of Christ with literal truth to the nature of the country in which He lived. To the end Holman Hunt remained the most consistent of all to the principles of Pre-Raphaelitism.

For a little while after his departure the influence of Holman Hunt lingered in England. " Autumn Leaves " and " The Blind Girl," both painted in 1855, are true Pre-Raphaelite pictures, and they were the last paintings by Millais that Ruskin blessed. But gradually, as he went on his way alone, Millais deteriorated, and though his work rapidly won public favour so that his career henceforward was, from a worldly point of view, one of uninterrupted success, his pictures ceased to be inspired by the noble seriousness of Holman Hunt or by the poetry of Rossetti. What had been sentiment degenerated into sentimentality, and as his subject-matter became commoner in quality, so an increasing laxity crept into his style of painting. " Bubbles," the child picture so extensively popularised as an advertisement by a firm of soap-makers, is the best known example of his later style, but the achievements which come nearest to the distinction of his early work are some of his portraits, notably that of John Charles Montague, an ex-sergeant of the 16th Lancers, whom Millais painted in the uniform of " The Yeoman of the Guard." This picture was painted in 1876, and thirteen years earlier Millais had been elected R.A. In 1885 he was created a baronet, and in 1896, after the death of Lord Leighton, he was made President of the Royal Academy ; but already his health was failing, and shortly after his election he died, on August 13 of the same year, and was buried in St. Paul's Cathedral by the side of his mighty predecessor, Sir Joshua Reynolds.

§ 3

Meanwhile Rossetti had been treading another path, forsaking the naturalism of Holman Hunt, but avoiding the anecdotal triviality that tempted Millais ; his pictures became more and more dream-like in their imaginative aloofness from life. The popularity that Millais courted was shunned by Rossetti, who, relying on the patronage of Ruskin and other admirers, ceased to exhibit his pictures except in his own studio.

In 1857 Rossetti went to Oxford with the intention of executing wall-paintings in the Debating Hall of the Union Society, snd there he gathered round him a brilliant band of pupils, chief among whom were two undergraduates from Exeter College, William Morris and Edward Burne-Jones (1833–98). Unfortunately the English climate is fatal to true fresco painting, but though the Oxford decorations rapidly perished, and to-day are hardly visible, they remain historic as marking the starting-point of a new phase of Pre-Raphaelitism, in which the naturalist element was lost and its place taken by a more deliberately decorative and romantic mediævalism. Of this new school Rossetti was as definitely the leader and inspirer as Holman Hunt had been of the original Brotherhood, and though for many years the pictures produced by Rossetti and his followers continued to be commonly described as " Pre-Raphaelite." it is now clear that their productions really had little to do

"THE DAY-DREAM," BY ROSSETTI.
South Kensington Museum, London.

A beautiful example of Rossetti's third and last phase, during which his model and inspiration was the beautiful wife of his disciple, William Morris.

439

with the original Pre-Raphaelitism, but formed part of what became known later as the " Æsthetic Movement."

In 1862 Eleanor Siddal, who for ten years had been Rossetti's model and constant inspiration, died, and at first the bereaved husband was so prostrated with grief that he was totally unfitted for work. But two years later he recommenced painting in oils, and reached the highest point in his " Lady Lilith " of 1864, and " The Beloved " (see page 432), painted in 1865-6. Though nominally a subject from the Song of Solomon, this voluptuous presentation of feminine beauty, which for sheer loveliness rivals a Botticelli, is far removed from the simple and comparatively stern Biblical paintings of the artist's youth. The subject is clothed in the garb of mediævalism, enveloped in the romance of a fairy-tale, and heightened by a brilliance of colour unsurpassed in the painter's work.

Rossetti's pictorial work may be divided into three periods, each of which is dominated by an ideal of womanhood derived from a living woman ; in the first period she is his sister Christina, in the second his wife Eleanor Siddal, and the inspiration of the third was Mrs. William Morris. Of the many pictures she inspired one of the most beautiful is " The Day-dream " (page 439) in the Ionides Collection at South Kensington, but though he painted her in many characters, he never painted Mrs. Morris as Dante's Beatrice. That character was sacred to his wife, and it was in memory of her that he began to paint in 1863— though it was not finished till much later—the " Beata Beatrix," now in the Tate Gallery. The picture, according to Rossetti, " is not intended at all to represent death, but to render it under the semblance of a trance, in which Beatrice, seated at a balcony overlooking the city [Florence], is suddenly rapt from earth to heaven."

Rossetti died at Birchington in 1882, but his ideals were faithfully carried on by the most celebrated of his pupils, Edward Burne-Jones, who had been intended for the Church, but after meeting Rossetti at Oxford felt he must be a painter. One great difference between their pictures lay in their different ideals of womanhood, for while the women of Rossetti were full-blooded and passionate, those of Burne-Jones were of so refined a spirituality that to many people they appear anæmic. Otherwise the paintings of Burne-Jones are as remote from naturalism as the later works of Rossetti; he also gives us dream pictures of an imaginary mediævalism; and while Rossetti, as became his Italian descent, found his ideal in the Florence of Dante's time, the Welshman Burne-Jones fittingly found his in the legendary court of King Arthur. Both, however, were

"THE MILL," BY SIR E. BURNE-JONES.

South Kensington Museum, London.

This vision of an imaginary world remote from actual life shows how Burne-Jones's idea of womanhood differs from that of Rossetti, and how far removed are his pictorial ideals from the naturalism of Millais and Holman Hunt.

inspired by the same feeling for chivalry and romance, and the distance that had been travelled from Holman Hunt's naturalism may be traced in the famous confession of Burne-Jones that he longed to paint " the light that never was on sea or land."

In 1884 he exhibited one of his best known and most popular works, " King Cophetua and the Beggar-Maid " (see page 436), at the Grosvenor Gallery, and two years later, at the age of fifty-three, he was tardily elected A.R.A., but he was never much in sympathy with the Academy, seldom exhibited there, and in 1893, five years before he died, he resigned his Associateship.

In addition to his pictures and water-colours, Burne-Jones designed a number of tapestries and stained-glass windows for his lifelong friend William Morris, whose unbounded artistic energy found more congenial occupation in reviving crafts than in practising painting. In Morris the mediævalism of Rossetti found a furiously eager and thoroughgoing exponent, and though many of his ideas were unpractical, his inauguration of the Arts and Crafts Society was one of the most fruitful art movements of the Victorian era, and to him more than to any other man we owe not only the revival of tapestry and stained glass but a great improvement on fine printing, in furniture, pottery, wall-papers, and interior decoration generally.

Holman Hunt, the eldest of the Pre-Raphaelites, survived them all, and after painting a series of sacred pictures unique in English art for their religious fervour and geographical exactitude, he died in September 1910 at the great age of eighty-three.

XVIII

THE VICTORIAN AGE

THE ART OF LANDSEER, LEIGHTON, POYNTER, ALFRED STEVENS, ALBERT MOORE, ORCHARDSON, AND G. F. WATTS

§ 1

SEVERAL of the artists already mentioned in this Outline — among them being Turner, Cotman, and David Cox — were alive and working when Queen Victoria ascended the throne in 1837, but we are not in the habit of thinking of any of these as typical artists of the Victorian era. Even the Pre-Raphaelites, whose art, as described in the last chapter, shed so much lustre on the Queen's long reign, were a group apart from the general trend of the times, and none of these painters—with the one exception of Millais in his later years—showed in his art those peculiar characteristics which we are now inclined to label broadly as " Victorian."

Just as in politics the reign of Victoriɾ was distinguished, before all things, by the growth of **Democracy,** so painting during this reign approached more closely than it had ever done before to popular ideals. Under Queen Victoria English painting became a homely, easily understandable art, appealing to the people by clear representation of simple themes often founded on everyday life, and almost always tinged by a sentiment perceptible and congenial to the humblest intelligence. Subject was of paramount importance, every picture told a story, and the story was usually of a simple nature that required no erudition for its comprehension, one that all who ran could read.

Of a host of pictures of this description only a few can be mentioned here. The quintessence of Victorianism may be found in the paintings of William Powell Frith (1819–

"HOPE," BY G. F. WATTS.

Tate Gallery, London.

Blindfolded, with lyre in hand, and sitting on the globe in the dim twilight of the world, Hope " strives to get all the music possible out of the last remaining string."

This beautiful allegory is the masterpiece of an artist who sought in all his works to " appeal to the imagination and the heart, and kindle all that is best and noblest in humanity."

1909), whose " Derby Day," now in the Tate Gallery, created a sensation in 1858, and whose " Railway Station," painted four years later, is a still more dramatic assemblage of the " all sorts and conditions of men " who go to make the world. No knowledge of the Old Masters or of the technique of painting is needed to enjoy Frith's " Railway Station " ; everybody can recognise the bridal couple being " seen off " by their friends, the boy who is going to school, the new recruit taking leave of his parents, and the criminal who is being arrested at the moment when he thought to escape. This picture is not only full of the incidents which may be seen at any railway station ; it is full of the simple human emotions which all have experienced and all can understand.

Very much the same qualities—though the subjects are entirely different—can be found in the works of Sir Edwin Landseer, R.A. (1802–1873), who was reputed to have been Queen Victoria's favourite painter, and was certainly one of the most popular and most successful painters of his day. Edwin Henry Landseer was born in London and was one of a family of artists. He was the third son of John Landseer, A.R.A., a painter and engraver ; his brother Charles Landseer (1799–1879) also became a successful painter of historical and animal pictures ; and his eldest brother, Thomas Landseer, became an expert engraver, whose prints after his brother's pictures materially contributed to the wide-spread fame and popularity which Edwin Landseer enjoyed. Animals specially appealed to the young artist, and some of his earliest studies were made in a menagerie at Exeter Exchange, where the Strand Palace Hotel now stands. The first distinction he received was a premium from the Society of Arts for his drawing of " A Horse for Hunting," and at the age of fourteen he was admitted as a student to the schools of the Royal Academy, where he had already made his debut as an exhibitor with a painting of " The Heads of a Poynter and Puppy."

Up to about 1820 his subjects had chiefly been dogs and horses, but he soon added other animals to his repertory. Among his father's friends was the historical painter

Benjamin Robert Haydon (1786–1846), and on the advice of this artist Landseer, while still an Academy student, learnt to dissect and make anatomical studies of animals. Taking advantage of the death of a lion in one of the menageries, he diligently studied its anatomy, and the knowledge thus gained gave him a power in the drawing of that animal notable in his future works. The first fruits of these studies were his pictures " A Prowling Lion " in the Academy of 1821 and " A Lion Disturbed " in the following year. In 1824 he exhibited " The Cat's Paw," a picture of a monkey seizing a cat's paw to take roasting chestnuts from a fire, this being one of the first of his animal paintings in which an obvious moral was happily combined with humour.

In this year, when Landseer was twenty-two, he accompanied his friend and fellow-student C. R. Leslie (1794–1859) on a visit to Scotland, where the two young artists had the honour of staying with Sir Walter Scott at Abbotsford. Landseer drew the dogs of the author of *Waverley*, and was introduced by the novelist to the deer forests of Scotland. Henceforward the " monarch of the glen " became one of Landseer's favourite subjects, and deerstalking was the sport which he loved beyond all others; but it is said that the sportsman was often vanquished by the artist, and that when a particularly noble animal came in sight, Landseer was apt to fling down his rifle and pick up instead his sketch-book and pencil.

In 1826 he was elected A.R.A., and his prosperity being now assured he left his father's house and established himself at 1 St. John's Wood Road, where he lived unmarried till the day of his death. Landseer now widened the field of his art, and painted pictures of various subjects, among them being several portraits. One of the most successful of the last was " Lord Cosmo Russell," a picture of a little boy on a rough pony scampering over the heather; but while he never lacked patrons even for portraiture, his fame and popularity depended chiefly on his animal pictures, and particularly on his paintings of dogs. A witty canon of St. Paul's, who was advised to have his portrait painted by

"DIGNITY AND IMPUDENCE," BY SIR EDWIN LANDSEER, R.A. (1802–73).
Tate Gallery, London.

Landseer, who was Queen Victoria's favourite painter, is the most famous interpreter in art of canine intelligence and fidelity. In this, the most popular of his pictures, the artist humorously contrasts the stateliness of the bloodhound with the " cheekiness " of a little Scotch terrier.

447

Landseer, laughingly declined with the remark, " Is thy servant a dog that he should do this thing ? "

In 1834 he exhibited at the Royal Academy " Bolton Abbey in the Olden Time," one of the best known and most popular of all his works, which has been made familiar throughout Great Britain not only by engravings but also by innumerable copies in needlework. In 1837 he increased his already great reputation by his picture of a faithful dog watching beside a coffin, entitled " The Old Shepherd's Chief Mourner," a work of intense pathos, and in the following year he painted a noble Newfoundland dog as " A Distinguished Member of the Humane Society." No painter ever surpassed Landseer in rendering all the varied aspects of canine character, and while in some of his pictures he attained a sublimity of pathos so that some captious critics accused him of making his dogs " too human," in others he showed a subtle humour which is irresistible. Probably no English picture has ever enjoyed a wider popularity than " Dignity and Impudence " (see preceding page), in which Landseer amusingly contrasts an old blood-hound of the Duke of Grafton breed with a little Scotch terrier called " Scratch." Landseer loved dogs and kept a troop of them in his home at St. John's Wood.

From 1839 onwards the artist enjoyed a considerable intimacy with the Royal Family. He taught both Queen Victoria and the Prince Consort to etch and painted many pictures for them, one of his largest being " The Drive, Shooting Deer on the Pass." He had been elected R.A. in 1831 and in 1850 he was knighted. He was a sculptor as well as a painter, and in 1859 he was commissioned to execute the lions for the base of Nelson's Column in Trafalgar Square. On this work the artist was engaged, off and on, for some half a dozen years, and his lions were finally uncovered at Trafalgar Square in 1869. Two of the studies which Landseer made at the Zoo for these lions are now in the National Gallery (Nos. 1349 and 1350).

Three years earlier, on the death of Sir Charles Eastlake (1793–1865), Landseer had been offered the Presidency of the Royal Academy, but he declined the honour, for though

"FAITHFUL UNTO DEATH," BY SIR E. J. POYNTER, P.R.A.
(1836–1919).

Walker Art Gallery, Liverpool.

This inspiring picture of a Roman sentinel, steadfastly remaining at his post amid the scenes of terror which accompanied the destruction of Pompeii by the eruption of Mount Vesuvius is generally regarded as the masterpiece of one of the most eminent of the Victorian classical painters.

29

"LOVE IN IDLENESS," BY SIR LAWRENCE ALMA-TADEMA, R.A. (1836-1912).

Among the classical painters of his time, Alma-Tadema, who was born in Holland, won wide popularity by illustrating the lighter side of life in ancient Greece and Rome. This dream-like picture of wistful maidenhood is a characteristic example of his art, and exhibits the scrupulously

450

Photo: Henry Dixon & Son.   Reproduced by permission of Messrs. Thos. Agnew & Sons.

"SYMPATHY," BY BRITON RIVIÈRE (1840–1920).

This favourite picture of a little girl in disgrace and her canine comforter never fails
to appeal to all who love children and dogs and have remarked the unspoken
sympathy which exists between them.

a general favourite, popular alike at Court, in society, and with the public, he was subject to fits of depression brought about by an almost morbid sensitiveness and a certain constitutional delicacy. Towards the end of his life he suffered continually from nerves, and his general state of health was sadly impaired by a railway accident in November 1868. This accident not only left a scar on his forehead but affected his memory, so that his last years were much clouded. He died in his house in St. John's Wood on October 1, 1873, and was buried in state at St. Paul's Cathedral.

The tradition of painting animals with affectionate insight, founded by Landseer, has been followed with success by many other British artists, prominent among them being Briton Rivière (1840–1920), who, after being influenced at first by the pictures of the Pre-Raphaelites and by Tennyson's poetry, soon turned his attention to the painting of pictures in which animals played an important part. His well-known " Sympathy " (see preceding page), in the Tate Gallery, is a characteristic Victorian picture in the Landseer tradition, but in gayer and more agreeable colours. It tells its own story clearly, and can never fail to appeal to all who love children and dogs and have noted the unspoken sympathy which exists between them.

§ 2

Victorian painting was essentially a story-telling art, but the stories were not limited to one country or to one century. The classical revival, the delight in pictures representing the life of ancient Greece and Rome, which marked, as we have seen, the art of France during the Revolutionary Period, did not show itself in England till nearly half a century later. The man who introduced this style of picture into England was Frederick Leighton, who, though born at Scarborough in 1830, spent the greater part of his early life abroad. Leighton was the son of a physician and spent his boyhood in Italy. When he was only ten years old he studied drawing at Rome, and afterwards lived in Florence,

" LOVE AND LIFE," BY G. F. WATTS (1817–1904).

Tate Gallery, London.

Love, strong in immortal youth, guides Life upwards over a
rocky path, sheltering her with his broad wings from stormy winds.
Even in this barren soil violets spring up where Love has trod.

An exquisite allegory by the most thoughtful of Victorian
painters.

where he was taught by several Italian artists. When he was eighteen he visited Brussels, and in the following year he continued his art studies in Paris, where he attended a life-school and copied pictures by Titian and Correggio in the Louvre. In 1850 he went to Germany, visiting Dresden and Berlin, but staying longest at Frankfort, where he worked for two years under a painter named Steinle, and was to some extent influenced by the painters Cornelius and Overbeck, who were mentioned in the last chapter. From Germany he returned to Paris, where he had a studio in the Rue Pigalle. At this time he was much enamoured of the earliest Italian artists, and his first oil-painting, executed at Frankfort, represented " Giotto found by Cimabue among the Sheep." It was from Paris that Leighton sent to the Academy of 1855 his picture of " Cimabue's Madonna carried in Procession through the Streets of Florence." This picture, with its precise drawing, elaborate design, and fresh, clear colour, created a tremendous sensation in London, and when it was bought by Queen Victoria the reputation of the painter was immediately made. It was not till five years later, however, that Leighton left Paris and settled in London.

Leighton was now thirty years old, and he was an accomplished, much-travelled man of the world. He had charming, courtly manners, and his prestige in the arts was equalled by his social success. He executed a number of illustrations for the Brothers Dalziel, but he had no lack of other patrons, and received numerous commissions for decorative paintings and subject pictures. He gave himself largely to the illustration of Greek history and legend, two of his most famous pictures in this style being " Daphnephoria " and " The Return of Persephone," now in the Leeds Art Gallery. He was generally considered to have recaptured the spirit of Greek art better than any artist since Raphael, and " The Bath of Psyche " (see page 460) is a famous example of the almost waxen perfection of his figures, and of his manner of idealising the nude.

The graceful sense of form noticeable in his paintings was also displayed in Leighton's works of sculpture, of which the best known are " The Sluggard " and " Athlete with Python," both in the Tate Gallery. From the moment he set foot in England, Leighton's career was a series of unbroken successes. He was elected A.R.A. in 1864, R.A. in 1868, and ten years later, after the death of Sir Francis Grant in 1878, he was elected President of the Royal Academy and received a knighthood. He was created a baronet in 1886, and on January 1, 1896, a few months before his death, he was made Baron Leighton of Stretton, being the first British painter elevated to the peerage.

Leighton never married. He built himself a handsome house, with an Arab Hall, from his own design, at No. 2 Holland Park Road, and his home, now known as Leighton House, is preserved as a memorial of his art.

Looking backward, we may surmise that the wide popularity enjoyed by Leighton and his followers was not altogether unrelated to the revival of interest in antiquity and archæology which, beginning in the reign of Queen Victoria, has continued undiminished to this day. At a time when the mind of the public was roused by reports in the newspapers of the discoveries made by excavators in Greece, Egypt, and elsewhere, it is not surprising that visitors to the Academy should have made favourites of those pictures which sought to portray life as it was in Greece or Egypt in the olden days.

Among a number of scholarly artists who were influenced by the example of Leighton, one of the most distinguished was his eventual successor in the presidency of the Royal Academy, Sir Edward John Poynter (1836–1919). This artist was born in Paris and was the son of an architect, Ambrose Poynter, who was himself a skilful painter in water-colours and had been an intimate friend of R. P. Bonington. E. J. Poynter studied art first in the Academy schools and afterwards in Paris, where one of his most intimate friends and fellow-students was the illustrator George du Maurier, author of *Trilby*. Poynter first exhibited at the Academy in 1861, and during the earlier part of his life he designed a number of decorative works, among them being mosaics for the Houses of Parliament

Photo: Frederick Hollyer.

"MAMMON," BY G. F. WATTS.

Tate Gallery, London.

A powerful indictment of ruthlessness in the pursuit of wealth. The artist shows us the god of riches, with ass's ears, in gold brocade and crown, seated on a blood-red throne surmounted by skulls, with money bags in his lap. With heavy hand he crushes the head of Woman, whose green garment (symbolic of hope) has fallen from her, while Man is stripped and prostrate beneath his foot.

MRS. MARY ANN COLLMANN, BY ALFRED STEVENS (1817-75).

National Gallery, London.

Painter, sculptor, and architect, Alfred Stevens recalled the universality which distinguished the giants of the Renaissance. Towards the end of his life he was entrusted with the execution of the Wellington Monument for St. Paul's Cathedral, but for many years his genius was frittered away by his being compelled to earn his living by designing minor objects for architects and commercial firms. This noble portrait of the wife of an architect who employed him at one time, shows the regal dignity and perfection of his painting.

and for St. Paul's Cathedral. He also, like Leighton, executed illustrations—some of which appeared in *Once-a-Week*—and painted portraits as well as landscapes; but though his activities were many and various, he was best known by his paintings of Greek, Roman, and Egyptian subjects. His first great popular success, and probably the most moving picture he ever conceived, was painted in 1865; " Faithful unto Death " (see page 449), now in the Walker Art Gallery, Liverpool, shows a Roman soldier standing unmoved at his post while Pompeii is being destroyed by earthquake and volcanic eruption, and in this picture the artist not only shows exactitude in archæological detail, but also expresses a nobility of purpose which every human being can understand and admire. In 1867 he painted " Israel in Egypt," but in later years he seldom approached the high seriousness of these early pictures, and though he maintained his popularity with scholarly and agreeable renderings of classical scenes, like " A Visit to Æsculapius " in the Tate Gallery, the subjects of these pictures tended to become lighter and sometimes trivial.

In addition to his work as a painter Sir E. J. Poynter was overwhelmed by official duties. He was elected A.R.A. in 1869 and two years later he was appointed the first Slade Professor at University College, London, a post which he held till 1875, when he became Director of the Royal College of Art at South Kensington, over which he presided for seven years. Meanwhile he had in 1876 been elected R.A., and henceforward his influence in the Academy council steadily increased. In 1894 he was appointed Director of the National Gallery, London, and he held this post till 1905, although in 1896 he had been appointed President of the Royal Academy, in succession to Millais. He was knighted in 1896 and made a baronet in 1902.

The wealth of Victorian England not only fostered native art, but naturally drew to these shores a number of foreign artists. Among them was one of the most famous of our modern classical painters, Sir Lawrance Alma-

Tadema. This artist was born in Holland in 1836, and after studying art in Antwerp gave his attention to historical painting. He began with early French and Egyptian subjects, but commenced his series of Greek subjects about 1865. In 1869 he sent his painting " The Pyrrhic Dance " to the Academy in London, where it was so well received that the painter decided to settle in England and became naturalised in 1873.

In the hands of Alma-Tadema the classical picture became historical in detail but playful and fanciful in subject. The Victorian anecdote reappeared in a Greek or Roman dress, as in his picture " A Silent Greeting " at the Tate Gallery, in which a Roman warrior places a bunch of roses in the lap of a sleeping lady. " Love in Idleness " (see page 450) is a characteristic example of his art and shows the wonderfully painted marble accessories which he was so fond of introducing into his pictures. Though full himself of antiquarian knowledge, and often called upon by Irving and other theatrical producers to assist in giving verisimilitude to the costumes and scenery for historical plays, Alma-Tadema never wearied the public with his learning, and his pictures were in the nature of agreeable dreams which made no serious demands upon the intellect or high emotions of the spectator. In the course of a long and successful career Alma-Tadema was elected A.R.A. in 1876, R.A. in 1879, knighted in 1899, and received the Order of Merit in 1905. He died while staying at Wiesbaden in 1912.

While all these artists enjoyed fame and fortune in their lifetime, other artists of equal or superior gifts were less appreciated by their contemporaries, though in several cases their fame is higher to-day than that of the popular favourites of their day. If we number Albert Moore (1841–93) among the Victorian classical painters, we must be careful to draw a distinction between his art and that of Leighton, Poynter, and Alma-Tadema. For, whereas these three artists emphasised the illustrative element in painting, Albert Moore laid more stress on its decorative element. Moore was not anecdotal, and for this reason his

THE BATH OF PSYCHE," BY LORD
LEIGHTON, P.R.A. (1830–96

Tate Gallery, London.

decorative compositions did not make so easy and obvious an appeal to his contemporaries; but he was filled with the Greek spirit of beauty, and his painting " Blossoms " (see page 463) is now one of the most admired of the quasi-classical pictures in the Tate Gallery. Moore was born at York and was the son of an artist, but though he was trained in the Academy schools and began to exhibit at the Academy in the 'sixties. he was not well received there, and subsequently exhibited chiefly at the Grosvenor Gallery and the Old Water-colour Society. He was never elected a member of the Academy, but associated with Whistler and other independent artists. An admirable draughtsman and designer, Albert Moore was also gifted with a refined and delicate sense of colour equalled by few of his contemporaries.

His brother Henry Moore (1831–95), an excellent marine painter, received more official recognition ; he was elected A.R.A. in 1886, R.A. in 1893, and in 1885 his " Catspaws off the Land," in the Tate Gallery, was bought for the nation.

Photo : T. & R. Annan.

"THE TENDER CHORD," BY SIR W. Q. ORCHARDSON, R.A.
(1835–1910).

This engaging picture of a Victorian young lady, arrested by some memory evoked by
" the tender chord," is a typical example of the domestic art of this distinguished Scottish
painter, who retained the respect of his brother artists by his polished powers of painting
and design, and won the affection of the public by his power to suggest a story and convey
a sentiment.

and never covetous of great wealth, Watts was able in hi
middle years to paint exactly as he pleased without thinkin
of sales and patrons. He painted portraits, but he neve
painted any person he did not respect and admire, and th
noble series of portraits of the great men of his time whic
he gave to the National Portrait Gallery shows how littl

NAPOLEON ON BOARD THE *BELLEROPHON*, BY W. Q. ORCHARDSON, R.A

Tate Gallery, London.

A dramatic, thought-provoking vision of the deposed Emperor on his way to St. Helen
The officers of his staff, from left to right, are Col. Planat, General Montholm, Surged
Maingaut, Count Las Cases, Generals Savary, Lallemand, and Bertrand. The bo
Las Cases leans upon the rail.

even in portraiture, did Watts paint for money. Similarly
the pick of his allegorical paintings, a cycle of the histor
of humanity, was kept for years in his own gallery at Littl
Holland House, till in 1897 he generously presented th
collection to the Tate Gallery. Watts was essentially
philosophical artist and he has not inaccurately been de
scribed as " a preacher in paint," for, in his opinion, it wa
not enough for an artist to portray noble aspirations, h

must also " condemn in the most trenchant manner prevalent vices," and utter " warning in deep tones against
lapses from morals and duties."   All aspects of Watts's art
may be seen to advantage in the room devoted to his works
at the Tate Gallery, where his beautiful " Hope " (see
page 444) and his " Love and Life " (see page 453) reveal
noble aspirations of humanity, while his unforgettable
" Mammon " (see page 456) and " The Minotaur " condemn prevalent vices and warn against lapses from morals.

As a sculptor Watts is represented at the Tate Gallery
by his bronze bust of " Clytie," but his most important
work in this medium is his equestrian group " Physical
Energy," originally designed as a monument to Cecil
Rhodes and set up over the empire-builder's grave on the
Matoppo Hills, South Africa.   A replica of this fine statue
has been placed in Kensington Gardens.

The life of Watts was long and full of honours.   He was
elected A.R.A. and R.A. in the same year, 1867 ; twice he
was offered and refused a baronetcy, but two years before
his death he accepted the Order of Merit.   He died in 1904
at the great age of eighty-seven, his last years having been
spent chiefly in his country house at Compton, Surrey,
where a large permanent collection of his works is still
visible to the public.

§ 5

Watts for nobility of thought and conception and Stevens
for grandeur of design and execution will, in all probability, be considered by posterity to have been the two
most eminent artists of the Victorian era, but though it may
be less easy to find, among the painters, the outstanding
giants who mark the same period in literature, the very
number of names as distinguished as they are familiar show
how active and flourishing the arts were during the Queen's
long reign.   Many artists who enjoyed, and still enjoy, a
wide popularity must necessarily be omitted from this
OUTLINE, but no survey, however hasty, of Victorian painting can ignore the band of Scottish artists who won fame
in the south as well as in the north.   Among them we may

mention the historical and romantic painter John Pettie
(1839-93) ; Peter Graham, the cattle painter ; John
MacWhirter, the popular painter of the Highlands ; William
M'Taggart, unrivalled in his delicate yet vigorous renderings
of foaming seas and windy shores ; and Sir W. Q. Orchardson, the leader of this band of Scottish students, and one of
the most polished, typical, and popular of all Victorian
artists.   William Quiller Orchardson (1835-1910) was born
in Edinburgh and came to London about 1862, and thereafter maintained and held his position as one of the most
popular of Academy exhibitors.   He excelled in a variety of
subjects ; his " Sir Walter Gilbey " and " Master Baby "
—a group of his wife and child—rank among the great
portraits of the nineteenth century ; " Napoleon on Board
the *Bellerophon* " (see page 466) is one of the best known and
most admired of modern historical paintings ; but perhaps
the best loved of all his works are those paintings of contemporary life, like " The Tender Chord " (see page 465),
which, without being positively " anecdotal," yet suggest
a story and convey a sentiment.   It was the distinction of
Orchardson that his story-telling was never crude and
obvious, his sentiment was always gentle and refined, his
execution was suave and accomplished, so that his pictures,
often representing moods of wistful reverie, charmed the
eye of the beholder and at the same time conjured up a
scene which dwelt in the memory and made its own appeal
to the imagination.

XIX

THE ROMANTIC MOVEMENT IN FRANCE

THE ART OF DELACROIX, GÉRICAULT, COROT, MILLET, AND THE BARBIZON SCHOOL

§ 1

SOME thirty years before the Pre-Raphaelite Brother-hood began its triumphant fight in England for the free expression of new ideals in art, a similar struggle between old and new schools of artists was waged with extraordinary vehemence in France. We saw in Chapter XVI how under the Revolution and the Empire a cold Classicism was the dominating tendency in French painting, and how gradually there arose among the younger artists a reaction against this traditional art. The spirit of unrest, which profoundly agitated France after the restoration of the Bourbons and culminated in the revolutionary explosion of 1848, first began to show itself in the art and literature of the younger generation. On one hand were the defenders of tradition, of the "grand style" of Academic painting, defenders of the classic ideal based on the sculpture of ancient Greece and Rome ; on the other were ardent young reformers, intoxicated with the colour and movement of life itself, who found their inspiration, not in the classics, but in romantic literature, in Dante, Shakespeare, Goethe, Byron, and Sir Walter Scott. Passion, movement, the imaginative expression of life were the aims of this group of artists, who became known as the Romantics.

"Who will deliver us from the Greeks and Romans ? " was a catchword among the young enthusiasts who found more beauty in life and Nature than in the masterpieces of ancient sculpture. The deliverer was found in the ranks of the reactionaries, in a young artist who was the pupil of Guérin the classicist. Jean Louis André Théodore Géricault was born at Rouen in 1791 and came to Paris about 1806, studying first with Carle Vernet and afterwards with Guérin. His method of drawing was so different from that approved by the school of David, that it exasperated his " correct " and academic master, who told Géricault he had better give up art because it was evident he would never succeed in it.

One day as Géricault was walking along a road near St. Cloud, a dapple-grey horse in a cart turned restive and plunged about in the sunshine. Géricault whipped out his sketch-book and jotted down notes of the movement of the animal and the play of light and shade on his dappled coat, and these notes gave him the idea of a great picture. He would paint an equestrian portrait, not the stiff image of a man on a wooden horse, but a vivid presentment of the plunging, sun-illumined animal he had seen. He persuaded his friend Lieutenant Dieudonné to pose for the rider, and he had a cab-horse brought round each morning that he might freshen his eye with the points of the horse. Working with the highest enthusiasm and energy Géricault, in the space of a fortnight, produced his " Officier des Chasseurs à Cheval," now in the Louvre. This picture created a sensation in the Paris Salon of 1812.

Two years afterwards Géricault repeated his success with a companion picture, " The Wounded Cuirassier," and after a short period of military service—when he had further opportunities of studying his favourite equine models—he went in 1817 to Italy, where he " trembled " before the works of Michael Angelo, who henceforward became his inspiration and idol.

When Géricault returned to France in 1818, he found all Paris talking about nothing but a naval disaster of two years earlier, an account of which had just been published by two of the survivors. The drama of the shipwreck of the *Medusa* seized upon the imagination of the artist, who determined to make it the subject of a picture. He spent months in collecting material for this work. He found the carpenter of the *Medusa* and induced him to make a model

"THE GLEANERS," BY J. F. MILLET.

The Louvre, Paris.

This master of democratic art painted the common life of the peasant in the field with a depth of feeling, sympathy, and understanding that had never previously been approached. There is epic grandeur in the figures of these three women, whose sturdy forms are contrasted with the still beauty of the sunlit landscape.

of the famous raft by which the survivors were saved. He spent days in hospitals studying the effects of illness and suffering. He persuaded two of the surviving officers of the ship to give him sittings, and painted one leaning against the mast and the other holding out his two arms towards the rescuing ship on the horizon. All his models were taken from life, and it is interesting to note that his friend, the famous artist Eugène Delacroix, posed for the man who lies inert on the left with his head against the edge of the raft.

These methods of painting—though afterwards employed by the Pre-Raphaelites—were then a complete innovation in painting, and the painting was so novel in conception, so contrary to the received ideas of the time, that when it was at length completed and shown in the Salon of 1819 it was at first greeted with nothing but abuse. Nevertheless, this picture marks a turning-point in the history of French painting; it brought strong feeling and pulsating life into the barren and frozen official art, and gave new ideals to the younger generation.

At the time the genius of Géricault was more highly appreciated in England than in France, and after the exhibition of his masterpiece the artist visited London, where his drawings and paintings of horses were intensely admired, and Géricault did signal service to the art of both countries by returning to Paris full of praise for the painting of Bonington and Constable, whose pictures he introduced to and made known in Paris. Unfortunately for the world this great genius was short-lived. Early in 1823 he was stricken down by a mortal illness, and after eleven months of terrible suffering, borne with fortitude and composure, he died in January 1824 at the early age of thirty-three. His place at the head of the Romantic School was taken by Delacroix, who had been his friend and fellow-student in the studio of Guérin.

Ferdinand Victor Eugène Delacroix was born at Charenton in 1798, but spent his early years at Marseilles, where he gained that love of vivid colour and bright sunshine which afterwards distinguished his painting. His father, an ex-foreign minister under the Directory and subsequently

Photo : Braun.

"THE BARRICADE," OR "LIBERTY GUIDING THE PEOPLE," BY
DELACROIX (1798-1863)

The Louvre, Paris.

This remarkable picture by the great leader of the Romantic Movement in France is a
true rendering of an incident during the street-fighting of the revolution in July 1830—
when the Parisians deposed the unpopular Charles X and placed his cousin Louis Philippe,
Duke of Orleans, on the throne—and at the same time the heroine of the Barricade may
be regarded as an allegorical figure of Liberty guiding the People.

prefect of Marseilles and Bordeaux, did not take kindly to the idea of his son becoming a painter, but he died before his son came of age, and Eugène Delacroix then found shelter with a married sister in Paris, where he overcame family opposition and was allowed to study art.

His father, however, had left him penniless, and the young artist was so poor that in 1822, after painting his first great picture, " The Barque of Dante," he could not afford to buy a frame, but sent the canvas to the Salon surrounded by four laths which he had coloured with yellow powder. There it was seen by Baron Gros, who generously recognised the great talent of the poor artist, and not only persuaded the administration to give the picture a handsome new frame, but hung it in a place of honour in the Salon Carré.

" The Barque of Dante " made the painter famous at once, and did not offend the Classicists. Gros said the picture was " Rubens reformed," and paternally advised the artist, " Come to us ; we will teach you how to draw." Delacroix was grateful to Gros for his kindness, but went his own way, and two years later he shocked the Classicists and delighted the Romantics by his picture " The Massacre of Scio."

It will be remembered that Constable's " Hay Wain " was exhibited in the Paris Salon of 1824, and when Delacroix saw it he was so overwhelmed by its colour that he obtained permission to retouch his own " Massacre of Scio." In a fortnight he completely repainted this picture, using the purest and most vivid colours he could find, with the result that it now became as brilliant in colour as it had already been in action and movement. The turbulent energy in this painting was too much for the Classicists, and Gros, playing on the title, said, " This is the massacre of painting." On the other hand, enthusiastic young critics lauded the picture with extravagant praise, one of them asserting that it showed up " all the horror of despotism " in art as in life.

In this picture, which was the real beginning of his lasting fame, Delacroix proved himself to be one of the world's great colourists, and laid the foundations of the new handling of colour which became the greatest pictorial triumph of the nineteenth century. Colour in his hands was no dead thing, it became something alive, scintillating and vibrating ; his results were obtained not only by the happy choice of individual tints, but still more by the science with which he knew how to juxtapose one colour against another so as to accentuate the brilliancy of each and secure a glowing harmony.

The art of Delacroix is distinguished by three things—its colour, its poetry, and its decorative qualities. He turned naturally to Dante, Shakespeare, and Byron for subjects, not so much because they provided him with good themes to illustrate, as because in their poetry he found those passionate ideals and aspirations which animated his own mind. When actual events aroused a similar intensity of emotion, he painted them also. Though usually he eschewed political subjects, the Revolution of July 1830 moved him to paint his famous picture " The Barricade," now known as " Liberty Guiding the People " (see page 473), a picture which is at once a fragment of actuality and the embodiment of an ideal. For this is a true historical picture in so far as it does represent with fidelity a typical incident during the street-fighting of the Revolution ; and at the same time the heroine of the barricade, with her Phrygian cap, streaming tricolour, and musket, is an allegory of Liberty, liberty for the people and liberty for art. Exhibited in the Salon of 1831 this picture perplexed the authorities, who could neither deny its excellence as a work of art nor altogether approve of its firebrand politics. The Director of Fine Arts temporarily solved the problem by purchasing the picture for the nation, and then turning its face to the wall ! To-day the picture is one of the chief treasures of the French School in the Louvre.

In the same year Delacroix made a journey to Morocco which had a considerable effect on his art, for he delighted alike in the brilliant colours and picturesque costumes of this sunny land, and on his return exhibited a number of pictures of Eastern subjects, which were enthusiastically received, and, inspiring other artists to do likewise, he gave birth to a school of artists known as the " Orientalists."

"THE RAFT OF THE *MEDUSA*," BY GERICAULT (1791-1824).

The Louvre, Paris.

Inspired by the heroic endurance of the survivors from a sensational shipwreck in 1816, this picture of a contemporary event, painted with scrupulous fidelity to the facts as obtained from eye-witnesses, marks a turning-point in the history of

Delacroix himself, however, was too big and varied a genius to confine himself to one subject, and having given a lead to the Orientalists he now devoted much of his time to decorative painting.

Though regarded by his great rival Ingres and by the

Photo : W. A. Mansell & Co.

THE POOL," BY COROT (1796–1875).
The Louvre, Paris.

The most poetic of landscape painters, Corot was long neglected by his contemporaries. Beginning life as a commercial traveller, he exhibited his first painting when he was thirty-one, but he never sold a picture till he had turned sixty.

classical painters as a revolutionary, Delacroix was full of respect for tradition, only whereas David and Ingres adhered to the tradition of Raphael and Leonardo da Vinci, Géricault and Delacroix upheld the tradition of Michael Angelo, Titian, Veronese, and Rubens. Though his own researches into colour were perhaps his most valuable legacy to the art of France. the intention of Delacroix was not to break with tradition but to bring back the colour and methods of the old masters into modern painting. The romanticism of Delacroix was a half-way house between the old Classicism and the Realism that was coming, and as he in his youth had challenged the position of Ingres and the Classicists, so in his later years his own romanticism was challenged by Courbet the Realist.

Owing to this long battle between the classics and the romantics, the doors of the Academy were closed against Delacroix for five-and-thirty years, and it was not till he was sixty—and so barred by age from holding a professorship at the École des Beaux-Arts—that he was at last admitted as a member of the Institute. The artist did not long enjoy the distinction, for he died at Paris in 1863.

§ 2

While Géricault, Delacroix, and other " Romantics " were liberating the painting of history, poetry, and real life from the trammels of Classicism, another group of French painters was engaged in rescuing landscape painting from the deadness and artificiality which had overtaken it since the days of Poussin and Claude Lorrain.

Among the earliest of the French artists to paint Nature as she is, and not as the pedantic " classics " thought she ought to be, was Jean Baptiste Camille Corot (1796–1875). Born in Paris, the son of a small linen-draper having a shop in the Rue de Bac, Corot was for eight years a commercial traveller in the cloth trade. It was not till he was twenty-six that he was reluctantly allowed by his family to abandon trade and devote himself to painting. His father made him an allowance of sixty pounds a year, and till he was nearing fifty this was practically all Corot had to live upon.

In 1822 he entered the studio of Victor Bertin (1775–1825), a painter of classical landscape so successful in his day that the French Government, attracted by his own work and that of his pupils, created a new Prix de Rome for Landscape Painting. This prize was usually carried off by Bertin's pupils, who thus came to regard Rome as the

Photo : Braun.

"THE LADY IN BLUE," BY COROT

The Louvre, Paris.

Universally admired as a landscape painter, Corot is less known as a figure painter because these subjects are rarer and until recently have been hidden away in private collections. This beautiful work, painted when the artist was a veteran of seventy-eight, is one of his last pictures and reveals his exquisite skill and refinement in portraiture

finishing school of their artistic education. The turning-point in Corot's life came in 1826, when he also went to Rome, and there he formed a friendship with another French painter, Aligny (1798–1871), who had some influence on his early efforts. Aligny, though a classical painter, had a much more honest feeling for Nature than most of his kind, and though his pictures are rigid in execution they show unusual carefulness in composition and detail. The early Roman paintings of Corot are distinguished by precise drawing, careful composition, and a deliberate soberness of detail, but they also have a lovely limpidity of colour unequalled in the work of his contemporaries, and a delicate feeling for light and air. Breaking away from the brown convention of his day, Corot painted southern landscape and architectural subjects in delicate tints of pale blues and greens, light biscuit-colour and pearly greys.

For some seven or eight years Corot remained in Italy, gradually forming a style which was absolutely his own and in which, while remaining true to the actual facts of Nature, he expressed her most poetical aspects. Occasionally he also painted pictures with small figures, and these, with their precision and delicate colour and subtle lighting, were nearer akin to the Dutch style of Vermeer and other seventeenth-century masters than to the accepted styles of Italian figure painting.

It is strange to think that the paintings of Corot—for which millionaires now eagerly offer thousands of pounds—were for long years utterly neglected by his contemporaries. He exhibited regularly in the Paris Salon from 1827, but his exhibits aroused neither censure nor admiration—they were simply ignored. *For thirty years he never sold a picture.* The first critic to notice his work was the poet Alfred de Musset, who praised his picture in the Salon of 1836, but with the exception of two favourable notices received in 1837 and 1847, he was generally as neglected by the press as by the public. It was not till he was sixty that Corot began to capture the attention of the critics and collectors.

The one great compensation that Corot possessed during

these years was the affection of a number of his brother
artists, who both admired the artist and loved the man.
Corot possessed a sunny, tender, tranquil nature that
endeared him to all who came in contact with him. He
was never embittered by his want of success, but lived the
life of a peasant, happy in his art. "Le Père Corot"
became the beloved patriarch of a colony of artists who
had settled in the little village of Barbizon in the forest of
Fontainebleau, a spot attractive to artists by the richness
and variety of its sylvan scenery and at the same time
reasonably near to the exhibition centre, Paris. In this
district Corot painted the most famous pictures of his
later days, *e.g.* "The Pool" (see page 477) and "Souvenir
of Mortefontaine" (see page 485). He particularly delighted in the poetic effects of early morning and approaching eve, "when all Nature sings in tune," and during the
glare of the noonday sun he would retire indoors, for effects
of brilliant sunshine did not make the same appeal to him.
He preferred the minor to the major chords of Nature's
colouring, and was the supreme interpreter of her moods
of wistfulness, mystery, and reverie.

Though the dreamy poetical beauty of Corot's later
landscapes, with their willowy trees and mysterious atmosphere, made an unprecedented appeal to American and
British collectors towards the end of the nineteenth century,
so that extravagant prices were paid for typical examples
—in one year more so-called "Corots" were said to have
been imported into the United States than Corot himself
could ever have painted—it is only in comparatively recent
years that the supreme excellence of Corot's early works
and figure paintings have become recognised.

More immediately successful than Corot was his friend
Jules Dupré (1812–89), whom Corot called "the Beet-
hoven of Landscape." Dupré was the son of a porcelain
manufacturer at Nantes and, like several other distinguished
artists of the time, began his career by painting on china.
He was one of the pioneers of "natural" landscape in
France, turning away from the medley of the classical
painters to render with fresh observation and expressive

31

Photo: Braun.

"SPRING," BY COROT.

This delightful picture of a young girl gathering flowers shows the power of Corot in interpreting moods of wistfulness and reverie, whether in Nature or human beings.

Photo : Braun.

"THE SOWER," BY MILLET (1814–75).

This world-famous figure is a noble expression of Millet's feeling for the dignity of labour, and can also be regarded as a universal symbol of the Present sowing the Future.

detail the characteristic beauties of rural France, her pastures, forests, and villages.

One of the most vigorous and famous of the Barbizon School, Théodore Rousseau (1812–67) was born in the same year as Dupré and, like him, was an enthusiastic admirer of Constable. Rousseau was the son of a Paris tailor and, though town-born, he experienced the fascination of the forest in his early boyhood, when he stayed with an uncle who had sawmills near Besançon. This uncle persuaded his parents to allow Théodore to study art, and accordingly the young man was placed in a Paris studio. From his masters, mediocre painters of classic landscape, Rousseau learnt less than from Nature, and a very early picture, painted in the open air at Montmartre—then almost country—showed a remarkable mastery in rendering air, light, and the details of Nature. In 1831 his first landscape was accepted and hung in the Salon; in 1833 he began his studies in the Forest of Fontainebleau, and again exhibited with credit; and in 1834 his picture of " A Cutting in the Forest of Compiègne " was awarded a medal, and was bought by the young Duke of Orleans. This early success, far from bringing him fortune, proved disastrous, for the older landscape painters, jealous of his growing reputation and his power, cruelly determined henceforward to exclude his work from the Salon. Accordingly in 1836 his magnificent " Descente des Vaches "—a great picture of herds of cattle coming down in autumn from the high pastures of the Jura—was rejected by the Salon. The picture is now one of the chief treasures of the Mesdag Museum in The Hague.

For fourteen years the work of Rousseau was excluded from the Salons; as a result of this attack Rousseau in 1837 left Paris for Barbizon, where he was joined by other independent painters. After the Revolution of 1848 the work of Rousseau began to be known and appreciated, but though his pictures now began to sell and he was awarded a first medal in 1849 and the Legion of Honour in 1852, he made no change in his life and continued at Barbizon till his death in 1867.

Corot, with characteristic modesty, once said : " Rousseau is an eagle ; as for me, I am only a lark who utters little cries among the grey clouds." There was indeed a great difference between the two men, for Rousseau did not look at Nature with the dreamy gaze of a poet, but with the fiery glance of a scientist who would wrest all her secrets

Photo : W. A. Mansell & Co.

"SOUVENIR OF MORTEFONTAINE," BY COROT.
The Louvre, Paris.

One of Corot's most famous masterpieces, this picture is an example both of his poetic feeling and of his adherence to classic methods of composition. Note how the picture is divided diagonally into two triangles of light and shade, an arrangement which contributes to the feeling of repose which the painting inspires.

from her. He delighted in the infinite details of Nature, and while preserving her breadth and majesty, he delicately differentiated between plants and weeds, mosses and lichens, brushwood and shrubs. Nothing was too great for his soaring imagination, nothing too small for his earnest attention. His vigorous rendering of form and his searching characterisation of Nature may be seen in " The Oaks " (see page 491).

Friendship and admiration for Rousseau had a great effect on the life of Virgilio Narcisse Diaz de la Pena (1808–76), commonly known as Diaz. This painter was born at Bordeaux, whither his father, a political refugee, had fled from Spain, and after his death, which occurred soon afterwards, Mme Diaz removed to Sèvres, where she supported her young family by giving lessons in Spanish and Italian. When he was fifteen years old he was apprenticed to learn china painting, but he soon tired of working at the factory, and spent all his spare time in painting romantic Eastern scenes from his imagination. About 1830, while still earning his living by painting on porcelain, Diaz met Rousseau in Paris, and this acquaintance ripened into a lifelong friendship. Taught by Rousseau how to use pure and brilliant colours so that his pictures glowed like jewels, the pictures of Diaz appealed to the public by their subjects and were soon sought after. At first Diaz painted nymphs and bathers, mythological subjects and oriental scenes, the last so brilliant in colour that it is difficult to believe Diaz never saw the Orient and never travelled farther than a few hundred miles from Paris.

Though he had little to complain about on his own account, Diaz shared the fortunes of his friend Rousseau, and accompanied him to Barbizon in 1837. There he gave his mind almost entirely to landscape, and made a new reputation by his brilliant forest pictures with light glancing on the tree stems.

Like Diaz and Dupré, the famous cattle painter Troyon (1810–65) began as a painter on porcelain. His father, who had been employed at the Sèvres Porcelain Factory, died early, and while quite young boys Troyon and his brother earned a living by painting on china at the manufactory, and in their spare time sketched from Nature in the surrounding country. It was not till he was thirty-two that Constant Troyon was able to leave Sèvres and commence his studies in Paris, and for some years his progress was hampered by the somewhat niggling style of painting he had acquired from the habit of decorating porcelain, but devoting himself especially to the painting of animals he gradually acquired strength and breadth, though he was nearly forty before he gained the power that has since made him famous. When he did find himself, however, the success of Troyon was immediate. He was speedily recognised by his contemporaries as the greatest animal painter since Cuyp and Paul Potter, and the demand for his work was so great that Troyon sometimes employed other painters to put in backgrounds and accessories. Troyon excelled in showing living beasts in their natural surroundings, and the landscapes in his cattle pictures are not mere " back-cloths " but genuine studies which interpret with sincerity the weather, the time of day, and the season of the year. His most famous masterpiece is his great painting " Oxen going to Work " (see page 489) in the Louvre, in which the superb rendering of the animals is equalled by the splendour with which the artist has rendered the full glory of the early morning landscape.

Though much influenced by Corot, who regarded him almost as a son, Charles François Daubigny (1817–78) evolved another distinct type of landscape and excelled in his poetic renderings of placid river scenes. His father was a journeyman painter of mediocre ability, and as a boy Daubigny painted decorations on clock-cases, glove-boxes, fans, and other articles of luxury. When he was seventeen he and a friend saved up a little over fifty pounds with which they set out on foot for Italy, and there maintained themselves for nearly a year. Returning to Paris, Daubigny gave himself for a time to figure subjects, but about 1840 he turned definitely to landscape, which he discovered to be his true vocation. His favourite sketching-ground was near Valmondois on the Oise, where he had spent happy days in his childhood. Though his landscapes were exhibited regularly in the Salon from 1841 to 1847, Daubigny had a hard struggle during these years, but in 1848 he received a second medal for his five landscapes in the Salon, and thereafter the State began to buy his pictures for provincial museums and his sales generally improved.

" On the Banks of the Oise " (see next page) is a beautiful and characteristic example of the art of Daubigny, and

"ON THE BANKS OF THE OISE," BY DAUBIGNY (1817–78).

A characteristic example of the peaceful river scenes which this artist painted with tender fidelity and poetic feeling.

"OXEN GOING TO WORK," BY TROYON (1810–65).

The Louvre, Paris.

The masterpiece of the most celebrated painter of cattle in the nineteenth century, this picture is remarkable not only for the lifelike rendering of the beasts but also for its brilliant expression of the full glory of a summer morning.

reveals that exquisite calm and repose which is a feature of many of his paintings, though occasionally he painted stormy scenes ; for Daubigny was not limited in his subjects, but painted various aspects of Nature. He was one of the pioneers in the truer rendering of Nature's own colouring, and his famous saying, " We never paint light enough," became a watchword to the younger generation of artists.

§ 3

The great struggle for liberty and truth in art, begun by the Romantics and landscape painters already mentioned, was carried a stage further by Jean François Millet (1814–75), who was the first to paint the peasant, not as a sort of "stage property" in a landscape, but as he truly lived and moved. Millet came of peasant stock, and during his boyhood worked hard in the fields with his father, whose home was in the hamlet of Gruchy, near Cherbourg. When he was eighteen, his father, recognising the lad's talent, allowed him to study art in Cherbourg, but as the eldest son he returned to manage the farm on his father's death in 1835. His heart, however, was still in his art, and seeing this his mother and grandmother heroically determined not to allow him to sacrifice himself, but soon persuaded him to return to Cherbourg. There his talent was recognised by the Municipality, who gave him a grant of forty pounds, and with this he went to Paris in 1836 and entered the studio of the historical painter Paul Delaroche (1797–1856). During the next twelve years, spent partly in Paris and partly in Normandy, Millet experienced nothing but trouble, distress, and discouragement. Though always in poverty, he married in 1841, and his wife died in 1844 ; at the end of 1845 he married again, and found a devoted and courageous helpmate in his second wife.

At this period of his life Millet chiefly painted portraits and small pictures of classical or mythological subjects, and already his colour—in which he was considerably influenced by Correggio—began to attract attention and the admiration of other artists. He became friendly with

THE OAKS," BY THÉODORE ROUSSEAU (1812–67).

The Louvre Paris.

The most vigorous of the Barbizon School, Rousseau as we may see in this picture, delighted in the infinite variety of Nature, and while strongly characterising her details, yet contrived to preserve her breadth and majesty.

Diaz, and through Diaz got to know Rousseau and others. In 1847 his picture " Œdipus taken from the Tree " was favourably noticed in the Salon by Théophile Gautier, who prophesied that the painter would become famous, and in the following year Millet's picture of a peasant woman was given a place of honour in the best room at the Salon. It looked as if the painter was on the point of achieving a popular success, for he had also been finding a ready sale for small pictures of nude figures, which he painted with great skill. But about this time he accidentally overheard somebody speaking of him as " Millet, who paints nothing but naked women," and this chance remark so upset him that he then and there determined never again to paint the nude. Already town life and town manners were distasteful to him ; he longed for country air to breathe and the peasant people whom he knew and loved to paint.

In 1849 he decided to change his manner of life, and with his wife and babies he removed to Barbizon, where Rousseau and Diaz were already settled. In this peaceful village Millet made his home, and found his true vocation in chronicling in a series of noble paintings the dignity of peasant labour. To the Salon of 1850 he sent his unforgettable picture of " The Sower " (see page 483), a work of epic grandeur which seems to symbolise the Present preparing the Future in the guise of an agricultural labourer fulfilling his common task. During the next ten years Millet painted some of his greatest pictures, " The Gleaners" (see page 471) in 1857, " The Angelus " in 1859, but all this time Millet was harassed by money difficulties, and with a growing and increasing family he had a hard struggle for mere existence. His new pictures were not popular ; not only did they fail to find purchasers, but they were often attacked because many of them were thought to be " socialistic," and " The Gleaners " was particularly abused on its first appearance as a work expressing subversive political principles. Millet and his family might have starved at this time, but for the good deeds stealthily done by his more fortunate comrades. In 1855 Rousseau secretly bought one of his pictures for £160, and Troyon also bought several of Millet's works, pretending that he was acting for an American collector who had no real existence. By this tactful generosity Millet was prevented from ever knowing how much he owed to the devotion of his friends.

It was not till the Great Exhibition at Paris in 1867 that Millet came into his own, and his opportunity came then because his friend Théodore Rousseau was President of the Jury. In this exhibition Millet was represented by " The Angelus," " The Gleaners," and seven other important paintings. He was awarded a first-class medal for the collection, and in the following year was made a Chevalier of the Legion of Honour. He was now at the height of his fame, but the honours and fortune which followed came too late to be enjoyed. The artist was deeply smitten by the death of Rousseau in December 1867, and his own health began to fail in 1870. During the disastrous Franco-Prussian war he retired to Cherbourg, where his work was interrupted by frequent illnesses. When he returned to Paris, the new Republican Government gave Millet a commission in 1874 to paint a set of decorative panels of " The Four Seasons " for the Panthéon, but though he at once began charcoal sketches for these subjects he was never able to execute the paintings. Throughout the autumn his health declined, and surrounded by his devoted family he died on the 20th January 1875.

Closely associated with Millet, whom he accompanied to Barbizon, was Charles Jacque (1813–94), who, though less powerful than Troyon, was one of the best animal painters of his time. He excelled in painting flocks of sheep in the open or on the edge of a forest. The painting of peasant life, inaugurated by Millet, was continued by Bastien Lepage (1848–84) and the still more popular Jules Breton (1827–1906), who, though weaker in drawing and less rich in colour, reaped where Millet had sown. Associated with Diaz, and still more fantastic than this painter in the exotic pictures of his earlier years, was Adolphe Monticelli (1824–86). Born at Marseilles, Monticelli brought the warmth of Southern colouring and imagination to Barbizon : he was the most romantic of the romantic landscape painters, and his canvases, loaded with rich pigment, from which radiant fairy-like figures emerge and seem to quiver with life, are magical masterpieces of jewel-like colour.

Belonging to a slightly later generation, but encouraged in his youth by Corot, Daubigny, and Millet, the exquisite

"THE HARBOUR OF TROUVILLE," BY BOUDIN (1825–98).
National Gallery, London. .

A link between the Barbizon School and the Impressionists, Boudin excelled in rendering the pearly tints of clear grey days. His marine paintings are pitched in a higher key of colour than that usually employed by the Barbizon painters.

sea painter Eugene Boudin (1825–98) is a link between the Barbizon School and the Impressionists. Boudin was born at Honfleur, where his father was a sea-captain, and during his early years he assisted Troyon by painting the skies in some of his pictures. This was a department of painting in which Boudin excelled, and his rendering of the clouds and the blue vault of heaven excited the keen admiration of Corot, who hailed his young contemporary as " the monarch of the sky." Boudin spent the greater part of his life in the neighbourhood of his birthplace, and never tired of painting the shipping, shores, and harbour scenes of this part of the Normandy coast. His paintings are pitched in a slightly higher key of colour than those of Corot and Daubigny, and the prevalence of luminous pearly greys in his work have caused his paintings—together with similar paintings of similar subjects by his slightly older contemporary, the Dutchman Bartholde Jongkind— to be known as *la peinture gris*, *i.e.* the " grey " school of painting. " The Harbour of Trouville " (see opposite page) in the National Gallery is a beautiful example of Boudin's delicate realism and of his sensitive feeling for the wind in the sky and the light on the water.

XX

THE MODERN DUTCH SCHOOL

§ I

FOR more than a hundred years after the deaths of Hobbema and Willem van de Velde, Holland produced no painter of European importance. The Dutch School, which during the seventeenth century had risen, as we have seen, to the highest eminence, sank during the eighteenth century into trivial virtuosity. Pictures became conjuring feats rather than true works of art, for they evoked neither tender sentiments nor noble thoughts, but only excited wonder by their manual dexterity. In craftsmanship many of these paintings were remarkable in their meticulous detail, and while some painters—like Willem van Mieris (1662–1747), whose " Fish and Poultry Shop " is in the National Gallery—carried on the traditions left by Jan Steen and Gerard Dou, still more made a reputation among their contemporaries by their minute rendering of fruit and flowers. These they painted with the patient skill of a miniaturist, and they delighted in introducing into their pictures flies and other small insects whose tiny, but marvellously realistic forms, had to be discerned with the aid of a magnifying-glass. Among the artists who excelled in this style of painting may be mentioned the woman-painter of Amsterdam, Rachel Ruysch (1664–1750), and her contemporary, Jan van Huysum (1682–1749), both of whom are represented in the National Gallery. Here we may see how skilfully they both painted flowers, how cunningly the one introduces a butterfly, the other a snail ; but we soon weary of this pettifogging cleverness, which

" A FRUGAL MEAL," BY JOSEF ISRAELS.

Glasgow Art Gallery.

One of the greatest democratic painters of the nineteenth century, Israels interpreted the indoor, home life of the peasant as the Frenchman Millet recorded his labour in the fields. Making a stay in the little fishing village of Zantvoort, near Haarlem, Israels discovered the human drama and pathos in everyday life. In this characteristic picture he shows us " the treasure of the humble," and invests a homely repast with the solemnity and poignancy of a sacrament.

may amuse our eyes for a few moments, but can never touch our hearts.

It was not till towards the middle of the nineteenth century that any great revival of painting showed itself in Holland. One who helped to prepare the ground for the new generation was Johannes Bosboom (1817–91), who painted impressive pictures in oils and water-colours of the interiors of Dutch churches and cathedrals. He was influenced by the seventeenth-century painter Emanuel de Witte (1607–92), who had also painted these subjects not only with great accuracy of linear perspective but with broad effects of light-and-shade ; Bosboom painted these interiors still more broadly and invested them with a dim atmosphere of grave grandeur and solemnity.

Bosboom always gives us a more or less generalised vision, and contrasted with the particularity of the painters who immediately preceded him, he may be said to have given a new direction to Dutch painting.

Another pioneer and forerunner of the modern movement was Willem Roelofs, who was born at Amsterdam in 1822, and went to France, where he made the acquaintance of Corot and other members of the Barbizon School. For some time Roelofs lived with these artists in the now famous village, and painted the forest of Fontainebleau in their company ; then he returned to the Netherlands, taking with him new ideals of landscape painting. Though he lived chiefly in Brussels, Roelofs had a considerable influence on Dutch painting. He was never an imitator of Corot, Daubigny, or Troyon, though he learnt something from all of them, as we may see in his picture " A Summer's Day " (see opposite page), and it was through him that a knowledge and appreciation of their paintings first spread through Belgium and Holland. Roelofs helped to found at Brussels in 1868 the *Société Libre des Beaux Arts* (Free Society of Fine Arts), of which Corot, Daubigny, and Millet became honorary members, and to this exhibition both Dutch and Belgian artists contributed. It became the rallying-point of the younger generation and of those painters who were beginning to be affected by the Barbizon pictures which

Photo : W. A. Mansell & Co.

"A SUMMER'S DAY," BY WILLEM ROELOFS (1822-97).

One of the pioneers of the Modern Dutch School, Roelofs worked at Fontainebleau with the painters of Barbizon and introduced their ideals of landscape painting into the Netherlands. This picture is a fine example of his tender fidelity to Nature and of the radiant beauty of his lighting.

so many of them had seen in Paris.   After living in Brussels for forty years Roelofs moved to The Hague, where he died in 1897.

§ 2

The debt of the modern Dutch painters to France cannot be ignored, but we must remember that Holland possessed in Rembrandt one of the greatest of the Old Masters, and though his influence seemed to slumber for two centuries in his own country, it was shortly to prove itself to be alive once more.   The greatest figure in this school is Josef Israels, and his art must be regarded as a blending of the influence of Rembrandt with that of Jean François Millet, plus the remarkable personality of the painter himself.   Israels was one of the earliest as well as one of the greatest of the modern Dutch painters.   He was born on January 27, 1824, at Groningen, of Hebrew parents, his father being a money-changer and broker.   As a boy his first ambition was to be a rabbi ; at an early age he studied Hebrew and buried himself in the Talmud, and he was well in his 'teens before he displayed a marked leaning towards art.   Meanwhile his father intended Josef for a business career, but while working under his father as a stockbroker's clerk, Josef Israels surreptitiously obtained lessons in painting from local artists, and though their talent was but mediocre their pupil soon began to display such unmistakable gifts that parental opposition was overcome and he was allowed to go to Amsterdam to study art.   He lodged with an orthodox Jewish family in the Ghetto, and all that he saw in the Jewish Quarter himself, combined with the religious paintings and etchings of Rembrandt based on the life in that quarter—which had altered so little since Rembrandt's time—made a profound impression on him, and had a more lasting influence than anything he learnt from his master, Jan Kruseman, who, though a successful portrait-painter of his time, was a dry and uninteresting artist.   In 1845 Israels left Amsterdam to study in Paris, but here again he was not very fortunate in his master.   He entered the studio of Picot, who had been a pupil of David, and so far from being in touch with the ideals of the " men of 1830,'' he was brought up to admire historical paintings in the classical style. When Israels returned to Amsterdam in 1848 he was chiefly influenced by the French historical painter Delaroche, and he began painting historical and dramatic subjects in which, beneath the French polish, the influence of Rembrandt was nevertheless discernible. But Israels had not yet found himself, and it was some years before he did. The critical period in the artistic career of Israels was about 1856. In 1855 he showed in the Paris Salon a historical picture, " The Prince of Orange for the first time opposing the Execution of the Orders of the King of Spain " ; in 1857 his exhibits at the Paris Salon were " Children by the Sea " and " Evening on the Beach," two tender impressions of commonplace, everyday scenes on the coast near Katwijk. These last pictures are by the Israels we know ; the picture of 1855 might have been by almost any historical painter of the period. How did this change come, and what brought it about ?

It was life, not art nor any artist, that changed the whole spirit of Israels' painting. He had a serious illness while he was living at Amsterdam, and when convalescent went to Zantvoort, a little fishing village close to Haarlem, to recruit his health. He lodged there with a ship's carpenter, and living the life of these simple, kindly seafaring folk, Israels was struck by the drama, pathos, and tragedy in the common lot. At Zantvoort he made the same discovery that Millet had made at Barbizon, namely, that to a sympathetic and understanding spectator the common life of the people even in a remote, secluded village is as full of romance, thrills, and tragedy as the pages of any history book. Israels discovered that " the events of the present are capable of being painted and the sorrows of the poor are as deep as the tragical fate of ancient heroes." A new vein of artistic expression was now opened to him, and henceforward he painted the life of the poor and humble, and found in typical, everyday episodes motives for expressing with peculiar intensity his wide human sympathy.

It may be said, therefore, that the art of Josef Israels,

Photo : W. A. Mansell & Co.

"A HAPPY FAMILY," BY JOSEF ISRAELS (1824-1911).

In this exquisitely lighted picture of the humble home of a Dutch fisherman, the painter gives us a touching study

502

Photo: *W. A. Mansell & Co.*   ALONE IN THE WORLD," BY JOSEF ISRAELS.

"The sorrows of the poor are as deep as the tragical fate of ancient heroes." In this moving picture of a wife who has just lost her beloved husband, Israels expresses his deep feeling for the daily tragedy of life.

503

though he received his training in Paris, was far more the fruit of his own experience of life than the outcome of French influence. We feel that even if Millet had never existed, Israels would not have painted otherwise than he did, and though the subject-matter of their respective pictures are akin, there are considerable differences between them. Millet painted his peasants out-of-doors in the light of the sun ; Israels pictured his fisher-folk by preference indoors, in dim interiors. Hence his pictures are usually more subdued in colour than those of Millet. Israels painted low life in low tones and built up his visions of life, whether in oil-paintings, water-colours, or etchings —and he worked in all three mediums—by broad masses of light and shade. Further, his tendency is to be more tragic than Millet, and many of his pictures have not inaccurately been described as " piercing notes of woe." One of his most famous pictures, " Alone in the World " (see preceding page), contains the essence of his art. In the treatment, in the rays of light dimly illuminating the gloom which befits the subject, we see the influence of Rembrandt ; while in the bowed figure of the lonely widow, with her open Bible by her side, we have a poignant expression of the artist's deep feeling for the daily tragedy of life.

In 1870 Josef Israels left Amsterdam and moved to The Hague, where he lived till he died on August 12, 1911, respected, honoured, and world-famous. He was a painter who appealed equally to the general public and to connoisseurs, and though so many of his works are tragic, this never interfered with his popularity, because he pictured the tragedies of common life which all have experienced and all can understand. Further, if he reached his highest intensity of expression in rendering sorrow, suffering, endurance, and the pathos of old age, Israels was not wholly tragic in his art. Pictures like " A Frugal Meal " (see page 497) and " A Happy Family " (see page 502) show the reverse of the medal, the compensations of poverty, and the happiness of the humble. But even in these scenes of domestic contentment there is something touching, and

" A SEASCAPE," BY H. W. MESDAG (1831–1915).

Originally a banker by profession, Mesdag retired from business at the age of thirty-five and henceforward devoting himself to art he became the foremost marine painter in Holland. This picture is a fine example of his vigorous rendering of the life and movement of the waves and of his skill in placing shipping, so that his picture is at once absolutely natural and also decorative.

the philosophy of Israels seems to bid us to ponder on the life of people who can be happy with so little.

When Josef Israels was a young man, working as a clerk under his father, one of his frequent duties was to take a money-bag to the bank of a Mr. Mesdag. This banker had a son Hendrik Willem Mesdag, born at Groningen on February 25, 1831, who also became a famous painter. For many years H. W. Mesdag practised art as an amateur, and it was not till he had amassed a considerable fortune in business that he retired from banking and devoted himself entirely to painting. Thus Mesdag was not only in the independent position of being able to paint what he pleased, without thinking of the taste of buyers, but he was also wealthy enough to help his brother artists whose works he admired.

In 1866, when he was thirty-five years of age, Mesdag went to Brussels, where his friend and relative Alma-Tadema was then residing. Roelofs also was living in Brussels, and it was under his guidance that the banker began the serious studies which should fit him to make art henceforward his profession. Mesdag stayed three years at Brussels and returned in 1869 to The Hague, no longer an active man of business but an artist. He was not only a painter himself but a collector of paintings, and in course of time he formed a very important collection of modern pictures, chiefly of the Barbizon and Modern Dutch Schools, which in 1903 he generously presented to the public. The Mesdag Museum at The Hague is a lasting monument of his own taste and of the genius of his contemporaries. As a painter Mesdag gave himself almost exclusively to the painting of the sea, and his marines are remarkable for their luminosity, truth, and the vigour of their handling. " A Seascape " (see preceding page) is a good example of his power of suggesting the life and movement of the waves and of his skill in placing shipping, so that his picture is at once absolutely natural and yet decorative in design.

The numerous painters of the Modern Dutch School— almost as numerous as the " Little Masters " of the seventeenth century—may broadly be divided into two classes, the figure of genre painters for whom Israels was the chief influence, and the landscape painters who were inspired by Roelofs and the French painters of Barbizon. Among the genre painters we may mention Albert Neuhuys, born at Utrecht in 1844, who approaches closely to Israels in his grave tender renderings of humble interiors ; David Adolf Constant Artz (1837–90), who, in addition to interiors, painted the fisher-folk of Scheveningen out-of-doors, frequently at moments when they were resting on the sandhills ; and Bernardus Johannes Blommers, born at The Hague in 1845, who developed in his own way the lighter side of the art of Israels. There is nothing tragic in the pictures of Blommers, whose favourite subjects are children playing on the sands at Scheveningen or paddling in the water. " On the Beach " (see next page) is a typical example of the happy seaside scenes in which the artist displays alike his love of children and his knowledge of sea and sky.

§ 3

Of the landscape painters of modern Holland, the nearest to Corot—nearest in the delicacy of his colouring and in the lyrical note that rings out clearly in all his work—is Anton Mauve (1838–88). The son of a Baptist minister, Mauve was born at Naandam and brought up in a strict Protestant home, where art was not encouraged. It was much against the will of his parents that he eventually took up art, and he made little progress under his first master, Van Os, a dry academic painter whose stiff style had little attraction for his sensitive, rather dreamy pupil. The earliest paintings of Mauve were tightly drawn and highly finished, but later, after he had made the acquaintance of Israels, Willem Maris, and other artists in Amsterdam, he completely changed his style, his handling became looser and broader, and he restricted his palette to delicate greys, greens, light fawns, and pale blues. When he was thirty he exhibited at the Free Society in Brussels, and he was influenced by the French artists who exhibited there, particularly by Corot and by Daubigny, whose works he saw

' ON THE BEACH," BY B. J. BLOMMERS (1845-1914).

A typical example of the happy art of this painter, displaying his love of children and his knowledge of sea and sky. A disciple of Israels, Blommers developed the lighter side of that master's art.

"THE SISTERS," BY MATTHEW MARIS (1839-1917).

Matthew Maris, the second of three brothers. all of whom won fame as painters, was the most romantic of the modern Dutch painters. This beautiful example of his art was painted in 1875 at London, where the artist made his home from 1872 till the time of his death.

in the house of Mr. Mesdag and other places in Holland. Mauve soon began to excel in landscape, rendering the soft hazy atmosphere that lingers over the meadows of Holland with infinite tenderness and poetic truth. The sand-dunes near Scheveningen were for many years his favourite sketching-ground, and it was there that he painted one of the most popular of his pictures, "The Sand Cart" (see opposite page). It is a painting that captivates us at once by its winning simplicity, its entire truth, and the atmosphere of repose which it exhales ; and this reposefulness is a general characteristic of the art of Mauve, though his subjects are usually taken from workaday life. We do not think of him primarily as an animal-painter, though his love of animals is made clear by the frequency with which he introduces them into his pictures. But Mauve's animals never seem to have been painted solely for their own sake ; they are part and parcel of the landscape, in which they take a natural place, fulfilling their allotted function as aids to human activity. Each of Mauve's landscapes has the animals appropriate to it. He painted horses—for many years his "Watering Horses," belonging to Mr. J. C. J. Drucker, was lent to the National Gallery—but he also painted donkeys on the seashore, cows in meadows and on the road, sheep at pasture and in their pens. The fine collection of Mauve's work in the Mesdag Museum at The Hague contains examples of all these subjects. Towards the end of his life Mauve painted sheep more frequently than any other animals, the reason being that after living at Amsterdam and The Hague he settled at Laren, which is in the heart of the sheep country to the north-east of Amsterdam. Mauve took all rural and sea-shore life for his province : he painted fishermen and fish-wives at a fish-auction on the beach, he painted groups of peasants gathered together at a timber sale, drawing the various types of faces with great insight and humour, but in all his pictures life is pleasant and work proceeds placidly in an atmosphere of peace and contentment.

Photo · W. A. Mansell & Co. "THE SAND CART," BY ANTON MAUVE (1838–88).

This tender rendering of a typical incident in the workaday life of the seashore captivates us by its winning simplicity, its entire truth, and its atmosphere of repose. Mauve was the most lyrical of the Dutch painters, and his pictures have a serene quality of placid contentment.

§ 4

Three of the most famous and most interesting of the modern Dutch painters were members of one family, all born at The Hague and the sons of a struggling printer. This printer, Maris by name, was of foreign extraction, being the son of a Bohemian soldier of fortune who left his native city of Prague, married a Dutch wife, and settled in the political capital of Holland. The printer also had some experience of fighting, for in 1830 he was called up as a conscript to fight on the side of the Netherlands in the war which resulted in the independence of Belgium. After this war the printer returned to a life of unbroken toil, married, and had three sons. Of these the eldest was Jacob (or James) Maris, born in 1837, next came Matthys (or Matthew), born in 1839, while the youngest, Willem, was born in 1844. In speaking of these brothers we shall here use the English equivalents of their names by which they are usually known in Great Britain and the United States.

All three sons showed at an early age remarkable talents for drawing, and notwithstanding his poverty their father appears to have realised the wisdom of allowing each to follow his artistic bent. In their early years James and Matthew were closely associated. In 1855 the talent of the latter came to the notice of Queen Sophie of Holland, who made him an allowance, and the thrifty father considering that this allowance was enough for two, both James and Matthew were able to spend a year studying and painting at the Antwerp Academy. At Antwerp the two brothers lived in the same house as Alma-Tadema, and through him they got to know his relative Mesdag, the banker-painter, Josef Israels, and other Dutch artists. But in these early days neither brother was much affected by the art of his immediate contemporaries. They laboured strenuously to master the technicalities of their art, and James was guided in his first efforts by a master named Van Hove. This artist, though of mediocre ability, was a very conscientious draughtsman, and under his influence James Maris produced pictures remarkable for the minuteness of

the details.   One of his early pictures, " Interior of a Dutch
House," painted when the artist was twenty-three, is in the
Mesdag Museum, and is quite in the style of Pieter de
Hoogh.   In the middle distance, on the left, is a sunny
nook ; in the foreground is the figure of a servant-girl standing in the entrance hall, holding in her right hand a basket
and in her left a pewter can.   All these details are painted
with scrupulous exactness, and the same characteristics may
be found in other domestic scenes and interiors which he
painted in these early years.

It was not till he was nearing thirty that James Maris
changed his manner of painting and acquired the style
which eventually brought him fame.   In 1865 he went to
Paris, where he remained for six years, and there, under
the influence of the Barbizon masters, he gradually broadened
his style, abandoning his former intimacy of detail and now
aiming at a more general effect of grandeur.   Henceforward he devoted himself almost exclusively to landscape,
and though the change of his style was brought about by
French painting, his mature work is akin to that of Ruysdael
in the nobility and majesty of its outlook.   We can hardly
escape thinking of Ruysdael's " Mill " when we see " The
Stone Mill " by James Maris in the Mesdag Museum ;   a
picturesque stone mill, with an open gallery round it, makes
a stately figure against a sky with white drifting clouds.
In the foreground are sandhills, in the distance the red
roofs of a village, but though the accessories taken together
make up a scene quite distinct from that shown in Ruysdael's
famous picture, both pictures have a touch of sublimity in
the dignity of their design.   Equally characteristic of the
way in which this artist subordinates particular objects to
the general effect is his painting of " Dordrecht " (see
page 515).   All details are merged in these masses of light
and shade, yet everyone who has seen this town at eventide
will agree that the painter has given us the essential
characteristics of the " Venice of the North," its Groote
Kerke, its shipping, its wide canals, and the rolling grey
sky overhead, and has presented these with incomparable
dignity and grandeur.

33

"THE GIRL AT THE WELL," BY MATTHEW MARIS

One of the earliest pictures painted at London by this artist, who in 1872 had rooms in St. James's Terrace, Regent's Park. It is a remarkable blend of romantic imagination with realistic treatment.

Photo: T. & R. Annan.

"DORDRECHT," BY JAMES MARIS (1837–99).

A majestic vision at eventide of the "Venice of the North," with its Groote Kerke, its wide canals, and its shipping. It is a fine example of the manner in which this artist. the eldest of the three brothers, subordinated details to the grandeur of the general effect.

William Maris is more limited in his range than either of his brothers, and though in their early days the work of all three showed a certain similarity of style, William's work altered least in style and in subject. He is nearer to Roelofs than either of his brothers, and his favourite subjects were landscapes with cattle, which he painted, as a rule, in full daylight, so that his pictures are rather brighter and gayer in colour than those of his brothers. A meadow extending along the border of the sandhills, in which are seen a few stunted trees and some cows, a pond perhaps in the immediate foreground, and a cloudy sky overhead, this is a typical William Maris subject. Less poetic than Mauve, less grand than his brother James, and less romantic than his brother Matthew, William Maris was a happy realist whose rich coloured pictures are full of sunshine and mirror the luxuriant greens of Holland's pasture-lands.

Matthew Maris stands apart from his brothers and from all the Dutch artists of his generation. He was different in his temperament, different in his life, and different in his art. Tracing it to his foreign extraction, to his Austrian, or, as we should now say, to his Czecho-Slovak blood, Professor Muther says there broke out in Matthew Maris a " Teutonic mediæval mysticism " from which his brothers were free. Matthew no doubt possessed a romantic mystical temperament, but it is possible that he was influenced by the romantic mediævalism of Rossetti. It was in England that Matthew Maris painted his most characteristic pictures, and in England, where he lived for forty-five years, he drifted apart from his brethren in his art as in his life.

The beginnings of Matthew were almost parallel with those of James. The two brothers studied, as we have seen, at The Hague and Antwerp, and they were together in Paris. One incident must be chronicled which appears to have had far more influence on Matthew than on James. In 1858 the two brothers were back from Antwerp at The Hague, and three years later, having made some money by copying pictures, the two set out together on a tour through the Black Forest to Switzerland, returning through France

By courtesy of Barbizon House.   "ENFANT COUCHÉE," BY MATTHEW MARIS.

An example of " the delightful quality of faiëry and enchantment which so strangely characterises some of the works
of Matthew Maris." It has a quality " for ever young and simple as of the glorified vision of a child."

by Dijon to the Puy-de-Dôme. Matthew was tremendously impressed by the romantic castles and buildings he saw in Central France ; to his poetic imagination they were enchanted palaces. The recollection of this tour never faded from his mind, and in pictures painted years afterwards we catch echoes of the turrets and battlements which remained fixed in his memory. We may see evidence of this in the background of " Feeding Chickens " (see page 520), painted in 1872.

Nevertheless it is important to note that there is not the same note of romanticism in pictures he painted only two years earlier. In 1868 Matthew joined his brother James in Paris, and we may see in the National Gallery a little picture he painted there in 1870. " Montmartre," as it is called, shows us dust-carts tipping rubbish on the side of a hill which has a windmill at the top. It is beautifully painted, perfect in its refined realism, but it is not romantic.

When the Franco-Prussian war broke out, James Maris returned to Holland. Matthew remained, went through the siege of Paris, and, like other residents, was enrolled in the Municipal Guard and called out for duty. His post was on the fortifications, opposite Asniéres and just under Mont Valérien, and he suffered considerably from the bitter cold during night duty. Military life was not congenial to this gentle artist, and the thought of killing anybody was abhorrent to him. He confessed afterwards, " I never put a bullet in my gun, but only pretended to do so ! "

His war experiences certainly did Matthew Maris no good ; they saddened him and tended to make him shrink into himself, so that he became more and more of a recluse. After the siege Matthew Maris came to London in 1872, and there he remained to the end of his days. He had rooms at first in the house of an art decorator named Daniel Cottier in St. James's Terrace, Regent's Park, and Cottier, a strong active business man, had much influence over him, telling him what sort of pictures he ought to paint. Although Cottier, an admirer of Rossetti, undoubtedly encouraged the romantic element in the Dutch artist, Matthew Maris rebelled at painting under his direction and professed that he was thoroughly unhappy in his house. Yet between 1872 and 1875, when he was under the spell of Cottier, Matthew Maris painted what are generally considered to be his finest pictures. Among them we may mention " The Girl at the Well " (see page 514) and " Feeding Chickens " (see next page), painted in 1872 ; " The Christening " and " Enfant Couchée " (see page 517), in 1873 ; " He is Coming "—a most Rossetti-like vision of a little princess at her spindle with a prince seen approaching through the open door—in 1874 ; and " The Sisters " (see page 509) in 1875. Yet even these works, full of indescribable poetry and romantic beauty, failed to satisfy the artist, who in after years would speak of them as " potboilers " which he had been compelled to paint by a tyrannical taskmaster.

Though discontented and professedly unhappy, Matthew Maris was slow to leave what he regarded as a house of bondage, and it was not till 1887—and then chiefly because Mrs. Cottier was in ill-health—that he finally left. He went to 47 St. John's Wood Terrace, intending to remain there only a fortnight, while he looked around for a more convenient studio, and he stayed there nineteen years. In 1906 he found a home at 18 Westbourne Square, Paddington, in a half-flat with a small painting-room, and in this modest abode, tended by a faithful housekeeper, he remained till he died on August 17, 1917. He seldom went out and he had few visitors, the most intimate friends of his later years being the Dutch picture-dealer, Mr. E. J. Van Wisselingh and his wife, a Scottish lady, daughter of Mr. Craibe Angus, of Glasgow, who had been one of the earliest British patrons of Matthew Maris. His later paintings became more and more mysterious ; instead of the clear outlines of his earlier pictures, forms were seen dimly as through a mist, and these pictures he would work over and over many times, each re-painting seeming to cast a new veil over faces and figures that became more and more spiritual. Had he wished, Matthew Maris might

"FEEDING CHICKENS," BY MATTHEW MARIS.

This picture, painted in 1872, shows how the artist could invest a commonplace incident of farm life with the magic of poetry. The "enchanted towers" in the background are probably a memory of the romantic castles and buildings in Central France which made a lasting impression on the artist when he saw them in 1861 while travelling from Dijon to the Puy-de-Dôme.

have had fortune as well as fame, for there were ardent collectors in many countries eager to secure examples of his works, but his means were straitened largely because he could with difficulty bring himself to part with a picture and desired to keep them all in his painting-room. In 1911 a Dutch admirer of his work, Mr. Thomsen, of The Hague, offered to the compatriot of whom he was proud a small pension. This the painter accepted, and the pension was continued till his death.

An abnormal being, Matthew Maris was " alone in the world " because he chose of his own accord to live the life of a hermit shut up with his dreams.

XXI

THE INFLUENCE OF THE FAR EAST

JAPANESE COLOUR-PRINTS AND THE ART OF WHISTLER

§ 1

TO attempt any historical survey of the art of the East is beyond the scope of this OUTLINE, but since several of the most distinguished Western painters of the nineteenth century were profoundly influenced by the art of China and Japan, it is necessary to make some brief mention of the wonderful art of the Far East and to record the genesis of its appreciation in Europe in order that we may perceive the part it played in shaping the style of certain modern masters.

Painting in water-colours on silk, or less often on paper, was practised in China from the earliest years of the Christian era. One of the oldest Chinese pictures known to exist is a scroll-painting called " Admonitions of the Instructress " in the British Museum. This has been pronounced by experts to be a work of the fourth century, but it has none of the characteristics of a primitive work executed when an art is in its infancy. The mastery of natural attitude and of the relation of figures to each other and the delicate expressiveness of the drawing prove that behind the art which produced it is a long history of development.

Chinese painting attained its highest excellence during the Sung Dynasty, *i.e.* approximately between A.D. 950 and 1250, and to this period belongs the masterly painting of " Two Geese " (see page 525) in the British Museum. The exquisitely refined drawing and simple naturalism in this dignified bird painting show the high state of civilisation in China at a time when Europe was only painfully

" THE LITTLE WHITE GIRL," BY JAMES McNEILL WHISTLER
National Gallery, London

For sheer beauty this portrait of his once favourite model, afterwards Mrs. Joanna Abbott, was never surpassed by Whistler. This picture inspired Swinburne to write his poem " Before the Mirror." In 1919 it was bequeathed by Mr. Arthur Studd to the National Gallery.

emerging from the Dark Ages. We have only to turn back to the first chapter of this work and to compare the paintings of Cimabue or of Giotto with this still earlier picture from the East, to realise how superior was the naturalism of the Chinese artist to that of the most gifted of the earliest European painters. The art of the Sung period excelled in landscape and animal painting, and it was " inspired by a mystical feeling for Nature (akin to that expressed by Wordsworth's poetry) which gives a serious beauty to its treatment of simple or seemingly insignificant subjects."

It is only in quite recent times, however, that Western artists have been attracted by the nobility of early Chinese art. In the nineteenth century Chinese paintings were scarce and little known in Europe, and the first examples of Oriental art made familiar to Europe were colour-prints from Japan. Though the Japanese to-day have a de-servedly high reputation as an artistic nation, China was their instructress in all the arts. The art of printing in colours from a number of wood blocks in succession was practised in China in the seventeenth century, perhaps earlier, but it was not till the eighteenth century that it flourished in Japan. In that country the demand for a popular art had fostered a school of painting devoted to themes of daily life, and the woodcut provided a cheap means of multiplying designs. At first, in the early part of the eighteenth century, these woodcuts were coloured by hand, then prints were made in two colours, rose-red and green, and in 1764 the first full-coloured prints, known as " brocade prints," were issued. Harunobu (1705–72) was the first master to use the new invention, which during the next hundred years was to produce the most beautiful examples of colour-printing that the world has seen.

From the time of Harunobu to the death of Utamaro in 1806, a succession of artists poured forth a series of these popular pictures, which were sold for the merest trifle, chiefly to the working classes of Japan. The painters of Japan catered for aristocratic tastes and were patronised by the wealthy and eminent, but the makers of colour-prints were democratic both in origin and aim and were regarded socially as artisans rather than artists. The aristocratic painters of Japan, like those of China, were symbolists, whose work conveyed subtle allusions to educated Orientals ; but the designers of colour-prints were realists, who rendered the common life of everyday people. Among the Japanese this art, despised by the higher classes, was named the " Mirror of the Passing World." With the common people of Japan the drama was an overwhelming passion, and consequently the subjects of innumerable colour-prints are taken from the stage, which provided endless themes. In all the earlier Japanese colour-prints figures predominate, but after the death of Utamaro a great artist arose in Hokusai (1760–

Photo : W. A. Mansell & Co.

"TWO GEESE," BY A CHINESE ARTIST OF THE SUNG PERIOD

(A.D. 950–1250).

British Museum, London.

1849), who invented a new landscape style. Hokusai was followed by other great landscape artists, Hiroshige (1796–1858) and his successor Hiroshige II, who worked *c.* 1840–65, and the splendid landscape designs by these artists were the first to make their influence felt in Europe.

Hokusai is now generally regarded as one of the world's great artists, worthy to rank with Rembrandt, Durer, and other giants. His " River Scene " (see page 533), with the great bridge over the water and Fujiyama in the distance, shows his unsurpassed skill in the technique of his art, the largeness of his view, and the intense human interest with which he invested every scene he painted. A master of the first order as a draughtsman, Hokusai was also a daring pioneer as a colourist, being the first to combine the particular greens, blues, yellows, and browns which distinguish his famous series " Thirty-six Views of Fuju-yama," to use the telling contrast of red, bright blue, and brown seen in his " Views of the Loochoo Islands," and to harmonise with infinite tenderness a whole gamut of greens and blues in his great designs based on carps. Hokusai lived to a great age, his death occurring when he was approaching his ninetieth birthday, and shortly before he expired he murmured, " If Fate had given me but five more years, I should have been able to become a true painter." He was not only one of the greatest and most poetic of the world's artists, he was one of the most modest.

The beginning of the artistic influence of Japan on Europe is generally dated from the International Exhibition held at London in 1862, when the examples of Japanese art there shown made a profound impression on all who studied them. Seidlitz, in his *History of Japanese Colour Prints*, gives the same date, but this authority traces the first discovery of Japanese art in Europe to a Japanese shop in the Rue de Rivoli, Paris. This shop, known as " La Porte Chinoise " and owned by a dealer named Soye, was frequented by a number of artists who delighted in the colour-prints by Hokusai, Hiroshige, and others which they found there. To this shop came Manet, Degas, Monet, and other French artists afterwards to become famous, and to it also came a young American artist, James McNeill Whistler. The Japanese have a perfect instinct of decoration, and consequently these colour-prints made an immediate and powerful appeal to a young artist who already had within him the instinct of decoration. In the work of Hokusai and Hiroshige, Whistler recognised those qualities which above all he desired to have in his own work.

§ 2

Among the artists of the nineteenth century Whistler holds a unique position. He was the first great painter of American birth to win universal renown. His life was a long struggle against hostile criticism and misunderstanding, and he defended his art and his ideals with the pungent brilliancy of a wit and with the undaunted pugnacity of a soldier. By example and precept he eventually revolutionised English ideas about art and interior decoration. He compelled people who stubbornly repeated " Every Picture tells a Story," to realise at long last that *every picture ought to sing a tune*, that is to say, it ought to utter forth a melody of line and a harmony of colour ; in a word, he compelled all England and the United States to recognise the decorative as well as the illustrative element in painting. More than any other English-speaking man Whistler opened our eyes to the true value of Velazquez and Hokusai, and he invented a new style of portraiture in which Spanish realism was exquisitely wedded to a Japanese sense of decoration. A stranger within our gates, he revealed England to the English and recorded both in his etchings and in his paintings poetic aspects of London's riverside, aspects to which hitherto all artists had been blind, aspects the beauty of which all can now see.

Whistler was born on July 10, 1834, at Lowell, in Massachusetts, and was baptized there with the Christian names of James Abbott. This second name he dropped in later life and substituted for it his mother's maiden name, McNeill. His father, Major George Washington Whistler, after leaving the United States army, became a railway

"AT THE PIANO," BY WHISTLER (1834–1903).

This early work, painted in 1859, was the first picture the artist exhibited in London. It shows us Whistler's

engineer, and in 1842 journeyed to Russia with his wife and family : he had been appointed chief adviser of the railway under construction between Moscow and Petrograd. The most important consequence to James Whistler of this boyhood stay in Russia was that in Petrograd he learnt to speak French fluently. His father died in 1849, when the widow returned with her children to the United States.

Following in his father's footsteps, James Whistler in 1851 entered the military college of West Point, but after three years of desultory study he was dismissed, chiefly owing to his deplorable failure in chemistry. The first question in his oral examination floored him completely, and later in life Whistler humorously said, " If silicon had been a gas I might have become a general in the United States army." Even from his Russian days Whistler had shown a remarkable capacity for drawing, and his delight in sketching prompted his relatives, after his West Point failure, to obtain for him a post as draughtsman in the Government Coast Survey Department at Washington, thinking that this occupation might be more congenial to him. To some extent it was, for here he learnt to engrave and etch, and he executed an excellent plate of a view, taken from the sea, of cliffs along the coast; but the fancy heads and figures which he irrelevantly added in the margin showed that he could not take his topographical studies seriously as a preliminary to map-making, but only as an excuse for sketching. In February 1855 he resigned his position, and the end of the year found him an art student in Paris.

Many painters have spent joyous student-days in Paris, but few of them bear the traces of it in their lives as Whistler did. He had barely turned twenty-one when he arrived in Paris, and his high-spirited temperament and sense of fun delighted in all the antics which then distinguished the Bohemians of the Latin Quarter. In those days the art students lived a life apart, making themselves noticed by wearing unorthodox clothes, playing all sorts of practical jokes, affecting to despise the common mortal, and never

34

so happy as when they succeeded in shocking and bewildering what they called the " bourgeois." Whistler plunged hot-foot into this way of life, and, as the distinguished French critic M. Théodore Duret, who knew him well, has remarked, there was grafted on him " the habit of a separate pose, whimsical attire, a way of despising and setting at defiance the ' vulgar herd ' incapable of seeing and feeling like an artist. This combination of the distinctive characteristics of a French art student and the manner of an American gentleman, in a man otherwise full of life, spirit, and individuality, made of Whistler a quaint original who could not fail to be remarked everywhere."

But all the time he was amusing himself he worked, not so much in the studio of Gleyre—his official place of training, but irregularly attended—as in the streets and cafés of Paris and in his rooms. He divided his time between etching and painting, and in the former he appeared almost as a master in the first " French Set " published as early as 1858. In the following year he produced his first great achievement in painting, " At the Piano " (see page 528), which, though rejected by the Paris Salon of 1859, was hung at the Royal Academy in 1860 and subsequently purchased by the Academician John Philip, R.A. In this picture, which represents his half-sister, Mrs. Seymour Haden, seated, playing the piano, against which her little daughter Annie, in white, is standing, Whistler already shows the influence of Velazquez. Philip was well known as an intense admirer of this master, and it was doubtless the Spanish qualities in Whistler's painting which led the older artist to buy it. Two years later Whistler set out for Madrid with the intention of seeing the pictures by Velazquez in the Prado, but on the way he stopped at a seaside resort, where he nearly got drowned while bathing and had to return to Paris without going to Madrid.

In 1863 he made his second attempt to exhibit in the Paris Salon, and again the jury rejected his picture, the full-length portrait of a young Irish girl, known as " Jo," dressed in white, holding a white flower, and standing against a white curtain. " The White Girl," as it was first called,

" LA PRINCESSE DE LA PORCELAINE," BY WHISTLER.

One of the masterpieces of Whistler's pronounced Japanese period, this picture is a costume portrait of Miss Christina Spartali, daughter of the Greek Consul-General in London. It was formerly in the possession of the shipowner, Mr. F. R. Leyland, and occupied a central position in the famous " Peacock Room " decorated for him by Whistler.

was the beginning of a series of pictures in which Whistler deliberately experimented in improvising a colour harmony based on the infinitely delicate gradations of one dominant colour. It was afterwards entitled " Symphony in White No. I."

So many paintings by artists of great talent were rejected by the Salon this year that the Emperor Napoleon III intervened, and by his order a selection of the rejected works was shown in a special room which became famous as the *Salon des Refusés*. Of this epoch-making exhibition more will be said in the next chapter, when dealing with French painters who were Whistler's contemporaries, but for the moment it must suffice to say that among the works there exhibited was " The White Girl," which elicited high praise from the more advanced critics.

From 1859 Whistler had divided his time between Paris and London, and though he had many friends and admirers in the former city, he was hurt at the lack of official recognition. In 1863 he fixed his residence in London, where several of his family were already established. Whistler's father had married twice, and one of the daughters by his first wife had married the English surgeon Seymour Haden, who afterwards made a great reputation as an etcher. Whistler's mother had also now left America and was living in London with her second son William, a doctor. James Whistler himself had not only stayed and exhibited in London, but had worked there, for in 1859 he had already begun the series of etchings known as " The Thames Set," which marks the culminating point of his first etching period. " Black Lion Wharf " (see page 543) may be taken as an example of the perfection of his technique in 1859, of the lightness and elasticity of his line, and of the vivacity of the whole. Though he afterwards produced etchings, perfect of their kind, in quite another style, Whistler never did anything better in their own way than some of the plates in " The Thames Set."

Whistler settled down in Chelsea, and became friendly with his neighbour Rossetti, who shared his taste for blue-and-white Chinese porcelain and for Japanese colour-prints, and during his first years in London the artistic influence of the Far East became more pronounced in Whistler's art. He surrounded himself with Oriental objects and introduced them constantly into his pictures. In 1864 he painted " The Gold Screen," against which sat a young woman in Japanese costume, surrounded by other variously

Photo : W. A. Mansell & Co.

" RIVER SCENE WITH BRIDGE AND FUJIYAMA IN THE DISTANCE," COLOUR PRINT BY HOKUSAI (1760–1849).
British Museum, London.

An impressive example of the naturalistic and decorative powers of the greatest of the democratic artists of Japan. We have only to compare it with " Old Battersea Bridge " (see page 536) to learn how Whistler was influenced by the design of Hokusai.

coloured objects from the Far East. About the same time he painted " La Princesse du Pays de la Porcelaine " (see page 531), in which brilliant colours are again afforded by a Japanese dress. The original of this portrait was Miss Christina Spartali, daughter of the Greek Consul-General in London. Her sister Marie Spartali, afterwards Mrs. Stillman, had been a pupil of Rossetti and sat to him for " Fiametta " and other paintings. Owing to the family likeness common to the two sisters, it has been said that at this time Whistler was subject to Rossetti's influence, but the resemblance between their works is a superficial one due only to the likeness of their respective models.   There is no evidence that Whistler borrowed any of Rossetti's methods, and the chief influences during the years in which Whistler formed his style of painting were Courbet and Manet—as we shall see in the next chapter—Velazquez and the masters of Japan.   In etching he was principally influenced by Rembrandt and Méryon.

" The Princess of the Porcelain Country," accepted by the Salon in 1865, was the first work by Whistler to be shown in any official exhibition in Paris.   Other pictures of this Japanese period were " The Lange Leizen," in the Academy of 1864, " The Balcony," in the Academy of 1870, and, most beautiful of all, " The Little White Girl " (see page 523), also known as " Symphony in White No. II," shown at the Academy in the same year.   The Japanese fan in the girl's hand is the only direct confession of Oriental influence in this picture, which otherwise unites the Spanish gravity and realism of " At the Piano " with the gay-coloured decorativeness of a Hokusai or Hiroshige.   After having seen this picture in Whistler's studio, Swinburne wrote the poem afterwards included in *Poems and Ballads* :

BEFORE THE MIRROR

Come snow, come wind or thunder,
  High up in air,
 I watch my face and wonder
  At my bright hair.
 Nought else exists or grieves
 The rose at heart, that heaves
With love of her own leaves, and lips that pair.

 I cannot tell what pleasures
  Or what pains were,
 What pale new loves and treasures
  New years will bear ;
 What beam will fall, what shower
 With grief or joy for dower,
But one thing knows the flower, the flower is fair.

Whistler also painted a " Symphony in White No. III " : in this two girls, one in cream, one in white, recline on a white sofa, while a fan on the floor and the flowers of an azalea in a corner repeat the dominant whites. The motive of the artist in choosing these colour-schemes and calling the pictures " symphonies " was at this time beyond the comprehension of even professional art critics, and one of them wrote of this picture in the *Saturday Review* :

In the " Symphony in White No. III " by Mr. Whistler there are many dainty varieties of tint, but it is not precisely a symphony in white. One lady has a yellowish dress and brown hair and a bit of blue ribbon, the other has a red fan, and there are flowers and green leaves. There is a girl in white on a white sofa, but even this girl has reddish hair ; and of course there is the flesh colour of the complexions.

To this Whistler promptly retorted :

Bon Dieu ! did this wise person expect white hair and chalked faces ? And does he then, in his astounding consequence, believe that a symphony in F contains no other note, but shall be a continued repetition of F, F, F ? . . . Fool !

This was one of the earliest of Whistler's critical encounters, taking place when the picture was exhibited at the Academy in 1867, and the critics were soon to learn that here was a painter who could hit back with interest.

As the successive exhibition of Whistler's pictures enabled the tendencies and peculiarities of his work to be more clearly seen, the public, the critics, and the Royal Academy itself became more and more hostile to him, and finally took up an attitude of undisguised ill-will. In 1872 his painting of his mother (see page 542), now universally recognised to be one of the great portraits of the century, was narrowly rejected by the Academy, and its final acceptance was only due to the staunch championship of the veteran Sir William Boxall, R.A., who threatened to resign from the Council if the picture were not hung. Doubtless Whistler's habit of giving his works titles borrowed from musical terms prejudiced the public against them. An extremist far more in his titles than in his actual manner of painting, Whistler went so far as to call his picture of

NOCTURNE—BLUE AND GOLD—"OLD BATTERSEA BRIDGE,"
BY WHISTLER.

Tate Gallery, London.

One of the celebrated nocturnes exhibited at the Grosvenor Gallery in 1877, when Ruskin
accused Whistler of "flinging a pot of paint in the public's face." The painter was
awarded only a farthing damages in the libel action which ensued; but two years after
Whistler's death, this picture, for which he had asked 200 guineas, was purchased at
2000 guineas for the National Gallery.

his mother, "Arrangement in Grey and Black." He defended this title by saying :

That is what it is. To me it is interesting as a picture of my mother ; but what can or ought the public to care about the identity of the portrait ?

In his desire to emphasise the importance of decorative

Photo : W. A. Mansell & Co.

"CREMORNE LIGHTS," BY WHISTLER.

National Gallery, London.

'When the evening mist clothes the riverside with poetry, as with a veil, and the poor buildings lose themselves in the dim sky, and the tall chimneys become campanili, and the warehouses are palaces in the night, and the whole city hangs in the heavens, and fairyland is before us."—J. McNeill Whistler.

design and colour in painting, Whistler became a little inhuman. As one of his younger critics pertinently observed, we can find an "arrangement of grey and black" in a coal-scuttle ; we find far more in Whistler's "Mother," we find reverence for age, character, tenderness, and affection. It has become one of the great pictures of the world, not only because it is a pleasing pattern of colours, but because it is a true work of deep emotion tenderly expressed.

No longer welcome at the Royal Academy, Whistler was fortunate in soon securing a new exhibition centre. Sir Coutts Lindsay, a rich banker and amateur painter who patronised the arts, had the Grosvenor Gallery built in Bond Street, and at the first exhibition opened there in May 1877 Whistler was represented by seven pictures. These included the portrait of Carlyle, now at Glasgow, a painting similar in style to the artist's " Mother," described as " An Arrangement in Brown," a full-length of Irving as Philip II of Spain, described as " Arrangement in Black No. III," and four nocturnes, two in blue and silver, one in blue and gold, and one in black and gold. Whistler had not confined his studies of the Thames in mid-London to his etched work ; he had used these subjects for paintings in the 'sixties, among them being " Old Battersea Bridge " and " Chelsea in Ice," but in this new series of evening effects by the riverside he shocked the conventions of the day more than he had yet done by his " symphonies."

These poetic paintings of night represent the extreme point of originality to which Whistler went. Particularities of scene and landscape exist in these nocturnes only as accessories ; the real subject is the limpidity of the atmosphere, water illumined by the pale rays of the moon, mysterious shadows, the great silhouettes of dark nights, the darkness intensified sometimes by a splash of fireworks against the sky. To-day, though Cremorne is no more, we can recognise the truth as well as the beauty in " Cremorne Lights " (see preceding page), for Whistler has now taught us to use our own experience in looking at these pictures of moonlight and lights reflected in the water. But at the time of their first appearance these nocturnes were incomprehensible to most people, who looked in them for topographical details which the veil of night would naturally conceal. In an eloquent and moving passage in his lecture, known as the " Ten o'Clock," Whistler afterwards explained what he saw and painted by the Thames at eventide :

When the evening mist clothes the riverside with poetry, as with a veil, and the poor buildings lose themselves in the dim sky, and the tall chimneys become campanili, and the warehouses are palaces in the night,

PORTRAIT OF MISS CICELY HENRIETTA
ALEXANDER, BY WHISTLER.

This charming portrait of the younger daughter of Mr. W. C.
Alexander is one of Whistler's most daring colour-schemes, a
bright harmony of grey and green. Note the butterflies in the
left-hand top corner, which give a note of summer-time gaiety
to the composition and repeat Whistler's own " trade-mark,"
the butterfly signature on the wall.

and the whole city hangs in the heavens, and fairyland is before us—then the wayfarer hastens home ; the working man and the cultured one, the wise man and the one of pleasure, cease to understand as they have ceased to see, and Nature, who, for once, has sung in tune, sings her exquisite song to the artist alone, her son and her master, her son in that he loves her, her master in that he knows her. .

But in 1877 Whistler's views on the poetry of night were unknown, and the magic of his brush could not immediately convert the public to appreciation of pictures the like of which had never before been seen in Europe. Something approaching them had been seen in Japan, as we may see by comparing Hokusai's bridge pictures with those of Whistler, but Hokusai and Hiroshige were not known then as they are to-day. Whistler's nocturnes were regarded by the majority as a smear of uniform colour in which no distinct forms could be considered. The painter was looked upon as a charlatan and buffoon, and among those who attacked him, sad to relate, was the stout defender of Turner and the Pre-Raphaelites. John Ruskin, no wiser in this respect than the others, permitted himself to write the following in *Fors Clavigera* on July 2, 1877 :

For Mr. Whistler's own sake, no less than for the protection of the purchaser, Sir Coutts Lindsay ought not to have admitted works into the gallery in which the ill-educated conceit of the artist so nearly approached the aspect of wilful imposture. I have seen, and heard, much of cockney impudence before now ; but never expected to hear a coxcomb ask two hundred guineas for flinging a pot of paint in the public's face.

Strange that Ruskin did not remember that the selfsame phrase about " flinging a pot of paint " had been used a generation earlier by a critic of one of Turner's sunsets. Then Ruskin had been on the side of the artist, now he did not understand and stood with the Philistines. Time has avenged the insult to genius uncomprehended, and the " Nocturne—Blue and Gold—Old Battersea Bridge " (see page 536), which Ruskin in 1877 thought not worth two hundred guineas, was in 1905 eagerly purchased for two thousand guineas and presented to the nation.

Whistler's exhibits brought him all the publicity any

artist could desire—all London was talking of his nocturnes —but the hostility of the critics, and particularly the savage onslaught of Ruskin, scared away purchasers. When he exhibited for the second time at the Grosvenor Gallery in 1878, Whistler found that Ruskin's denunciation was stopping the sale of his pictures and, after some hesitation, he decided to bring a libel action against him.

The case was heard on the 25th and 26th of November 1878 before Mr. Justice Huddlestone and a special jury. It created a great sensation, but Whistler was ill advised to bring the action, because artistic questions can never be satisfactorily settled in a court of law. Popular sympathy was with the critic, who had so often been right in the past, and Whistler's brilliant repartees in the witness-box did him no good, for they only tended to confirm the opinion that he was an amusing jester who was not to be taken seriously. In cross-examination the opposing counsel elicited the fact that the " Nocturne in Black and Gold " had been painted in two days, and then said, " The labour of two days, then, is that for which you ask two hundred guineas ? " " No," replied Whistler with dignity; " I ask it for the knowledge of a lifetime."

The point at issue really was whether the nocturnes were or were not works of art, and this was a matter obviously over the heads of the jury. Albert Moore, giving evidence for Whistler, praised his pictures highly and declared that they showed not " eccentricity " but " originality." William Rossetti also pronounced the nocturnes to be true works of art, but on the other side Frith declared they were not, and Burne-Jones agreed with him because, though he admitted that the nocturnes had " fine colour and atmosphere," he considered that they lacked " complete finish." Tom Taylor, the art critic of *The Times*, giving evidence for Ruskin, attempted to explain what Burne-Jones meant by finish, and for this purpose produced a picture by Titian. But when this was handed to the jury, one of them, mistaking it for a picture by Whistler, exclaimed, " Oh, come ! we've had enough of these Whistlers," and they all refused to look at it !

In the end Whistler was awarded the contemptuous sum of one farthing damages. This meant that he had to pay his own law costs, and since nobody would buy his

Photo : *W. A. Mansell & Co.*

"THE ARTIST'S MOTHER," BY WHISTLER.
Luxembourg, Paris.

When M. Bourgeois, Minister of Fine Arts, expressed a desire to purchase this work for the French Nation, Whistler replied : " The picture you have chosen is precisely the one I could most earnestly wish to see become the object of so solemn a consecration."

pictures now he was soon in money difficulties. He revenged himself by issuing a pamphlet, *Art and Art Critics*, in which his enemies were neatly and wittily put in their places, but this did not help him to live. To put an end to an untenable situation, early in 1879 he had to abandon his residence, " The White House," in Chelsea. He became a bankrupt and all his belongings were sold to satisfy his creditors.

Another man might have been crushed by the misfortunes which now crowded on him, but fortunately Whistler was an etcher as well as a painter, and at this moment, when his pictures were unsaleable, he again turned to etching. He came to an arrangement with a firm, which advanced him a sum of money on etchings he engaged to execute, and with this he went in 1879 to Venice, where he developed a new and beautiful style in etching. In com-

Photo : W. A. Mansell & Co.

" BLACK LION WHARF," BY WHISTLER.

One of the most famous etchings in his early " Thames Set," this work shows the precision and delicacy of Whistler's draughtsmanship in 1859. He was the first artist to perceive and record the picturesqueness of the Thames in mid-London.

parison with his earlier work, these Venice etchings were lighter in handling and more simplified in line ; but they palpitated with light and air and were fairylike in their delicacy of decoration. " San Giorgio " (see page 545) shows how spacious and satisfying an effect Whistler was now able to secure with a minimum of means.

These new etchings were not at first popular with the public and the critics any more than the nocturnes, but they were appreciated and purchased by many discriminating print-collectors, and when Whistler returned to Chelsea towards the end of 1880 his position gradually improved. In 1883 he held a second and larger exhibition of his Venetian pieces at the Fine Art Society, and prepared an extraordinary catalogue, in which under each numbered exhibit appeared quotations taken from influential journals and well-known writers, *all hostile*, and beginning with this extract from *Truth* : " Another crop of Mr. Whistler's little jokes." The exhibition, which was beautifully arranged and staged, together with this quaint catalogue, caused an immense sensation. Never before had an artist made fun of his critics to this extent. Visitors could not fail to recognise the refinement in works like " San Giorgio," and when they read a sentence like " Whistler is eminently vulgar " the criticism recoiled on the writer, not the artist. The tide began to turn, and a considerable opinion now became definitely favourable to Whistler. He began to paint again, people like Mrs. Meux, the wife of the brewer, and Lady Archibald Campbell came to him for portraits, and his position was immensely strengthened when his " Portrait of the Artist's Mother " obtained a medal and a brilliant success in the Paris Salon of 1883. Later this work was bought by the French Government for the Luxembourg.

For the next few years Whistler made Paris his principal exhibition centre. At the Grosvenor Gallery in 1881 his " Portrait of Miss Cicely Alexander " (see page 539) had been dreadfully abused by English critics ; in the Paris Salon of 1884 it was singled out for general approbation. For a brief season Whistler exhibited at the Royal Society of British Artists, of which he was elected President in June 1886, and under his presidency this Society held the most brilliant exhibitions in its history. But in 1888 there was a cabal against him by members discontented with his rule ; Whistler was compelled to resign, and was followed by a number of talented artists whom he had persuaded to join the Society. When asked to explain what had happened, the ex-President replied, " It is quite simple ; the artists have left and the British remain."

Photo : Rischgitz Collection.

"SAN GIORGIO," 1880, BY WHISTLER.

A brilliant example of Whistler's second manner in etching which he developed in Venice, where he stayed for some months after his bankruptcy. Again " fairyland is before us," and with the utmost economy of means the artist has suggested a characteristic aspect of Venice and its shipping, flooded with light and air.

The year after Whistler met with this rebuff in London, he was made a Chevalier of the Legion of Honour, which showed the esteem in which he was now held in France, and in 1892 he took a house at Paris in the Rue de Bac. He can hardly be said to have settled there, however, for he returned several times to London. In 1890 he had published a collection of letters and various controversial matter, including a report, with his own marginal comments, of the Ruskin trial, under the title of *The Gentle Art of Making Enemies*, and this publication not only increased his reputation as a wit but showed that he possessed a distinct literary style of his own. This was followed some years later by *The Baronet and the Butterfly*, a pamphlet giving the artist's version of a quarrel and lawsuit with Sir William Eden over a portrait of Lady Eden. Whistler had early adopted the device of a butterfly as his sign-manual and signature, but he was a butterfly with a sting, as he confessed himself to be in the little drawings with which he decorated his publications.

All the quarrels and encounters of his stormy life cannot be recounted here, but in the end he was victorious in London as in Paris. The purchase of his " Mother " by the French Government helped to turn the scale in England. A new generation of artists gave Whistler a banquet in London to celebrate the event, and in the same year (1892) the most important one-man-show of his pictures yet held anywhere was opened in the old Goupil Gallery in Bond Street. This included nearly all his most famous works, among them the disgraced nocturnes, but now only a minority objected to his pictures or his titles, and the success of the exhibition revealed the change which the course of years had brought about in London opinion. The Royal Academy was no longer the power it had been in his earlier days ; its prestige had declined, and there was now a powerful body of outside artists who admired Whistler. In 1898 the most eminent of these formed the " International Society of Sculptors, Painters, and Gravers," and invited Whistler to become its first President, a position he held till his death on July 17, 1903. The exhibitions of this new Society proved that Whistler was not only respected by artists, but had become fashionable with all persons of taste.

To sum up, it may be said that after forty years of incessant battling, Whistler enjoyed a decade of tranquil success, but his last years were saddened by private trouble. In 1888 he had married the widow of E. W. Godwin, an architect, and his wife's death in 1896 was a great blow to the artist. With his loneliness he grew restless, and though his continued devotion to his work saved him from melancholy, he travelled about a good deal. He was visiting Holland in the summer of 1902 when he was seized with a heart attack, and though he gained enough strength to return to London, and even to begin working again in the winter, a relapse in the following June prostrated him, and on Friday, July 17, after conversing good-humouredly during lunch, he was seized with syncope at 3 p.m. and died without suffering. France, Italy, Bavaria, and Dresden had all conferred distinctions on him ; but in America, his birthplace, and in England, where he lived and worked for the greater part of his life, Whistler received no official recognition.

§ 3

In his treatment of buildings, particularly in his earlier etchings, Whistler was undoubtedly influenced by the work of Charles Méryon, one of the earliest and greatest etchers of architectural subjects. The life of this artist is one of the saddest stories in modern art. Charles Méryon was born in 1821 ; he was the son of a French dancer, and his father is said to have been an Englishman of good family, but during his early life he had little assistance from either of his parents, and from his boyhood he had to struggle to make his own way in the Bohemian underworld of Paris.

During Méryon's lifetime, unfortunately, etchings were not so popular as they are to-day. For a century and a half after Rembrandt, etching, as a pure and separate art, lay comparatively unnoticed, but undeterred by want of

Insatiable vampire l'éternelle luxure
Sur la grande cité convoite sa pâture

"LE STRYGE," BY MÉRYON (1821–68).

The career of this great French etcher is one of the saddest tragedies in art history. Unable in his lifetime to sell his prints at tenpence apiece in sufficient numbers to save him from starvation, Charles Méryon died in a hospital literally from want of proper nourishment. A few years after his death his genius was so appreciated that his etchings were eagerly bought at £5 apiece, and in recent years collectors have paid over a thousand pounds for an etching which the artist could not sell for a franc.

548

patrons, poverty, and ill-health, Méryon devoted himself to the revival of this almost forgotten art, and became one of its greatest masters that the world has yet seen. To record on copper the beauty and interest of the architecture of Paris became the passion of Méryon's life, and his etchings are unique for the imagination and emotional force they display combined with scrupulously exact drawing of the architectural features which form his theme. His famous etching " Le Stryge " (see opposite page), showing us a view of Paris from Notre Dame, with one of the quaint gargoyles of the Cathedral occupying a prominent place in the foreground, reveals not only the perfection of his technique, with its fine, nervous line and rich velvety blacks, but also the blend of realism and imagination which characterises this artist's work.

These masterly views of Paris were offered for sale by the artist at the price of one franc (then worth about tenpence in English money), but even at this ridiculous figure they did not find enough purchasers to enable him to keep body and soul together. Privation, hardship, and want of proper nourishment inevitably told on his health, and eventually his nerves gave way and he was put away as insane in the hospital of Charenton. But though of a nervous temperament, his brain was not diseased, and after some months of good feeding in the hospital Méryon became normal, and it was seen that his breakdown was wholly due to starvation. He was allowed to leave Charenton and began to work again, drawing and etching in Paris, but the unhappy genius had no better fortune and seemed unable to secure the minimum amount of food that a human body requires. Again he starved, with the same result, his mind became unhinged and he was taken back to Charenton, where he died in 1868.

By a cruel irony of fate the etchings began to be appreciated almost immediately after the etcher's death. Never before or since has the art world seen so rapid and sensational an increase in value. The explanation is that the interest excited by the plates of Whistler and Seymour Haden led to a feverish hunt after other etchers, and so the fame of Méryon was established. Within a few years of his death the etchings he had vainly tried to sell for tenpence apiece were changing hands at five pounds; the prices of them rose rapidly and steadily from tens to hundreds of pounds, and within recent years rich collectors have paid more than a thousand pounds to secure a fine impression of an etching by Méryon.

XXII

REALISM AND IMPRESSIONISM IN FRANCE

THE ART OF COURBET, MANET, DEGAS, RENOIR, MONET, AND
RODIN

§ 1

THE French Impressionists were the offspring of the
Realists, and to trace their artistic pedigree we
must return to painting in France in the middle of the
nineteenth century. It was shown in Chapter XIX how
the Romantics had rebelled against a false Classicism, but
only the barest hint was given of how the struggle for
liberty and truth in art reached a further stage in the
forties by the development of a new group of artists known
as the Realists. The leader of this movement and the man
who perhaps did more than any other to change the whole
modern outlook on art was Gustave Courbet (1819–77).

Courbet was the son of a wealthy farmer of Ornans in
the Doubs. His father intended him for the law, and with
this object sent him to Paris. Arrived there, Courbet
threw law to the winds and set about learning the one thing
that interested him, painting. A rigid republican, both
by education and inclination, Courbet was penetrated by a
passionate sympathy for the working classes, and he found
the subjects for his pictures in the ordinary life of the
people. Further, holding tenaciously that painting, " an
art of sight," ought to concern itself with things seen, he
was as opposed to Romanticism as the Romantics had been,
in their day, to Classicism. Intensely earnest and serious
by nature, Courbet regarded it as mere frivolity to make
pictures out of imaginary incidents in poems and romances
when all the pageant and pathos of real life waited to be
painted. His point of view is made clear by a reply he

once made to a patron who desired that he should execute a painting with angels in it for a church. " Angels ! " said Courbet, " but I have never seen angels. What I have not seen I cannot paint."

After the Revolution of 1848 Courbet's new style of democratic painting had a temporary success. In 1849, before the political reaction had begun, he was awarded a medal at the Salon for his picture, " After Dinner at Ornans." This medal placed him *hors concours,* that is to say, it gave him the right of showing pictures in future Salons without his works having to obtain the approval of the Selecting Jury. Courbet took full advantage of this privilege in the following year, and to the Salon of 1850, in addition to two landscapes and four portraits, he sent two large pictures entitled " The Stone-breakers " and " A Funeral at Ornans " (see page 558). The political reaction was in full tide, and the two last pictures raised a storm of fury, because their subjects were supposed to be " dangerously Socialistic." It will be remembered that it was in the Salon of the same year that J. F. Millet showed his first great democratic painting, " The Sower."

" A Funeral at Ornans " became one of the milestones in the progress of modern painting, for, notwithstanding the abuse showered on Courbet, the sincerity of his work appealed to a younger generation of artists. Here was a man who saw life steadily as a whole, and painted life just as he saw it. Each figure in it from the clergy to the mourners, from the gravedigger to the dog, is painted simply but with a truth and power that make it a living thing. Courbet was the first of modern painters to break away from the classic traditions of Italy and turn towards the open-air realism of Velazquez and Frans Hals. He not only had much direct influence on Whistler and on Manet, but pointed out to them the road along which they should travel.

In 1855 Courbet painted a picture which summed up his life of the past seven years. He called it " The Studio of the Painter : a Real Allegory." On the right of this large canvas were the types he had been painting, the

Photo : by courtesy of " Colour."

"PINE-TREE AT ANTIBES," BY CLAUDE MONET.

This view from a promontory on the Riviera is a beautiful example of true impressionist or "luminist" painting, in which the artist uses the radiant hues of the rainbow to get the actual colours of sunshine and small "broken touches" of paint to suggest the vibration of light. Note how full of colour are the shadows, also the decorative balance of the composition, which betrays a hint of Japanese influence.

beggar, the labourer, the tradesman, the priest, the poacher, the gravedigger ; on the left was a group of his personal friends, among them Baudelaire and Proudhon ; between the groups was Courbet himself painting a landscape of Ornans.

In an introduction to the catalogue of a private exhibition of his works held in the same year, Courbet explained his endeavour to replace the cult of the ideal by a sentiment of the real :

> To translate the manners, the ideas, and the aspect of my own times according to my perception, to be not only a painter but still more a man, in a word, to create a living art, that is my aim.

During the reign of Napoleon III Courbet became more and more incensed against all authorities, political or artistic. The former thought him revolutionary because of his subjects, the latter because his style was based on Dutch and Spanish painting instead of on the accepted Italian masters. Nevertheless, his position as leader of the Realist school was such that in 1870 he was nominated Chevalier of the Legion of Honour. Courbet wrote a violent letter to the Ministry refusing to accept this decoration, and when the Commune broke out in 1871 he took a prominent part in the Revolution and became President of the Commission of Fine Arts. Courbet has been much blamed because during his brief presidency he allowed to be pulled down the Column commemorating Napoleon I in the Place Vendôme. This was part of a scheme to efface from Paris all traces of the Empire, whether First or Third, and though the Column was a historic monument it had no great artistic interest. On the other hand it was Courbet who, during the fury of the Commune, not only preserved intact the art treasures of the Louvre, but with difficulty secured the safety of the Arc de Triomphe. He was full of concern for this monument because of its great artistic qualities, notably the sculpture by Rude with which it was decorated, and he managed to persuade those who urged its demolition that the Arc de Triomphe ought to be

'LE BON BOCK," BY EDOUARD MANET (1832–83).

A splendid example of the realistic portraiture of the artist's middle period. It represents M. Belot, an engraver, who gave his friend eighty sittings before this lifelike picture was completed. *Bock* is the common term in France for a glass of beer; hence the title may be rendered in English as " A Good Drink."

spared because it stood not so much for the glory of Napoleon as for the heroism of the revolutionary armies of France.

Still, when the Commune had been suppressed with an iron hand, the good deeds of Courbet during the insurrection were forgotten : the unfortunate artist was arrested in connection with the demolition of the Vendôme Column, condemned to six months' imprisonment and to defray the whole cost—some 400,000 francs—of the reconstruction of the Column.   This utterly ruined him, and though Courbet eventually succeeded in crossing the frontier he was broken in health and spirits.   He died in exile in 1877.

§ 2

Manet was the heir of Courbet with this difference, that the temper of his art was more aristocratic. He also built up his pictures by the direct application of planes of colour rather than by working up an underpainting based on linear design and light-and-shade ; he also used the blonde palette of Velazquez and Hals, and he also chose his subjects from the life around him ; but he painted the people and life of the middle-classes, while Courbet had concentrated on the proletariat.

Edouard Manet was born at Paris in 1833.   His father was a magistrate and, like Courbet, Manet was originally destined for the bar, but he eventually overcame family opposition, and when he was about eighteen he was permitted to enter the studio of Couture (1815–79).   Thomas Couture was an accomplished artist whose rich coloured paintings were a discreet compromise between Romanticism and Classicism, but his orthodox instruction appealed little to Manet, who from the beginning desired to observe Nature closely and reproduce it according to his own feeling. After travelling in Germany, Austria, and Italy to study the Old Masters, Manet finally found in the paintings by Velazquez and Goya at the Louvre the answer to all his questionings and aspirations for light and truth.   Influenced by these masters and by the example of Courbet, he gradually evolved a new technique which presented modern aspects by modern methods. Observing how one colour melted into another in Nature, he declared "There are no lines in Nature," and in his pictures he abandoned the convention of the outline and shaped his forms by a modelling obtained by subtle gradations of tints which fused into one another. The problem of just illumination was to Manet a matter of primary importance. Once when he was asked to point out the principal figure in a group he had painted, he made a reply that has become historic. "The principal person in a picture," said Manet, "is the light."

Manet made his first appearance at the Salon in 1861 with a portrait of himself and his young wife and another painting, "The Spanish Guitar-player." Over both the cry of "Realism" was raised, and Realism was unpopular at the moment, nevertheless the Jury, inspired by Delacroix, gave Manet an Honourable Mention. But during the next two years the partisans of the classical tradition obtained the upper hand again, and Manet was excluded from the Salon of 1863. So many artists of admitted talent, however unpopular, had their works rejected *en bloc* by the Salon jury this year, that the Emperor Napoleon III, inspired by a praiseworthy liberal thought, insisted that these innovators should at least have the right to exhibit together in a special room. Thus there came into being what was known as the *Salon des Refusés*: among the exhibitors there, in addition to Manet and Whistler, were Alphonse Legros, Fantin Latour (1836–1904), celebrated both as a portraitist and as a painter of flowers, Harpignies, Renoir, Claude Monet, and many others who have since become famous. One of the paintings in this exhibition, a sunset by Claude Monet, entitled "Impressions," excited much laughter among the crowd that came to jeer at the "rejected," and henceforward the custom arose of alluding to the new school of painters as "Impressionists." Originating as a term of derision, the word remained in use, and the painters to whom it was applied adopted it as an official label which would serve, as well as any other, to cover their varied aims.

Photo: Braun.

"A FUNERAL AT ORNANS," BY GUSTAVE COURBET (1819–77).

The Louvre, Paris.

In this great picture of a country funeral, every figure from the clergy to the mourners, from the kneeling gravedigger to the dog is

Prior to the *Salon des Refusés* Edouard Manet had little or no knowledge of Claude Monet, who was seven years his junior, but now the similarity between their names and the abuse showered upon both drew the two men together. Through Monet, Manet came to know Renoir and Sisley, who had been fellow-students with Monet in the studio of Gleyre, Whistler's master, and this group was joined, among others, by two older artists, Camille Pissarro and Degas. As in the case of the Pre-Raphaelites, it was friendship and unjust derision which created the solidarity of the Impressionists, though the individual painters had by no means identical aims. Manet, we now realise, was far more a Realist than an Impressionist, and it is important to remember that he passed as an innovator years before Impressionism existed or was even thought of. It was more than ten years after the *Salon des Refusés* before Manet became influenced by the new ideas of colour evolved by Pissarro, Monet, and Renoir. In his fine portrait " Le Bon Bock " (see page 555), painted in 1873, Manet still reveals himself as the heir, not only of Courbet, but of Velazquez, Hals, and Goya. Nothing could be further from the once popular notion of an " Impressionist " picture as a daub hastily put together, than this careful, if unconventional, portrait of his friend the engraver Belot enjoying a glass of beer. M. Belot gave Manet no less than eighty sittings before this portrait was finished. It is freer than Courbet, with a greater simplifying of planes and values, but it is no revolution, it is a continuation and development of Courbet's realism.

Quite different in style is " A Bar at the Folies-Bergère " (see page 561), painted in 1882. We may say at once that the chief difference between the two pictures is in the colour, for—to borrow a term from the wine-list—the colour in " Le Bon Bock " is " still," while that in the " Bar " picture is " sparkling," sparkling especially in the wonderful painting of the bottles and glasses as we may see even in a photograph. Both pictures are magnificent, both are marvellously lifelike, but in the second there is a more searching pursuit of colour, in shadow as well as in light, and a more vivacious statement of its actuality.   In a word, it is a typical " Impressionist " picture : and here we may well pause to inquire what is meant by " Impressionism."

§ 3

If we look at all the bottles in "A Bar at the Folies-Bergère " we shall notice that the treatment of detail here is totally different from the treatment of detail, say, in Millais's " Ophelia " (cf. page 427).   In his picture Millais looked at each leaf, flower, and branch separately, and set them down separately on his canvas like a sum in addition. But all the bottles in Manet's picture are seen simultaneously in relation to each other : it is a synthesis, not an addition.   Impressionism, then, in the first place, is the result of *simultaneous vision* that sees a scene as a whole as opposed to *consecutive vision* that sees Nature piece by piece. Let us suppose, for a moment, that we are staying at a house on the banks of the Seine opposite the church at Vernon.   Let us suppose that, having arrived there in darkness the previous evening, we jump out of bed in the morning, open the window, and put out our head to see the view.   Monet's picture " The Church at Vernon " (see page 569) shows us what we should see *at the first glance* ; the glance, that is to say, when we see the scene as a whole, before any detail in it has riveted our attention and caused us unconsciously to alter the focus of our eye in order to see that detail more sharply.   Another way of putting the matter is to say that in an Impressionist picture there is only one focus throughout, while in a Pre-Raphaelite picture there is a different focus for every detail.   These two methods of painting represent different ways of looking at the world, and neither way is wrong, only whereas the Pre-Raphaelite looks *particularly* at a series of objects, the Impressionist looks *generally* at the whole.

This way of viewing a scene broadly, however, is only a part of Impressionism.   It was not a new invention, for Velazquez saw and painted figures and groups in a similar way, therefore Impressionists like Whistler and Manet (in his earlier works), who adopted this broad style, were in this respect developing an existing tradition rather than inventing a new one. But a later development of Impressionism, which was a complete innovation, was the new palette they adopted. From the time of Daubigny, who said, " We never paint light enough," the more progressive

Photo : Braun.

"A BAR AT THE FOLIES-BERGÈRE " BY MANET.

Painted the year before he died, this picture of a bar in a popular Parisian music-hall shows the final style of an artist who said, " The principal person in a picture is the light." Though crowded with glittering details all sparkling with reflected light, the picture is a true impression of a scene viewed " steadily and as a whole."

painters had striven to make the colours in their pictures closer to the actual hues of Nature. Delacroix was one of the pioneers in the analysis of colour. When he was in Morocco he wrote in his Journal about the shadows he had seen on the faces of two peasant boys, remarking that while a sallow, yellow-faced boy had *violet* shadows, a red-faced boy had *green* shadows. Again, in the streets of Paris, Delacroix noticed a black and yellow cab, and observed

36

that, beside the greenish-yellow, the black took on a tinge of the complementary colour, violet. An advertisement issued by a well-known soap firm will have made many readers familiar with the phenomenon of complementary colour. The name of the soap was printed in bright red letters on a white paper, and we were asked, after gazing at this steadfastly for a few moments, to look up at a white ceiling, when we should see the name of the soap in *green* letters. Every colour has its complementary, that is to say, an opposing colour is evoked by the action of the human eye after we have been gazing at the said colour ; consequently all colours act and react on one another. Delacroix discovered that to obtain the full brilliance of any given hue it should be flanked and supported by its complementary colour. He did not attain to full know- ledge ; it was left for a later generation to make nicer dis- tinctions and to recognise that if violet is the right com- plementary for a greenish-yellow, an orange-yellow requires a turquoise blue, and so on.

The nineteenth was a scientific century during which great additions were made to our knowledge of optics. The French scientist Chevreuil wrote a learned book on colour, which was studied with avidity by the younger painters. It became clear to them that colour was not a simple but a very complex matter. For example, we say that grass is green, and green is the *local colour* of grass, that is to say, the colour of grass at close range, when we look down on it at our feet. But grass-covered hills seen at a great distance do not appear green, but *blue*. The green of their local colour is affected by the veil of atmo- sphere through which we view it in the distance, and the blue we see is an example of *atmospheric colour*. Again, the local colour of snow is white, but everybody who has been to Switzerland is familiar with the " Alpine glow " when the snow-clad peaks of the mountains appear a bright copper colour owing to the rays of the setting sun. This " Alpine glow" is an example of *illumination colour*, and since the colour of sunlight is changing throughout the day, everything in Nature is affected by the colour of the light which falls upon it.

"THE UMBRELLAS," BY RENOIR (1841–1919).

Tate Gallery, London.

The strange spectacle presented by an array of umbrellas on a rainy day in a public place has here inspired the artist to give one of his most original and ingeniously designed impressions of Parisian life. Renoir excelled in rendering the actual colour of sunshine on human flesh and figures, and this picture is as true to Nature's own colouring as it is true to life in its intimate observation of human character and behaviour

The landscape painter, then, who wishes to reproduce the actual hues of Nature, has to consider not only " local colour," but also " atmospheric colour " and " illumination colour," and further take into consideration " complementary colours." One of the most important discoveries made by the later Impressionist painters was that *in the shadows there always appears the complementary colour of the light*. We should ponder on all these things if we wish to realise the full significance of Manet's saying, " The principal person in a picture is the light."

This new intensive study of colour brought about a new palette and a new technique. For centuries all painting had been based on three primary colours, red, blue, and yellow ; but science now taught the painters that though these might be primary colours in *pigment*, they were not primary colours in *light*. The spectroscope and the new science of spectrum-analysis made them familiar with the fact that white light is composed of all the colours of the rainbow, which is the spectrum of sunlight. They learnt that the primary colours of light were green, orange-red, and blue-violet, and that yellow—though a primary in paint—was a secondary in light, because a yellow light can be produced by blending a green light with an orange-red light. On the other hand green, a secondary in paint because it can be produced by mixing yellow with blue pigment, is a primary in light. These discoveries revolutionised their ideas about colour, and the Impressionist painters concluded they could only hope to paint the true colour of sunlight by employing pigments which matched the colours of which sunlight was composed, that is to say, the tints of the rainbow. They discarded black altogether, for, modified by atmosphere and light, they held that a true black did not exist in Nature : the darkest colour was indigo, dark green, or a deep violet. They would not use a brown, but set their palettes with indigo, blue green, yellow, orange, red, and violet, the nearest colours they could obtain to the seven of the solar spectrum.

Further, they used these colours with as little mixing as possible. Every amateur in water-colour knows that the more he mixes his paints, the more they lose in brilliancy. The same is true of oil paints. The Impressionists refrained, therefore, as much as possible from mixing colours on their palettes, and applied them pure in minute touches to the canvas. If they wanted to render secondary or tertiary colours, instead of mixing two or three pigments on the palette, they would secure the desired effect by juxtaposed touches of pure colours which, at a certain distance, fused in the eye of the beholder and produced the effect of the tint desired. This device is known as *optical mixture*, because the mixing is done in the spectator's eye. Thus, whereas red and green pigment mixed on a palette will give a dull grey, the Impressionists produced a brilliant luminous grey by speckling a sky, say, with little points of yellow and mauve which at a distance gave the effect of a pearly grey. Similarly the effect of a brilliant brown was given by the juxtaposition of a series of minute touches of green, red, and yellow ; and this association of minute touches of three pure colours set up a quivering vibration which had greater luminosity than any streak of brown pigment. It was an endeavour to use paints as if they were coloured lights.

Various names have been given to this technique. It has been called " Divisionism," because by it the tones of secondary and tertiary colours were divided into their constituent elements. It has been called " Pointillism," because the colour was applied to the canvas in points instead of in sweeping brush-strokes. It has been called " Luminism," because the aim of the process is primarily to express the colour of light with all its sparkle and vibration. This last is the best name of all, because it serves to emphasise the new outlook of the new painters. The tendency before the Impressionists was to regard colour from the standpoint of black and white. Thus, in considering a grey, it would have been asked is it a dark grey or a light grey, does it approach black or white ? The Impressionists took quite a different attitude and asked whether it was a bluish grey, or a greenish grey, or a purplish grey, or a reddish grey : in a word, not whether it was light

"A DANCER ON THE STAGE," BY DEGAS (1834–1917).

Pastel in the Luxembourg.

This pastel, which gives a wonderful impression of a ballet-dancer almost floating into the brilliant light of the stage from the obscurity of the " wings," should be compared with the earlier painting by the same artist on the opposite page. It is miraculous in its suggestion of quivering movement.

THE DANCING LESSON," BY DEGAS.

A passionate interest in movement and life drew Degas to the study of professional dancers, and his pictures of the Ballet are world-famous and unique. In this comparatively early work he shows us the hard realities which lie behind the fairyland of the stage. The varied attitudes of the dancers, in difficult positions, reveal his mastery of drawing, while the aerial spaciousness of the scene as a whole results from his perfect rendering of light and air.

or dark, but to which colour in the solar spectrum it most closely approached.

To the Impressionists shadow was not an absence of light, but light of a different quality and of different value. In their exhaustive research into the true colours of shadows in Nature, they conquered the last unknown territory in the domain of Realist Painting.

To sum up, then, it may be said that Impressionist Painting is based on two great principles :

1. *The substitution of a Simultaneous Vision that sees a scene as a whole in place of a Consecutive Vision that sees Nature piece by piece.*

2. *The Substitution of a Chiaroscuro based on the colours of the solar spectrum for a Chiaroscuro based on Black and White.*

This new technique, with all the research and experiment which is implies, was not the invention of one man, but the outcome of the life studies of a whole group of men. Most prominent among those who brought Impressionist painting to perfection in theory and practice were Camille Pissarro, Claude Monet, and Auguste Renoir.

§ 4

Camille Pissarro (1830–1930) was born at St. Thomas in the Danish West Indies and came to Paris with his parents when he was twenty-five. He became a pupil of Corot, and his earlier works show the influence of Corot as regards style and colour and of Millet in subject and drawing. He was the eldest of the Impressionists, being two years older than Manet ; but throughout his life Pissarro was an ardent student, never ceasing to investigate and experiment, always ready to listen to the theories and to observe the practice of a junior who claimed to have discovered a new truth. Though darker in colour than his later work, a small landscape now in the Musée des Arts Decoratifs at Paris, painted by Pissarro in 1869, shows that even at this time he was experimenting in the division of tones. Unfortunately nearly all the earlier paintings of Camille

Pissarro are lost, for his home and studio were in the line of approach of the destroying Prussians in 1870. Owing to the war Pissarro and Monet came to London in 1871, and there they saw the later paintings of Turner, which con-

Photo : Braun.

"THE CHURCH AT VERNON," BY MONET (*b.* 1840).

A typical landscape by this famous Impressionist showing his immediate concern with a fugitive effect of light. All details in the landscape are subordinated to the illumination which falls upon them. Even deprived of their magical colour, the reflections in the water show the vibration of light, the sense of movement and life, obtained by Monet's method of painting with broken touches.

firmed their ideas about colour and encouraged them to paint brighter and still brighter.

Claude Monet was ten years younger than Pissarro. Though born in 1840 at Paris, where his father was a merchant, he spent much of his boyhood at Havre, where he learnt a good deal about painting from Boudin. After completing his military service in Algeria, Monet returned to

Paris and entered the studio of Gleyre. Here he formed a close friendship with two fellow-students, Renoir and Sisley, and became acquainted later with Manet, as has already been related. Monet's earliest paintings, however, are not lighter than those by Boudin and Corot, and he was first influenced by these and others of the Barbizon School.

Auguste Renoir (1841–1919) was born at Limoges, where his father was a tailor in a small way of business, and at the age of thirteen young Auguste began to earn his living as a painter on porcelain. This early apprenticeship left a certain trace on his art which was always decorative and even elegiac in spite of its later realism. In time Renoir saved up enough money to go to Paris and become a pupil of Gleyre, but while his friends were landscapists Renoir was first and foremost a figure painter.

Alfred Sisley (1839–99) was born in Paris of English parents, and his development was parallel to that of Monet, whose work his own pictures closely resemble. We may say that all these young men, together with Pissarro, were discontented with the state of painting before 1870. They looked at their pictures and they looked at Nature; but while they realised how far their painting fell short of their intention, they had not yet found the way to secure greater brilliancy and truth. That way was discovered during the 'seventies, after Pissarro and Monet had seen the Turners in London and returned to Paris. It is possible to exaggerate the influence of Turner on the new movement, for it had really begun earlier with Delacroix, but the sight of the Turners undoubtedly hastened its accomplishment as far as Pissaro and Monet are concerned. Not the beginning of Impressionism, but the first public revelation of Impressionism, was an exhibition held at Nadar's galleries, Boulevard des Capucines, in 1874. Here were gathered together works by many of the " rejected " of 1863, Manet being the best known of them and generally considered the leader of the movement, and also works by new adherents to Impressionist doctrine. The exhibition provoked much controversy, but it was sufficiently talked about to be something of a success, and thereafter for several years a

Salon des Impressionistes was an annual event. But in 1874 the science of colour was still in its infancy, and if the exhibitors were " Impressionists " they were not all " luminists." Even Renoir's famous picture of people in a theatre-box, painted about this time, is sombre in colour, in comparison with the scintillating canvases he was to paint later.

Another contributor to this exhibition, whose picture, " The Dancing Lesson " (see page 567), attracted much attention, was Degas. Friendship with Manet drew Degas into this circle, though he never entirely accepted all the principles of Impressionism. Edgar Hilaire Germain Degas (1834–1917) was born in Paris, the son of a banker, and, like Courbet and Manet, was originally destined for a legal career. In 1855, however, he entered the École des Beaux Arts, and also studied under Lamothe, a pupil of Ingres. All his life Degas, who was brought up in the classical tradition, had the deepest veneration for Ingres. He was also an admirer of Holbein and Clouet, whose pictures he copied. In 1856 he went to Rome and remained two years in Italy studying the work of the early Italian masters. Returning to Paris, he began as an historical painter, his last picture in this style being " A Scene of War in the Middle Ages," shown in the Salon of 1865. But about this time he came into contact with Manet, and through him with Pissaro, Monet, Renoir, and others who frequented the Café Guerbois in the Batignolles, and there endlessly discussed their artistic aims and ideals. Because of this centre for social intercourse the Impressionist group was at one time nicknamed " The School of Batignolles." Owing to the powerful new influences surrounding him, Degas was led to abandon his historical works and devote himself to painting scenes of modern life. Always intensely interested in the rendering of movement, Degas was first attracted to subjects he found on the race-course, one of the earliest successes in his new manner being " A Carriage at the Races." He also painted washerwomen at their work, scenes in cafés and in theatres, and revealed himself as an artist passionately absorbed in the spectacle

Photo : W. A. Mansell & Co.

"ST. JOHN THE BAPTIST," BY RODIN (1840–1917).

South Kensington Museum, London.

Falsely accused of having taken a cast from life and shown it as an original statue, Rodin modelled this heroic figure larger than life to prove his ability in modelling. It was first intended to portray nothing more than " A Man Walking," but while he was working on it Octave Mirbeau told the sculptor it was an ideal St. John, and Rodin accepted the title.

of city life, though with rather a cynical outlook.   Degas was the greatest draughtsman among the Impressionists, and in his pictures of modern life he relied upon line more than any other of the friends with whom he exhibited, Like Whistler, he was much influenced by Japanese colours prints, which gave him new ideas of pattern and design.

After the Franco-Prussian war, during which he served in the artillery, Degas concentrated on the Ballet, a subject for which he became famous throughout the world, and which occupied his best attention for twenty years.   In these works Degas stands revealed as an uncompromising Realist.   What he usually shows us is not the glamour and illusion of the Ballet from the spectator's standpoint; Degas gets behind the scenes and exposes the work and discipline which lie behind this artificial fairyland ;   he strips the dancers of their tinsel, compelling us to see that they are not lovely young nymphs, but plain, tired, hard-worked women, often middle-aged.   The beauty of his pictures is to be found not in any prettiness of his models, but in the lighting, the arrangement, the drawing, and later, in the colour, in the convincing truth of his vision, and in the decorative charm of his design.   In the later 'seventies and thenceforward, Degas worked more frequently in pastel than in oils, and in these later pastels he adopts the prismatic hues of Luminism, based on the rainbow colours of the solar spectrum, so that these works, in addition to their masterly drawing and decorative design, have the additional beauty of shimmering, iridescent colour. A superb example of his later style is the pastel " A Dancer on the Stage " (see page 566) in the Luxembourg, Paris. Here, for once in a way, Degas forgets his cynicism and shows us the magical glamour of a *première danseuse* quivering with movement, bathed with light, and happy apparently in her moment of success.   After 1886 Degas retired almost completely from the public eye, living the life of a recluse on a fifth floor in Montmartre ; refusing for the most parts to sell his works or even to show them to collectors, though his fame continually increased and the value of his earlier works rose to sensational prices.   Before his death his picture " Dancers at the Bar," which he had originally sold for £20, was bought by an American collector for £17,400, this being the record price obtained to-day at public auction for a picture by any living artist. But Degas was equally contemptuous of praise or criticism, and to the end he declined all honours.

Claude Monet, who is still alive, has also seen pictures he sold for £4 bring thousands of pounds in America and elsewhere. Devoting himself to the painting of landscapes in bright sunlight, he has carried the pitch of painting into a higher key than any artist before him had done. " Pine-Tree at Antibes " (see page 553) is a beautiful example of his style at its maturity ; radiant colours are laid side by side in small broken touches to suggest the vibration of light, while the decorative arrangement shows that Monet also has taken hints for design from the artists of Japan. Light is always the " principal person " in Monet's land-scape, and since he is always aiming at seizing a fugitive effect, he has insisted on consistency of illumination at particular hours of the day and season. With this object he adopted, since the early 'eighties, a habit of painting the same subject under different conditions of light. He would set out early in the morning with a carriage-load of canvases, and arriving at his destination he would start his day's work, changing his canvas every couple of hours as the light changed. In this way he painted a series of views, all of the same subject, but all different in colour and lighting. Among the most famous of these series are those known as " Haystacks," " The Poplars," " The Thames at Waterloo Bridge," " Rouen Cathedral," and " Water-lilies," the last being a scene in his own riverside garden at Giverny. When he was a young man M. Monet once said, " I want to paint as a bird sings," and all his pictures have this delicious lyrical quality. While he adopted the rainbow palette and the technique of the small touch—" the pro-cedure by the touch " as it is called in France—Monet has never been dogmatic in his use of divisionism.

The elaboration of Divisionism into a rigid scientific theory of painting was the work principally of two younger

BALZAC, BY RODIN.

The upper part of Rodin's statue of Balzac which caused a sensation in the Salon of 1898. This powerful rendering of the great novelist, loosely wrapped in his dressing-gown, shows the extreme limit of impressionism in sculpture.

men, Georges Seurat (1859–91) and the living artist Pau
Signac, born at Paris in 1863. But for his early deatl
Seurat, who was a genius in design as well as a great colourist
would have obtained a foremost place in modern art. I
was Seurat about 1880 who definitely established th
superiority, for the purposes of brilliance and intensity, o
" optical blending " to actual blending on the palette
The division of tones, which was never more than a con
venience to painters like Monet and Sisley, became a lav
not to be departed from in the work of Seurat and Signac
This new scientific development of Impressionism becam
known as " neo-Impressionism." For a time Pissarro als
practised this method of Divisionism with scrupulous exact
ness, but eventually he adopted a broader and freer manner
though still retaining the general principle of divide
colour. In addition to Seurat and Signac, the chief ex
ponents of neo-Impressionism have been Henri-Edmon
Cross (1856–1910) and the living Belgian painter, Thé
van Rysselberg. This method of painting and the scientifi
theories on which it is based are fully described in M. Pau
Signac's book *D'Eugène Delacroix au Néo-Impressionism*
(Paris, 1898).

§ 5

By the first principle of Impressionism, the substitu
tion of simultaneous for consecutive vision, sculpture wa
affected as well as painting. From the time of Louis XIV
France had always had talented and accomplished sculptor
at her command, but it was not till the era of Impressionisn
that she produced a great world-sculptor whose name wa
worthily coupled with that of Michael Angelo. Amon
the earlier French sculptors Jean Baptiste Pigalle (1714–85
was a pioneer of Realism, his vigorous and fertile imagina
tion giving his sculpture a certain accent of life and origin
ality. Jean Antoine Houdon (1741–1828), his pupil, wa
famous for the power and truth of his portrait busts
François Rude (1784–1855) was a still greater liberator o
French sculpture from a cramping classicism which slavishl
imitated the antique. His famous group " Le Dépar

des Volontaires de 1790 " on the Arc de Triomphe shows Rude's realism and the nobility of his expression of patriotic feeling. Antoine Louis Barye (1796–1875), both painter and sculptor, the contemporary and friend of the Barbizon landscape painters, achieved high distinction by his life-like sculpture of animals, and his small bronzes are still eagerly sought after by collectors.

It was a pupil of Barye, an even greater modeller than himself, who was to achieve the greatest fame won by any sculptor since Michael Angelo. Auguste Rodin was born at Paris in the same year as Monet, 1840. He was of humble origin, and in his youth had to earn his living by working in a mason's yard, where he became familiar with the material he was destined to master. For years his only studio was his humble bedroom, and it was here that he modelled his early bust, " The Man with the Broken Nose," which, when exhibited at the Salon, was acknow-ledged to be a masterpiece of realism, modelled with a power and truth unknown for generations. When his beautiful statue, " The Age of Bronze," now in the Luxem-bourg, was exhibited in the Salon of 1877, the authorities were so astonished by its masterly modelling that the sculptor was accused of having taken a cast from life. To prove the falsehood of this accusation Rodin made his next statue, " St. John the Baptist " (see page 572) rather more than life-size, and again the modelling was miraculous in its perfection. If the " Age of Youth " with its polished rendering of the graceful form of adolescence reminds us of the best Greek sculpture, this second powerful and lifelike rendering of a mature man is comparable to the figures by the master-sculptors of the Renaissance.

It has often been asked why a statue by Rodin is different from any other statue, and the explanation is simple : instead of copying Greek sculpture as others had done, Rodin did as the Greeks did—he went direct to Nature. " Everything," he said, " is contained in Nature, and when the artist follows Nature he gets everything." Rodin taught his contemporaries that distinction in sculpture is obtained, not by selecting a certain type of figure, but by

37

the gift and art of modelling. "Sculpture," he once said, "is the art of the hole and the lump," and as he went on he proved that in order to present a true appearance of form it was necessary sometimes to fashion the "holes" and "lumps," not exactly as they existed in anatomy, but as they appeared to the human eye. In this way Rodin introduced impressionism into sculpture, showing us heads and figures as they appeared to the human eye enveloped in atmosphere and bathed in light. His famous monument "The Citizens of Calais" is remarkable, not only for the poignant expression of the different characters of the various figures, but also for the truth of atmosphere and movement in this procession winding its way along slowly and sadly. These are no graveyard figures, but living men moving and breathing in the air that surrounds them. Commemorating an historic incident when France and England were at war, this monument has become a happy and lasting token of the *Entente Cordiale*, for in addition to the monument at Calais a replica of it has been erected on the Victoria Embankment, London, close to the House of Lords, thanks to the generosity of English admirers of the French sculptor.

The rugged technique by which Rodin obtained his wonderful effects of atmospheric reality was long in establishing itself in public favour, yet there have been few sculptors animated with a more profound respect for the material of their art. It was Rodin's love of marble itself which led to a new development of his art, in which he would leave rough the matrix from which his sculpture was hewn, so that delicate heads and figures seemed to grow like flowers out of the marble of their origin. A memorable example of his work in this style is "Thought," in which a feminine head of exquisite refinement and spirituality emerges from a rough-hewn block of marble.

Rodin reached his extreme limit of impressionism in sculpture with his colossal statue of "Balzac" (see page 575), which, when exhibited in the New Salon of 1898, threw the world of art into a condition bordering upon frenzy. The man who twenty years before had been declared too skilful to be genuine was now accused of not knowing the elements of his craft.   Yet the sublime simplicity of this figure, loosely wrapped in a dressing-gown, with the up-turned face, the lion-maned head of genius, soaring, as it were, to heaven, revealed Rodin at his highest not only as a master of impressionist modelling, but also as a psychologist who could conceive and create an unforgettable expression of the very soul of genius.

XXIII

POST-IMPRESSIONSIM, CUBISM, AND FUTURISM

THE ART OF CÉZANNE, VAN GOGH, GAUGUIN, MATISSE,
AND PICASSO

§ I

WHAT is " Post-Impressionism " ? This term was invented by the English painter and art critic, Mr. Roger Fry, to cover various art movements which came *after* Impressionism, and since some of these movements have been developments of Impressionism, while others have been a reaction from it, confusion can only be avoided by considering separately the principal movements and the artists associated with them.

The reader of this OUTLINE will have observed that, from the days of Giotto down to the close of the nineteenth century, the development of the main stream of European painting was in the direction of a more perfect representation of the appearances of natural forms. In the nineteenth century two causes contributed to change the direction of painting. One was the invention of Photography, which set painters wondering what part the representative element really played in a picture; the other was the new Colour-science of the Impressionists, who seemed to have pushed truth of representation to a point where further developments were impossible. Ambitious painters sighed, like Alexander, for new worlds to conquer : the problems of foreshortening, of perspective, of the true colour of shadows, all had been solved triumphantly by their predecessors. What was there left to be done by a painter who did not wish to imitate the work of any other artist ? It was inevitable that a reaction should set in. Painting, according to the neo-Impressionist formulas described in the last

" PORTRAIT OF THE ARTIST," BY VINCENT VAN GOGH.

Shop-assistant, schoolmaster, and missionary before he became a painter, Van Gogh is one of the most romantic and pathetic figures in modern painting.   This early portrait of himself shows the fanatical sincerity of his character, and the passionate vehemence of his individual style of painting.

chapter, had become, as we have seen, a highly complicated and scientific business. A new generation began to argue that, after all, painting was not a science but an art, and that its primary function was not the accurate representation of Nature but the expression of an emotion. A fresh start was made in a new direction. Emphasis was now to be laid on expressing an idea rather than on rendering appearances, and it was held that by reducing the facts or phenomena to a minimum the idea might be able to shine forth more brightly. The vessel of art having become overloaded, it was thought advisable to lighten the ship by throwing some of the cargo overboard.

Already there had been a forerunner in this direction. Honoré Daumier (1808–79), though chiefly known to his contemporaries as a pungent caricaturist and lithographer, also executed oil-paintings which have become highly esteemed since his death. These pictures, sometimes satirising the Law Courts whose " justice " roused him to fury, often based on some illuminating incident in the history of Don Quixote and Sancho Panza, were unlike any other pictures of his time, and always expressed an idea with a maximum of intellectual force and a minimum of colour and pictorial means.

Half a century before his time, he had the courage to eliminate trappings and redundancies from his painting, and to give us plastic conceptions of rugged simplicity. In so doing he anticipated the most interesting and fruitful of modern pictorial movements.

It was from the heart of Impressionism itself that the most powerful reaction began, and the artist usually regarded now as the " Father of Post-Impressionism " is Paul Cézanne (1839–1906), who during his lifetime exhibited with the Impressionists and was long thought to be one of them. But though the friend and companion of Pissarro, Renoir, and Monet, Cézanne differed from them in many ways. To begin with, he was a southerner, born at Aix in Provence, while all the others belonged to Northern France ; secondly, while accepting their colour theories, he never wholly adopted in practice their prismatic palette ; thirdly, while they were primarily occupied with registering fugitive effects of light, he was always most concerned with eternal verities. His aim is best explained in his own words : " I wish to make of Impressionism something solid and durable, like the art of the Old Masters."

If we look at his landscapes (see pages 587 and 594), or his " Card Players " (page 585), or his portrait of himself (see next page), we do not think first of the light by which these things are seen, but rather of the weight, density, and solidity of the forms depicted. The art of Cézanne is simpler and less complicated than that of Monet and Pissarro ; his analysis of colour is more summary, his expression ruder and more forcible. His colour is entirely his own, and the prevalence of browns in his pictures itself separates him from the other Impressionists ; but this brown with him is not a convention, it is true to the colour of the sun-scorched landscape of his home, of the South of France, in which he chiefly worked. His paintings may seem clumsy in handling beside the delicate work of Renoir and Sisley, but by reason of his whole-hearted sincerity and honesty of purpose they make a deep and strong impression. Cézanne was not a conscious revolutionary ; his pronounced style was the result of a strong, incorruptibly honest mind struggling to express what his eye could see without any preconceived ideas as to the manner of expression. His private life was simple and uneventful, devoted to unremitting toil which was never recognised or honoured. After studying in Paris he returned to the South of France, where he lived and married on an allowance of £12 a month made him by his father, a banker. After his father's death he inherited a share of his fortune, but made little change in his manner of living. He did not paint to make money, but to learn more about Nature and life, and to express what he felt vaguely in his soul. It is related of him that after he had finished a study out-of-doors, he would often leave his painting against the nearest bush. With the last brush-stroke, his interest in the painting ceased : he had done all he could ; and it was his wife who surreptitiously followed in his footsteps and garnered in the canvases so difficult at that time to sell.

Photo: E. Druet.

"PORTRAIT OF THE ARTIST," BY PAUL CÉZANNE (1839–1906).

This is the painter who said : " I wish to make of Impressionism something solid and
enduring, like the art of the Old Masters." His rugged painting of himself in middle age
gives us an impression of substance and weight which proves that the artist has achieved
his object.

these contentions, for in the first place nothing is more beautiful or weaker than a flower, and in the second it is a commonplace of construction that an arch is stronger than a horizontal on two perpendiculars. Nevertheless, blind to the error of their major and minor premise, the Cubists with a parade of logic proceeded to the conclusion that a painting wholly composed of straight lines is stronger and therefore more beautiful than a painting containing curved lines. Picasso's " Head of a Lady in a Mantilla " (see next page) illustrates the first phase of Cubism, in which the human body is cut up into geometrical forms. It is a " crystallisation " of a human head, which looks less like a painting than a wood-carving executed by a savage with a blunt instrument, yet once our eyes have grown accustomed to the strange barbarism of the technique we have to acknowledge that this head is not altogether wanting in expression.

The first phase of Cubism is simple in comparison with the second, for if the first consisted in cutting up natural objects into geometrical shapes, the second consisted in shuffling the pieces. This curious development, with which the name of Picasso is chiefly associated, professed to show, not merely one aspect of objects, but a number of sectional aspects seen from different standpoints and arbitrarily grouped together in one composition. By this method the painting of a simple object like a teacup is transfigured into an unrecognisable fugue—consisting of fragments of the cup as seen from above, from the sides, and, as held up in the air, from below. These ingenious conglomerations, professing to give us " the greater reality " of things seen, leave us as bewildered, confused, and uninformed as a metaphysician's analysis of truth and error. As an example of the second phase of Cubism we give Picasso's " Portrait of M. Kahnweiler " (see page 601), in which all we can recognise are fragmentary frontal aspects of his waistcoat (with watch-chain), left eye, left ear, and one side of his nose drowned in a chaotic sea of various aspects of receipt-files and other unrecognisable objects. Thus a movement which originated in an attempt

Photo : E. Druet.

"HEAD OF A LADY IN A MANTILLA," BY PABLO PICASSO.

An example of the first phase of Cubism (see preceding page) in which all curved lines are eliminated in order to give greater "strength" to a picture. and human features are consequently cut up into geometrical forms. Executed at a period when primitive and savage art was idolised by advanced artists, this head looks less like a painting than a wood figure carved by a savage with a blunt instrument.

" PORTRAIT OF M. KAHNWEILER," BY PABLO PICASSO.

An example of the second phase of Cubism when, owing to the arbitrary shuffling of the geometrical shapes into which natural forms had already been cut up, only infinitesimal fragments of objects can be identified by the uninitiated. In this " puzzle-picture " a glimpse of a waistcoat with watch-chain can be seen in the centre, above it are indications of an eye, nose, and ear, but the rest of M. Kahnweiler appears to be smothered under the papers and files of his office.

to secure a primitive simplicity was led astray by false doctrines, till it finally wandered into a blind alley of complexity, for the complications of neo-Impressionist painting were child's play in comparison with the entanglements of the puzzle-pictures of the later Cubists.

Following upon the distortions of M. Matisse and the strange pictures of the Cubists, in which the facts of vision were either ignored or so juggled with that they became incomprehensible, it is not surprising that yet another school of painters arose who abandoned representation as an indispensable element in picture-making and argued that painting should be as free as music to give emotional pleasure without any appeal to association of material ideas. This claim that painting should be abstract, and not concern itself with the concrete, was argued by the Polish artist Wassily Kandinsky, working at Munich in 1914, more convincingly in his book *The Art of Spiritual Harmony* than in his kaleidoscopic pictures. In theory it seems plausible enough that if a musician is free to weave melodies without reference to natural sounds, a painter should be free to construct compositions without reference to natural forms. It is also true that the emotional pleasure we derive from the stained-glass windows of an old cathedral does not depend on the subject painted. We are enchanted with the radiant beauty of the pattern of colour. So far so good, but now comes the point that no artist living or dead has yet succeeded in convincing the world that these stained-glass windows would give us any keener or purer emotional pleasure if they had no subject, or been able himself to produce an abstract painting more beautiful in colour and pattern than paintings based on concrete forms.

Kandinsky, however, went a step further, and claimed that his abstract paintings were not mere dream-patterns, but had a meaning for the initiated in that they were based on the psychological effect on the observer of various lines and colours. But these effects are by no means definitely established, they are still a subject for speculation, and till they are fixed by the common consent of mankind, experiments in the " art of spiritual harmony " must necessarily

Photo : E. Druet.

" MOTHER AND CHILD," BY PABLO PICASSO.

It seems remarkable that the painter of this picture should have been one of the founders of Cubism and author of the strange paintings on pages 600–601. This picture, with its refined draughtsmanship, shows the normality of Picasso's art before his passion for novelty and experiment led him to the invention of Cubism.

be uncertain and inconclusive. Indeed, in Kandinsky's own " Compositions "—as his abstract paintings are entitled —outward and visible signs alone give us a clue to the inward and spiritual meaning, and it is by discerning faint traces of a gun-carriage, a puff of smoke, and falling houses in one of his pre-War pictures, painted in 1913, that we

Photo : Emmett.

" A LADY AND HER DOG," BY GIACOMO BALLA.

An example of a Futurist painting in which an endeavour is made to represent movement by showing in various positions the moving paws and tail of the dog, the swing of his chain, and the step of his owner's feet. Here painting attempts to rival and surpass the achievements of the rapid-motion camera.

obtain a sense of that " clash and conflict of ideas in the spiritual world " that the painting is said to express.

The sectional representation of divers aspects of different objects was developed, with an added emphasis on the expression of movement, by the group of Italian painters known as the " Futurists." Futurism was a literary as well as an artistic movement, and it was largely a protest against the tyranny of the past on the part of ardent nationalists, who resented that the present achievements of their country should be obscured by the glory of its past. The leader of the movement was a writer, Signor Marinetti, and his skilled pen justified the extraordinary practices of his artist friends by sonorous phrases. A pictorial record of the commonplace fact that the seat of a chair is visible after the sitter has got up and walked away, was majestically alluded to as an example of " the plastic interpenetration of matter." As regards colour, the Futurists accepted the divisionism and complementarism of the neo-Impressionists, but in the rendering of form they sought to introduce new principles : " Universal dynamism must be rendered in painting as a dynamic sensation ; movement and light destroy the materiality of bodies." An amusing example of the " dynamic decomposition of matter " is Giacomo Balla's painting " A Lady and her Dog " (see opposite page), which may be regarded as a synthesis of rapid-motion photography. A multiplicity of paws and tails indicates that the animal is trotting with wagging tail, four ghostly chains suggest the whirling of his lead, and an army of shoes presents the movement of his owner's feet. In concentrating their endeavours on the expression of movement, the Futurists attempted to convert painting from an art of space to an art of time. Their daring experiments have produced few pictures likely to stand the test of time, but possibly an exception may be made for Signor Balla's " Centrifugal Force." This painting of revolving spheres shooting forth golden sparks into an azure void was not only decorative in design and colour, but also nobly expressive of the Force that shoots meteorolites through the universe. An abstract painting that succeeds in expressing an abstract idea is clearly legitimate art, but pictures of this calibre are unfortunately the exception among abstract paintings.

Nevertheless it would be wrong to assert that the experiments of the modern extremists in painting have been wholly valueless. Technically they have widened the horizon of painting and opened the road to a new

Realism in which the firm structure and rigid design of the Cubists can be combined with a truth and beauty of colour derived from the Impressionists. Psychologically their work is of profound interest to every student of history. Coming events cast their shadow before them on the field of art. The patient reader who has followed this history thus far will have observed the increasing endeavour on the part of painters to give an expression of Strength. In examining their works he will have noticed that, however greatly they may vary in their aspects and styles, nearly all of them contain an element of Violence. These Fauviste, Cubist, and Futurist paintings never soothe us to rest ; they aim at galvanising us into action. All of them must be regarded as symptoms, as expressions in art of the unrest, agitation, and suppressed violence seething subterraneously in Europe prior to the outbreak of the Great War. The effect of the War on art will be considered in the next chapter, but long before August 1914 premonitions of the coming hostilities were given in the tumult of modern painting.

XXIV

ART DURING THE GREAT WAR OF 1914–18

A SURVEY OF THE WORK OF OFFICIAL WAR ARTISTS AND OTHERS

§ 1

IT was shown in the last chapter how at the beginning of the present century the art world was deluged with theories and " isms," while several of the pictures illustrated afforded evidence that a sinister violence and subterranean unrest became manifest in European painting before it exploded in European politics and precipitated a great war. On the Continent—and to a slighter extent in England also—the " wild-men " of painting had betrayed in form and colour that spirit of merciless aggression which eventually provoked Armageddon. The principal British contribution to the extreme left of modern painting was a development of Cubism known as " Vorticism," and it is not altogether without significance that the leader of this movement, Mr. P. Wyndham Lewis, should have begun in the early spring of 1914 a series of abstract paintings with titles taken from *military* textbooks. His " Plan of Campaign " (see page 611), exhibited at London in June 1914, was based not on any vision of landscape and figures, but on such a diagram of a battle disposition as we may find in any history book. The parallel lines and blocks stand for the divisions of contending forces, and the heavy blocks in the upper right-hand corner are supposed to represent the extended left wing of one army outflanking and falling with superior strength on the right wing of the other army. This is the " plan of campaign." Here again we have a curious premonition of the War expressed in paint. The case of Mr. Wyndham Lewis typifies the general effect the Great War had on art. When a student at the Slade School

Mr. Lewis made himself remarked by the uncommon power of his drawing. Caught up in the vortex which swept so many ambitious young artists into the whirlpool of " abstract painting," because of their desire to attain novelty at all costs, Mr. Lewis was led in the years immediately preceding the Great War to paint " abstract " pictures, incomprehensible to the multitude and difficult for even the initiated to understand. Then in 1918, after two years experience with the heavy artillery in France, he returned to London and returned to realism. " The Gun Pit," which he painted for the Canadian War Memorials, was no abstract picture, but a perfectly comprehensible painting based on vision, on his remembered experience with the big guns and of the big-built men who worked them.

The chief effect of the Great War on painting, therefore was to bring about a return to realism, but it was a new realism modified, as we shall see, by certain principles derived from movements which, in themselves, appeared to be extravagant. Not only did the Great War restore to sanity many of the most promising of the younger artists, it also prepared the public to accept and understand their works Youthful artists, who in peace-time might have waited til middle age before their talent was recognised, became famous in a year or two. The wall of prejudice was broken down by the unparalleled upheaval of our normal world so that even conservative minds were ready to consider impartially a new vision of new events. Further, though there was no slackness on the part of the younger artists in joining the colours, the artistic activity of Great Britain may be said to have reached its zenith during the years of the Great War. Never before had so much official and State patronage been given to British artists, never before did the British public so clearly recognise that picture-making was not a mere pastime but an activity which had its own function and purpose of usefulness to humanity.

As early as 1914–15 the first public recognition of the artist's value to the State in war-time came in connection with the recruiting campaign. " Art for art's sake " was dead and done with, but in its place was substituted a new

"THE ROAD FROM ARRAS TO BAPAUME," BY C. R. W. NEVINSON, A.R.A.

From the Painting in the Imperial War Museum.

The son of a famous war-correspondent, Mr. Nevinson was the first artist to make a reputation by his original and intense interpretation of scenes on the battlefields. This painting of a road familiar to thousands of British soldiers is a typical example of his later pictures of the Great War, in which mannerisms and inessential details have alike been suppressed, and the main characteristics of the remembered scene are stated with emphatic simplicity and clearness.

gospel of " Art for the Idea's sake." Art was recognised as an element of education and social progress, because nothing else in the world could impress an idea so vividly and lastingly on the human memory. During the first winter and spring of the Great War close on a hundred posters were commissioned from various artists by the Parliamentary Recruiting Committee, and 2,500,000 copies of these posters were distributed throughout the United Kingdom. In addition to these official posters, generous contributions were made to the campaign by several private firms. The recruiting posters issued by the London Electric Railways will be long remembered for their efficiency and artistic qualities, notably Mr. Brangwyn's " Remember Belgium " (see page 617) and Mr. G. Spencer Pryse's " The Only Road for an Englishman " (see page 614). Later the use as a poster during the War Savings Campaign of a reproduction of Whistler's portrait of his Mother (see page 542) —as a gentle reminder that " Old Age Must Come "—was significant of a growing belief on the part of Authority that the most artistic picture can make the widest public appeal.

Simultaneously with the appearance of the recruiting posters on the hoardings, came the war cartoons in the newspapers. It is impracticable to give a list of the British artists who did excellent work in this direction—every reader will remember notable drawings.

Meanwhile what of painting ? It was said rather bitterly in 1916 that " no visitor to the Royal Academy would know that there was a war on." It may be admitted frankly that the exhibitions in these years looked much the same as those in years of peace. Pictures of the War were infrequent, and when present they were rarely successful. The failure of the older artists to grapple with the situation was neither surprising nor shameful. They did not possess the requisite experience. Some endeavoured to be topical, and envisaged the War after their memory of Crimean pictures, changing the uniforms into khaki but repeating the old arrangements. But sword-waving officers, swaggering cavalrymen, and neatly brushed infantry were no longer convincing even to civilians. Standing before an

"PLAN OF CAMPAIGN," BY P. WYNDHAM LEWIS.

A curious premonition of the Great War, this painting—exhibited at
London in June 1914—is based on the diagram of a battle disposition
which we may see in any history book. The parallel lines and
blocks stand for divisions of contending forces, and the heavy
blocks in the upper right-hand corner are supposed to represent the
superior forces of the army turning and crushing the right wing
of the other.

Academy picture of a charge, a wounded New Zealander was overheard to remark : "That's absurd ! one man with a machine-gun would wipe out the lot." New methods of warfare demanded new methods of painting for their efficient expression. The battle in art, as at the Front, was for the young, and the first man to capture the imagination of London by his war pictures was a young artist hitherto practically unknown.

§ 2

Before 1914 Mr. Christopher R. W. Nevinson was only known to the few as a young artist of promise. After studying at the Slade School of Art, he had formed ties of friendship in Paris with the Italian artist Gino Severini, and so had become influenced by Futurism. He was also interested in Cubism, and though he never definitely adhered to "Vorticism," he exhibited once with Mr. Wyndham Lewis, Mr. Edward Wadsworth, Mr. William Roberts, and other Vorticists. During the early stages of the Great War Mr. Nevinson was driving a motor-ambulance behind the Belgian Front, and being invalided with rheumatic fever early in 1915 he was able to resume painting during his convalescence. Thus he was practically the first artist who had the opportunity to exhibit in London pictures of the Great War based on personal experience of the realities of modern fighting. It was in the spring of 1915 that Mr. Nevinson showed his first three war pictures in the exhibition of the London Group at the Goupil Gallery, and though these betrayed Futurist and Cubist influence, they were perfectly intelligible as illustrations of actual incidents.

Dr. Johnson maintained that there was some good to be got out of every book, and similarly it may be argued that there is some good to be got out of every artistic theory. It was the peculiar distinction of Mr. Nevinson to leave aside all the extravagances of Futurism and Cubism, and snatch from them the two things which helped him to render realistically a new world in a new way. The particular good thing in the work of the Italian Futurists was their successful suggestion of movement. By a generous use of slanting lines in the composition, Mr. Nevinson gave a vivid sense of movement and life to his early painting " Returning to the Trenches." His French soldiers, with packs on their backs, their bodies and rifles sloping in the direction in which they were marching, were not portrayed as they would be shown in a photograph : the aim here was not to portray a group of individual soldiers, but to express the onward rush of an advancing army, and this impression was vividly and irresistibly conveyed. Further, the use of straight lines and avoidance of curves—characteristics derived from Cubism—suggested that the movement was that of a vast machine rather than of a collection of human beings.

The distinguished art critic, Mr. A. Clutton Brock, has pointed out in one of his essays that for fifty years or more a belief has been growing on us that man is a machine and " should be conscious of the fact that he is one." The popular play " R.U.R." was an expression of this consciousness in dramatic form ; in painting it was confessed by the Cubist method which, as Mr. Clutton Brock has said,

does express, in the most direct way, the sense that in war man behaves like a machine or part of a machine, that war is a process in which man is not treated as a human being but as an item in a great instrument of destruction, in which he ceases to be a person and is lost in a process. The cubist method, with its repetition and sharp distinction of planes, expresses this sense of a mechanical process better than any other way of representation.

Familiarity with the working of the " war-machine " prepared the mind of the public to accept that vision of the world as a complicated piece of mechanism which is the essence both of Cubism and Futurism. The Great War offered to the Cubists one of the few subjects which their technique was fitted to express, and the marvel is that this opportunity, missed by the French and Italian inventors of the new method, was seized upon with conspicuous success by a handful of almost unknown British artists.

From the first Mr. Nevinson stood out from all previous

" THE ONLY ROAD FOR AN ENGLISHMAN," BY G. SPENCER PRYSE.

Still remembered for its effectiveness during the Recruiting Campaign of 1914–15, this poster with its dignified design and noble appeal, shows how vividly art can be used to implant an idea in our minds.

painters of war by reason of his power in suggesting movement, and the implication in his pictures that modern war
was not the affair of human individuals, but the creaking
progress of a complicated machine.   His remarkable painting of the interior of a hospital, " La Patrie " (see illustration
below), which was purchased by Mr. Arnold Bennett, is
tragical in its intensity, but it is the tragedy of automata

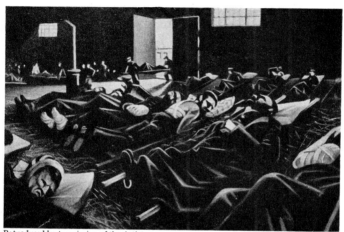

Reproduced by permission of the Artist.

" LA PATRIE," BY C. R. W. NEVINSON, A.R.A.

An intensely tragic vision of " the broken débris of the war-machine." The treatment of
the figures shows a modified use of the Cubist method, which is helpful here as an
indication that " war is a process in which man is not treated as a human being but
as an item in a great instrument of destruction."

crushed and mangled in the revolutions of a pitiless machine.
Other artists have painted the interiors of base-hospitals,
pictures of men bandaged but smiling, and attended by a
bevy of comely nurses, so that the spectator might imagine
it was rather pleasant than otherwise to be wounded ; but
Mr. Nevinson permits no falsifying of the facts ; he shows
us the reality of the thing, the broken debris of the war-
machine, the pain and the suffering and, above all, the

relative insignificance of the individual pawn in this mighty war-game.

The versatility of Mr. Nevinson and the way in which he alters his style to suit his subject is seen in " A Group of Soldiers " (see page 618). The great truth about the English " Tommy " after 1915 was that he was the British working-man in disguise, and here with unerring accuracy Mr. Nevinson has penetrated to the man behind the uniform, and unveiled the man of toil, the unit of the machine. Some have demurred that in the foremost figures the hands are exaggerated but, while the point is open to debate, a slight exaggeration is permissible as emphasising the fact that these men belong to the horny-handed class. In this group, where there is no movement to be registered, Futurist devices would be out of place and they are avoided, but there is still a faint trace of Cubism in the definite angles of the simple modelling, and this helps to give a monumental sense of strength and doggedness to the sturdy figures.

In landscape, as well as in his figure paintings, Mr. Nevinson contrived to get at the reality behind the thing seen. " The Road from Arras to Bapaume " (see page 609) is neither impressionistic nor photographic, but it gives the essential truth of a scene acutely remembered. All the inessential details have been suppressed, with the result that the main recollections of the truth—the white, switchback track of Roman straightness, the lopped-down tree-trunks, the stream of moving traffic, and the limitless expanse—are recorded with increased strength and intensity. This is one of Mr. Nevinson's later pictures of the Great War and while he no doubt enjoyed greater facilities and privileges when he returned to France in 1917 as an " official artist " than he had done in 1914–15 as a motor-mechanic, the essential qualities in his pictures remained the same. His reputation was made with the earlier pictures, in which the mannerisms were most marked ; in the later works these mannerisms were pruned to a vanishing point, and realities were stated without any serious loss in strength and with increased clarity.

It is no wonder that the war-pictures of Mr. Nevinson took London by storm in the early days of the Great War. He was the first to show the grim inner realities of modern fighting, and others who dealt only with appearances seemed in comparison remote from the heart of the subject. When other young artists were released from the fighting line, a new series of visions of men as automata expressed

Reproduced by permission of the London Underground Railways

" REMEMBER BELGIUM," BY FRANK BRANGWYN, R.A.

This striking poster was specially drawn by Mr. Brangwyn for the famous series of artistic recruiting appeals issued by the London Electric Railways.

the new outlook of a new generation, but their work did not begin to appear in exhibitions till nearing the time of the Armistice in 1918.

The first serious rival to Mr. Nevinson appeared in April 1916, when a large painting, " The Kensingtons at Laventie " (see page 624), by Mr. Eric H. Kennington, was exhibited in Regent Street. Mr. Kennington, a young painter of promise in whom William Nicholson had taken an interest, was an artist of quite another type. He

" A GROUP OF SOLDIERS," BY C. R. W. NEVINSON, A.R.A.

From the painting in the Imperial War Museum.

After 1915 the British soldier was the British workman in disguise. In the above picture the artist has unveiled the man behind the uniform and expressed this truth with convincing simplicity and force. Faint traces of Cubism, revealed in the definite angles of the modelled forms, help to give strength and doggedness in the sturdy figures.

"A SKETCH IN ALBERT," BY SIR MUIRHEAD BONE.

A drawing made on the spot by the first "Official Artist" sent by the British Government to the Western Front in the Great War. Sir Muirhead Bone, who is our premier living etcher, gives a vivid impression here of the ravaged state of this Belgian town, and invests its ruin with a dignity of his own.

was untouched by the most modern movements, except that he had a leaning towards simplicity of drawing and emphasis of design : this and a knowledge of the Great War from within was all he had in common with Mr. Nevinson. After only three months' training in England as a Territorial, Private Kennington went to France at the beginning of November 1914 with the 13th Battalion of the London Regiment (" The Kensingtons "). He returned to England in 1915, when he was discharged unfit for further service, and then began to paint this great picture of a typical moment in the life at the Front during the terrible winter of 1914–15. The moment chosen for representation in this picture was when his platoon, after serving for four days and nights in the fire trenches, enduring the piercing cold of twenty degrees of frost and almost continuous snow, had at last been relieved. The men have emerged from the communication trench terminating in a ruined farmyard, and are forming up along the ruined village street. Each figure in the picture is an actual portrait, and the artist has given the following description of his work :

Corporal J. Kealey is about to give the order " Fall in, No. 7 Platoon." . . . In the first four—reading from right to left—are Pte. Slade, resting with both hands on his rifle ; Lce.-Cpl. Wilson, Pte. Guy, and Pte. McCafferty, who is turning to look at the other men falling in behind. . . . On the extreme left is Pte. H. Bristol. . . . Directly behind Pte. Guy are two men in waterproof sheets : Pte. Kennington [the artist] in a blue trench helmet and Pte. W. Harvey. . . . On the ground is Pte. A. Todd. . . . He has fallen exhausted by continual sickness, hard work, lack of sleep, long hours of " standing-to," and observing.

This picture shows quite another aspect of realism. It is a stately presentation of human endurance, of the quiet heroism of the rank and file. The deadliest enemy here is the piercing cold, which seems to pervade the whole picture. Apart from its human emotional appeal, this large picture —in which the figures are two-thirds life-size—possesses a peculiar technical interest in that it is painted on glass. The advantage of this method is that the pigment is hermetically sealed, and so long as the thick plate-glass endures unbroken the colour of the surface will remain for centuries